YOUNG CHILDREN
OF BLACK IMMIGRANTS
IN AMERICA:
Changing Flows, Changing Faces

Randy Capps and Michael Fix, Editors

Migration Policy Institute

December 2012

Migration Policy Institute
Washington, DC

© 2012 Migration Policy Institute

Library of Congress Cataloging-in-Publication Data

Young children of Black immigrants in America: changing flows, changing faces / edited by Michael Fix and Randy Capps.

       p. cm.

   Includes bibliographical references.

   ISBN 978-0-9831591-1-7 (pbk.)

1.   Children of immigrants--United States. 2.   Children, Black--United States. 3.   Child develop-ment--United States. 4.   Children--Health and hygiene--United States. 5.   Immigrants--United States. 6.   Africans--United States. 7.   West Indians--United States. I. Fix, Michael. II. Capps, Randy.

   HQ792.U5Y685 2012

   305.230869120973--dc23

                    2012023829

Cover Photo: Modified version of "Low Angle View Of A Father Touching His Son (10-12) On The Shoulders" (stk30771abf) via Photos.com.

Cover Design: April Siruno, MPI

Typesetting: Erin Perkins, LeafDev

Suggested citation: Capps, Randy and Michael Fix. 2012. *Young Children of Black Immigrants in America: Changing Flows, Changing Faces*. Washington, DC: Migration Policy Institute.

Printed in the United States of America.

TABLE OF CONTENTS

INTRODUCTION 1
Michael Fix, Randy Capps, and Kristen McCabe

PART ONE: DEMOGRAPHY OF A RAPIDLY GROWING IMMIGRANT
POPULATION TO THE UNITED STATES

CHAPTER 1: Contemporary Black Caribbean Immigrants in the United States .. 21
Kevin J.A. Thomas

CHAPTER 2: New Streams: Black African Migration to the United States 45
Randy Capps, Kristen McCabe, and Michael Fix

CHAPTER 3: Young Children in Black Immigrant Families from Africa
and the Caribbean 75
Donald J. Hernandez

PART TWO: FAMILY CIRCUMSTANCES, EARLY CHILDHOOD
OUTCOMES, AND SCHOOL READINESS

CHAPTER 4: Black and Immigrant: Exploring the Effects of Ethnicity and
Foreign-Born Status on Infant Health 119
Tiffany L. Green

CHAPTER 5: Parenting Behavior, Health, and Cognitive Development among
Children in Black Immigrant Families: Comparing the United States and
United Kingdom 145
Margot Jackson

CHAPTER 6: Patterns and Predictors of School Readiness and Early Childhood
Success among Young Children in Black Immigrant Families 183
Danielle A. Crosby and Angel S. Dunbar

CHAPTER 7: Circumstances and Outcomes among Black Immigrant Mothers and
their Young Children: Evidence from Palm Beach County, Florida 229
Lauren Rich, Julie Spielberger, and Angela Valdovinos D'Angelo

CHAPTER 8: Transnational Parenting: Child Fostering in Ghanaian Immigrant
Families 265
Cati Coe

PART THREE: EDUCATIONAL EXPERIENCES AND ACADEMIC
ACHIEVEMENT

CHAPTER 9: Beyond Black: Diversity among Black Immigrant Students in New
York City Public Schools 299
Fabienne Doucet, Amy Ellen Schwartz, and Elizabeth Debraggio

CHAPTER 10: The Academic Development of Black Foreign-Born Students in
Miami-Dade County Schools 333
Dylan Conger and Megan Hatch

CHAPTER 11: Will the Paradox Hold? Uncovering the Path to Academic Success
for Young Children of Black Immigrants 355
Carola Suárez-Orozco

ACKNOWLEDGMENTS 371
ABOUT THE EDITORS AND AUTHORS 373
ABOUT THE YOUNG CHILDREN OF BLACK IMMIGRANTS INITIATIVE 381
ABOUT MPI'S NATIONAL CENTER ON IMMIGRANT INTEGRATION POLICY 383

INTRODUCTION

CHANGING FLOWS, CHANGING FACES

Randy Capps, Michael Fix, and Kristen McCabe

Migration Policy Institute

The child population in the United States is rapidly changing and diversifying — in large part because of immigration. Today, nearly one in four US children under age 18 is the child of an immigrant.[1] Latino, Black, Asian, and multiracial children together are nearing a majority of the nation's children. These "minority" children already account for more than half of US children under age 1.[2]

Not surprisingly, scholarship has focused on the largest immigrant groups: the children of Latinos and Asians. Far less academic attention has been paid to the rapidly changing Black child population, and in particular to the young children of Black immigrants from birth through age 10. Yet the children of Black immigrants represent an increasing share of the Black child population in the United States.

From 1990 to 2009, the number of foreign-born Blacks in the United States more than doubled, from 1.4 million to 3.3 million. This growth, driven by increased levels of immigration from Africa and ongoing migration from the Caribbean, is gradually transforming the composition of the country's Black population.[3] Black immigrants accounted for about 1 percent of the total Black population in 1960, 5 percent in 1990, and 8 percent by 2009.[4] The make-up of the Black child population is changing in turn: since 1990, the number of Black immigrants' children

---

1   Migration Policy Institute (MPI) Data Hub, "The United States" (Social & Demographic Characteristics), www.migrationinformation.org/datahub/state.cfm?ID=US.
2   US Census Bureau, "Most Children Younger than Age 1 are Minorities, Census Bureau Reports," (news release, May 17, 2012), www.census.gov/newsroom/releases/archives/population/cb12-90.html.
3   See Chapter 2 in this volume, Randy Capps, Kristen McCabe, and Michael Fix, *New Streams: African Migration to the United States.*
4   US Census Bureau, "Table 8. Race and Hispanic Origin of the Population by Nativity: 1850 to 1990," www.census.gov/population/www/documentation/twps0029/tab08.html; US Census Bureau, American FactFinder, 2009 American Community Survey, Table S0201: Selected Population Profile in the United States.

ages 10 and younger has more than doubled. By the late 2000s, about 813,000 young children lived in Black immigrant families, representing 8 percent of all young children in immigrant families and 12 percent of all young Black children in the United States.[5]

Black immigrants in the United States are strikingly varied in their origins, languages, cultural and socioeconomic backgrounds, and patterns of integration. No single country accounts for more than one-fifth of this population. Further, Black migration to the United States comes through differing channels that reflect varying levels of human and social capital and carry differing entitlements to public benefits. Black immigrants enter as family members, as workers, as refugees seeking humanitarian relief, and as "diversity" immigrants from underrepresented sending countries. In general, Black immigrants are more likely than other immigrant groups to enter as refugees and are less likely than Hispanic immigrants to enter the country illegally or overstay their visas and become unauthorized. African immigrants are overrepresented among immigrants entering through the diversity visa lottery.[6]

A broad and deep literature makes clear that parental economic, social, and other resources are critically important for development during early childhood. These resources vary considerably among Black immigrant parents depending on a variety of factors described in this volume. As a result, when viewed in the aggregate, young children of Black immigrants often come out in the middle on indicators of development and well-being when compared with children in other demographic groups, native-born and immigrant alike. At the same time, we also see widely varying outcomes when Black immigrants' children are broken out by sending country, mode of entry, or generation.

I.   Focus of the Volume

A core goal of this volume is to address gaps in knowledge about how young children of Black immigrants are faring in terms their health, well-being, school readiness, and academic achievement. Its chapters explore the migration and settlement experiences of Black immigrants to the United States, focusing on contextual factors such as family circumstances, parenting behaviors, social supports, and school climate that influence outcomes during early childhood and the elementary and middle-school years.

The chapters were commissioned as papers by the Migration Policy

---

5   See Chapter 3 in this volume, Donald J. Hernandez, *Young Children in Black Immigrant Families from Africa and the Caribbean.*

6   *The Immigration Act of 1990* established the diversity visa lottery to allow entry to immigrants from countries with low rates of immigration to the United States; there is an annual allotment of 55,000 diversity green cards.

Institute (MPI) and presented at a research symposium held in 2011 at MPI with support from the Foundation for Child Development. The goals of the symposium and of this volume have been to bring together an interdisciplinary network of scholars to synthesize the existing literature on young children of Black immigrants (birth through age 10), report new research results, and — hopefully — to lay the foundation for future research and policy discussions on children of Black immigrants. Taken together, the chapters present demographic overviews of Black immigrants in the United States and their young children and offer perspectives on developmental outcomes across a range of domains. The chapters compare young children in Black immigrant families with peers from a variety of racial/ethnic and nativity backgrounds including US-born Black children, those with US-born white parents, and children with Asian and Latino immigrant parents.[7] To the extent that data sources allow, the chapters highlight variations across Black immigrant-origin groups in the United States. Although much of the research is national in scope, some studies focus on urbanized areas where Black immigrants are heavily concentrated, such as New York City and Florida's Miami-Dade and Palm Beach counties. One of the chapters provides an international comparison between the United States and United Kingdom. Central questions the book addresses include:

- What are the origins of Black immigrants? How do factors such as English language proficiency, educational attainment, earnings and income, housing conditions, family structure, modes of immigration, legal status, and citizenship status vary by their origins? What are the implications of these factors for young children's health, well-being, development, and academic trajectories?

- What are the birth and early childhood health outcomes for children in Black immigrant families? Do children of Black immigrants exhibit some of the same advantages shown by other children of immigrants — for instance, the relatively strong birth outcomes of Asian and Latino immigrants' children?

- What social supports and public services do Black immigrant parents secure for their children? What are their utilization rates for prenatal care, center-based child care, public health insurance, and other supports? How strongly is the use of these supports associated with child outcomes?

- How well prepared are the children of Black immigrants for their entry into kindergarten? What are their developmental trajectories during the preschool years? How do they perform at kindergarten entry relative to other groups of children? What factors are associated with better and worse performance?

---

7   In this chapter the "white" population refers to non-Hispanic whites.

- How successful are the children of Black immigrants in public elementary and middle schools? How do their academic outcomes compare with other children? What variations can be seen across Black immigrant children? How are academic outcomes related to differences in English language proficiency, family socioeconomic background, and other measurable factors?

Many answers to these questions have important policy implications for education, health care, child care, early childhood development, immigrant integration, and refugee assistance. While the book focuses principally on children of Black immigrants, most chapters provide informative — and sometimes worrying — contrasts with children from a variety of different racial/ethnic backgrounds including the children of US-born Blacks, children with US-born white parents, and children with Asian and Latino immigrant parents. We believe, then that the volume offers new evidence about relative advantage and disadvantage among the nation's increasingly diverse child population overall.

II. Structure of the Volume

The book is divided into three parts. The first provides a demographic overview of the Black immigrant population, focusing on the migration and settlement experiences of Black African and Caribbean immigrants and the family resources available to their young children. In Chapter 1, Kevin Thomas of Pennsylvania State University outlines the historical origins of Caribbean immigrants to the United States and describes their racial diversity, countries of origin, languages spoken, modes of immigration, legal status, educational attainment, and US labor market incorporation. In Chapter 2, Randy Capps, Kristen McCabe, and Michael Fix of MPI provide a parallel analysis of African immigrants. In Chapter 3, Donald Hernandez of Hunter College, City University of New York (CUNY), examines the demography of young children of Black immigrants, their family circumstances, and access to social supports.

Part Two includes both national and more localized studies that describe the family circumstances, health, development, and school readiness of children in Black immigrant families during the years leading up to enrollment in elementary school. In Chapter 4, Tiffany Green of Virginia Commonwealth University investigates whether the birth outcomes of children with Black immigrant mothers are better than would be expected given their socioeconomic status — a pattern observed among Mexican immigrant mothers in the United States that is referred to as the "epidemiologic paradox." In Chapter 5, Margot Jackson of Brown University analyzes parenting behaviors and their relationship to early health and cognitive outcomes among children of Black immigrants in the United States and the United Kingdom. The extent to which child outcomes are shaped by the national policy context (i.e., a presumably more generous, protective welfare state in the United Kingdom versus the one found in the United States) is a central question presented by this international comparative study. In Chapter 6, Danielle Crosby and Angel Dunbar of the University of North Carolina at Greensboro examine levels of school readiness among young children of Black immigrants and identify the contextual factors — such as family circumstances, parenting practices, and enrollment in center-based care — that encourage early school success. In Chapter 7, Lauren Rich, Julie Spielberger, and Angela Valdovinos D'Angelo of Chapin Hall at the University of Chicago conduct a similar analysis of Black immigrants' children in Palm Beach County, FL, a county with one of the largest Haitian populations in the United States.

In Chapter 8, Cati Coe of Rutgers University offers an alternative assessment of the living and child-care arrangements of Black immigrants' children, relying on ethnographic data from the United States and Ghana. Coe describes the circumstances and goals of Ghanaian immigrant parents who send their children to Ghana to be raised in the care of other relatives. The parents' reliance on "child-fostering" systems are rooted in Ghanaian child-rearing practices and linked to parents' work experiences and lack of affordable child-care options in the United States.

The third part of the book examines the educational experiences and academic achievement of Black immigrant children during the elementary- and middle-school years. While the earlier chapters generally focus on US-born children with immigrant parents ("the second generation"), the chapters in this section focus on children who were born outside the United States ("the first generation"). In Chapter 9, Fabienne Doucet, Amy Ellen Schwartz, and Elizabeth Debraggio of the Steinhardt School of Culture, Education, and Human Development, CUNY, analyze the racial/ethnic isolation of Black immigrant children in New York City public schools along with their reading and math scores, and their schools' educational climate. In Chapter 10, Dylan Conger and Megan Hatch of George Washington University examine student progress in reading from grades 3 through 8 and the influence of home language on relative academic progress and achievement. Chapters 9 and 10 examine some of the integration challenges that immigrant students face in US public schools and how they affect academic performance, with a particular focus on Haitian immigrant students. In the final chapter of the volume, Carola Suárez-Orozco of the University of California, Los Angeles, reviews the challenges Black immigrants' children face in the US educational system, how they compare with those faced by other immigrant groups, and the salience of the "immigrant paradox" theory for young children of Black immigrants.

III. Defining the Population

The authors throughout this volume focus on children from birth to age 10 with at least one Black immigrant parent. Children of immigrants may be first- or second-generation. The third generation is composed of those born in the United States with US-born parents. Nearly all children of immigrants under age 6 (95 percent) are US-born, but substantial numbers of older children are first-generation immigrants.[8] The authors' analyses of the first generation generally include students in grades 1 through 8.

Black race is less precisely defined than immigrant generation. Concepts of race can vary depending on the social context, and mainstream notions of race in US society may differ from those held by immigrant-origin groups. In this volume, Black race is usually defined by answers to the US Census Bureau's population surveys, other large-scale surveys, and administrative data from public school districts and hospitals. Respondents generally identify their own race in these data sources, though parents may report the race of their children or other family members. While Census Bureau surveys such as the American Community Survey allow multiracial respondents to report multiple races, other data sources may not, and some individuals with multiracial backgrounds may only report a single race or ethnicity with which they identify.

Data Sources

The chapters in this volume draw conclusions about the well-being of young children of Black immigrants based on a variety of data sources, including national-level surveys, qualitative case studies, and administrative records from schools and hospitals. Children of Black immigrants represent just 2 percent of all US children, and multiple data sources provide a more robust, well-rounded portrait than we might expect for such a small, diverse group of children. Comparing results across chapters, however, should be done with caution as the chapters vary in the populations and geographic areas analyzed, as well as the data sets and methodologies employed.

Three chapters exploit longitudinal, birth-cohort data sets. Jackson (Chapter 5) employs two nationally representative birth-cohort surveys: one in the United States (the Fragile Families and Child Well-being Study) and one in the United Kingdom (the Millennium Cohort Study). Crosby and Dunbar (Chapter 6) also use a nationally representative US birth-cohort study (the Early Childhood Longitudinal Study, Birth Cohort or ECLS-B), while Rich and her colleagues (Chapter 7) use a similar survey of a cohort born in Palm Beach County, FL. In all three

---

8   MPI DataHub, "The United States" (Social & Demographic Characteristics, Table 4. Children in Immigrant Families in the United States (1990, 2000, and 2010)), www.migrationinformation.org/datahub/state.cfm?ID=US#tables.

chapters, data are drawn from random samples of hospital births and are used to track young children from birth through age 5 or 6.

Because they all involve data on children born in the United States (or the United Kingdom in the case of the Millennium Cohort Study), these three chapters necessarily focus on second–generation children.

In contrast, the two chapters employing public school data focus on first- rather than second-generation children. They do so because schools generally do not record parents' birthplace, preventing the identification of second-generation students. Doucet and her colleagues (Chapter 9) analyze longitudinal data from two years' worth of records from New York City, the nation's largest public school district. Conger and Hatch (Chapter 10) use data from several years' worth of school records from Miami-Dade County, the fourth-largest school district in the United States.

Data from these multi-year longitudinal studies — whether based on school records or a birth cohort — allow the authors to assess how children of Black immigrants fare relative to their peers at a single point in time and analyze changes in relative standing over time.

IV. Principal Findings

Below we summarize the volume's major findings, grouping them into five subtopics: (1) the characteristics of Black immigrants and their implications for child well-being; (2) birth outcomes and early childhood health; (3) access to benefits and services; (4) early developmental outcomes and preparation for kindergarten; and (5) academic performance in elementary school.

1. Characteristics of Black Immigrants and Implications for their Children's Well-Being

One animating theme of the volume is the diversity of Black immigrants' children and the resulting wide variation in their well-being and trajectories. Taken together, the demographic overview chapters by Thomas, Capps and colleagues, and Hernandez point to a number of protective factors that influence the development of Black children of immigrants.

- *Black immigrant parents — especially those from Africa — have relatively high levels of educational attainment and English proficiency.* The four-year college completion rate for Black African immigrants (38 percent) exceeds that for the overall US population (27 percent), while the rate for Caribbean immigrants is lower (20 percent). Three-quarters of Black immigrants speak English as their first language or speak

English very well, substantially above the proficiency rate for immigrants overall (48 percent). Their educational attainment and English proficiency represent important advantages for Black immigrant parents in promoting the early development of their children, preparing them for school, and interacting with teachers and other educators. These factors are also associated with higher earnings and better socioeconomic status in the United States.

- *Black immigrant parents have relatively high employment rates, and the families they head have a lower poverty rate than US-born Black or Latino counterparts.* Three-quarters of Black immigrant adults work, a higher rate than for immigrants overall and the US-born. Employment is particularly high among Caribbean immigrant mothers, many of whom are single parents. Relatively high employment and educational attainment contribute to a lower poverty rate for children in Black immigrant families (19 percent) versus those in US-born Black families (35 percent), Latino immigrant families (28 percent), and US-born Latino families (23 percent). The poverty rate for children in native-born white families is 10 percent — roughly the same as children born to Black parents from Nigeria, Jamaica, Ghana, and small English-speaking Caribbean countries such as Barbados, Bermuda, Grenada, Trinidad and Tobago, and St. Vincent and the Grenadines.

- *Black immigrants overall are less likely to be unauthorized than Latino immigrants.* Most Black immigrants are insulated as a result of their legal immigration status from the restrictive and comparatively new state and local enforcement activities that are felt most acutely by Latino immigrant communities. Lawful permanent resident (LPR) status usually confers eligibility for health insurance, child-care subsidies, and other public benefits. About one-quarter of Black African immigrants enter as refugees, a status granting them access to health insurance, cash assistance, education, training, and other resettlement services. African immigrants receive about half of all diversity visas, and these visas secure legal permanent residence and a path to citizenship. Most Caribbean immigrants are admitted as relatives of US citizens or permanent residents, attesting to the well-settled and connected nature of their communities. Black Caribbean immigrants are more likely than African immigrants and immigrants overall to be US citizens — a sign of their longer tenure in the United States and their integration.

- *Children of Black immigrants — both those of African and Caribbean origin — enroll in center-based pre-kindergarten programs at notably high rates.* Along with native Asian families, children ages 3-4 in Black immigrant families have the highest rate of prekindergarten enrollment (56 percent). This rate is slightly higher than children in US-born Black or white families (both about 50 percent) and considerably higher than those in Latino immigrant families (36 percent). Participation in high-quality early care and education promotes language, cognitive, and social development, and it may be particularly valuable for the development of children whose parents who do not speak English fluently.

These protective factors do not extend, however, to all children in Black immigrant families. Some groups of Black immigrants' children are relatively disadvantaged, including those born to parents from Haiti, the Dominican Republic, Sudan, and Somalia. Many grow up in low-income families where parents have lower levels of education and English fluency than children in Black immigrant families overall. Some refugee origin-country families, such as those from Somalia and Sudan, have fled persecution and conflict and experienced trauma, including the loss of family members in their home countries. Many refugee children migrate with interruptions in their formal education.

There are two areas in particular where children of Black immigrants overall face greater risks than other children of immigrants: family structure and housing. Black children of immigrants are significantly more likely to live in single-parent families than children of Hispanic, Asian, or white immigrants, with the highest rates found among children with parents from the Dominican Republic, Jamaica, and the smaller English-speaking Caribbean countries. Children of Black immigrants are less likely than white and Asian children to live in homes that their parents own. Except for children of Latino immigrants they are also more likely to live in crowded conditions (i.e., with more than one person per room) than other children. Crowding and low homeownership rates reflect both the relatively low earnings of Black immigrants (despite their educational attainment and English proficiency) as well as their concentration in high-cost cities on the East Coast. Living in single-parent homes and crowded housing has been associated with poorer developmental and academic outcomes.

2. Birth Outcomes and Early Childhood Health

A key question addressed in four chapters (Green, Jackson, Crosby and Dunbar, and Rich et al) is whether children of Black immigrants exhibit the same epidemiologic paradox observed among children with Mexican-born mothers: i.e., better birth outcomes than the native-born white population despite lower socioeconomic status. Green's analysis of vital statistics from several major East Coast states finds only qualified support for the paradox: children born to Black immigrant mothers tend to have better outcomes (measured in terms of birth weight and prematurity) than those born to US-born Black mothers, but they have worse outcomes than most other major racial/ethnic groups. Rich and her colleagues find that Black, mostly Haitian, immigrant mothers in Palm Beach County have worse outcomes in terms of pregnancy and birth complications and rates of prematurity than Latina immigrants, but better outcomes than US-born Blacks. In their analysis of US data, Crosby and Dunbar also find that children of Black immigrants are less likely to be low birth weight than children of Black US-born parents. Similarly, Jackson finds that nationally, Black immigrant mothers have babies with higher birth weights than native-born Black mothers but lower ones than those with Latino immigrant mothers. Taken together, these studies consistently indicate that babies born to Black immigrants fare better than those born to US-born Blacks and worse than those born to Latina immigrant mothers.

Three chapters find that Black immigrant mothers broadly adopt health-promoting protective behaviors during and after pregnancy. The chapters by Green and by Crosby and Dunbar report that Black immigrant mothers are less likely than any other group of mothers to smoke during pregnancy, and Crosby and Dunbar find they are less likely than any group of US-born mothers to use drugs or alcohol during pregnancy. The chapters by Jackson and by Crosby and Dunbar report that breastfeeding — which has been linked to better child health and cognitive development — is more common among Black immigrant mothers than most other groups of mothers.

The findings across the chapters about the health of Black immigrants' children after infancy are mixed, with no clear pattern emerging. Crosby and Dunbar's analysis raises one particularly worrying health concern regarding Black immigrants' children: they find that about 40 percent of them are overweight when they start kindergarten; 20 percent are obese. These rates are similar to those for Black and Latino children of natives.

3. Access to Benefits and Services

From birth through early childhood, children of Black immigrants seem to have relatively broad access to services and benefits such as health insurance coverage, nutrition supplement programs, and center-based child care. Each is associated with cognitive development and school readiness.

Hernandez finds, for example, that 90 percent of Black immigrants' children have health insurance coverage. This is above the rate for Latino children of immigrants (82 percent) but marginally lower than other groups of children. Along similar lines, Rich and her colleagues find that Black immigrant mothers are more likely to obtain health insurance coverage through Medicaid than Latina immigrant mothers, though less likely to do so than US-born Blacks. They also find that Black immigrants are more likely than Latina immigrant and US-born

Black mothers to participate in Special Supplemental Nutrition Assistance for Women, Infants and Children (WIC), a federal program that has been shown to promote positive health and cognitive development in young children.

One striking and consistent finding across a number of the chapters is the high rate of center-based child care among children of Black immigrants. Crosby and Dunbar, for example, find that 87 percent of children with Black Caribbean immigrant parents attend center-based child-care facilities during the year before kindergarten, among the highest rates of any demographic group. Children with Black African immigrant parents were somewhat less likely to use center-based care (71 percent). Hernandez finds that 3- and 4-year-old children of Black immigrants are enrolled in prekindergarten programs at a higher rate than every demographic group except children of Asian immigrants. Using Palm Beach County survey data, Rich and her colleagues find that preschool-age children of Black immigrants are more than twice as likely to attend Head Start and other center-based child-care programs as children of Latina immigrants and are as likely to do so as Black or Latino children of natives.

Coe's chapter on child fostering offers a cautionary note about the access of Black immigrant parents to quality child care in the United States. In her case study of Ghanaian immigrant parents, Coe finds several factors that complicate child rearing in the United States. Many Ghanaian immigrant parents work long hours, preventing them from staying home to take care of young children. Some of the families in her sample have insufficient incomes to purchase child care on the US market, but are ineligible for public child-care subsidies. At the same time, current US immigration rules make it difficult for Ghanaian families to sponsor relatives such as grandparents who might assist with child care. Faced with uncertain and potentially unstable child-care arrangements, some Ghanaian immigrant parents choose to send their children to Ghana to be raised by other relatives. This system of shared parenting — or "child fostering" — is well developed in Ghana, and so parents see the risks and sorrows of separation as being necessary to overcome the material difficulties they face in raising their children in the United States. However, the long-term implications for the integration of fostered children when they return to the United States are unknown.

Black children of immigrants have substantially higher utilization rates of center-based child care, public health insurance, and nutrition programs when compared to Latino children of immigrants. These results owe in part to the fact that Black immigrant parents are less likely to be unauthorized immigrants than Latino immigrant parents, and thus do not face the same eligibility barriers or fears of public program participation. Black immigrant parents are also more likely to be proficient in English, reducing communication and cultural differences with service providers. Access to these forms of support can provide a good foundation for the cognitive development and school readiness of the children of Black immigrants.

One area of service use where the authors' findings are less consistent is prenatal care. Studies by Jackson and by Crosby and Dunbar find that nationwide, Black immigrant mothers are about as likely as other mothers to obtain prenatal care early in their pregnancy. Green, however, finds in her study of births in East Coast states that Black immigrant mothers are *less* likely than any other group of mothers in the study to initiate prenatal care during the first trimester. Thus the findings on initiation of prenatal care conflict depending on geographic area studied and data source used, underscoring the need for further research.

4. Early Developmental Outcomes and Preparation for Kindergarten

The examination of center-based child care and social supports lays the foundation for the volume's analysis of Black immigrant children's early cognitive development and their school readiness. The chapters by Jackson, Crosby and Dunbar, and by Rich and her colleagues show better early education outcomes for children of Black immigrants than those of Latino immigrants or US-born Black parents. On most measures, though, they show worse outcomes than children of US-born white and Asian parents.

Crosby and Dunbar find that at age 2, Black immigrants' children fall behind their peers with East Asian, European immigrant, and US-born white parents on an observation-based assessment of their problem-solving skills, speech, comprehension, and other cognitive measures. But by kindergarten entry Black immigrants' children catch up with the children of US-born white parents and substantially outpace children with US-born Black and Latino parents (both immigrant and native) on reading tests. In regression models that control for socioeconomic status, children of Black immigrants actually outperform most other groups in reading, including Latino children and those with Black and white US-born parents.

Analysis of the Palm Beach County sample by Rich and her colleagues supports the conclusion that Black immigrants' children are relatively well prepared for school. Children of Black immigrants — most with Haitian parents — scored significantly higher than Latino children of immigrants, and marginally higher than children with US-born Black parents, on the county's two kindergarten readiness assessments. Notably, children of Black immigrants in the county's most economically distressed neighborhoods perform about as well as the countywide population of kindergarten entrants regardless of race/ethnicity on the reading test. The authors attribute the relatively strong performance of Black immigrants' children to their enrollment in center-based child care, their parents' relatively high education and employment rates, and the number of books in the home.

Here again, the results of differing analyses do not always yield consistent results. Using nationally representative data Jackson finds that children in Black families, regardless of parental nativity, are less prepared for kindergarten than US children overall. At age 5, children in Black immigrant families score significantly lower on a picture-based vocabulary test than do children in white and Asian families, and somewhat lower than children in US-born Black families. Only children in Latino immigrant families have lower scores. Jackson compares US results with data from the United Kingdom, where 5-year olds with Black immigrant parents score lower than those with UK-born parents on a similar vocabulary test. As in the United States, the UK sample includes one large immigrant group with lower scores than children of Black immigrants; in the UK case this is children of South Asian immigrants.

While the findings across the three chapters sometimes conflict, they generally show an advantage for children of Black immigrants in their cognitive development and school readiness when compared with children from lower-income and lower-socioeconomic status backgrounds — i.e., children of Latino immigrants and children with US-born Black parents. Still, children with white and Asian parents tend to perform as well or better than children of Black immigrants on most measures in the national data. The studies indicate that parental education, employment, parenting practices, and center-based child-care participation promote the school readiness of children in Black immigrant families.

5. Academic Performance in Elementary School

Another focus of the book is the academic outcomes of Black immigrant children in public elementary and middle schools. The chapters that explore academic outcomes focus on first-generation immigrant students because school administrative data do not identify second-generation students.

Using data on New York City public school students in grades 3 through 8, Doucet and her co-authors find that Black immigrant students generally perform worse than Asian and white immigrant students but better than Latino immigrant counterparts on standardized reading and math assessments. Black Caribbean students, in particular those from Haiti and the Dominican Republic, have among the lowest scores. The authors point to the fact that almost half of Haitian- and Dominican-born Black students are English Language Learners (ELLs), and that test scores tend to be lower for ELLs than other students. African immigrant students perform slightly better but still below the citywide average. However, when regression models are used to control for

English proficiency and exposure to English at home, Haitian students perform as well or better than their English-speaking Caribbean counterparts.

The authors attribute Black immigrants' relatively poor test performance to limited English proficiency, interrupted schooling, and low socioeconomic status. But these factors cannot account for all of the differences in tests scores the authors observe. Their qualitative work in several New York City schools also suggests that some of the schools are not attuned to the classroom needs of Black or immigrant students.

Conger and Hatch offer a different assessment of Black immigrant children's academic progress in the Miami-Dade public schools based on six years of longitudinal data. Black immigrant and US-born Black students score the lowest of any group of students on third grade reading tests. Between third and eighth grade the reading scores of US-born Blacks decline, as do the scores of Black immigrant students from English-speaking homes (about half of whom are from Jamaica). By contrast, Black immigrant students whose home language is not English (most of whom are Haitian) see their reading test scores rise. Latino immigrant students' scores also rise, while the scores of native-born Latino students decline. The authors conclude that ELL students generally start with lower test scores but are more likely than English-proficient immigrants to make gains over time.

The findings from these studies of two of the nation's largest urban school districts suggest that Black immigrant children face significant hurdles to strong academic performance — including English language proficiency, school segregation, and an often unfavorable climate of reception in the schools. It is important to bear in mind that the two studies focus on first-generation students, who may not have had the advantages of center-based child care and other early childhood supports that US-born children of immigrants often receive.

Suárez-Orozco then compares some of the advantages and disadvantages faced by first- and second-generation immigrant students. The immigrant paradox would hold that first-generation students should perform better than their US-born second-generation peers. Second-generation Black students may be more susceptible to the effects of racial discrimination than the first generation students, who may be able to retain stronger associations with their countries of origin. Studies have shown that first-generation students generally have better attitudes toward their teachers as well as better school attendance and attachment. But second-generation students have some distinct advantages including English-language proficiency, broader familiarity with US culture, and US citizenship. Suárez-Orozco contends that given the recency and diversity of Black immigrant flows that it is too soon to tell whether and how broadly the immigrant paradox applies to Black children of immigrants.

V. Conclusions and Directions for Future Research

The authors in this volume present a broad set of findings on the health, development, and academic performance of young children of Black immigrants. Their findings are based on robust analyses of national and local data sets and include case studies of several jurisdictions with the largest Black immigrant populations in the country. While they draw a number of fresh and compelling conclusions from their research, the study populations remain relatively small and diverse and the research should be seen as a first, incremental step toward a broader understanding of the issues confronting Black immigrant families and their children. It is our hope that this volume will lay a foundation for future research and policy development on this increasingly significant population.

The chapters identify several factors associated with health, development, and early academic performance for Black immigrants' children. Some bear on the selectivity of immigrants — that is, their motivation, education, and socioeconomic background prior to migration. In general, African immigrants can be viewed as comparatively highly selected because they travel long distances, making illegal migration more difficult than from the Caribbean or Latin America. Additionally, many African immigrants must meet the modest educational admission requirements imposed by the diversity visa program.

Another complex factor that influences the health, development, and early academic achievement of Black immigrants' children is their reception in the United States. Since relatively few Black immigrants are unauthorized, few are affected by restrictive immigration policies and enforcement policies at the federal, state, and local levels. Further, since most Black immigrants speak English fluently, they and their children do not experience the same levels of linguistic isolation as some other immigrant populations. Taken together, legal status and English skills translate into broader access to public programs and other forms of social support.

When it comes to the climate of reception, we should also emphasize the spatial concentration of the Caribbean, and to a lesser extent African, populations in the United States. Their concentration in a few states (including New York, Florida, Maryland, and Massachusetts) means that the responsiveness of these states' integration policies to the needs of children of Black immigrants are likely to have an important impact on their well-being and life trajectories. Integration policies include those influencing credential recognition of highly educated but often underemployed Black immigrant parents, funding for dual language learning pre-school programs, and, as we have seen, the responsiveness of teachers and schools to Black immigrant children's language and other learning needs.

A complex related contextual variable lies at the intersection of immigrant integration and racial discrimination. Here the evidence is harder to come by, especially in large-scale survey data. Whether and how Black immigrants' children are affected by discrimination and perceptions of discrimination remains an important topic for further research that adopts different methodologies.

One set of findings that almost all the chapters place in stark relief involves the relative disadvantages of children in Latino immigrant and US-born Black families. Though this volume was intended to focus on Black immigrants' children, the findings here consistently make it clear that the children of Latino immigrants and US-born Blacks remain the nation's most vulnerable child populations. Some of the policies designed to support the well-being and development of these children — policies such as improving access to health care and social services, facilitating enrollment in early education programs, and improving the education of ELL students in the case of Latino children — would also be valuable for children in Black immigrant families.

A related set of findings involves the change in position of Black immigrants' children relative to other children on several key indicators when controlling for socioeconomic status. It appears that much of the disadvantage of children of Black immigrants is related to socioeconomic status (or in the case of educational outcomes for non-English-speaking Black immigrants, language). When socioeconomic status and language are controlled in the models, children of Black immigrants generally outperform children of Latino immigrants and Black natives, and they sometimes perform on par with Asian and white children. Black immigrant families may provide protective factors— factors which are difficult to measure in existing data sets — that help insulate children from the negative effects of poverty and linguistic isolation. Thus it is important to provide results with and without controls for socioeconomic status and language, as several of the authors have done in this volume.

This volume was commissioned by the Foundation for Child Development with the intent of laying the groundwork for research on young children in Black immigrant families. As we look over the chapters several lines of inquiry in particular seem to hold potential. One would be to probe the apparent conflicts in the findings that surface from the analyses described in this volume. As we have noted, differing studies of indicators such as the initiation of prenatal care and school readiness produce differing results that hinge on the subpopulations studied, the data sets used, and the comparison populations selected.

Another potential area of inquiry would be to look beyond the epidemiologic paradox to examine whether the mostly positive birth outcomes of children of Black immigrants erode over time. The evidence on child health presented in the volume is mixed, though obesity is a concern among Black immigrants' children just as it is among Latino immigrants' children.

A further topic of future research might be the progress of children of Black immigrants whose families entered as refugees. Their share of the total refugee population has been higher in the most recent decade than in the past: for instance 29 percent of refugees had African nationalities in the 2000s versus 7 percent in the 1990s.[9] Moreover, refugees generally are among the most disadvantaged immigrant groups. One animating question here might be the degree to which the benefits and services provided under the refugee resettlement program have helped them overcome that disadvantage and promoted their social and economic integration.

Another possible research direction — suggested above — would be to examine perceived discrimination on the part of younger children of Black immigrants along with its effect on identity formation and, in turn, on educational achievement, physical and mental health, and other outcomes.

Finally, as Margot Jackson's chapter underscores, comparative research on children of Black immigrants can be quite valuable. Future analyses might follow her work and the work of others who have examined how settlement of similar populations in differing states, metro areas, and countries with differing mixes of integration and immigration enforcement policies affect development and integration — thereby offering insights into practice and policy models.[10] ⟿

---

9   US Department of Homeland Security (DHS), *2011 Yearbook of Immigration Statistics*, Table 14 (Washington, DC: DHS, 2012), www.dhs.gov/yearbook-immigration-statistics; DHS, *2002 Yearbook of Immigration Statistics*, Table 17 (Washington, DC: DHS, 2003), www.dhs.gov/archives.

10   Maurice Crul, "Pathways to Success for the Second Generation in Europe," *Migration Information Source*, September, 2007, www.migrationinformation.org/Feature/display.cfm?ID=592.

Works Cited

Capps, Randy, Kristen McCabe, and Michael Fix. 2012. New Streams: African Migration to the United States. In *Young Children of Black Immigrants in America: Changing Flows, Changing Faces*, eds. Randy Capps and Michael Fix. Washington, DC: Migration Policy Institute.

Crul, Maurice. 2007. Pathways to Success for the Second Generation in Europe. *Migration Information Source*, September 2007. www.migrationinformation. org/Feature/display.cfm?ID=592.

Hernandez, Donald J. 2012. Young Children in Black Immigrant Families from Africa and the Caribbean. In *Young Children of Black Immigrants in America: Changing Flows, Changing Faces*, eds. Randy Capps and Michael Fix. Washington, DC: Migration Policy Institute.

Migration Policy Institute (MPI) Data Hub. 2011. The United States (Social & Demographic Characteristics). www.migrationinformation.org/datahub/state. cfm?ID=US.

_____. 2011. The United States (Social & Demographic Characteristics, Table 4. Children in Immigrant Families in the United States (1990, 2000, and 2010). www.migrationinformation.org/datahub/state.cfm?ID=US#tables.

US Census Bureau. Table 8. Race and Hispanic Origin of the Population by Nativity: 1850 to 1990. Accessed September 26, 2012. www.census.gov/population/ www/documentation/twps0029/tab08.html.

_____. 2012. Most Children Younger than Age 1 are Minorities, Census Bureau Reports. News release, May 17, 2012. www.census.gov/newsroom/releases/ archives/population/cb12-90.html.

US Census Bureau, American FactFinder. 2009. American Community Survey, Table S0201: Selected Population Profile in the United States. Accessed September 30, 2012.

US Department of Homeland Security (DHS). 2003. *2002 Yearbook of Immigration Statistics*. Washington, DC: DHS. www.dhs.gov/archives.

_____. 2012. *2011 Yearbook of Immigration Statistics*. Washington, DC: DHS. www.dhs.gov/yearbook-immigration-statistics.

PART ONE

DEMOGRAPHY OF A RAPIDLY GROWING IMMIGRANT POPULATION TO THE UNITED STATES

CHAPTER 1

CONTEMPORARY BLACK CARIBBEAN IMMIGRANTS IN THE UNITED STATES

Kevin J. A. Thomas

The Pennsylvania State University

Introduction

Caribbean societies have long been part of international migration movements. Along with the demise of their native populations following early contact with Europeans, the demographic profile of Caribbean societies was transformed by additional immigration from Europe and the arrival of sub-Saharan African slaves[1] in the early 1500s.[2] During the period of slavery, however, there was limited migration of Black slaves from the Caribbean to the United States. According to historical evidence, some slaves were transferred to US plantations after first being acclimated to the harsh conditions of the Caribbean islands.[3] In sum, for the almost three centuries following the arrival of Africans in the Caribbean, there was little voluntary migration of Blacks between the Caribbean and the United States.

Large-scale voluntary movements started to occur almost immediately after the end of slavery in the British Caribbean during the 1830s, as former slaves explored opportunities to secure better living conditions elsewhere.[4] Initially, these movements were restricted to inside the region, and involved freed slaves moving from labor-surplus to labor-

---

1   Alejandro Portes and Ramón Grosfoguel, "Caribbean Diasporas: Migration and Ethnic Communities," *Annals of the American Academy of Political and Social Science* 533 (1994): 48–69.
2   Mary C. Waters, *Black Identities: West Indian Immigrant Dreams and American Realities* (Cambridge, MA: Harvard University Press, 1999).
3   D. Elliott Parris, "Contributions of the Caribbean Immigrant to the United States Society," *Journal of Caribbean Studies* 2 (1981): 1–13.
4   Bonham C. Richardson, "Caribbean Migrations 1838-1985" in *Modern Caribbean*, eds. F. W. Knight and C. A. Collier (Chapel Hill: University of North Carolina Press, 1989), 203–28.

scarce Caribbean colonies.[5] Since then, successive generations have used migration as a means to improve living standards and to mitigate the economic hardships of the post-slavery period. In the process, increasingly large numbers of Caribbean Blacks migrated to destinations in Europe, primarily the United Kingdom.

It was not until the end of the Spanish-American War in 1898 that the United States emerged as a major destination for Black international migrants from the Caribbean.[6] Among the initial wave were Caribbean natives who had been employed by US firms in the construction of the Panama Canal. Many of these immigrants settled in New York after their economic sojourn to Central America, although about one-third of them eventually returned to their homelands.[7] For much of the past two centuries, Caribbean immigration to the United States has also been influenced by America's hegemonic relationship with countries in the region, since most of them, with the important exception of Jamaica, have been under US political control at some point in their history.[8]

Despite economic and political links between the United States and the Caribbean, immigrants from the region accounted for only a small percentage of all US immigrants until recently. Between 1820 and 1970, for example, only 2 percent of all immigrants in the United States were from the Caribbean (meanwhile, the corresponding proportion of African immigrants was even smaller, at around 0.1 percent).[9] Many Caribbean Blacks who arrived during this period were labor migrants whose services were heavily recruited by the US agricultural industry. For example, in the late 1800s workers migrated to Florida in large numbers in response to the high demand for labor among US fruit harvesting industries.[10]

I.   Trends, Diversity, and Origins

While the initial Caribbean contribution to total immigration to the United States was relatively small, it grew steadily over the 20th century.[11] In particular, between 1920 and 1950 the number of Caribbean immigrants to the United States increased by more than 540 percent.[12]

---

5   Suzanne Model, *West Indian Immigrants: A Black Success Story?* (New York: Russell Sage Foundation, 2008).

6   Ibid.

7   Richardson, "Caribbean Migrations 1838-1985."

8   Portes and Grosfoguel, "Caribbean Diasporas."

9   Roy Simon Bryce-Laporte, "Black Immigrants — The Experience of Invisibility and Inequality," *Journal of Black Studies* 3, No. 1 (1972): 29–56.

10   Raymond A. Mohl, "Black Immigrants: Bahamians in Early Twentieth Century Miami," *Florida Historical Quarterly* 65, No. 3 (1987): 271–97.

11   These quotas were set for nations in the Eastern Hemisphere, not the Western Hemisphere, and so did not apply to immigration from the Caribbean.

12   Portes and Grosfoguel, "Caribbean Diasporas."

Immigration reforms in 1965, which lifted national origin-country quotas and replaced them with a system based on family reunification and employment, further increased the size of the Caribbean immigrant population. A decade after the 1965 reforms, the number of Caribbean immigrant arrivals to the United States was almost equal to those from Mexico and Canada.[13] These movements were also facilitated by advanced communication and transportation links between the United States and the Caribbean.[14] As a result of these developments, migration from the Caribbean became less risky. Thus, legislative, infrastructural, and technological developments combined to dramatically increase migration flows between the Caribbean and the United States during the course of the 20th century. Consequently, between 1981 and 1990, an estimated 1.2 million Caribbean immigrants arrived in the United States; this number is about 1,000 percent larger than the number of arrivals between 1921 and 1930.[15]

The increased Caribbean migrant flows to the United States after the 1960s included a significant number of unauthorized immigrants from selected Caribbean countries. Some studies suggest that in the late 1970s, Jamaica, Haiti, and the Dominican Republic were among the top 14 countries of origin for unauthorized immigrants to the United States.[16] Estimates also indicate that in 1980, these countries, along with Cuba and Trinidad and Tobago, accounted for as much as 7.1 percent of the total unauthorized immigrant population of the United States.[17]

Despite the rapid growth in size of the Caribbean immigrant population throughout much of the 20th century, Black immigrants from the region have arrived in smaller numbers than their counterparts from Africa since the year 2000. Yet, because of their longer history of immigration to the United States, Black immigrants from the Caribbean still outnumber the Black African immigrant population. In 2008-09, for example, there were 1.7 million Black Caribbean immigrants in the United States compared to 1.1 million Black Africans (see Table 1). Likewise, the total number of Caribbean Blacks exceeded the combined total number of Black immigrants from South America, Europe, and other world regions. Collectively, Caribbean countries account for the majority of the Black immigrant population in the United States. In 2009, one in every two Black immigrants was from a Caribbean-origin country.

---

13 Roy Simon Bryce-Laporte, "Introduction: New York City and the New Caribbean Immigration: A Contextual Statement," *International Migration Review* 13, No. 2 (1979): 214–34.

14 Richardson, "Caribbean Migrations 1838-1985," 203–28; Mary Mederios Kent, "Immigration and America's Black Population," *Population Bulletin* 62, No. 4 (December 2007).

15 Portes and Grosfoguel, "Caribbean Diasporas: Migration and Ethnic Communities."

16 Bryce-Laporte, "Introduction: New York City and the New Caribbean Immigration."

17 Jeffrey S. Passel and Karen A. Woodrow, "Geographic Distribution of Undocumented Immigrants: Estimates of Undocumented Aliens Counted in the 1980 Census by State," *International Migration Review* 18, No. 3 (1984): 642–71.

Table 1. Black Immigrants in the United States by Region of Origin, 2008-09

	Total Immigrant Population (000s)	Black Immigrant Population (000s)	Share of Blacks among All Immigrants (%)
All US immigrants	*38,234*	*3,267*	*9*
Born in Africa	1,457	1,081	74
Born in the Caribbean	3,437	1,701	49
Born in South America	2,578	174	7
Born in Mexico or Central America	14,285	191	1
Born in Europe	5,113	58	1

Note: Black immigrants are those who responded "Black" either alone or in combination with any other race in response to the American Community Survey (ACS) in 2008-09.
Source: Migration Policy Institute (MPI) analysis of 2008 and 2009 ACS, pooled.

One distinguishing feature of the immigrant population from the Caribbean, relative to that from Africa, is that the former is more racially diverse. Estimates for 2009 indicate that about half (49 percent) of all Caribbean immigrants identified themselves as Black. (See Table 2.) Over 90 percent of immigrants from several sending countries (including the two largest — Jamaica and Haiti) identified themselves as Black. On the other hand, Black immigrants accounted for only 4, 14, and 47 percent of immigrants from Cuba, the Dominican Republic, and Dominica, respectively. Black immigration from these three countries has accelerated recently, further increasing the diversity of the Caribbean immigrant population. Between 1980 and 2009, the number of Black immigrants from Dominica increased by 1,500 percent while the number from the Dominican Republic and Cuba increased by 600 percent and 187 percent, respectively.

Table 2. Black Immigrants as Share of All Immigrants in the United States from Caribbean Origins, 2008-09

	Total Immigrants (000s)	Black Immigrants (000s)	% Black
All US Immigrants	38,234	3,267	9
Born in the Caribbean	3,437	1,701	49
St. Kitts-Nevis	12	12	100
Haiti	541	534	99
Barbados	50	48	96
Jamaica	638	612	96
St. Lucia	19	18	95
Antigua-Barbuda	18	17	94
St. Vincent	18	17	94
Grenada	31	29	94
Bahamas	29	26	90
Other West Indian countries	34	29	85
Trinidad and Tobago	220	181	82
Other Caribbean countries	23	16	70
Dominica	34	16	47
Dominican Republic	785	110	14
Cuba	985	34	3

Source: MPI analysis of 2008 and 2009 ACS, pooled.

In recent decades, Black Caribbean immigrant flows have mostly originated in English-speaking countries. The significance of these movements increased toward the end of the 1960s as Caribbean nationals from former British colonies faced restrictions on the immigration of Commonwealth nationals to Britain.[18] As a result of these restrictions, immigration from Jamaica and former English colonies in the Caribbean surged toward the end of the decade. Beginning in the 1960s, there were also notable increases in immigration from non-English speaking countries; the number of Dominican and Haitian immigrants rose substantially, accompanied by increased refugee flows from Cuba following the Cuban revolution in 1959.[19]

---

18 Portes and Grosfoguel, "Caribbean Diasporas."
19 Adela Pellegrino, "Trends in Latin American Skilled Migration: 'Brain Drain' or 'Brain Exchange'?" *International Migration* 39, No. 5 (2001): 115–32; Portes and Grosfoguel, "Caribbean Diasporas."

Immigrants from English-speaking Caribbean countries still make up the majority of Black Caribbean immigrants in the United States. Jamaica alone accounted for 36 percent in 2008-09 (see Table 3), while Trinidad and Tobago, Barbados, and Grenada collectively accounted for 19 percent. At the same time, the size of the immigrant population from non-English Caribbean countries has accelerated rapidly in recent decades. The number of Black immigrants from Haiti increased 514 percent between 1980 and 2008-09, while the Black Dominican population grew by 686 percent. In fact, Haitians accounted for 31 percent of all Black Caribbean immigrants in 2008-09, up from 19 percent in 1980.

Table 3. Black Caribbean Immigrants by Country of Origin, United States, 1980 to 2008-09

Year	Population (000s)					Share of Total from Region (%)				
	1980	1990	2000	2006	2008 -09	1980	1990	2000	2006	2008 -09
Black Caribbean immigrants	453	897	1,428	1,636	1,701	100	100	100	100	100
Jamaica	179	314	534	620	612	40	35	37	38	36
Haiti	87	216	414	484	534	19	24	29	30	31
Trinidad & Tobago	57	98	164	194	181	13	11	11	12	11
Dominican Republic	14	95	85	68	110	3	11	6	4	6
Barbados	27	40	51	51	48	6	4	4	3	3
Cuba	12	22	30	33	34	3	2	2	2	2
Grenada	7	16	26	30	29	2	2	2	2	2
Other West Indian countries	3	15	25	39	29	1	2	2	2	2
Bahamas	12	19	25	26	26	3	2	2	2	2
St. Lucia	1	7	13	17	18	0	1	1	1	1
Antigua-Barbuda	4	12	18	14	17	1	1	1	1	1
St. Vincent	3	12	21	20	17	1	1	1	1	1
Dominica	1	10	13	15	16	0	1	1	1	1
Other Caribbean countries	43	16	-	15	16	9	2	-	1	1
St. Kitts-Nevis	2	7	10	9	12	0	1	1	1	1

Note: Black immigrants are those who responded "Black" either alone or in combination with any other race to the ACS race question in 2000, 2006, 2008, and 2009. In 1980 and 1990, respondents could not report more than one race (i.e., report a multiracial identity), and so the responses for these years are for Black race only.
Source: MPI analysis of data from the 1980, 1990, and 2000 US Census of Population and Housing; 2006 ACS, and 2008-2009 ACS, pooled.

Between 2006 and 2009, however, the overall number of Black Caribbean immigrants fell by about 4 percent. This decline was possibly a response to the economic recession in the United States. Between 2006 and 2008-09, the number of Black immigrants from Trinidad and Tobago decreased by 7 percent (falling from 194,000 to 181,000), while the population of Black immigrants from Jamaica remained nearly the same.

II. Modes of Entry and Legal Status

Estimates based on data from the Pew Hispanic Center indicate that Black immigrants from the Caribbean are the least likely to be unauthorized among all Black immigrants in the United States.[20] Specifically, about 16 percent of Caribbean-born Blacks were unauthorized in 2006-08, compared with 21 percent of Black Africans and 29 percent of Black immigrants from other regions (see Figure 1). Given its larger size overall, however, the unauthorized segment of the Black Caribbean immigrant population was still larger in absolute terms than that of Black Africans.

In general, about half (49 percent) of all Caribbean Blacks in 2006-08 were naturalized citizens — the largest proportion among Black immigrants and a higher share than US immigrants overall (32 percent). Black Caribbean immigrants were also slightly more likely to be legal permanent residents (LPRs) (28 percent) than Black Africans (26 percent) and were equally as likely to be LPRs as immigrants overall. The relatively large proportion of naturalized citizens among Caribbean immigrants reflects the fact that, on average, they have more years of US residence than most other Black immigrants.[21] One implication of their higher levels of citizenship and permanent residence status is that, among all Black immigrants, those from the Caribbean are possibly the least likely to be disqualified from public benefit programs.

At least 7 percent of all Black Caribbean immigrants are refugees or asylees. Most are Cubans, who, since the *Cuban Adjustment Act of 1966*, are automatically granted provisional admission (and can then gain legal permanent resident status after a year of US residence).[22] Recent

---

20 These estimates were calculated by the Migration Policy Institute (MPI) based on US Current Population Survey (CPS) data, augmented by legal status assignments by demographers at the Pew Hispanic Center.

21 After becoming legal permanent residents (LPRs), immigrants must typically spend five years in this status (three years if married to a US citizen) before becoming eligible to apply for US citizenship.

22 Tracy Fujimoto, "Elian Doesn't Live Here Anymore: One Little Boy in the Maze of US Immigration and Family Law," *University of Hawai'i Law Review* 23 (2000): 249–75; Ruth Ellen Wasem, *Cuban Migration and Policy Issues* (Washington, DC: Congressional Research Service, 2007), www.fosterquan.com/content/documents/policy_papers/CRSOnCubanMigrationIssues.pdf.

refugees include Cubans, admitted under the provisions of the *Cuban Migration Agreement of 1994*, as well as those from other refugee-sending countries such Haiti and the Dominican Republic. Since the 2010 earthquake in Haiti, an estimated 48,000 Haitian immigrants already in the United States have received protection from removal — and work authorization — under a blanket form of temporary humanitarian relief known as Temporary Protected Status (TPS).[23] Unlike refugees, TPS recipients are not eligible for public benefits, including public health insurance, in most states.

Figure 1. Citizenship and Legal Status of Black Caribbean Immigrants to United States, 2006-08

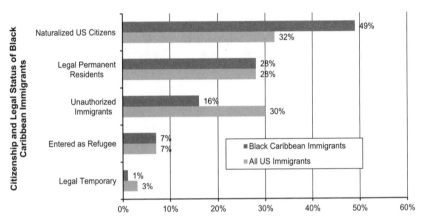

Source: MPI analysis of US Current Population Survey (CPS) 2006-08 data, pooled, augmented by assignments of legal status to noncitizens by Jeffrey S. Passel, Pew Hispanic Center.

Official estimates for the 2010 fiscal year, which report on nationality but not race, indicate that Caribbean immigrants of any race accounted for 13 percent of all LPRs admitted to the United States during the year — slightly more than African immigrants (10 percent).[24] Caribbean LPRs were less likely than Africans to be admitted under the diversity visa program, for employment, or through other channels. Sixty percent of Caribbean LPRs were admitted through family reunification channels compared to 48 percent of Africans.

---

23 US Department of Homeland Security (DHS), "Secretary Napolitano Announces the Extension of Temporary Protected Status for Haiti Beneficiaries," (press release, May 17, 2011), www.dhs.gov/ynews/releases/pr_1305643820292.shtm.

24 DHS, Yearbook of Immigration Statistics, 2010 Revised March 30, 2011, "Table 10: Persons Obtaining Legal Permanent Resident Status by Broad Class of Admission and Region and Country of Birth: Fiscal Year 2010" (Washington, DC: DHS, 2011), www.dhs.gov/files/statistics/publications/LPR10.shtm.

According to demographer Mary Mederios Kent[25] more than 80 percent of recent immigrants from the Caribbean admitted under family reunification provisions were from English-speaking countries and Haiti. In 2010, 41 percent of immigrants from Caribbean origin countries and territories were legally admitted as the immediate relatives of US citizens (see Figure 2). Another third (34 percent) were admitted under other family-sponsored preferences, which are subject to annual numerical limits and have been challenged in congressional immigration reform debates.

While Caribbean immigrants who obtained LPR status in 2010 were most likely to be admitted as the immediate relatives of US citizens, refugee and asylee admissions accounted for the second largest number of persons from the Caribbean granted permanent residence. Caribbean immigrants (24 percent) were more likely to obtain permanent residence as refugees or asylees than either Africans (22 percent) or immigrants overall (13 percent). In 2010, virtually all Caribbean refugees and asylees were from Cuba (91 percent) and Haiti (9 percent).

Figure 2. Persons Granted Legal Permanent Residence by Class of Admission,* FY 2010

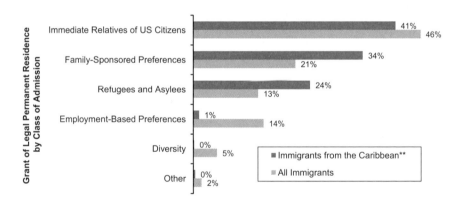

* These admissions include both immigrants obtaining permanent residency upon arrival in the United States as well as those who apply for and receive LPR status after substantial periods of residency in the country without such status.

** Includes Caribbean immigrants of all races; the legal admissions data disaggregate admissions by country of origin and not by race.

Source: Author's representation of data from US Department of Homeland Security (DHS), "Table 10: Persons Obtaining Legal Permanent Resident Status by Broad Class of Admission and Region and Country of Birth: Fiscal Year 2010," *Yearbook of Immigration Statistics, 2010* (Washington, DC: DHS, revised March 30, 2011).

25 Kent, "Immigration and America's Black Population."

III. Geographic Settlement Patterns

Black Caribbean immigrants are less geographically dispersed than their African counterparts. However, unlike African immigrant groups they have been very successful in using their spatial concentration in selected states to increase their economic and political influence in local communities.[26] In 2009, two-thirds of all Caribbean immigrants lived in two states — New York and Florida, with 38 percent and 28 percent respectively — accounting for the majority of the Black foreign-born population in these states and nearly one-fifth of both states' total Black population (18 percent and 17 percent). Along with New York, other northeastern states such as Massachusetts (4 percent), Maryland (3 percent), and Connecticut (3 percent) are host to substantial numbers of Black immigrants from the Caribbean.

Over the years, Caribbean immigrant groups have clustered in specific US states. As in the first half of the 20th century, Dominicans and Jamaicans remain heavily concentrated in New York, while Florida maintains its long tradition of attracting refugees from Cuba. There are large concentrations of Black Haitian immigrants in the Miami–Fort Lauderdale area and around south Florida, including those living in enclave communities such as Little Haiti.[27] Caribbean settlement in Florida is, however, distinct when compared with other states in the US South and Midwest. Compared to Africans and other Black immigrants, for example, Caribbean Blacks are less likely to live in states such as Arkansas, Louisiana, Oklahoma, Mississippi, and Missouri.

IV. Human-Capital Characteristics

Following the immigration reforms of 1965, Caribbean immigration to the United States involved a significant degree of educational selectivity. In other words, there were differences in the educational characteristics of Caribbean nationals who chose to migrate to the United States compared to those who chose to remain in their countries of origin. This was especially true for immigrants from English-speaking Caribbean countries. For example, while Jamaican and Trinidadian immigrants were generally more highly educated than their origin-country counterparts, the opposite was true for immigrants from the Dominican Republic.[28] Furthermore, immigrants from English-speaking Caribbean countries arriving during this period were more likely to be

---

26 Cédric Audebert, "Residential Patterns and Political Empowerment among Jamaicans and Haitians in the U.S. Metropolis: The Role of Ethnicity in New York and South Florida," *Human Architecture: Journal of Sociology and Self-knowledge* 6, No. 4 (2009): 53–68.

27 Audebert, "Residential Patterns;" James A. Dunlevy, "On the Settlement Patterns of Recent Caribbean and Latin Immigrants to the United States," *Growth and Change* 22, No. 1 (1991): 54–67.

28 Adela Pellegrino, "Trends in Latin American Skilled Migration."

highly educated and employed in white-collar occupations than their counterparts who arrived in earlier decades.[29]

Recently, however, notable declines have occurred in educational selectivity among Caribbean immigrants. More recent Caribbean Blacks tend to have had relatively lower socioeconomic status in their countries of origin.[30] In contrast, contemporary immigrants from Africa tend to be among the more educated members of their origin countries.[31] These differences may partly explain why Caribbean Blacks are not as well educated, overall, as their immigrant counterparts from Africa.

For example, in 2005-09, Black Caribbean immigrants were generally overrepresented among less-educated groups in the United States. About one in five Caribbean Blacks ages 25 or over had less than a high school diploma compared to one in seven Black Africans (see Table 4). Compared to US natives (12 percent), Caribbean Blacks were about twice as likely to lack a high school degree (22 percent). Immigrants with less than a high school diploma or equivalent credential also accounted for a considerable proportion of Black immigrants from countries such as the Dominican Republic (36 percent), Cuba (35 percent), and Haiti (26 percent). These patterns reflect two possibilities. First, Caribbean Blacks with low levels of educational attainment may be more likely to come from non-English-speaking Caribbean countries because of their close proximity of the United States; the highly educated migrants from these countries may have more flexibility to go elsewhere. Second, contemporary immigrants from the Caribbean with comparatively low educational credentials are more likely to come from refugee-sending countries, in particular Haiti. This pattern is consistent with studies showing that recent Caribbean refugees are substantially less educated than their counterparts who arrived in the 1960s.[32]

Caribbean Blacks are also underrepresented among the highly skilled when compared to US natives, Black African immigrants, and immigrants overall. On average, Black immigrants born in the Caribbean were less likely to have a master's, doctorate, or professional degree in 2005-09 (7 percent) than US-born Blacks (10 percent) and Black African immigrants (15 percent). They were also about half as likely to have college degrees (13 percent) than Black African immigrants (23 percent). Immigrants from English-speaking Caribbean countries such as Bahamas, St. Kitts-Nevis, and Antigua and Barbuda were the most

29 Elizabeth Thomas-Hope, "Skilled Labour Migration from Developing Countries: Study on the Caribbean Region," (International Migration Papers 50, International Labor Office, Geneva, 2002), www.ilo.org/public/english/protection/migrant/download/imp/imp50e.pdf.

30 Douglas S. Massey, "Commentary," *Federal Reserve Board of New York Economic Policy Review* 11, No. 2 (2005): 121–2.

31 Joseph Takougang, "Contemporary African Immigration to the United States," *Irinkerindo: A Journal of African Migration* 2 (2003).

32 Portes and Grosfoguel, "Caribbean Diasporas."

likely to have a four-year college degree, while those from the non-English speaking countries of Haiti, Dominican Republic, and Cuba were the least likely to have such a degree.

Table 4. Educational Attainment for Adults (Ages 25 and Over) by Origin (%), 2005-09

	Educational Attainment				
	Less than High School	High School or GED	Some College	4-Year College (no professional degree)	Master's, Doctorate, or Professional Degree
US TOTAL	15	29	28	17	10
Native born	12	31	30	18	10
Foreign born	32	23	18	16	11
Black immigrants	20	28	27	16	9
Black immigrants born in Africa	13	21	29	23	15
Black immigrants born in the Caribbean	22	32	27	13	7
Bahamas	12	26	32	19	10
St. Kitts-Nevis	19	32	21	18	10
Other Caribbean countries	19	30	24	15	12
Dominica	23	29	26	14	9
Other West Indian countries	16	35	26	15	8
Grenada	19	37	24	12	8
Jamaica	20	32	27	13	7
Trinidad and Tobago	14	36	29	14	7
Barbados	17	34	27	14	7
Antigua and Barbuda	20	32	25	15	7
Cuba	35	32	19	8	6
St. Vincent	20	35	25	14	6
Haiti	26	30	27	12	5
Dominican Republic	36	27	21	11	5
St. Lucia	21	39	22	12	5

Source: MPI analysis of 2005-09 ACS, pooled.

Caribbean Blacks are more likely to be English-proficient than their African counterparts (see Table 5). A smaller proportion of the former are also likely to be bilingual; in fact, close to 60 percent of Black Caribbean immigrants speak exclusively English at home. These patterns reflect the fact that the majority of Caribbean countries are former British colonies. As the estimates indicate, 90 percent of immigrants from major English-speaking Caribbean-origin countries — such as Jamaica, Trinidad and Tobago, and Barbados — use English as their primary language at home. Moreover, 11 of 13 Caribbean-origin groups in Table 4 have English monolingual levels that exceed the average for all immigrants and that for Black Africans.

Table 5. English Proficiency for Immigrants Ages 5 and Over by Origin (%), 2005-09

	Yes, speaks only English	Speaks Another Language at Home			
		Yes, speaks English very well	Yes speaks English well	Yes, speaks English but not well	Does not speak English
Foreign born, total	16	32	21	20	11
Black immigrants, total	46	29	14	8	3
Black African immigrants	21	49	20	8	2
Black Caribbean immigrants	59	19	12	8	3
Grenada	97	2	0	0	0
Barbados	96	3	0	1	0
St. Vincent	96	3	1	0	0
Antigua-Barbuda	96	3	0	0	0
Trinidad and Tobago	95	3	1	0	0
St. Kitts-Nevis	95	4	0	0	0
Jamaica	93	6	1	0	0
Other West Indian countries	88	9	2	1	0
Bahamas	77	20	3	1	0
Other Caribbean countries	72	22	5	1	0
Dominica	62	26	6	3	3
St. Lucia	59	34	5	2	0
Cuba	8	26	20	26	20
Haiti	7	40	30	18	5
Dominican Republic	5	31	24	26	14

Source: MPI analysis of 2005-2009 ACS, pooled.

As expected, English proficiency levels are much lower among immigrants from Spanish-speaking Cuba and from French-speaking Haiti, groups that have many poorly educated refugees. Within household contexts, fewer than 10 percent of immigrants from Haiti and Cuba use English exclusively. Both groups speak other non-English languages at home, such as French Creole and Spanish. Among these groups, limited English language skills are likely to have negative implications for their integration into society, given the positive influence of English proficiency on various socioeconomic outcomes of immigrants.[33]

V. Employment and Earnings

In 2005-09, Black Caribbean immigrants were as likely to participate in the labor force as Black African immigrants (see Table 6). Among individuals between the ages of 18 and 64, the percentage employed was about 75 percent for both groups. Caribbean Blacks also had labor force participation rates that exceeded the averages for US natives and all immigrants combined. However, there were important variations in labor force participation across the Caribbean Black immigrant population. On the whole, these variations were not necessarily driven by systematic differences in labor force participation among immigrants from English and non-English Caribbean countries. For example, while Cuban Blacks had the lowest percentage employed (64 percent), Haitian Blacks had an employment rate (77 percent) that was consistent with the average for all Caribbean Blacks (75 percent).

There are pronounced gender disparities in labor force participation among both Black African and Caribbean immigrants. Female employment rates were as much as 13, 11, and 9 percentage points lower than those of males among immigrants from St. Vincent, Haiti, and the Dominican Republic, respectively. Still, on average, Black Caribbean women (73 percent) were more likely to participate in the labor force than Black African-born (68 percent) and all US-born (68 percent) females. This was partly due to the higher employment rates of female immigrants from countries such as Jamaica, Grenada, and St. Kitts. In absolute numbers, there were more employed Black Caribbean women than men (533,000 versus 468,000), a pattern also seen in two of the leading sending countries: Jamaica and Trinidad and Tobago.

---

33 Kevin J. Thomas, "Familial Influences on Poverty Among Young Children in Black Immigrant, U.S.-born Black, and Nonblack Immigrant Families," *Demography* 48, No. 2 (2011): 437–60.

Table 6. US Civilian Employment Rates for Adults (Ages 18 and Over),* by Origin and Gender, 2005-09

	Population (000s)			Employment Rate		
	Total	Men	Women	Total	Men	Women
All US adults ages 18 to 64	187,610	93,114	94,496	71	76	67
Native-born adults	157,467	77,617	79,850	72	75	68
Immigrant adults	30,143	15,497	14,645	71	82	60
Black immigrants	2,556	1,247	1,309	75	78	71
Black African immigrants	847	459	388	75	80	68
Black Caribbean immigrants	1,338	608	730	75	77	73
St. Kitts-Nevis	9	4	5	80	83	78
Grenada	24	10	14	78	77	78
Jamaica	484	213	270	77	77	77
Other West Indian countries	27	12	15	77	77	77
Haiti	414	198	216	76	79	72
Barbados	38	18	21	76	78	75
St. Vincent	15	6	9	74	80	70
Antigua-Barbuda	15	6	9	74	75	74
Other Caribbean countries	13	6	7	74	83	67
Trinidad and Tobago	153	66	88	73	76	70
Dominica	14	6	8	73	76	70
Dominican Republic	72	34	38	70	74	66
Bahamas	22	10	12	69	68	69
St. Lucia	16	6	9	69	66	71
Cuba	22	13	8	64	66	61

Notes: * Employment rates are for the civilian population only. Adults in the armed forces are excluded from the denominator. Population totals for men and women may not add up exactly due to rounding.

Source: MPI analysis of 2005-09 ACS, pooled.

Collectively, Caribbean Blacks had higher median earnings than all immigrants, the overall Black immigrant population, Black Africans, and Blacks from Central America (see Table 7). Caribbean Blacks had higher median earnings. The Caribbean advantage relative to Black Africans is particularly surprising. Higher levels of schooling tend to be associated with higher earnings, and Caribbean Blacks had lower average schooling levels than Black Africans. Despite this schooling disparity, the median earnings of Caribbean Blacks were about 14 percent higher than those of their Black African counterparts, suggesting that economic returns to schooling are higher among the former than the latter. These results are also striking given the fact that Caribbean immigrant workers are more likely to be women than Africans.

Four factors may explain these earnings differences. First, compared to Caribbean Blacks, Black Africans with non-US university degrees receive lower financial returns from their schooling.[34] Second, since immigrant earnings are positively associated with language proficiency, so higher levels of English proficiency among Caribbean than African Blacks may contribute to income differences. Third, Caribbean immigrants have on average been in the United States longer than African immigrants, and those from Jamaica, Trinidad, and other English-speaking West Indian countries are the most established. Fourth, the average age of Caribbean immigrants is higher than for Africans, with a larger share in the prime earning years of 45 to 54.

---

34 F. Nii-Amoo Dodoo, "Assimilation Differences among Africans in America," *Social Forces* 76, No. 2 (1997): 527–46.

Table 7. Median Annual Earnings for US Civilian Workers (Ages 16 and Over),* by Origin, 2005-09

	Total (thousands)	Median Annual Earnings (US $)
All US workers ages 16 and over	141,295	$32,000
Native-born workers	119,095	$33,000
Immigrant workers	22,200	$26,000
Black immigrants	1,962	$29,000
Black African immigrants	639	$27,000
Black Caribbean immigrants	1,044	$30,000
Barbados	31	$36,000
Other West Indian countries	22	$35,000
Other Caribbean countries	10	$35,000
Antigua-Barbuda	11	$35,000
Grenada	19	$33,000
Jamaica	390	$32,000
Trinidad and Tobago	115	$32,000
St. Vincent	12	$32,000
St. Kitts-Nevis	8	$31,000
Bahamas	16	$30,000
Dominica	11	$30,000
St. Lucia	11	$27,000
Haiti	322	$25,000
Cuba	15	$24,000
Dominican Republic	52	$22,000

* Median annual earnings are for civilian workers with nonzero earnings only. Adults in the armed forces and those with negative or zero earnings are excluded.

Source: MPI analysis of 2005-09 ACS, pooled.

VI. Demographic Characteristics: Age and Sex Distribution

The majority of Caribbean immigrants to the United States have traditionally been women.[35] In 2009, Caribbean Blacks were predominantly female (55 percent), unlike Black immigrants from Africa and US natives. This female dominance is particularly notable among immigrants from Antigua and Barbuda, St. Lucia, and Grenada. The exception to this pattern is found among Cubans, at least 55 percent of whom were male.

Table 8. Age Distribution of Black Immigrants, 2005-09

	Age Distribution (%)							
	< Age 11	Age 11-17	Age 18-24	Age 25-34	Age 35-44	Age 45-54	Age 55-64	Age 65 +
Total US population	15	10	10	13	14	15	11	13
Total native-born population	16	10	10	12	13	14	11	13
Total foreign-born population	3	4	9	20	22	18	12	12
Black immigrants	3	5	9	19	22	20	12	9
Black immigrants born in Africa	5	7	12	23	24	18	8	3
Black immigrants born in the Caribbean	2	4	8	17	21	22	15	13

Source: MPI analysis of 2005-2009 ACS, pooled.

Black Caribbeans were more likely to be in their older working years (ages 45-64) and to be elderly than Black African immigrants. At the same time, the proportion of Africans between the young adult ages of 18 and 34 exceeded that found among US natives and immigrants from the Caribbean.

The percentage of Caribbean immigrants who are children below age 10 is less than half that of the US-born population (6 versus 16 percent). Both the African and Caribbean immigrant populations are less likely to consist of children than US natives. This is generally true for immi-

---

35 Harriette Pipes MacAdoo, Sinead Younge, and Solomon Getahun, "Marriage and Family Socialization among Black Americans and Caribbean and African Immigrants," in *The Other African-Americans: Contemporary African and Caribbean Immigrants in the United States,* eds. Yoku Shaw-Taylor and Steven A. Tuch (Lanham, MD: Rowan and Littlefield Publishers): 93–116.

grants as most children in immigrant families are US-born. African and Caribbean immigrants are both less likely to be adolescents or young adults than US natives. It is important to note that Black immigrants born in Africa and the Caribbean are more likely than US natives to be in their child-bearing years and that the US-born children of immigrants face many of the same integration challenges as the young foreign-born.

Among Black immigrants, Caribbean Blacks have the smallest share in young childhood. Less than 1 percent of immigrants from Trinidad and Tobago, Barbados, Bahamas, and St. Kitts-Nevis are children below age 10. Compared to Black immigrants overall and Black Africans, Black Caribbeans have the lowest percentage of children below age 18. These age-distribution patterns are consistent with evidence suggesting that children in the Caribbean Black population are highly involved in return migration flows, as many Caribbean immigrant families in the United States send their children back to their origin countries to allow them to experience their teenage socialization processes back home.[36] Furthermore, return migration among Caribbean children is sometimes driven by their parents' desire to have them complete part of their education in their origin countries.[37] In general, these children are usually allowed to migrate back to the United States and to be reunited with their families during their late adolescence.

VII. Family Structure

For the most part, Black immigrants live in family contexts that are quite different from those of US natives and other immigrant populations. Research suggests that the children of Black immigrants are the least likely among children of immigrants to live in two-parent households.[38] As Table 9 indicates, the percentage of household heads (with or without children) who are single is higher among Black immigrants than among immigrants on average.

---

36 Marjorie Faulstich Orellana, Barrie Thorne, Anna Chee, and Wan Shun Eva Lam, "Transnational Childhoods: The Participation of Children in Processes of Family Migration," *Social Problems* 48, No. 4 (2001): 572–91.

37 Dwaine Plaza, "Transnational Return Migration to the English-speaking Caribbean," *Revue européenne des migrations internationales* 24, no.1 (2008): 115-37.

38 Peter David Brandon, "The Living Arrangements of Children in Immigrant Families in the United States, *International Migration Review* 36 (2002): 416-36.

Table 9. Family Structure among Black Immigrants of Caribbean Origin, 2005-09

	Family Structure (%)				
	Single: No Children under 18	Married: No Children under 18	Single with Children under 18	Married with Children under 18	Extended
Total US population	40	27	9	20	4
Native born	41	28	9	19	4
Foreign born	32	21	10	29	7
Black immigrants	40	14	16	22	8
Black immigrants born in Africa	41	11	15	28	5
Black immigrants born in the Caribbean	40	15	17	18	10

Notes: Analysis limited to household heads ages 16 and older. Married individuals are defined as those who are married with a spouse present.
Source: MPI analysis of 2005-2009 ACS, pooled.

A decomposition of single-parent households into those with and without children under 18 sheds additional light on the family structure of Black immigrants. In terms of single-parent households without children, Africans (42 percent) and Caribbean Blacks (41 percent) are broadly similar. Within immigrant sub-populations, however, up to half of Kenyan, Ugandan, and Cuban household heads live in such households.

The higher percentage of single-parent households with children among Black immigrants than among immigrants overall or among US natives is of particular policy concern. Black immigrants are disadvantaged in this regard because single-parent households are associated with various socioeconomic vulnerabilities, including high levels of poverty, limited parental supervision, and poor schooling outcomes.[39] Studies show, for example, that Black Caribbean children in single-parent households have lower test scores than their counterparts in two-parent families.[40] Beyond their exposure to the disadvantages of racial minority status, therefore, Black immigrants face additional vulnerabilities associated with the structural characteristics of the households in which they live.

---

39 Nancy Landale, Kevin J. A. Thomas, and Jennifer Van Hook, "The Living Arrangements of the Children of Immigrants," Future of Children 21, No. 1 (2011): 43–70.

40 Philip Kasinitz, Juan Battle, and Inés Miyares, "Fade to Black? The Children of West Indian Immigrants in South Florida," in Ethnicities: Children of Immigrants in America, eds. Rubén Rumbaut and Alejandro Portes (Berkeley, CA: University of California Press, 2001), 267–300.

For both African and Caribbean Blacks, the percentage of single-parent households with children is about twice that of the US average. Caribbean Black households are slightly more likely to be single-parent households with children (17 percent) than Black African households (15 percent). Some studies suggest that the prevalence of such households among Caribbean immigrants reflects the fact that such households are also highly prevalent in Caribbean-origin countries.[41] Among Africans, single-parent households are more common among Cape Verdeans, Guineans, and immigrants from refugee-sending countries such as Somalia and Liberia. Among Caribbean-origin countries, immigrants from the Dominican Republic and St. Lucia are most likely to live in a single-parent household with children.

Although one-fourth of US households overall involved married couples with no children, such families are generally uncommon among Black immigrants. Rather, as observed among all immigrants, married-couple households among African and Caribbean immigrants are more likely to have children under 18 than no children at all. The larger proportion of married households with children among Black immigrants is likely a product of family reunification processes and a higher rate of births to immigrant than native women in the years immediately following their arrival in the United States. In general, however, African immigrants are more likely to live in married households with children (28 percent) than Black immigrants from the Caribbean (18 percent).

At the same time, extended family arrangements are more common among Black immigrants than among US natives. Extended households serve an instrumental purpose in meeting the short-term needs of immigrants by allowing them to pool resources and providing child care, although their long-term benefits remain unclear.[42] Table 9 suggests that the short-term benefits of extended households are more common among the Caribbean immigrant population (9.5 percent) than among Africans (4.9 percent). A likely explanation for this disparity is the comparatively lower costs of migration between the United States and the Caribbean, which allows Caribbean immigrants to bring more members of their extended family to the country than their African immigrant counterparts. Furthermore, since Caribbean immigrants have a longer history of migration than African immigrants, they are also likely to have a larger proportion of family members who immigrate to the United States using non-marriage immigration channels.

VIII. Conclusions

Black Caribbean immigration to the United States is rooted in strong historical, cultural, and economic linkages between the two regions.

---

41 Ibid.
42 Landale, Thomas, and Van Hook, "The Living Arrangements of the Children of Immigrants."

Future immigration flows are likely to be influenced by the dynamics of America's social and political relationships with Caribbean countries and the ways in which these dynamics affect immigration policy. Continued refugee migration from Cuba, for example, is likely to be determined by the changing dynamics of US-Cuban relations. At the same time, the United States and Caribbean countries are still very much connected by strong familial relationships between Caribbean immigrants in the United States and their relatives back home. If current laws persist, such connections will provide an important basis for the continuation of legal Caribbean immigration to the United States in the coming decades.

Changes in the family preference categories in US immigration law could strongly affect future flows from the Caribbean, as the majority of the current legal permanent resident flow from the Caribbean comes through these channels. The Temporary Protected Status program has been important for Haitian immigration in recent years, and whether this program is extended or maintained will have an impact on the numbers of Haitians living in the United States as well as their legal status composition.

Regardless of how legal migration flows are affected by immigration reforms, however, the proximity of the Caribbean to the United States suggests that Caribbean countries will continue to play a role in illegal migration to the United States. Recent trends also underscore the fact that Black Caribbean immigration may be more responsive to changes in the US economy than Black African immigration. While immigration flows from several Caribbean countries declined during the recent economic recession, the immigration of Black Africans increased during this period. The determinants of these trends are difficult to identify using available data. However, it is reasonable to believe that once the recession ends, Black Caribbean immigration will return to its prerecession levels.

While Black Caribbean immigrants are overrepresented among the less educated and underrepresented among the highly educated, they report strong English language skills, become US citizens at high rates, and exhibit high levels of labor force participation. Notably, Black Caribbean immigrants report higher earnings than their African counterparts, despite the fact that Black African immigrants are among the best-educated immigrant groups in the United States.

The geographic concentration of Black Caribbean immigrants in states such as New York and Florida, long destinations for Caribbean immigrants, may lend integration advantages to the population, in part because of their potential influence over politics and public policy. Yet compared to immigrants and natives, Black Caribbean immigrants are particularly likely to live in single-parent families with children under 18, a living arrangement that complicates family socioeconomic status and child well-being. ⤴

Works Cited

American Community Survey (ACS). 2005-09. Accessed from Steven Ruggles, J. Trent Alexander, Katie Genadek, Ronald Goeken, Matthew B. Schroeder, and Matthew Sobek. *Integrated Public Use Microdata Series: Version 5.0* [Machine-readable database]. Minneapolis: University of Minnesota, 2010.

Audebert, Cédric. 2009. Residential Patterns and Political Empowerment among Jamaicans and Haitians in the U.S. Metropolis: The Role of Ethnicity in New York and South Florida. *Human Architecture: Journal of Sociology and Self-knowledge* 6 (4): 53–68.

Brandon, Peter David. 2002. The Living Arrangements of Children in Immigrant Families in the United States. *International Migration Review* 36: 416–36.

Bryce-Laporte, Roy Simon. 1972. Black Immigrants — The Experience of Invisibility and Inequality. *Journal of Black Studies* 3 (1): 29–56.

_____. 1979. Introduction: New York City and the New Caribbean Immigration: A Contextual Statement. *International Migration Review* 13 (2): 214–34.

Dodoo, F. Nii-Amoo. 1997. Assimilation Differences among Africans in America. *Social Forces* 76 (2): 527–46.

Dunlevy, James A. 1991. On the Settlement Patterns of Recent Caribbean and Latin Immigrants to the United States. *Growth and Change* 22 (1): 54–67.

Fujimoto, Tracy. 2000. Elian Doesn't Live Here Anymore: One Little Boy in the Maze of US Immigration And Family Law. *University of Hawai'i Law Review* 23: 249–75.

Kasinitz, Philip, Juan Battle, and Inés Miyares. 2001. Fade to Black? The Children of West Indian Immigrants in South Florida. In *Ethnicities: Children of Immigrants in America,* eds. Rubén Rumbaut and Alejandro Portes. Berkeley, CA: University of California Press.

Kent, Mary Mederios. 2007. Immigration and America's Black Population. *Population Bulletin* 62, no. 4 (December).

Landale, Nancy, Kevin J. A. Thomas, and Jennifer Van Hook. 2011. The Living Arrangements of the Children of Immigrants. *Future of Children* 21(1): 43–70.

MacAdoo, Harriette Pipes, Sinead Younge, and Solomon Getahun. 2007. Marriage and Family Socialization among Black Americans and Caribbean and African Immigrants. In *The Other African-Americans: Contemporary African and Caribbean Immigrants in the United States,* eds. Yoku Shaw-Taylor and Steven A. Tuch. Lanham, MD: Rowan and Littlefield Publishers.

Massey, Douglas S. 2005. Commentary. *Federal Reserve Board of New York Economic Policy Review* 11 (2): 121–2.

Model, Suzanne. 2008. *West Indian Immigrants: A Black Success Story?* New York: Russell Sage Foundation.

Mohl, Raymond A. 1987. Black Immigrants: Bahamians in Early Twentieth Century Miami. *Florida Historical Quarterly* 65 (3): 271–97.

Orellana, Marjorie Faulstich, Barrie Thorne, Anna Chee, and Wan Shun Eva Lam. 2001. Transnational Childhoods: The Participation of Children in Processes of Family Migration. *Social Problems* 48 (4): 572–91.

Parris, D. Elliott. 1981. Contributions of the Caribbean Immigrant to the United States Society. *Journal of Caribbean Studies* 2: 1–13.

Passel, Jeffrey S. and Karen A. Woodrow. 1984. Geographic Distribution of Undocumented Immigrants: Estimates of Undocumented Aliens Counted in the 1980 Census by State. *International Migration Review* 18 (3): 642–71.

Pellegrino, Adela. 2001. Trends in Latin American Skilled Migration: "Brain Drain" or "Brain Exchange"? *International Migration* 39 (5): 115–32.

Plaza, Dwaine. 2008. Transnational Return Migration to the English-speaking Caribbean. *Revue européenne des migrations internationales* 24 (1): 115-37.

Portes, Alejandro and Ramón Grosfoguel. 1994. Caribbean Diasporas: Migration and Ethnic Communities. *Annals of the American Academy of Political and Social Science* 533: 48–69.

Richardson, Bonham C. 1989. Caribbean Migrations 1838-1985. In *Modern Caribbean,* eds. F. W. Knight and C. A. Collier, 203–28. Chapel Hill: University of North Carolina Press.

Takougang, Joseph. 2003. Contemporary African Immigration to the United States. *Irinkerindo: A Journal of African Migration* 2.

Thomas, Kevin J. 2011. Familial Influences on Poverty Among Young Children in Black Immigrant, U.S.-born Black, and Nonblack Immigrant Families. *Demography* 48 (2): 437–60.

Thomas-Hope, Elizabeth. 2002. Skilled Labour Migration from Developing Countries: Study on the Caribbean Region. International Migration Papers 50, International Labor Office. www.ilo.org/public/english/protection/migrant/download/imp/imp50e.pdf.

US Census of Population and Housing. 1980, 1990, and 2000. Accessed from Steven Ruggles, J. Trent Alexander, Katie Genadek, Ronald Goeken, Matthew B. Schroeder, and Matthew Sobek. *Integrated Public Use Microdata Series: Version 5.0* [Machine-readable database]. Minneapolis: University of Minnesota, 2010.

US Department of Homeland Security (DHS). 2011. Secretary Napolitano Announces the Extension of Temporary Protected Status for Haiti Beneficiaries. Press release, May 17, 2011. www.dhs.gov/ynews/releases/pr_1305643820292.shtm.

_____. 2011. *Yearbook of Immigration Statistics,* 2010 Revised March 30, 2011. Table 10: Persons Obtaining Legal Permanent Resident Status by Broad Class of Admission and Region and Country of Birth: Fiscal Year 2010. Washington, DC: DHS. www.dhs.gov/files/statistics/publications/LPR10.shtm.

Waters, Mary C. 1999. *Black Identities: West Indian Immigrant Dreams and American Realities.* Cambridge, MA: Harvard University Press.

CHAPTER 2

NEW STREAMS: BLACK AFRICAN MIGRATION TO THE UNITED STATES

Randy Capps, Kristen McCabe, and Michael Fix

Migration Policy Institute

Introduction: A Long History of Black African Migration

B lack African migration to North America dates back to the earliest days of European colonization. The first recorded passage of slaves from Africa to this region occurred in 1519, to Puerto Rico — now a US territory. Between 1519 and 1867, when the slave trade ended, an estimated 10 million African slaves had been taken from Africa to the Western Hemisphere, with 360,000 landing in what today is the United States.[1] Thus, forced African migration preceded the formation and independence of the United States, and the country has always had a significant Black population. In the 2010 census, 38.9 million US Blacks comprised 12.6 percent of the country's total population, up slightly from 12.3 percent in 2000.[2]

Large-scale voluntary migration from Africa to the United States is a relatively recent phenomenon. The earliest recorded voluntary Black migration from Africa originated from Cape Verde in the early 1800s and was associated with commercial whaling.[3] With the ending of slavery and the slave trade in the late 1800s and subsequent severe restrictions on flows from Africa (along with restrictions from Southern Europe and Asia), there was very little immigration from Africa to

---

1   David Ettis, "The Volume and Structure of the Transatlantic Slave Trade: A Reassessment," *The William and Mary Quarterly* 58, no. 1 (2001): 17–46.

2   Karen R. Hughes, Nicholas A. Jones, and Roberto R. Ramirez, "Overview of Race and Hispanic Origin: 2010," *2010 Census Briefs* C201BR-02 (Washington, DC: US Census Bureau, 2011), www.census.gov/prod/cen2010/briefs/c2010br-02.pdf.

3   Marilyn Halter, *Between Race and Ethnicity: Cape Verdean American Immigrants*, 1860-1965 (Champaign, IL: University of Illinois Press, 1993).

the United States until the end of the 20th century.[4] The 1965 reforms to US immigration law removed national origin quotas that placed very low caps on migration from outside Northern Europe, and created the current system in which most legal immigrants come through family reunification channels.[5]

I. A Rapidly Rising New Immigrant Population

In 2009 African immigrants *of all races* numbered about 1.5 million, or 4 percent of the nation's total of 38 million immigrants,[6] fewer than immigrants from Latin America, Asia, or Europe.

Seventy-four percent of African immigrants (1.1 million) identified themselves as Black in 2009.[7] Black African immigrants comprised 3 percent of all immigrants and a similar share of the total US Black population of 39 million.

Though currently small in number, Black Africans are among the fastest-growing immigrant populations in the United States. In 1980 the total Black foreign-born population was 816,000, only 64,000 of whom had been born in Africa (see Table 1). By 2009 the total Black immigrant population had quadrupled to 3.3 million, while the African Black immigrant population had risen by a factor of 16, to 1.1 million. About half of this increase occurred within the past decade, as there were only 574,000 Black immigrants of African origin in 2000.

---

4   Kevin J. A. Thomas, "What Explains the Increasing Trend in African Emigration to the U.S.?" *International Migration Review* 45, no. 1 (2011): 3–28.

5   The 1965 *Immigration and Nationality Act*, US Public Law 89-236.

6   Unless otherwise noted, the data presented in this chapter are based on Migration Policy Institute (MPI) analysis of data from the decennial US Census of Population for 1980, 1990, and 2000, and the 2008 and 2009 American Community Surveys (ACS), pooled.

7   Throughout the chapter, except where noted, Black immigrants are those who responded "Black" either alone or in combination with any other race to the race question in the Census or ACS.

Table 1. Black Immigrants* by Region of Origin, United States, 1980 to 2008-09

	1980 (000s)	1990 (000s)	% Change 1980 to 1990	2000 (000s)	% Change 1990 to 2000	2008-09 (000s)	% Change 2000 to 2008-09
All immigrants	14,079	19,682	40	31,133	58	38,234	23
All Black immigrants	816	1,447	77	2,435	68	3,267	34
Black African immigrants	64	184	188	574	212	1,081	88
Black Caribbean immigrants	453	897	98	1,428	59	1,701	19
Black immigrants from other regions	299	366	22	433	18	485	12

Note: *Black immigrants are those who responded "Black" either alone or in combination with any other race to the survey's race question in 2000 and 2008-09. In 1980 and 1990, respondents were not given multiple race options, and so the responses for these years are for the Black race only.

Source: MPI analysis of data from the 1980, 1990, and 2000 US Census of Population and Housing (census); 2008-09 American Community Surveys (ACS), pooled.

Black immigrants from Africa are outnumbered by their counterparts from Caribbean countries (1.1 versus 1.7 million in 2009), but Caribbean migration to the United States has slowed considerably in recent years.[8] Between 2000 and 2009, the Black African immigrant population grew by 92 percent, while the Black Caribbean immigrant population rose by only 19 percent. If the trends of the past decade continue, by 2020 Africa will likely replace the Caribbean as the major source region for the US Black immigrant population.

The United States has rapidly become one of the major destinations for African migrants. In 2010, according to World Bank estimates, the United States was the destination for an estimated 4 percent of all African migrants, ranking it fifth behind France, Côte D'Ivoire, South Africa, and Saudi Arabia — and just ahead of the United Kingdom, Spain, and Italy.[9] Remove the Ivory Coast and South Africa from the list, and the United States ranks third among destinations outside the African continent. Moreover, France and Saudi Arabia primarily receive Arab migrants from North African countries, while nearly three-quarters of US African immigrants are Blacks from sub-Saharan countries. Though the World Bank data do not further disaggregate African

---

8   In 2009 there were 485,000 Black immigrants from regions besides Africa or the Caribbean; most were from Central and South America.

9   Dilip Ratha, Sanket Mohapatra, Caglar Ozden, Sonia Plaza, William Shaw, and Abebe Shimeles, *Leveraging Migration for Africa: Remittances, Skills, and Investments* (Washington, DC: World Bank, 2011), http://siteresources.worldbank.org/EXTDECPROSPECTS/Resources/476882-1157133580628/AfricaStudyEntireBook.pdf.

migrants by race, it is likely that the United States has become — or will soon become — the destination for the largest number of sub-Saharan African migrants outside the continent.

II. Increasingly Diverse Origins

Historically, Black African immigrants to the United States have had their origins in West Africa and in Anglophone countries. In 2009 the Anglophone countries of Nigeria, Ghana, Kenya, Liberia, Cameroon, and Sierra Leone together accounted for 46 percent of all Black African immigrants (see Table 2), whereas in 1980 they had accounted for 62 percent. In 1980 Nigeria alone accounted for 37 percent of all Black African immigrants; by 2009, Nigeria's share had fallen to 19 percent. Today, no single country predominates as a source for Black African immigrants.

Table 2. Black African Immigrants by Country of Origin, United States, 1980 to 2008-09

	Number of Immigrants (000s)				% Black African Immigrants			
	1980	1990	2000	2008-09	1980	1990	2000	2008-09
Black African immigrants	*64*	*184*	*574*	*1,081*	*100*	*100*	*100*	*100*
Country of origin								
Nigeria	24	56	133	201	37	30	23	19
Ethiopia	5	34	66	143	9	18	12	13
Ghana	8	20	65	110	12	11	11	10
Kenya	2	6	29	68	3	4	5	6
Somalia	0	1	35	67	0	1	6	6
Liberia	3	10	39	64	5	6	7	6
Sudan	0	3	13	34	1	2	2	3
Sierra Leone	2	6	20	34	3	3	3	3
Cameroon	1	3	12	30	2	2	2	3
Cape Verde	2	4	10	22	3	2	2	2
Eritrea*	0	0	17	22	0	0	3	2
Senegal	0	2	9	16	0	1	2	1
Uganda	1	4	7	14	2	2	1	1
South Africa	1	3	5	11	1	2	1	1
Guinea	0	1	0	11	0	0	0	1
Zimbabwe	1	1	6	11	2	1	1	1

	Number of Immigrants (000s)				% Black African Immigrants			
	1980	1990	2000	2008-09	1980	1990	2000	2008-09
Tanzania	1	1	4	10	1	1	1	1
Egypt	0	0	4	7	0	0	1	1
Morocco	0	0	2	5	0	0	0	0
Other West Africa	1	3	0	52	1	1	0	5
Other East Africa	0	0	0	22	0	0	0	2
Other African countries	6	13	97	127	9	7	17	12

Note: * Before the 2000 census, Eritreans were classified as Ethiopians, because Eritrea did not gain independence from Ethiopia until 1993.

Source: MPI analysis of 1980, 1990, and 2000 census; 2008-09 ACS.

Most but not all African immigrants in the United States identify themselves on government surveys as Black (see Table 3). The share of Black immigrants from most sub-Saharan African countries exceeded three-quarters, with the most notable exception being South Africa, which has sent predominantly white immigrants to the United States. North African countries generally have smaller Black populations and few of their immigrants to the United States are Black. In contrast to Europe, the United States receives relatively few immigrants from North Africa, so the Black share of African immigrants to the United States is much higher than that of Europe.

Table 3. Black Immigrants as Share of All US Immigrants and Immigrants from African Origins, 2008-09

	Total Immigrants	Black Immigrants	% Black
All US immigrants	38,234	3,267	9
African immigrants	1,457	1,081	74
Cameroon	31	30	99
Ghana	111	110	99
Somalia	68	67	99
Nigeria	204	201	99
Ethiopia	146	143	98
Eritrea	23	22	98
Liberia	66	64	97
Guinea	11	11	97
Sierra Leone	36	34	95
Senegal	16	16	95
Other West Africa	55	52	95
Other African countries	145	124	86
Sudan	40	34	86
Kenya	82	68	83
Uganda	19	14	75
Other East Africa	33	22	67
Zimbabwe	17	11	64
Cape Verde	36	22	63
Tanzania	18	10	53
Other North Africa	15	2	15
South Africa	82	11	14
Morocco	53	5	9
Egypt	135	7	5
Algeria	16	1	3

Source: MPI analysis of 1980, 1990, and 2000 census; 2008-09 ACS.

III. Diverse Modes of Entry and Legal Statuses

Black African immigrants also have diverse modes of entry into the United States, and various legal statuses once they are here. The Pew Hispanic Center estimated that in 2007, 30 percent of all immigrants in the United States were unauthorized: they had either entered the United States illegally (usually across the border with Mexico) or over-stayed a valid visa.[10] Among Black African immigrants, the estimated unauthorized share is lower: 21 percent (see Figure 1). Pew's estimates suggest that there are about 200,000 unauthorized Black Africans in the United States, out of a total unauthorized population of 11 million or more. Illegal migration in the United States is highly controversial and is closely associated with Latino immigrants — especially those from Mexico and Central America — but not with Black immigrants. Unauthorized immigrants are generally barred from major government benefits and services, and have been increasingly subject to immigration raids or arrests by the police as well as the risk of deportation. A lack of legal status is also associated, generally, with more precarious employment, lower wages, and lack of private health insurance coverage. Thus the lower percentage of the unauthorized among Black African immigrants means that they generally have better prospects for integration than other groups (such as Mexicans) with a more precarious status.

---

10 US population surveys such as the census, ACS, and Current Population Survey (CPS) ask respondents about their citizenship, country of origin, and year of arrival in the United States. The surveys do not inquire about the legal status for noncitizens or refugee entrant status. The Pew Hispanic Center has developed methods to assign legal status to noncitizens in the CPS based on country of origin, year of US arrival, and other characteristics. Here we pool three years of CPS data, 2006-08, because of the smaller sample size in the CPS than the ACS.

Figure 1. Citizenship and Legal Status of Black African Immigrants, United States, 2006-08

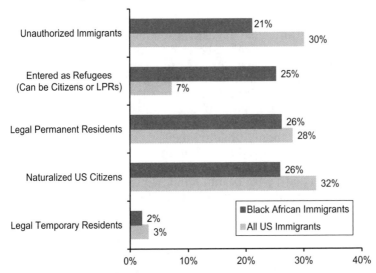

Source: MPI analysis of US Current Population Survey 2006-08 data pooled, augmented with assignments of legal status to noncitizens by Jeffrey S. Passel, Pew Hispanic Center.

Black African immigrants are much more likely than other immigrants to have entered the United States as refugees or gained asylum after coming to the country.[11] Since 1980, the United States has recognized the international definition of refugees as fleeing "persecution or a well-founded fear of persecution."[12] Within the past three decades, instability within several African countries has led to the admission of many immigrants from these sources as refugees — a designation allowing them to receive resettlement services and public benefits immediately upon their arrival and for a period of several months or years afterward (depending on the type of service or benefit). In 2007 about a quarter of all Black African immigrants in the United States had entered as refugees or received asylum (though many had since become permanent residents or citizens), versus 7 percent of all US immigrants. Five refugee source countries — Ethiopia, Somalia, Liberia, Sudan, and Eritrea — together accounted for 30 percent of all Black African immigrants in 2009.[13]

Another quarter of Black African immigrants are legal permanent

---

11 Refugees are so designated abroad, by the US Department of State, and enter the United States with that designation. Asylees may declare their intention to seek asylum when they arrive at a port of entry; others spend some time in unauthorized status before seeking asylum.

12 US Office of Refugee Resettlement (ORR), *Who We Serve* (Washington, DC: US Department of Health and Human Services, ORR), www.acf.hhs.gov/programs/orr/about/whoweserve. htm.

13 Some immigrants from these countries immigrated through employment, family reunification, or other provisions of US immigration law, but the majority came as refugees.

residents (LPRs) who did not come as refugees. These immigrants primarily entered the United States through one of three types of visa programs: family reunification, employment, or diversity.

While many earlier African immigrants have become US citizens, in particular those from Anglophone countries, the overall citizenship rate among the Black African population is relatively low. In 2007, 26 percent of Black African immigrants had naturalized, below the average of 32 percent for all immigrants. In most cases, LPRs must wait five years before they can apply to take the US citizenship test.[14] A relatively small share of Black African immigrants have met the five-year requirement: in 2009, 22 percent of Black African immigrants had arrived in 2005 or later, versus just 13 percent for immigrants overall. The highest shares of these post-2005 arrivals were found among immigrants from Cameroon (28 percent), Kenya (28 percent), and Zimbabwe (28 percent); Tanzania (27 percent); and Somalia (26 percent).

A small share of Black African immigrants have been admitted as temporary immigrants, including students and those with temporary work permits. In 2007 about 2 percent of Black African immigrants held these types of temporary visas, close to the average of 3 percent for all immigrants.

Finally, there are small groups of African immigrants that are allowed to stay in the United States temporarily due to political conflicts or natural disasters in their home countries. The US Congress has designated two types of temporary legal status — Temporary Protected Status (TPS) and Deferred Enforced Departure (DED) — on a country-by-country basis for short periods (usually 18 months to two years at a time), although the Congress often extends these designations for many years. TPS and DED allow immigrants to work in the United States and protect them from deportation. These statuses do not, however, put immigrants on a path to permanent residency, nor do they confer eligibility for health insurance or major public benefit programs. In December 2011 approximately 4,000 immigrants from Liberia, Somalia, Sudan, and South Sudan had been eligible for TPS or DED status. Most of such grants had gone to immigrants from Central American countries and Haiti (300,000–400,000).[15]

The annual flow of legal immigrants to the United States is about 1 million, with approximately 10 percent (100,000) coming from Africa. Family reunification is the most common mode of legal admission to

---

14 The waiting period is three years for legal permanent residents (LPRs) who have married US citizens.

15 Ruth Ellen Wasem and Karma Ester, *Temporary Protected Status: Current Immigration Policy and Issues* (Washington, DC: Congressional Research Service, 2010), www.fas.org/sgp/crs/homesec/RS20844.pdf; Ruth Ellen Wasem and Karma Ester, *Temporary Protected Status: Current Immigration Policy and Issues* (Washington, DC: Congressional Research Service, 2011), www.fas.org/sgp/crs/homesec/RS20844.pdf.

the United States, including people who enter through marriage or who are sponsored to immigrate by their parents, siblings, or adult children. In fiscal year (FY) 2010, two-thirds of the approximately 1 million immigrants legally admitted to the United States were admitted through family provisions (either as immediate relatives of US citizens or through other family preferences).[16] Another 14 percent were admitted for employment (or as spouses or children of those admitted for employment), and 13 percent were admitted as refugees (see Figure 2). Five percent were admitted through the diversity visa program, which was started in 1995 to increase representation from source countries with small numbers in the United States.[17]

Figure 2. Legal Admissions* by Class for All US Immigrants and African Immigrants, FY 2010

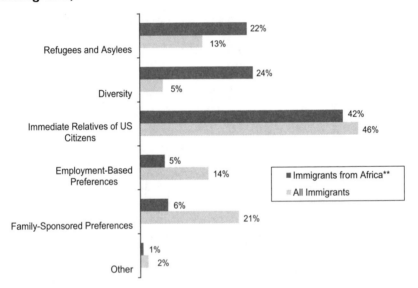

Note: * Legal admissions include both immigrants obtaining permanent residency upon arrival in the United States as well as those who apply for and receive LPR status after substantial periods of residency in the country without such status.
** Includes African immigrants of all races; the legal admissions data disaggregate admissions by country of origin and not by race.
Source: US Department of Homeland Security (DHS), "Table 10: Persons Obtaining Legal Permanent Resident Status by Broad Class of Admission and Region and Country of Birth: Fiscal Year 2010," in *Yearbook of Immigration Statistics* (Washington, DC: DHS, 2010, revised March 30, 2011), www.dhs.gov/files/statistics/publications/LPR10.shtm.

---

16 The US federal government's fiscal year (FY) 2010 ran from September 30, 2009, through October 1, 2010. The legal admissions data used here include both immigrants who were legally admitted upon their arrival in the United States as well as those who applied and had their status adjusted to LPR while already living in the country.
17 The diversity program was enacted by the *Immigration Act of 1990* (US Public Law 101-649), but the first diversity immigrant did not arrive until 1995.

African immigrants are much more likely to have been admitted through the diversity program or as refugees than immigrants from most other world regions. In FY 2010 almost half of the African immigrants (46 percent) were in these two admissions classes, versus just 18 percent of all immigrants (see Table 4).[18] As a consequence, relatively low shares of African immigrants were in the family reunification and employment classes. It is not surprising that African immigrants are overrepresented in the diversity program, given that they are underrepresented in the general immigrant population and the program is designed to promote pluralism in immigration flows.[19] While Africans comprised 10 percent of all legal admissions, they accounted for 48 percent of diversity immigrants in FY 2010 — a share that was up substantially from 32 percent in FY 1999. The overrepresentation of African immigrants among US refugees (17 percent) owes to several factors, including the large number of conflicts on the continent that have displaced refugees and the policies of public and private institutions that carry out resettlement in the United States and internationally.

Table 4. Legal Admissions,* by Class, for African Immigrants and Sub-Saharan Origin Countries, FY 2010

	Total Admissions	Immediate Relatives of US Citizens	Family-Sponsored Preferences	Refugees and Asylees	Diversity	Employment and Other
All immigrants	1,042,625	46	21	13	5	16
All immigrants from Africa**	101,355	42	6	22	24	6
Cape Verde	1,668	54	44	-	0	1
Malawi	164	72	7	2	7	13
Senegal	1,285	68	5	7	11	9
Gambia	859	65	5	17	3	9
Nigeria	13,376	60	11	1	22	7
Ghana	7,429	59	7	2	28	4
Angola	148	52	9	20	9	9
Mali	528	57	2	19	5	16
Burkina Faso	377	54	3	14	24	5
Ethiopia	14,266	47	5	19	28	1
Uganda	1,085	46	6	27	12	9

18   The legal admissions data do not identify the race of immigrants, and so African immigrants here include Black immigrants alongside those of other races. Overall, about one-quarter of African immigrants are not Black, and this share has been declining over time.

19   The diversity program allots 50,000 visas each year to countries with admissions of less than 50,000 over the prior five-year period. See Ruth Ellen Wasem, *Diversity Immigrant Visa Lottery Issues* (Washington, DC: Congressional Research Service, 2011), www.fas.org/sgp/crs/misc/R41747.pdf.

	Total Admissions	Immediate Relatives of US Citizens	Family-Sponsored Preferences	Refugees and Asylees	Diversity	Employment and Other
Sierra Leone	2,011	46	5	24	21	4
South Africa	2,758	46	3	0	10	41
Kenya	7,421	41	3	19	31	6
Togo	1,563	40	5	24	30	2
Benin	486	36	1	13	46	5
Zimbabwe	1,274	34	2	43	5	17
Côte D'Ivoire	1,621	33	2	41	17	7
Sudan	2,397	32	2	44	20	2
Tanzania	1,850	28	4	56	4	7
Guinea	1,379	29	1	56	8	6
Cameroon	4,161	26	3	32	37	2
Liberia	4,837	24	4	55	16	1
Eritrea	1,656	24	3	47	23	3
Congo, Republic	968	20	1	53	23	4
Rwanda	489	18	-	70	9	3
Somalia	4,558	16	1	82	1	1
Congo, Democratic Republic	1,764	8	1	59	31	2
Burundi	841	3	0	91	4	2
Balance of Africa (includes North Africa)	18,136	44	7	8	34	8

Note: * Legal admissions include immigrants obtaining permanent residency upon arrival in the United States as well as those who apply for and receive LPR status after substantial periods of residency in the country without such status.

** Includes African immigrants of all races; the legal admissions data disaggregate by country of origin and not by race.

Source: DHS, "Table 10: Persons Obtaining Legal Permanent Resident Status by Broad Class of Admission and Region and Country of Birth: Fiscal Year 2010."

The refugee and diversity programs have expanded the diversity of the African immigrant population in recent years. During previous decades, large Anglophone nations such as Nigeria, Ghana, Kenya, and Liberia dominated African immigration flows to the United States. But the list of countries sending significant numbers of immigrants to the United States has grown over time, with the diversity and refugee programs contributing increasing numbers, especially from non-English-speaking countries.[20] In FY 2010, the shares of immigrants admitted through family reunification channels were highest for African

20 Thomas, *What Explains the Increasing Trend.*

nations with the longest history of emigration to the United States, led by Cape Verde — the oldest source country (98 percent) — and followed by Malawi, Senegal, Gambia, Nigeria, and Ghana (all at two-thirds or more, see Table 4). All of these countries except for Malawi are in West Africa.

Countries with lower shares of family-based admissions are located across the continent. Shares of family admissions are lowest in countries where refugees comprise the largest class of admissions, most notably Zimbabwe, Côte D'Ivoire, Sudan, Tanzania, Liberia, Eritrea, Congo, Rwanda, Somalia, and Burundi. Diversity admission shares are highest for some small countries (such as Benin, Togo, and Burkina Faso) but also for the larger countries of Kenya, Ethiopia, and Ghana. The diversity program has been drawing larger numbers of immigrants from East Africa in recent years.

It is striking that immigration flows from some African countries — including major sending countries such as Ethiopia — are composed of high shares of family, refugee, and diversity immigrants.

IV. Black Africans Younger and More Likely to be Men than Immigrants Overall

Black African immigrants tend to be younger than both the US-born population and immigrants overall. In 2009, only 3 percent of Black African immigrants were ages 65 or older (see table 5). Black African immigrants were more likely to be working age (ages 18 to 64) than immigrants overall and the US-born population, and they were slightly more likely than immigrants overall to be children. The relative youth of Black African immigrants reflects their recency of arrival.

Table 5. Age Distributions of the US Population and Black African Immigrants, 2009

	Age Distribution (%)							
	Birth to 10	11 to 17	18 to 24	25 to 34	35 to 44	45 to 54	55 to 64	65 and older
Total US Population	15	10	10	13	14	15	11	13
Native born	16	10	10	12	13	14	11	13
Foreign born	3	4	9	20	22	18	12	12
Black immigrants	3	5	9	19	22	20	12	9
Black African immigrants	5	7	12	23	24	18	8	3

Source: MPI analysis of 2008-09 ACS.

Unlike the US population or Black immigrants overall, Black African immigrants are more likely to be men than women. In 2009, men accounted for 53 percent of the Black African-born population compared to only 48 percent of Black immigrants and 49 percent of the total US population. Black African immigrants are more likely to be men in part because so many are admitted through the diversity visa program. In 2009, 57 percent of diversity immigrants were men versus 45 percent of LPR admissions overall.[21]

Among Black African immigrants, the Senegalese born have the highest share of men: 68 percent. Only Black African immigrants from Sierra Leone, Cameroon, and Somalia are more likely to be women than men.

V. Geographic Settlement Patterns Similar to US-Born Blacks

Black African immigrants are heavily concentrated in a handful of states, and their distribution largely reflects the pattern for the total Black population, with two notable exceptions. African immigrants, like US blacks generally, are most heavily concentrated in New York, Texas, California, Florida, and Illinois — the five states with the largest overall populations. Substantial African immigrant and total Black populations also overlap in the southeastern states of Georgia, Virginia, and North Carolina and the northeastern states of Maryland, Ohio, and Pennsylvania (see Figures 3 and 4 for comparison). Unlike the Black population, however, large numbers of Black African immigrants have settled in Minnesota and Washington, while few African immigrants live in the five comparatively rural southeastern states (Louisiana, Alabama, Mississippi, Tennessee, and South Carolina) that have substantial US-born Black populations.

---

21   Wasem, *Diversity Immigrant Visa Lottery Issues.*

Figure 3. Black African Immigrant Population, by State, 2006-08

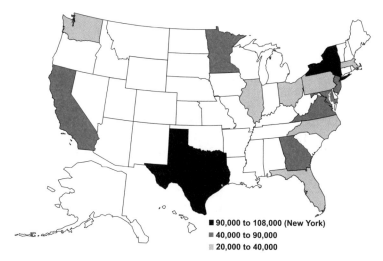

- 90,000 to 108,000 (New York)
- 40,000 to 90,000
- 20,000 to 40,000

Source: MPI analysis of 2006-08 ACS.

Figure 4. Total Black Population,* by State, 2010

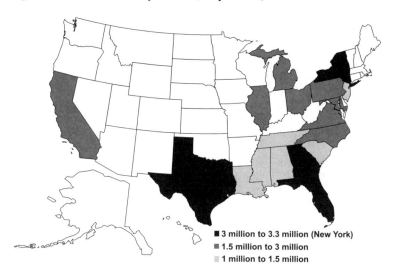

- 3 million to 3.3 million (New York)
- 1.5 million to 3 million
- 1 million to 1.5 million

Note: * Total Black population includes those answering the census that they were Black alone or Black in combination with any other race.

Source: US Census Bureau, "Table P-1: Race, 2010 Census National Summary File of Redistricting Data," http://factfinder2.census.gov/faces/nav/jsf/pages/index.xhtml.

VI. More Human Capital than Other US Immigrants

Black African immigrants are among the best-educated US immigrants. African immigrants are disproportionately admitted through the diversity program — which requires immigrants to have at least a high school degree or two years of experience in an occupation that requires at least two years or more of training to perform.[22] High travel costs could partially explain the relatively high share of skilled Africans among US immigrants. Relatively few Africans come to the country as unauthorized migrants (see Figure 1), and the unauthorized tend to be less well educated.

According to data from the World Bank's Global Skilled Migration Database, the United States benefits from disproportionately high-skilled African migration. In 2000 the United States accounted for 37 percent of African high-skilled migrants but only 15 percent of all African immigrants to Organization for Economic Cooperation and Development (OECD) countries.[23] Canada and Australia also attracted a relatively high share of high-skilled African migrants; by contrast, the United Kingdom, France, and other European countries were destinations for a greater share of low-skilled African migrants.

The overrepresentation of the highly skilled among US immigrants is particularly striking for several of Africa's largest source countries. The United States was the destination for 59 percent of Nigeria's high-skilled immigrants along with 47 percent of those from Ghana and 29 percent from Kenya.[24] For all three countries, the US share of skilled migrants exceeded its share of all migrants and appears to have come at the expense of the United Kingdom, which disproportionately received low-skilled migrants from these three Anglophone countries.

The overrepresentation of the highly skilled can be seen in the relatively high share of Black African immigrants with at least a four-year college degree. In 2007, 27 percent of the US population ages 25 and older had a four-year degree or more, versus 38 percent of Black African immigrants (see Table 6).[25] Immigrants from several Anglophone African countries were among the best educated: a majority of Black immigrants from Nigeria, Cameroon, Uganda, Tanzania, and

---

22 Because the diversity visa program requires only a high school education, it may be associated with the relatively low share of African immigrants without a high school degree, but it does not necessarily influence the share of African immigrants with a college degree.

23 The World Bank defines highly skilled migrants as those with a "tertiary" education, or those with a postsecondary degree. The World Bank report does not distinguish among African immigrants by race. See Ratha et al., *Leveraging Migration for Africa*.

24 Ibid.

25 The findings for the remainder of the paper are based on analyses of pooled ACS data for 2005 through 2009. Five years of data were pooled to produce adequate sample sizes for comparisons of indicators by country of origin.

Zimbabwe had at least a four-year degree. Black immigrants from Egypt, where the official language is Arabic, were also among the best educated.

While Black immigrants from most African nations are better educated than the overall US population, immigrants from a few — mostly refugee — origin countries have far lower levels of formal schooling. Black immigrants from Eritrea, Liberia, Cape Verde, and Somalia are all less likely to have a college degree than the general US population, and more than half the immigrants from Cape Verde and Somalia have a high school degree or less. Immigrants from Eritrea, Liberia, and Somalia are disproportionately refugees.

Table 6. Educational Attainment for Adults Ages 25 and Over, Black Immigrants, and Black African Immigrants by Origin, 2007

	Population (000s)	Educational Attainment (%)				
		Less than High School	High School or Equivalent Only	Some College or 2-Year Degree	4-Year College Degree (bachelor's)	Masters, Doctorate, or Professional
All US adults 25 and older	196,972	15	29	28	17	10
Native-born adults	165,754	12	31	3	18	10
Immigrant adults	31,218	32	23	18	16	11
Black immigrants	2,529	20	28	27	16	9
Black African immigrants	752	13	21	29	23	15
Nigeria	151	4	11	23	35	27
Cameroon	20	6	13	26	29	26
Egypt	5	8	23	17	40	13
Uganda	9	2	19	27	28	24
Tanzania	7	7	12	31	27	24
Zimbabwe	7	3	12	34	26	24
Kenya	41	4	16	38	26	16
South Africa	7	7	22	31	22	18
Other West Africa	37	19	23	25	20	14
Ghana	80	9	26	31	20	14
Senegal	12	17	22	28	23	10
Other East Africa	12	12	17	39	17	15
Sierra Leone	24	13	21	34	19	13

		Educational Attainment (%)				
	Population (000s)	Less than High School	High School or Equivalent Only	Some College or 2-Year Degree	4-Year College Degree (bachelor's)	Masters, Doctorate, or Professional
Sudan	23	20	21	27	23	9
Morocco	5	18	26	27	27	3
Other African countries	94	14	27	31	18	11
Ethiopia	99	13	27	32	18	10
Guinea	7	27	29	17	18	10
Eritrea	17	25	23	26	18	8
Liberia	43	13	24	38	18	7
Cape Verde	12	41	33	15	7	4
Somalia	39	44	26	19	7	3

Source: MPI analysis of 2005-09 ACS.

A similar pattern emerges for English proficiency among Black African immigrants, most of whom have strong English skills with a significant share being bilingual. Overall, 70 percent of Black African immigrants either speak English as their primary language or speak another language but are also fluent in English (see Table 7), substantially above the rate for all immigrants (48 percent). Yet, only 21 percent of Black African immigrants speak English as their primary language at home. A much larger share (49 percent) are bilingual: they speak another language but also speak English very well. Liberia and South Africa are the only two origin countries from which substantially more than a quarter of immigrants speak English as their primary language. For immigrants from other Anglophone African countries, English is generally not the primary language but a second, colonial language learned during formal schooling.

English proficiency rates are high for almost all African origin countries. Only two origin groups have proficiency rates below the average for all US immigrants (48 percent): Cape Verdeans (45 percent) and Somalis (42 percent). Immigrants from several other refugee countries have low English proficiency rates, but are still above average for all US immigrants: Guinea (49 percent), Eritrea (54 percent), Sudan (54 percent), and Ethiopia (57 percent). Overall, Black African immigrants have a strong advantage in the US workforce due to their relatively high English language skills.

Table 7. English Proficiency for Immigrants Ages 5 and over, Black Immigrants, and Black African Immigrants by Origin, 2007

	Population (000s)	Speak English at Home	Speak a Language other than English at Home (%)			
			Speak English Very Well	Speak English Well	Do Not Speak English Very Well	Do Not Speak English at All
Immigrants age 5 and older	*37,255*	*16*	*32*	*21*	*20*	*11*
Black immigrants	3,075	46	29	14	8	3
Black African Immigrants	991	21	49	20	8	2
Zimbabwe	10	19	73	7	1	0
South Africa	9	44	45	9	2	0
Nigeria	185	26	62	10	2	1
Liberia	64	66	21	9	4	0
Uganda	12	23	60	15	1	1
Kenya	62	18	63	15	3	1
Sierra Leone	30	25	54	17	3	1
Ghana	97	20	59	17	3	0
Cameroon	26	26	50	18	6	1
Other East Africa	18	27	46	15	10	2
Tanzania	9	17	53	22	3	5
Other African countries	127	24	42	21	11	2
Ethiopia	124	9	49	31	9	2
Senegal	14	11	46	31	11	1
Sudan	33	10	44	29	15	2
Other West Africa	48	11	43	29	15	2
Eritrea	19	8	46	29	13	4
Egypt	7	11	41	33	13	2
Morocco	6	10	41	28	17	4
Guinea	10	14	35	29	19	2
Cape Verde	15	7	38	28	18	9
Somalia	64	6	35	25	23	10

Source: MPI analysis of 2005-09 ACS.

VII. High Employment Rates But Relatively Low Earnings

The relatively high educational attainment and English proficiency of Black African immigrants appears to translate into high labor force participation, though not necessarily high earnings. Employment rates for Black African immigrants are higher than for immigrants overall or for US-born adults. In 2007, 75 percent of Black African immigrants ages 18 to 64 were employed, versus 71 percent of immigrants overall and 72 percent of US-born adults (see Table 8). The employment rate was 70 percent or higher for Black immigrants from all African origins except Guinea, Egypt, Morocco, Sudan, and Somalia — all five of which have relatively high shares of emigrants admitted as refugees.

Labor force participation was especially high for Black African women relative to other immigrant women. In 2007 Black African women had an employment rate of 68 percent, 8 points above the rate for all immigrant women. The employment rate for Black immigrant women was over 50 percent for all origin countries except Somalia, Egypt, Morocco, and Sudan — countries with large Muslim populations and with high shares of refugee admissions, as noted earlier.

Table 8. Employment Rates for US Civilian Men and Women Ages 18 to 64,* Black Immigrants, and Black African Immigrants by Origin, 2007

	Population (000s)			Employment Rate (%)		
	Total	Men	Women	Total	Men	Women
All US adults ages 18 to 64	*187,610*	*93,114*	*94,496*	*71*	*76*	*67*
Native-born adults	157,467	77,617	79,850	72	75	68
Immigrant adults	30,143	15,497	14,645	71	82	60
Black immigrants	2,556	1,247	1,309	75	78	71
Black African immigrants	847	459	388	75	80	68
Sierra Leone	26	12	13	82	83	80
Uganda	10	5	5	81	78	83
Kenya	48	25	23	80	83	76
Ghana	87	49	38	79	84	73
Zimbabwe	9	4	4	78	80	77
Nigeria	161	93	69	78	82	73
Senegal	13	9	4	77	85	60
South Africa	8	4	4	77	82	72
Ethiopia	109	55	54	76	83	70
Liberia	52	26	26	76	78	74
Cape Verde	13	6	6	74	72	77
Cameroon	23	12	11	74	73	76

	Population (000s)			Employment Rate (%)		
	Total	Men	Women	Total	Men	Women
Eritrea	17	9	8	74	81	67
Other West Africa	42	26	16	74	81	62
Tanzania	7	5	3	71	75	66
Other African countries	110	60	50	71	77	64
Other Eastern Africa	15	7	8	69	67	72
Guinea	8	5	3	69	75	58
Egypt	5	3	2	67	80	47
Morocco	5	3	2	67	79	50
Sudan	28	17	11	67	77	50
Somalia	50	24	26	54	66	44

Note: * Employment rates are for the civilian population only. Adults in the armed forces are excluded from the denominator.
Source: MPI analysis of 2005-09 ACS.

Black African immigrants' earnings are surprisingly low given their high levels of formal education and English proficiency. In 2007 median annual earnings for Black African immigrants were $27,000, just above the median for all immigrants ($26,000) and about 20 percent below the median for US-born workers ($33,000, see Table 9). Recall that the educational attainment of Black African immigrants is substantially higher than that of either US-born workers or US immigrants overall, and that their English proficiency is also high relative to immigrants overall. Thus, lower human capital is not likely to explain Black Africans' relatively low earnings.

Table 9. Median Annual Earnings for US Civilian Workers Ages 16 and Over,* Black Immigrants, and Black African Immigrants by Origin, 2007

	Population (000s)	Median Annual Earnings (US $)
Employed civilian workers age 16 and older	*141,295*	*32,000*
All native-born adults	119,095	33,000
All immigrants	22,200	26,000
All Black immigrants	1,962	29,000
Black African immigrants	639	27,000
Nigeria	128	36,000
Egypt	4	35,000
Uganda	8	34,000
Sierra Leone	21	31,000
Ghana	70	30,000
Cameroon	17	30,000
Zimbabwe	7	30,000
Tanzania	5	30,000
Kenya	39	28,000
South Africa	6	26,000
Other African countries	78	25,000
Liberia	40	25,000
Eritrea	13	25,000
Cape Verde	10	25,000
Senegal	10	25,000
Ethiopia	84	24,000
Other West Africa	31	24,000
Other East Africa	11	24,000
Sudan	19	21,000
Guinea	6	20,000
Morocco	4	20,000
Somalia	28	18,000

Note: * Median annual earnings are for civilian workers with nonzero earnings only. Adults in the armed forces and those with negative or zero earnings are excluded.

Source: MPI analysis of 2005-09 ACS.

Black African immigrants may be disadvantaged by their recent date of arrival or because their degrees and credentials cannot be translated meaningfully into high-skilled jobs in the United States. A relatively low share of Black African immigrants have become US citizens, and lack of citizenship may somewhat reduce their access to the best jobs — especially government jobs. On the other hand, relatively few Black African immigrants are unauthorized, and so they are less likely than Latin American immigrants (who are much more likely to be unauthorized) to be subject to job exploitation at the lower end of the labor market.

VIII. Underemployment of High-Skilled Africans in the US Workforce

Part of the explanation for African immigrants' low earnings may be underemployment among those who are highly skilled. In 2009 over a third of recent immigrants (those with fewer than ten years of US residency) who had a college degree or higher earned abroad were working in unskilled jobs (see Figure 5).[26] The employment of high-skilled African immigrants seems to improve alongside their years of residence in the United States: the share working in unskilled jobs drops to 22 percent after ten years in the United States, comparable to the level for Asian immigrants and substantially lower than those from Latin America.[27] However, immigrants from Asia and Latin America tend to have limited English proficiency, while those from Africa are disproportionately fluent in English — an attribute that should improve their opportunities for skilled employment. At the same time, though, difficulties with credentialing and racial discrimination in the US labor market are factors that potentially reduce Black Africans' opportunities for skilled employment.

---

26 These data include only immigrants who have earned their college degrees abroad, not those who have earned degrees in the United States. African immigrants include all those with origins on the continent, and the figures are not disaggregated by race.

27 Jeanna Batalova and Michael Fix, *Uneven Progress: The Employment Pathways of Skilled Immigrants in the United States* (Washington, DC: Migration Policy Institute, 2008), www.migrationpolicy.org/pubs/BrainWasteOct08.pdf.

Figure 5. Shares of High-Skilled US Immigrants Working in Unskilled Jobs, 2009

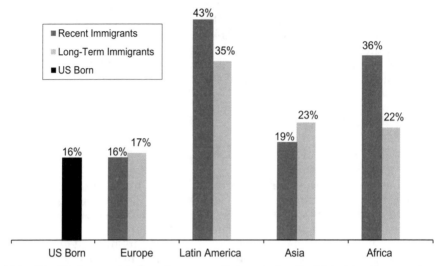

Notes: "Unskilled occupations" require no more than modest on-the-job training (for example, construction laborers, drivers, and maids). "High-skilled immigrants" here include only those who earned their college degrees abroad; US-trained immigrants are excluded. "Europe" includes Canada, Australia, and New Zealand. "Recent" immigrants have been in the United States for ten years or less, while "long-term" immigrants have been in the country for at least ten years.
Source: MPI analysis of 2009 ACS.

Underemployment, however, varies considerably across countries of origin. Immigrants who hold a bachelor's or professional degree are more likely to hold skilled jobs if they come from Anglophone countries with a relatively long history of sending immigrants to the United States — for instance, Ghana, Nigeria, Uganda, and South Africa.[28] African immigrants who have done their tertiary education in English or spent more time in the United States (where they may have upgraded their credentials and gained experience) find it easier transferring their credentials than immigrants who have not.

28 Aaditya Mattoo, Ileana Cristina Neagu, and Caglar Ozden, "Brain Waste? Educated Immigrants in the US Labor Market" (policy research working paper 3581, World Bank, Washington, DC, 2005).

IX. Conclusion: Prospects for Future African Immigration Flows

Demographic and economic trends should continue to increase emigration pressures in Africa. Currently, the migration rate from and within Africa is estimated at 2.5 percent of the continent's total population — significant, though below the worldwide rate of 3.1 percent and substantially below rates for Europe and Latin America.[29] Africa remains one of the poorest regions of the world, and economic pressures along with recurring political conflicts are likely to increase future migration. Additionally, due to high fertility rates, most African countries still have rapidly increasing young adult populations. It is projected that the African working-age population (15 to 64) could double and add 700 million more potential workers and emigrants between 2005 and 2050.[30] Despite rapid economic growth in Africa, this increase, equivalent to more than twice the current total US population, could dramatically increase emigration pressures at a time when the labor forces of Europe, the United States, and other industrialized regions are in a decline due to the aging of these countries' native-born populations.

If the past is any guide, future flows from Africa are not likely to be heavily composed of unauthorized immigrants because of the distance and expense involved in making the journey. Expanded legal flows could be accommodated under current US immigration policies, and in particular by the family reunification system, as there are no numerical limitations on admission via marriage to US citizens, and the individual country caps of 20,000 in other family preference categories have yet to be met.[31] At the same time, a decline in refugee admissions or the elimination of the diversity program could reduce African migration.

Despite the economic downturn that began in 2008, African migration to the United States has not subsided noticeably. The types of admission categories used by Africans are generally not closely tied to immediate economic conditions: for instance, only 2 percent of African immigrants have student visas or temporary work permits (see Figure 1), and only 5 percent of African LPRs are admitted directly for employment (see Table 4). While most African immigrants work, even if they have entered as refugees or through family or diversity channels, it is not clear whether the current weak US labor market has substantially affected their employment prospects. Despite their relative underemployment, African immigrants may be at a long-term advantage in the

---

29 Ratha et al., *Leveraging Migration for Africa.*
30 Ibid.
31 Currently, there are only individual country restrictions on family immigration from four countries that are overrepresented in US immigration flows: China, India, Mexico, and the Philippines. See US Department of State, *Visa Bulletin for June 2011,* IX, no. 33 (May 11, 2011), http://travel.state.gov/visa/bulletin/bulletin_5452.html.

US labor force because they are so well educated. Moreover, many have been employed in the health-care sector, which has been relatively immune to the recession. In 2007, 10 percent of Black African immigrant men and 33 percent of women worked in health-care occupations versus just 3 percent of all men and 13 percent of all women in the US labor force.

Yet, many high-skilled African immigrants remain underemployed in the United States. There is evidence that, over time, a larger share of this group are obtaining jobs commensurate with their skill levels, and so this population may become better integrated and more prosperous. At the same time, refugee flows may increase the number of less-well-educated African immigrants, and as flows increase and diversify over time, populations from other African nations may see their average levels of formal schooling fall (if the experience of Cape Verdean immigrants is any guide).

Regardless of changing economic conditions, reforms to the US immigration system would likely alter future African immigration flows. In the past 15 years, African immigrants have benefitted from the diversity program, which has been among the bargaining chips in comprehensive immigration debates since 2006 and has been targeted for elimination by the current chair of the House Immigration Subcommittee, Lamar Smith. There have also been debates over shifting legal immigration criteria away from family reunification and diversity toward immigrants' skills and the demands of the US labor market. If some of the family preference classes (for instance, parents and adult siblings of permanent residents) are cut or curtailed, such a change could marginally slow future African migration, although the great majority enter as the immediate relatives of US citizens – a category that has been historically safe from challenge. On the other hand, if the United States were to adopt a point system or other mechanism to promote more high-skilled immigration, the shift could increase the flow of college-educated immigrants from Africa.

In sum, Black Africans are one of the fastest-growing groups of US immigrants, and their flows do not appear to have been affected by the recession. Most are admitted as refugees, to reunite with family members, or through the diversity program — and none of these channels are linked to economic conditions. Black African immigrants are highly concentrated in a few states that have large Black populations overall, and in a few others with significant refugee populations.

Black Africans are among the best educated of all immigrants in the United States, and this country attracts a greater share of well-educated Africans than does Europe. Finally, well-educated African immigrants are frequently employed in low-skilled jobs, and this underemployment lowers their wages relative to other well-educated US workers.

Certain proposed changes to US immigration laws that are likely to be raised in future debates could reduce flows from Africa, most notably the elimination of the diversity visa program and reduced refugee admissions. Congress has discussed eliminating diversity visas and limiting family-based admissions as part of reforming the US immigration system. Passage of comprehensive immigration reform legislation is unlikely in the near future, as it has failed several times in the past few years. In the meantime, African migration to the United States is likely to continue increasing under the current system. ⤳

Works Cited

American Community Survey (ACS). 2005-09. Accessed from Steven Ruggles, J. Trent Alexander, Katie Genadek, Ronald Goeken, Matthew B. Schroeder, and Matthew Sobek. *Integrated Public Use Microdata Series: Version 5.0* [Machine-readable database]. Minneapolis: University of Minnesota, 2010.

Batalova, Jeanne and Michael Fix. 2008. *Uneven Progress: The Employment Pathways of Skilled Immigrants in the United States.* Washington, DC: Migration Policy Institute. www.migrationpolicy.org/pubs/BrainWasteOct08.pdf.

Ettis, David. 2001. The Volume and Structure of the Transatlantic Slave Trade: A Reassessment. *The William and Mary Quarterly* 58 (1): 17–46.

Executive Committee of the High Commissioner's Programme. 2004. *Protracted Refugee Situations.* Geneva: Executive Committee of the High Commissioner's Programme, Standing Committee. www.unhcr.org/40ed5b384.html.

Halter, Marilyn. 1993. *Between Race and Ethnicity: Cape Verdean American Immigrants, 1860-1965.* Champaign, IL: University of Illinois Press.

Hughes, Karen R., Nicholas A. Jones, and Roberto R. Ramirez. 2011. Overview of Race and Hispanic Origin: 2010. *2010 Census Briefs* C201BR-02. Washington, DC: US Census Bureau. www.census.gov/prod/cen2010/briefs/c2010br-02.pdf.

Immigration Act of 1990. US Public Law 101-649. http://thomas.loc.gov/cgi-bin/query/z?c101:S.358.ENR:.

Mattoo, Aaditya, Ileana Cristina Neagu, and Caglar Ozden. 2005. Brain Waste? Educated Immigrants in the US Labor Market. Policy Research Working Paper 3581, World Bank. Washington, DC.

Ratha, Dilip, Sanket Mohapatra, Caglar Ozden, Sonia Plaza, William Shaw, and Abebe Shimeles. 2011. *Leveraging Migration for Africa: Remittances, Skills, and Investments.* Washington, DC: World Bank. http://siteresources.worldbank.org/EXTDECPROSPECTS/Resources/476882-1157133580628/AfricaStudyEntireBook.pdf.

The 1965 Immigration and Nationality Act. US Public Law 89-236. http://library.uwb.edu/guides/USimmigration/79%20stat%20911.pdf.

Thomas, Kevin J. A. 2011. What Explains the Increasing Trend in African Emigration to the U.S.? *International Migration Review* 45 (1): 3–28.

United Nations High Commissioner for Refugees. 2012 UNHCR country operations profile – Kenya. www.unhcr.org/pages/49e483a16.html.

_____. 2012 UNHCR country operations profile - United Republic of Tanzania. www.unhcr.org/cgi-bin/texis/vtx/page?page=49e45c736&submit=GO.

US Census Bureau. Table P-1: Race, 2010 Census National Summary File of Redistricting Data. http://factfinder2.census.gov/faces/nav/jsf/pages/index.xhtml.

US Census of Population and Housing. 1980, 1990, and 2000. Accessed from Steven Ruggles, J. Trent Alexander, Katie Genadek, Ronald Goeken, Matthew B. Schroeder, and Matthew Sobek. *Integrated Public Use Microdata Series: Version 5.0* [Machine-readable database]. Minneapolis: University of Minnesota, 2010.

US Department of Homeland Security (DHS). 2010. Table 10: Persons Obtaining Legal Permanent Resident Status by Broad Class of Admission and Region and Country of Birth: Fiscal Year 2010. In *Yearbook of Immigration Statistics*. Washington, DC: DHS, revised March 30, 2011. www.dhs.gov/files/statistics/publications/LPR10.shtm.

US Office of Refugee Resettlement (ORR). *Who We Serve*. Washington, DC: US Department of Health and Human Services, ORR. www.acf.hhs.gov/programs/orr/about/whoweserve.htm.

US Department of State. 2011. *Visa Bulletin for June 2011*, IX, no. 33, May 11. http://travel.state.gov/visa/bulletin/bulletin_5452.html.

Wasem, Ruth Ellen. 2011. *Diversity Immigrant Visa Lottery Issues*. Washington, DC: Congressional Research Service. www.fas.org/sgp/crs/misc/R41747.pdf.

Wasem, Ruth Ellen and Karma Ester. 2010. *Temporary Protected Status: Current Immigration Policy and Issues*. Washington, DC: Congressional Research Service. www.fas.org/sgp/crs/homesec/RS20844.pdf.

CHAPTER 3

YOUNG CHILDREN IN BLACK IMMIGRANT FAMILIES FROM AFRICA AND THE CARIBBEAN

Donald J. Hernandez

Hunter College and the Graduate Center, City University of New York

Introduction

The number of US children of Black immigrants has grown rapidly over the past two decades. Driven by increasing migration from Africa and sustained flows from the Caribbean, the number of Black immigrants in the United States has more than doubled over the past 20 years.[1] As a result, the number of children from birth to 10 with a Black foreign-born parent has also more than doubled, rising from 363,000 in 1990 to 813,000 in 2005-09 (see Table 1).

Children of immigrants also comprise an increasing share of Black children. Between 1990 and 2005-09, children of any race with at least one foreign-born parent rose from 13 percent to 24 percent of all US children aged 10 and younger. During the same period, the share of Black children with immigrant parents rose from 7 percent to 12 percent. This trend holds important social implications, since, as described in this chapter, the US Black child population is becoming increasingly diverse in origins, languages spoken, and other characteristics.

In order to account for potential racial differences between parents and children within the same family, this chapter focuses on *Black children with Black immigrant parents.* The definition of "Black" children and parents here includes those self-reported in the data as either only

---

1   See Chapter 2 in this volume, Randy Capps, Kristen McCabe, and Michael Fix, *New Streams: Black African Migration to the United States.*

Black race or Black and another race (i.e., multiracial).[2]

The chapter's goal is to provide new and comprehensive data on the changing demography and circumstances of children in Black immigrant families. To this end, the chapter reviews several standard family, parent, and child indicators that influence child well-being. These indicators are available in the US Census Bureau's annual American Community Survey (ACS), the most comprehensive data set on the US population.[3] They include:

- Family structure

- Parental citizenship

- Home language and linguistic isolation

- Parental education and employment

- Income and poverty

- Housing conditions

- Enrollment in prekindergarten

- Health insurance coverage

Throughout the chapter, children of Black immigrants are compared on these indicators with children of Black natives and with children of white, Hispanic, and Asian immigrants and natives. The analysis also compares children of Black immigrants from Africa with those from the Caribbean and provides data on some individual origin countries.

The ACS data are generally taken from the last five years of pooled data that were available at the time this chapter was written (2005 through 2009) in order to maximize the sample size and precision of the estimates for small populations.[4] Where useful for the analysis, comparisons are made with earlier periods using the 1990 and 2000 Census of Population and Housing.

---

2   Prior to 2000, census forms did not permit respondents to report multiple racial identifications. Estimates provided for years before 2000 count only those individuals who reported their race as Black alone.

3   Data accessed using Steven Ruggles, J. Trent Alexander, Katie Genadek, Ronald Goeken, Matthew B. Schroeder, and Matthew Sobek, *Integrated Public Use Microdata Series: Version 5.0* [Machine-readable database]. Minneapolis: University of Minnesota, 2010, http://usa.ipums.org/usa/index.shtml.

4   The Census Bureau has released American Community Surveys (ACS) data for 2010, but these data were not available at the time the detailed results for this chapter were calculated. Several years of data are needed to produce estimates for smaller populations of Black children of immigrants with different parental origins, and because these small populations are the main focus of the chapter, data for 2005-09 are employed.

Table I. Children from Birth through Age 10 with Black Immigrant Parents: 1990, 2000, 2005-09

	Number of Black Children with Black Immigrant Parents (000s)	Share of All Black Children (%)	Share of All Children in Immigrant Families (%)	Number of All Black Children (000s)	Number of All Children in Immigrant Families (000s)
2005-09	813	12	8	6,548	10,419
2000	625	10	7	6,505	8,552
1990	363	7	7	5,434	5,112

Notes: Analysis includes children living with at least one parent. Race was calculated with IPUMS variables as follows: American Community Surveys (ACS) — RACED (with more than one race permitted); 2000 Census — RACDET00; 1990 Census — RACED (with only one major race permitted).
Source: Author's analysis of data from the 1990 and 2000 US Census of Population and Housing (census); 2005-09 American Community Surveys (ACS), pooled.

I. Sending Regions and Countries

This research focuses on Black children — both immigrant and US born — with at least one Black immigrant parent born in either the Caribbean or Africa. These children accounted for 86 percent (or 700,000) of the 813,000 children living in Black immigrant families in 2005-09 (see Table 2). Forty-seven percent of Black children in immigrant families have parents with origins in the Caribbean, while 39 percent have parents from Africa. Eighty percent of those with Caribbean origins are from Haiti (37 percent), Jamaica (34 percent), or Trinidad and Tobago (10 percent), and another 5 percent are from the Dominican Republic. Children of Black African immigrants have more diverse origins, with the largest proportions of parents from Nigeria (22 percent), Ethiopia (11 percent), Somalia (9 percent), Ghana (8 percent), Kenya (6 percent), and Liberia (5 percent).

Table 2. Black Children from Birth through Age 10, by Immigrant Origin: 2005-09

	Number (000s)	(%)
All Children in United States	42,561	-
Children of Immigrants[0]	10,419	24
All Black Children in United States	6,548	-
Black Children with Immigrant Parents1	813	8
Black Children with Immigrant Parent from:		
Caribbean[2]	384	47
Haiti[3]	141	37
Jamaica[3]	129	34
Trinidad and Tobago[3]	38	10
Dominican Republic[3]	19	5
Bahamas[3]	9	2
Other Caribbean[3]	9	2
Barbados[3]	9	2
Grenada[3]	7	2
St. Lucia[3]	6	2
Dominica[3]	5	1
St. Vincent[3]	5	1
Antigua[3]	4	1
Cuba[3]	3	1
St. Kitts[3]	2	1
Bermuda[3]	1	0
Africa[2]	316	39
Nigeria[4]	69	22
Other Africa[4]	64	20
Ethiopia[4]	33	10
Somalia[4]	30	9
Ghana[4]	26	8
Kenya[4]	18	6
Liberia[4]	15	5
Sudan[4]	12	4
Sierra Leone[4]	9	3
Cameroon[4]	8	3
Eritrea[4]	6	2
Senegal[4]	5	2
Guinea[4]	5	2
Cape Verde[4]	4	1

	Number (000s)	(%)
Uganda[4]	3	1
Zimbabwe[4]	3	1
Tanzania[4]	2	1
Egypt[4]	2	1
Morocco[4]	2	1
South Africa[4]	2	1
Algeria[4]	-	0

Notes: Analysis includes children living with at least one parent. Due to rounding, percentages may not add up to 100.
[0] Percent displayed is percent of all children; [1] Percent displayed is percent of all Black children; [2] Percent displayed is percent of Black children of immigrants; [3] Percent displayed is percent of Black children with Caribbean origins; and [4] Percent displayed is percent of Black children with African origins.
Source: Author's analysis of 2005-09 ACS, pooled.

II. Geographic Concentration

For children of immigrants overall, the five top states of residence are California, Texas, New York, Florida, and Illinois. But Black children in immigrant families are more heavily concentrated on the East Coast (see Table 3). Two-thirds live in Eastern states: 22 percent in New York, 18 percent in Florida, and 24 percent in Massachusetts, New Jersey, Maryland, Virginia, and Georgia combined. California and Texas each account for about 5 percent of Black children in immigrant families, and 3 percent live in Minnesota. The remaining 23 percent are dispersed across the remaining 40 states and the District of Columbia.

Table 3. States with Largest Numbers of Children of Black Immigrants from Birth through Age 10, by Parental Region of Birth

	Black Children of Black Immigrants			Black Children of Black Caribbean Immigrants			Black Children of Black African Immigrants	
	(%)	Number (000s)		(%)	Number (000s)		(%)	Number (000s)
US Total	100	813	US Total	100	384	US Total	100	316
NY	22	182	FL	32	123	NY	11	34
FL	17	142	NY	30	117	MD	9	30
NJ	6	48	NJ	7	27	TX	9	29
MD	6	46	MA	5	21	CA	7	23
GA	5	42	GA	4	16	MN	7	21
TX	5	41	CT	3	13	GA	6	20
CA	5	39	MD	3	12	VA	5	15
MA	5	37	PA	3	10	NJ	4	14
MN	3	23	TX	2	6	MA	4	12
VA	3	22	CA	1	5	OH	3	11

Notes: Analysis includes children living with at least one parent. Due to rounding, percentages may not add up to 100.
Source: Author's analysis of 2005-09 ACS, pooled.

The high concentration of children of Black immigrants along the East Coast is especially prominent among children with Caribbean parents, as children with African parents are more geographically dispersed. Among Black children with Caribbean origins, almost two-thirds live in just two states: Florida (32 percent) and New York (31 percent). Over one-quarter live in other East Coast states: 7 percent in New Jersey, 6 percent in Massachusetts, 4 percent each in Georgia and in Connecticut, and 3 percent each in Maryland and in Pennsylvania.

Black children in immigrant families from Africa are more spatially dispersed. New York had the highest concentration (11 percent), but no other state accounted for more than 10 percent.

III. Family Structure

A. Two-Parent Families

Most children of immigrants live in two-parent families, and children in two-parent families tend to be advantaged in their educational outcomes compared to children in one-parent families.[5]

Compared to their counterparts in native-born Black families, Black children in immigrant families are significantly more likely to live with two parents (71 versus 39 percent); they are also more likely to live with two parents than Hispanic children of natives (59 percent). They are less likely, however, to live in two-parent families than children of immigrants in the other major race-ethnic groups (see Figure 1).

Figure 1. Share of Children Living with Two Parents from Birth through Age 10, by Race-Ethnicity and Family Immigrant Status

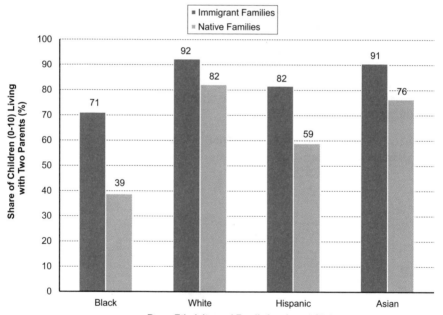

Note: Analysis includes children living with at least one parent.
Source: Author's analysis of 2005-09 ACS, pooled.

---

5   Andrew J. Cherlin, "Going to Extremes: Family Structure, Children's Well-Being, and Social Sciences," *Demography* 36, No. 4 (1999): 421–28; Sara McLanahan and Gary Sandefur, *Growing Up with a Single Parent: What Hurts, What Helps* (Cambridge, MA: Harvard University Press, 1994).

Black children in African immigrant families are more likely to live in two-parent homes than their peers in Caribbean immigrant families (76 versus 65 percent). The two-parent share of children among African immigrant families is nearly as high as for Hispanic immigrant and white native families.

To be more specific, the large majority of Black children with parents born in Ethiopia/Eritrea (79 percent), Nigeria (82 percent), and Sudan (81 percent) live with two parents. The share is lower for Black children with origins in Ghana (70 percent), Haiti (69 percent), and Somalia (68 percent), and for children with origins in Jamaica (62 percent) and other English-speaking Caribbean countries (65 percent) and the Dominican Republic (57 percent).

B. Extended-Family Households

Grandparents and adult household members may be available to help parents nurture and care for children in the home, allowing parents greater work flexibility. Black and Hispanic children in immigrant families are equally likely to have a grandparent in the home (11 percent versus 10 percent, see Figure 2). The proportions are somewhat higher for Black children in native-born families (14 percent) and for Asian children in both immigrant and native-born families (15 percent and 13 percent, respectively), and higher still for Hispanics in native-born families (17 percent). Among white children, only 6-7 percent have a grandparent in the home.

Figure 2. Share of Children from Birth through Age 10 with Grandparent in Home, by Race, Ethnicity, and Family Immigrant Status

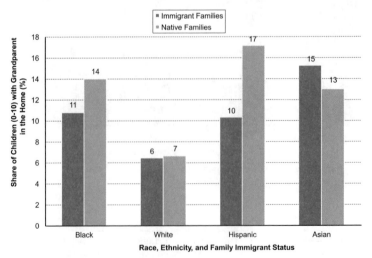

Note: Analysis includes children living with at least one parent.
Source: Author's analysis of 2005-09 ACS, pooled.

The shares of Black immigrants' children living in extended families vary by sending regions: 13 percent of children with Caribbean origins have a grandparent in the home, as do 8 percent of those with African origins. The proximity of the Caribbean to the United States and the long history of migration between the two help explain this difference.

C. Number of Children in the Family

Having brothers and sisters can be a mixed blessing. Growing up in a large family can be beneficial, because siblings share the companionship of childhood and may provide important supports throughout adulthood. But siblings can also be competitors for the limited time and financial resources of their parents, which can lead to reduced educational attainment, and to lower occupational achievement and income during adulthood.[6]

Black children in immigrant and native-born families are about equally likely to live in small families with one or two children (60 percent and 59 percent, respectively) or in medium-sized families with three or four children (34 percent). When compared with white, Hispanic, and Asian children, there is not much variation in the number of children per family.

In terms of sending regions, most Black children with Caribbean origins (63 percent) live in small families. Among Black children with parents born in Caribbean countries, no origin group has more than 6 percent of children living in large families with five or six children or more than 2 percent in families with seven or more children.

Meanwhile, Black families with parents from several African countries are larger. Comparatively few Black children with origins in Sudan and Somalia live in small families (32 percent and 26 percent, respectively). Fifty-one percent of Black children with Sudanese-born parents live in families with three to four children, and 17 percent live in families with five or more children (see Figure 3). The proportion of children in Somali families with five or more children (40 percent) is much higher than for any of the other groups.

---

6   Peter M. Blau and Otis Dudley Duncan, *The American Occupational Structure* (New York: Wiley, 1967); David L. Featherman and Robert Mason Hauser, *Opportunity and Change* (New York: Academic Press, 1978); Judith Blake, "Family Size and the Quality of Children, Demography 18 (1981), 321-42; Judith Blake, "Number of Siblings and Educational Mobility," *American Sociological Review* 50 (1985): 84-94. Judith Blake, "Differential Parental Investment: Its Effects on Child Quality and Status Attainment," in Jane B. Lancaster, Jeanne Altmann, Alice S. Rossi, and Lonnie R. Sherrod, *Parenting Across the Life Span: Biosocial Dimensions* (New York: Alsine De Gruyter, 1987), 351-75; Judith Blake, *Family Size and Achievement* (Berkeley, CA: University of California Press, 1989).

Figure 3. Share of Children (from Birth through Age 10 with Black Immigrant Parents) Who Have Five or More Siblings under Age 18 in the Home, by Parental Country or Region of Origin

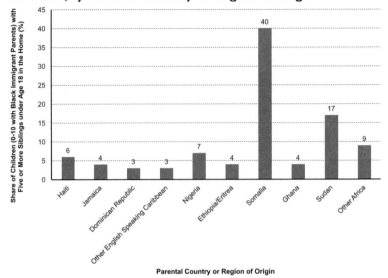

Note: Analysis includes children living with at least one parent.
Source: Author's analysis of 2005-09 ACS, pooled.

IV. Family, Social, and Economic Resources

A. *US Citizenship of Parents and Children*

US citizenship is important for children and their parents because it provides access to important public benefits and services, and the right to vote in local, state, and national elections.[7] By definition, all children in immigrant families have at least one immigrant parent; however, many of these children also live with a US-born parent or a parent who is a naturalized US citizen.

---

7   Randy Capps, Genevieve Kenny, and Michael Fix, "Health Insurance Coverage of Children in Mixed-Status Immigrant Families," in *Snapshots of America's Families III*, No. 12 (Washington, DC: The Urban Institute, 2003); Michael Fix and Jeffrey S. Passel, *Trends in Noncitizens' and Citizens' Use of Public Benefits Following Welfare Reform: 1994-97* (Washington, DC: The Urban Institute, 1999), www.urban.org/publications/408086.html; Michael Fix and Wendy Zimmerman, "When Should Immigrants Receive Benefits?" in Isabel V. Sawhill, ed., *Welfare Reform: An Analysis of the Issues* (Washington, DC: The Urban Institute, 1995); Donald J. Hernandez and Evan Charney, eds., *From Generation to Generation: The Health and Well-Being of Children in Immigrant Families* (Washington, DC: National Academy Press, 1998), www.nap. edu/catalog.php?record_id=6164#toc; Wendy Zimmermann and Karen Tumlin, "Patchwork Policies: State Assistance for Immigrants under Welfare Reform" (Occasional Paper No. 24, The Urban Institute, Washington, DC, 1999), www.urban.org/publications/309007.html.

Overall, 67 percent of Black immigrants' children live with at least one citizen parent — a higher rate than children of Hispanic immigrants (59 percent) but lower than children of Asian immigrants (71 percent) and children of white immigrants (79 percent, see Figure 4). Caribbean-born parents of young children are more likely to be US citizens than African-born parents. African parents' lower rates of citizenship may be associated with their relatively recent arrival, as it generally takes five years of legal US residency for immigrants to qualify for US citizenship.[8]

Figure 4. Share of Children (from Birth through Age 10) in Immigrant Families with US-Born Citizen Parent or Naturalized Citizen Parent, by Race, Ethnicity, and Parental Region of Birth

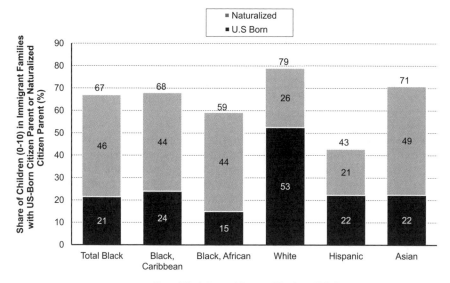

Notes: Analysis includes children living with at least one parent. Due to rounding, values may not add up to 100 percent.

Source: Author's analysis of 2005-09 ACS, pooled.

While Black children with Caribbean-born parents are more likely to have a naturalized parent, they are equally likely as children with African-born parents to have a US-born parent (44 percent). This share is substantially higher than among white and Hispanic children of immigrants (both below 30 percent), though slightly lower than Asian children of immigrants (49 percent). These figures reflect substantial intermarriage between immigrants and natives in the Asian and Black populations.

---

8   The waiting period for citizenship is three years for legal immigrants married to US citizens.

Rates of parental citizenship are lowest for Black children of Somali (51 percent) and Sudanese (54 percent) origins and highest for those of Jamaican and Nigerian origins (75 percent). These high rates are likely due to the fact that Jamaica and Nigeria have relatively long histories of US immigration. By contrast, Somali and Sudanese immigrants have arrived most recently, many entering as refugees. These factors may slow their intermarriage rates and perhaps their children's integration.

Despite these variations across parental origin countries, the findings described here suggest that Black children of immigrants live in families with parents who have made commitments to the United States by acquiring citizenship and/or marrying US citizens. Comparatively high rates of parental citizenship bode well for the integration of children with Black immigrant parents.

Regardless of parental origin or citizenship, the overwhelming majority (90 percent) of Black children of immigrants are US-born citizens. Ninety-three percent of Black children with Caribbean origins are citizens; the share for those with African origins is slightly lower (85 percent), potentially due to the fact that African immigrants — both parents and children — arrived more recently.

Even when children are US citizens, however, their parents are often noncitizens — and lack of citizenship can disqualify these parents from important benefits and services for their families. For instance, the 1996 federal welfare reform law and subsequent amendments restricted noncitizen access to cash welfare (Temporary Assistance for Needy Families, or TANF), food stamps (Supplemental Nutrition Assistance Program, or SNAP), and public health insurance (Medicaid); in particular, immigrants with fewer than five years of legal residency and all unauthorized immigrants were excluded from these benefits in most states. Often the US-born child is eligible while the parent is not, and this can result in a reduced benefit level for TANF and SNAP. Complex eligibility rules along with fears and misconceptions about the consequences of applying for benefits can also deter noncitizen parents from seeking assistance for their needy, qualified children.[9]

Rates of mixed citizenship and, therefore, mixed eligibility for public benefits within families are higher for Black immigrant families than all other families, except Hispanic immigrant families.

Fifty-five percent of Black immigrants' children live in mixed-citizenship nuclear families with at least one US citizen and one noncitizen. This is substantially lower than the corresponding proportion for Hispanic children in immigrant families (75 percent), but notably higher than for white or Asian children in immigrant families (48 percent and 42 percent, respectively). The proportion living in mixed-citizenship families is essentially the same for Black children with parents from

---

9   Michael Fix, ed., *Immigrants and Welfare* (New York: Russell Sage Foundation, 2009).

Africa (55 percent) and the Caribbean (56 percent). Children who live in mixed-citizenship families may face barriers to accessing public benefits that could be important for their well-being and development.

B. English Language Fluency and Linguistic Isolation

Parents with English language skills can often get better jobs, better assist their children with school and homework, and thus better contribute to the social and economic integration of immigrant families into US society. Overall the children of Black immigrants have a substantial advantage over most other groups of children in immigrant families because of their parents' relatively high levels of English proficiency, though there are variations here as well.

Eighty percent of Black immigrants' children have at least one parent who speaks English fluently: that is, who speaks English exclusively or "very well." The other 20 percent have parents who speak English "well," "not well," or "not at all" (see Figure 5).[10] Black immigrants' children are only slightly less likely than white immigrants' children to have English-fluent parents (84 percent), but substantially more likely to have fluent parents than Asian (70 percent) or Hispanic (42 percent) children of immigrants.

---

10   The Census asks respondents whether people in the household over age 5 speak English or another language at home. The level of spoken English fluency is queried for those who speak another language. Those who speak English at home or speak another language and speak English very well are considered proficient. Those who speak English well, not well, or not at all are considered limited English proficient (LEP).

Figure 5. Share of Children (from Birth through Age 10) in Immigrant Families with at Least One English-Fluent Parent, by Race-Ethnicity

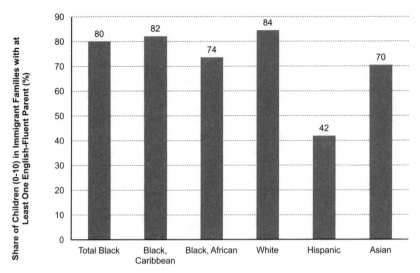

Note: Analysis includes children living with at least one parent.

Source: Author's analysis of 2005-09 ACS, pooled.

English fluency rates vary widely by parental origin. Among Black children with immigrant parents from Jamaica and other English-speaking Caribbean countries, 99-100 percent live with a mother or father who is English fluent. The proportions are somewhat lower for Black children with parents born in Nigeria (92 percent) and Ghana (84 percent), and fall to about two-thirds for Ethiopia/Eritrea (67 percent) and the lower levels for those with origins in Sudan (59 percent), the Dominican Republic (58 percent), and Haiti (59 percent). Black children of Somali-born parents are the least likely to have an English-fluent parent (44 percent). In fact, refugees and other immigrants from Somalia speak several different, less common languages, potentially complicating their integration and communication with the host society.

Linguistic isolation is a broader measure of English language fluency based on whether *all household members* aged 13 or older — including parents, older siblings, other relatives, and nonrelatives — speak English very well.[11] Using this broader measure, 15 percent of Black immigrants' children live in linguistically isolated households, somewhat higher than the rate for white children in immigrant families (12 percent), but notably lower than for Asian immigrants' children (24 percent) and Hispanic immigrants' children (44 percent, see Figure 6).

---

11   Children are considered linguistically isolated if no one in the household over age 13 speaks English exclusively or very well.

Figure 6. Share of Children (from Birth through Age 10) in Immigrant Families with Linguistically Isolated Households, by Race-Ethnicity

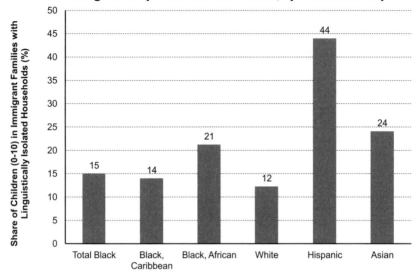

Note: Analysis includes children living with at least one parent.
Source: Author's analysis of 2005-09 ACS, pooled.

Only 6 percent of children with Nigerian origins and 11 percent with Ghanaian origins live in linguistically isolated households. This share rises to 27 percent for those with Ethiopian/Eritrean origins, 31 percent for Haitian, 32 percent for Sudanese, and 45 percent for children with Somali-born parents. Not surprisingly, the children of Somali and Sudanese immigrants are the most likely to be linguistically isolated, just as they are the most likely to have parents with limited English proficiency.

C. Parental Educational Attainment

It has long been known that children whose parents have completed fewer years of schooling tend to themselves leave school earlier and obtain lower-paying jobs when they reach adulthood.[12] Immigrant parents often have high educational aspirations for their children, but

---

12 William H. Sewell, Robert M. Hauser, and Wendy. C. Wolf, "Sex, Schooling, and Occupational Status," *American Journal of Sociology* 83, No. 3 (1980): 551–83; Featherman and Hauser, *Opportunity and Change*; William H. Sewell and Robert M. Hauser, *Education, Occupation and Earnings* (New York: Academic Press, 1975); Blau and Duncan, *The American Occupational Structure.*

may know little about the US educational system, particularly if they have low levels of education.[13]

Children in immigrant and native-born Black families are about equally likely to have a mother who has not graduated from high school (16 percent and 15 percent respectively) or a father who has not graduated from high school (both 12 percent, see Figures 7 and 8). The proportions are several percentage points higher for Hispanic children in native-born families (19 percent for mothers and 17 percent for fathers), but much higher for Hispanic children in immigrant families (48 percent for mothers and 51 percent for fathers). In contrast, 10 percent or less of white and Asian children has either a father or mother without a high school education, regardless of parental nativity.

At the higher end of the educational distribution, children of Black immigrants are much more likely than children of Black natives to have parents who are college graduates: 33 percent versus 18 percent for fathers and 26 percent versus 15 percent for mothers (see Figures 9 and 10). Hispanic children are much less likely to have parents who are college graduates, while college attainment rates for white and Asian parents are substantially higher.

When Black children of African and Caribbean immigrants are compared, an interesting gender pattern emerges: African immigrant fathers are much better educated than mothers, while the educational attainment rates of mothers and fathers from the Caribbean are similar. For instance, Black children of Caribbean immigrants are equally likely to have mothers and fathers without a high school education (13 percent). But children of African immigrants are twice as likely to have mothers as fathers without a high school education (20 percent versus 11 percent). Similarly, the shares of Caribbean-origin children with college-educated mothers and fathers are the same (23 percent), while African-origin children are much more likely to have college-educated fathers than mothers (45 percent versus 27 percent).

Once again, variations across origin countries are even more pronounced than those across regions. The highest high school graduation rates are found among Nigerian parents (only 1 percent of Nigerian-origin children have fathers or mothers who did not graduate), followed by children with origins in Jamaica (11 percent for fathers, 9 percent for mothers), other English-speaking Caribbean countries (9 percent for fathers, 8 percent for mothers), and Ghana (5 percent for fathers, 10 percent for mothers). By contrast, the proportion of children who have

13 Grace Kao, "Psychological Well-Being and Educational Achievement among Immigrant Youth," in *Children of Immigrants: Health, Adjustment, and Public Assistance*, ed. Donald J. Hernandez (Washington, DC: National Academy Press, 1999), 410–77; Rubén. G. Rumbaut, "Passages to Adulthood: The Adaptation of Children of Immigrants in Southern California," in *Children of Immigrants: Health, Adjustment, and Public Assistance*, ed. Donald J. Hernandez (Washington, DC: National Academy Press, 1999), 478–545; Hernandez and Charney, *From Generation to Generation.*

fathers who are not high school graduates is 13 percent for Sudanese children and 12 percent for Ethiopian/Eritrean-born children , while 20 percent of children with Ethiopian-/Eritrean-origin and 35 percent with Sudanese-origin parents have *mothers* who are not high school graduates. Children in Somali immigrant families are the most likely to have parents without a high school education and have the largest gap between fathers (30 percent) and mothers (53 percent).

Figure 7. Share Children (from Birth through Age 10) with Father Who Did Not Graduate from High School, by Race, Ethnicity, and Family Immigrant Status

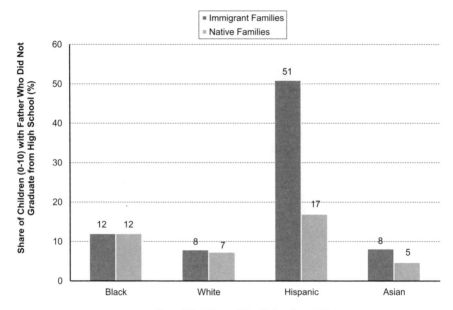

Note: Analysis includes children living with father.

Source: Author's analysis of 2005-09 ACS, pooled.

Figure 8. Share Children (from Birth through Age 10) with Mother Who Did Not Graduate from High School, by Race, Ethnicity, and Family Immigrant Status

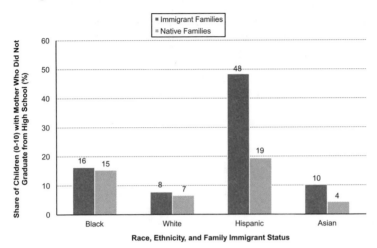

Note: Analysis includes children living with mother.

Source: Author's analysis of 2005-09 ACS, pooled.

Figure 9. Share Children (from Birth through Age 10) with Father Who Completed Bachelor's Degree, by Race, Ethnicity, and Family Immigrant Status

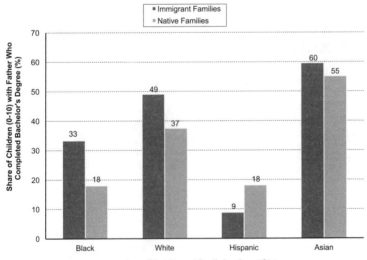

Note: Analysis includes children living with father.

Source: Author's analysis of 2005-09 ACS, pooled.

Figure 10. Share Children (from Birth through Age 10) with Mother Who Completed Bachelor's Degree, by Race, Ethnicity, and Family Immigrant Status

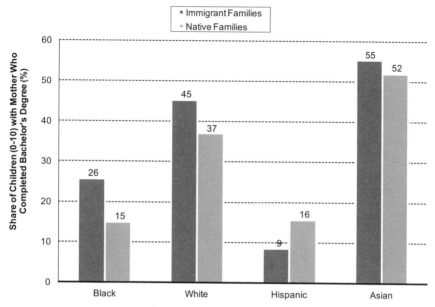

Note: Analysis includes children living with mother.
Source: Author's analysis of 2005-09 ACS, pooled.

Patterns of college attainment among Black immigrant parents are similar, though gaps between fathers and mothers are larger. Children of Nigerian immigrants are the most likely to have college-educated parents (73 percent for fathers and 53 percent for mothers). In fact, children of Nigerian immigrants are even more likely to have college-educated fathers than children of Asian immigrants (60 percent). At the other end of the spectrum, 14 percent of children in Somali immigrant families have college-educated fathers, and only 5 percent have college-educated mothers. College completion rates for immigrant parents from the Caribbean tend to fall between these two extremes. For most English-speaking Caribbean countries, there is no gender gap in college completion. Notably, Black children of Jamaican immigrants are more likely to have college-educated mothers than fathers (29 percent versus 24 percent).

D. Parental Workforce Attachment

Almost all fathers living with their young children (94 percent) work. This high rate of employment holds for most children in African and

Caribbean immigrant families (see Figure 11). Children in white, Hispanic, and Asian immigrant families are slightly more likely to have employed fathers (with rates ranging from 95 percent to 97 percent). Black children of US natives have a somewhat lower paternal employment rate (90 percent).

Figure 11. Share Children (from Birth through Age 10) with an Employed Father, by Race, Ethnicity, and Family Immigrant Status

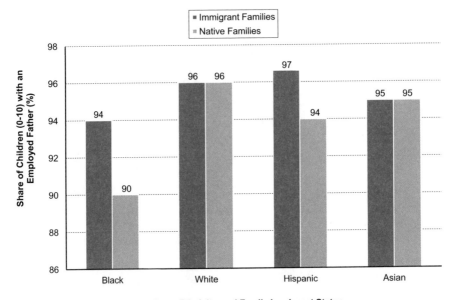

Note: Analysis includes children living with father.

Source: Author's analysis of 2005-09 ACS, pooled.

Other studies have also found that paternal employment is nearly universal among immigrant families, regardless of their race or ethnic origin.[14]

The employment of immigrant mothers varies more widely. Black immigrant mothers of young children are more likely to work than mothers in all other immigrant and race-ethnic groups — except for Black native mothers (see Figure 12). Eighty-one percent of Black Caribbean immigrants' children have working mothers, exceeding the high rate for Black natives' children (78 percent). The maternal employment rate is 70 percent or higher for Black children with parents from all major African and Caribbean sending countries, except Sudan (57 percent) and Somalia (47 percent).

---

14   For instance, see Donald J. Hernandez, Nancy A. Denton, and Suzanne E. Macartney, "Indicators of Characteristics and Circumstances of Children Ages 0-17 in Immigrant Families by Country of Origin and in Native-Born Families by Race-Ethnicity," University of Albany Center for Demographic and Social Analysis, 2011, www.albany.edu/csda/children.

Figure 12. Share Children (from Birth through Age 10) with an Employed Mother, by Race, Ethnicity, and Family Immigrant Status

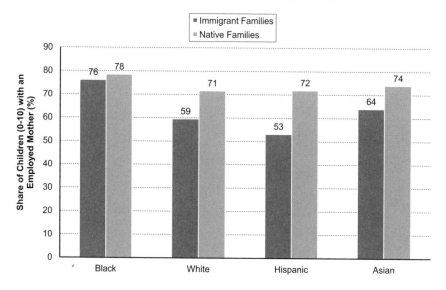

Race, Ethnicity, and Family Immigrant Status

Note: Analysis includes children living with mother.

Source: Author's analysis of 2005-09 ACS, pooled.

When it comes to full-time work, Black immigrant fathers do not fare as well as immigrant fathers in other race-ethnic groups. The share of Black immigrants' children with fathers who work full-time is 74 percent, lower by a few percentage points than for white, Asian, and Hispanic immigrant children (see Figure 13). Only Black natives' children have a lower share of fathers working full-time (68 percent). The rate of paternal full-time work falls within a narrow range (72 percent to 79 percent) for children with Black immigrant parents from all origins except Somalia (57 percent).

Figure 13. Share Children (from Birth through Age 10) with a Father Employed Full-Time and Year-Round, by Race, Ethnicity, and Family Immigrant Status

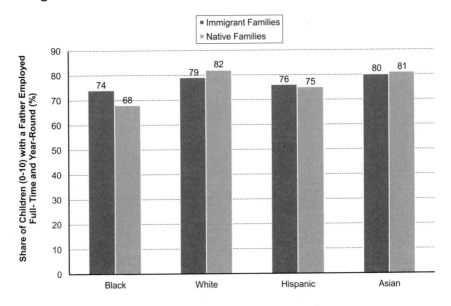

Race, Ethnicity, and Family Immigrant Status

Note: Analysis includes children living with father.
Source: Author's analysis of 2005-09 ACS, pooled.

In contrast to the pattern for fathers, Black children are the most likely to have mothers working full-time (45 percent for Black children of immigrants and 43 percent for Black children of natives, see Figure 14). Among children with Black immigrant parents, the children with the highest proportion of mothers working full-time are those with mothers born in Jamaica (56 percent), followed by English-speaking Caribbean countries and Haiti (49-50 percent), and then by Ghana and Nigeria (45-46 percent). The lowest proportions are among children with mothers born in Sudan (23 percent) and Somalia (14 percent). The lower levels of full-time employment for these two origin countries may be related to comparatively low shares of English-fluent mothers, high shares who have not graduated from high school, traumas experienced by mothers fleeing as refugees from war-torn regions, and culturally influenced social roles for women.

Figure 14. Share Children (from Birth through Age 10) with a Mother Employed Full-Time and Year-Round, by Race, Ethnicity, and Family Immigrant Status

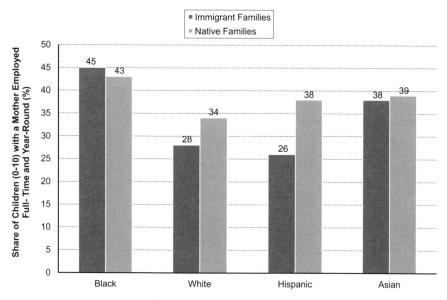

Note: Analysis includes children living with mother.

Source: Author's analysis of 2005-09 ACS, pooled.

Immigrant families do not rely solely on parents for income from work, as many have other workers in the home. For instance, 14 percent of Black children of immigrants have another adult worker in the home as do 12 percent of Asian children of immigrants and 21 percent of Hispanic children of immigrants. Children in native-born families and white children are less likely to have another working adult in the household. Black children in immigrant families are most likely to have another adult worker in the home if they have a parent born in Haiti (19 percent), Jamaica (17 percent), other English-speaking Caribbean countries (15 percent), the Dominican Republic (14 percent), or Ghana (14 percent).

E. Parental Earnings

Parental income is central to determining children's well-being, and 19 percent of Black children in both immigrant and native-born families have working fathers who earn less than twice the federal minimum wage — a wage level needed to support a family at above 150 percent of the federal poverty level (see Figure 15).[15] The share of white and Asian children with fathers earning below twice the minimum wage was much lower (11 percent and below). The share for Hispanic children of immigrants was the highest (32 percent). Among Black children of immigrants, those with fathers born in Ghana were the least likely to have fathers earning below twice the minimum wage (10 percent) while those with fathers born in Somalia were the most likely (41 percent).

Figure 15. Share of Children (from Birth through Age 10) with a Father Earning Less than Twice the Federal Minimum Wage, by Race, Ethnicity, and Family Immigrant Status

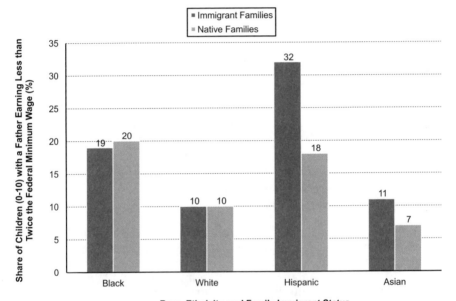

Note: Analysis includes children living with father.

Source: Author's analysis of 2005-09 ACS, pooled.

Mothers earn less than fathers across all major race-ethnic groups, and patterns across groups are similar. Twenty-nine percent of Black

15 The minimum wage was set at $5.15 in 2005-06, and increased to $5.85 in 2007, $6.55 in 2008, and $7.25 in 2009. Assuming 40 hours per week and 50 weeks' work, a person earning twice the federal minimum wage in 2009 would earn $29,000. Since the 2009 federal poverty thresholds were set at $17,258 for a family of three with two children, and $21,756 for a family of four with two children, the corresponding 200 percent poverty thresholds are $34,516 and $43,512. Thus, annual earnings at twice the value of the federal minimum wage in 2009 ($29,000) would allow a worker to keep his or her family at a level between 100 percent and 200 percent of the poverty threshold. Please note that these calculations are based on the federal minimum wage and do not take account of variations in minimum wages enacted at the state level.

immigrants' working mothers do not earn twice the minimum wage (see Figure 16). Hispanic children of immigrants had the largest share of mothers earning below twice the minimum wage (45 percent).

Figure 16. Share of Children (from Birth through Age 10) with a Mother Earning Less than Twice the Federal Minimum Wage, by Race, Ethnicity, and Family Immigrant Status

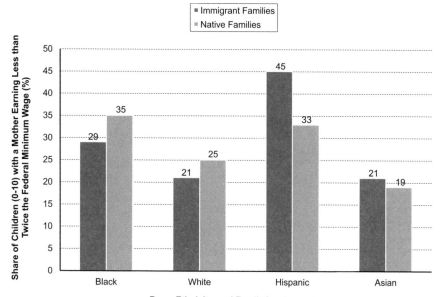

Note: Analysis includes children living with mother.
Source: Author's analysis of 2005-09 ACS, pooled.

F. Poverty

Children from low-income families often experience less success in school and lower earnings in adulthood.[16] In fact, over time family poverty has greater negative consequences for children than either limited parental education or living in a one-parent family.[17]

Nineteen percent of Black immigrants' children live in families with incomes below the federal poverty threshold (see Figure 17). Poverty rates are higher for Hispanic children of natives (23 percent) and Hispanic children of immigrants (28 percent). Black children of natives

---

16 Vonnie McLoyd, "Socioeconomic Disadvantage and Child Development," *American Psychologist* 53, No. 2 (1998): 185–204; Greg J. Duncan and Jeanne Brooks-Gunn, eds., *Consequences of Growing Up Poor* (New York: Russell Sage Foundation, 1997); Sewell and Hauser, *Education, Occupation and Earnings.*

17 Duncan and Brooks-Gunn, *Consequences of Growing Up Poor*; McLoyd, "Socioeconomic Disadvantage and Child Development."

have the highest rate (35 percent). Poverty rates for white and Asian children in immigrant and native-born families are much lower (7 percent to 10 percent). Black children in immigrant families with African origins are more likely than those with Caribbean origins to live in poverty (23 percent versus 18 percent).

Poverty rates for Black immigrants' children vary across African and Caribbean parents' countries of origin. Only Black children with parents born in Nigeria have poverty rates as low as white children (10 percent). Black children with parents born in Jamaica (14 percent), Ghana (15 percent), and other English-speaking Caribbean countries (16 percent) have the next lowest poverty rates, and poverty rates are highest for Black children with parents born in Sudan (35 percent) and Somalia (60 percent).

The share of families with income below twice the poverty level (what we refer to as the "low-income" level here) is greater. Using this definition, 45 percent of Black immigrants' children live in low-income families, a substantially smaller share than Black children of natives (63 percent), Hispanic children of natives (48 percent), or Hispanic children of immigrants (64 percent, see Figure 17). Black children with African-born parents are more likely than their counterparts with Caribbean-born parents to live in low-income families (49 percent and 43 percent, respectively).

Among the Black children of immigrants, children with Somali- and Sudan-born parents are the most likely to be low income (85 percent and 70 percent, respectively), followed by those with origins in Haiti and the Dominican Republic (56 percent and 52 percent, respectively). Rates are substantially lower among Black children with origins in Nigeria (29 percent), Ghana and Jamaica (35 percent), and other English-speaking Caribbean countries (38 percent).

Figure 17. Share Children (from Birth through Age 10) in Official Poverty and Below 200 Percent of Official Poverty, by Race, Ethnicity, and Family Immigrant Status

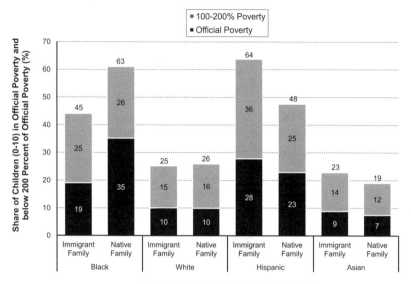

Race, Ethnicity, and Family Immigrant Status

Note: Analysis includes children living with at least one parent. Due to rounding, percentages may not add up to 100.

Source: Author's analysis of 2005-09 ACS, pooled.

Overall, children with parents from Nigeria, Ghana, Jamaica, and the rest of the English-speaking Caribbean fare best on most economic indicators, while those from Haiti and the African refugee-sending countries of Sudan and Somalia fare the worst.

G. Housing

Housing costs and conditions can influence the financial resources and time parents are able to devote to their children. Patterns of housing hardship often reflect income and poverty, as limited incomes may require families to live in rented rather than owned homes, spend a substantial share of income on housing, or double- or triple-up, resulting in crowded housing conditions.

Family homeownership. Homeownership can reflect both access to higher-quality housing and a commitment by families to their local communities. Nearly one-half (48 percent) of Black children in immigrant families live in homes owned by their parents (or other family members, see Figure 18). Thirty-five percent of Black children of natives live in their families' homes. Homeownership is much higher in white and Asian families — ranging from 69 percent to 75 percent.

Among children of Black immigrants, those with Caribbean origins are more likely to live in owned homes than those from African origins (49 percent versus 44 percent), reflecting their higher incomes and longer residence in the United States. Family homeownership is very high for Black children of Nigerian immigrants (67 percent). Children of Jamaican immigrants also have a relatively high rate of family homeownership (54 percent). Only 30 percent of Black children with Sudanese origins and 9 percent of those with Somali origins, however, live in owned homes. Thus, patterns of family homeownership track patterns of poverty.

Figure 18. Share Children (from Birth through Age 10) Living in Homes Owned by Parents or Relatives, by Race, Ethnicity, and Family Immigrant Status

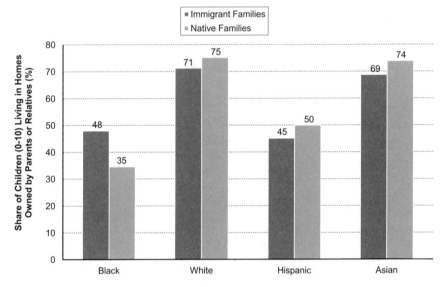

Note: Analysis includes children living with at least one parent.

Source: Author's analysis of 2005-09 ACS, pooled.

Housing cost burdens. Households that pay more than half of their income for housing are more likely to lack the resources to meet other basic needs, including supporting the development of their children. This high ratio of housing costs to income is referred to as a "severe housing-cost burden." Twenty-eight percent of Black immigrants' children live in families with severe housing-cost burdens, a rate exceeded only by Black children of natives (31 percent) and Hispanic children of immigrants (29 percent, see Figure 19). The severe housing cost burden rate is 12 percent for white children of natives.

Substantial shares of children from all backgrounds live in families with "moderate" housing burdens, defined as housing costs between one-third and one-half of family incomes. Taken together, over half of Black children of immigrants (56 percent), Black children of natives (55 percent), and Hispanic children of immigrants (58 percent) live in families with moderate or severe housing burdens.

Among the children of Black immigrants, those with Caribbean origins are about as likely as their peers with African origins to live in homes with severe (30 percent versus 28 percent) and moderate housing-cost burdens (28 percent each).

Black children with origins in Haiti or Somalia are the most likely to experience either severe or moderate housing-cost burdens (63 percent each), but their rate is only slightly higher than for Black children of immigrants from most other origins (53-56 percent); the lowest rate is for children with Nigerian origins (51 percent). Thus, rates of housing burdens for Black children of immigrants often exceed by a substantial margin their poverty rates and their rates of living in low-income families. These high housing burdens are accounted for at least partly by Black immigrants' concentration in East Coast states with high housing costs.

Figure 19. Share Children (from Birth through Age 10) in Families with Moderate and Severe Housing Burdens, by Race, Ethnicity, and Family Immigrant Status

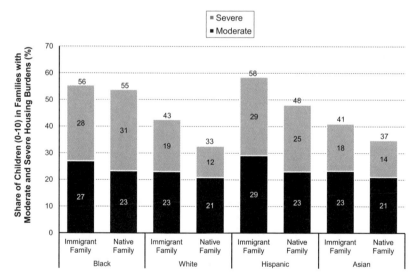

Notes: Analysis includes children living with at least one parent. Due to rounding, percentages may not add up to 100.

Source: Author's analysis of 2005-09 ACS, pooled.

Crowded housing. Low-income families may double up with other family members or nonrelatives, leading to overcrowding. Overcrowded housing is linked to several risk factors for children's health, well-being, and development. When household members have different schedules, children may sleep less or have irregular sleep patterns, resulting in poorer behavior and difficulty concentrating in school. Lack of privacy can create household stress and lead to less responsive parenting. Crowded housing has also been linked to a higher risk of infectious diseases among children.[18] Children are considered to be living in crowded housing if they live in a home with more than one person per room.[19]

Twenty-three percent of Black immigrants' children live in overcrowded housing, nearly twice the level for Black children in native-born families (13 percent, see Figure 20). White children in immigrant and native-born families are less likely still to live in overcrowded housing (13 percent and 6 percent, respectively), as are Asian children in native-born families (8 percent). Hispanic immigrants' children are the only group with a higher overcrowding rate (40 percent). Black children with African-born parents (28 percent) are more likely than their peers with Caribbean-born parents (21 percent) to live in crowded housing, but again substantial variation exists across parental countries of origin.

Overcrowding is lowest among Black children with immigrant parents born in Jamaica (15 percent), other English-speaking Caribbean countries (17 percent), and Nigeria (18 percent), and highest for those with origins in Haiti (29 percent), Sudan (42 percent), and Somalia (56 percent). Thus, overcrowding, like housing cost burdens, is relatively high among Black children with immigrant parents of many different origins. There is greater variation in overcrowding than cost burdens, however, with the least economically advantaged groups (Somalis and Sudanese) having overcrowding rates several times as high as better-off groups such as Nigerians and Jamaicans.

---

18 John N. Edwards, Theodore D. Fuller, Santhat Sermsri, and Sairudee Vorakitphokatorn, *Household Crowding and Its Consequences* (Boulder, CO: Westview Press, 1994); Gary W. Evans, Stephen J. Lepore, B. R. Shejwal, and M.N. Palsane, "Chronic Residential Crowding and Children's Well Being," *Child Development* 69, no. 6 (1998): 1514–23; Hernandez and Charney, *From Generation to Generation*; Gary W. Evans, Susan Saegert, and Rebecca Harris, "Residential Density and Psychological Health among Children in Low-Income Families," *Environment and Behavior* 33, vol. 2 (2001): 165–80; Gary W. Evans, Henry N. Ricciuti, Steven Hope, Ingrid Schoon, Robert H. Bradley, Robert F. Corwyn, and Cindy Hazan, "Crowding and Cognitive Development: The Mediating Role of Maternal Responsiveness among 36-Month-Old Children," *Environment and Behavior* 42, vol. 1 (2010): 135–48.

19 US Census Bureau, *Housing of Lower-Income Households*, Statistical Brief No. sb/94/18 (Washington, DC: US Census Bureau, 1994), www.census.gov/apsd/www/statbrief/sb94_18.pdf.

Figure 20. Share Children (from Birth through Age 10) in Overcrowded Housing, by Race, Ethnicity, and Family Immigrant Status

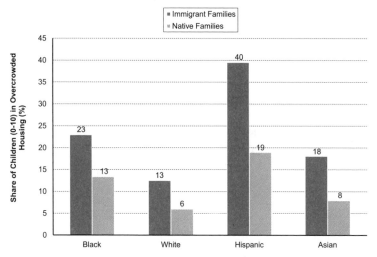

Note: Analysis includes children living with at least one parent.
Source: Author's analysis of 2005-09 ACS, pooled.

V. Access to Social Supports

A. Prekindergarten

Participation in high-quality early care and education promotes language, cognitive, and social development. Participation in high-quality preschool programs may be particularly valuable for the development of children in immigrant families with parents who do not speak English fluently.[20] The analysis of preschool enrollment described here is based on the assumption that prekindergarten is generally beneficial for children's academic and socioemotional development; data on the *quality* of preschool were unavailable for analysis.[21]

---

20 William T. Gormley, "Early Childhood Care and Education: Lessons and Puzzles," *Journal of Policy Analysis and Management,* 26, No. 3 (2007): 633–71; William T. Gormley, "The Effect of Oklahoma's Pre-K Program on Hispanic Children," *Social Science Quarterly* 89, No. 4 (2008): 916–36; William T. Gormley and Ted Gayer, "Promoting School Readiness in Oklahoma: An Evaluation of Tulsa's Pre-K Program," *Journal of Human Resources* 40, No. 3 (2005): 533–58; William T. Gormley, Ted Gayer, Deborah Phillips, and Brittany. Dawson, "The Effects of Universal Pre-K on Cognitive Development," *Developmental Psychology* 41, No. 6 (2005): 872–84.

21 The ACS data on preschool enrollment may exclude some children participating in Head Start and other forms of center-based care, as some respondents may categorize these programs as prekindergarten.

Black children of immigrants are more advantaged than most other children in terms of access to early education — at least prekindergarten. Young Black children aged 3-4 are slightly more likely than white children to be enrolled in prekindergarten (56 percent versus 54 percent for young children in immigrant families, and 50 percent versus 49 percent for those in native families — see Figure 21). Asian children of immigrants are equally likely to be enrolled in prekindergarten (56 percent), but enrollment rates are lower among all other race-ethnic groups. Hispanic children in immigrant families are the least likely to be enrolled in prekindergarten (36 percent).

Figure 21. Share Children Ages 3-4 Enrolled in Prekindergarten, by Race, Ethnicity, and Family Immigrant Status

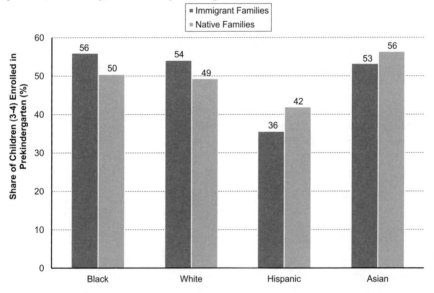

Note: Analysis includes children living with at least one parent.

Source: Author's analysis of 2005-09 ACS, pooled.

Among young children in Black immigrant families, prekindergarten enrollment is somewhat higher for those with Caribbean origins than African origins (61 percent versus 53 percent). The highest prekindergarten enrollment rates are for young Black children in immigrant families with parents from Jamaica, other English-speaking Caribbean countries, and Nigeria (ranging from 63 to 66 percent), followed by Ghana, Haiti, and Sudan (ranging from 54 to 59 percent, see Figure 22). Fifty percent of young children in Black immigrant families with parents from the Dominican Republic and Ethiopia/Eritrea are enrolled in prekindergarten, but the enrollment rate falls to 37 percent for those from Somalia. Thus, excluding children with Somali-born parents, the majority of Black children of immigrants in the relevant age range (3-4 years) are enrolled in prekindergarten. Given the very low parental education rates and precarious economic well-being of children in the Somali group, low preschool enrollment rates are troubling; among the children of Black immigrants, this group of children likely has the greatest need for high-quality early education.

Figure 22. Share Children (with Black Immigrant Parents) Ages 3-4 Enrolled in Prekindergarten, by Parental Country or Region of Origin

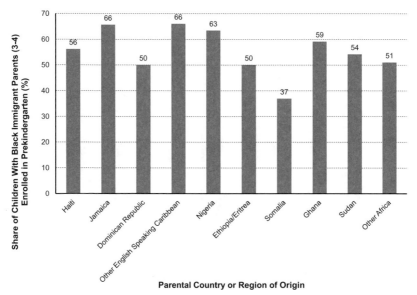

Note: Analysis includes children living with at least one parent.

Source: Author's analysis of 2005-09 ACS, pooled.

B. Health Insurance

Good health is correlated with success in school and work, and the availability of health insurance coverage is in turn tied to health outcomes. Because ACS did not begin reporting on health insurance data until 2008, only two years of data (2008-09) were available at the time this analysis was written.

Health insurance coverage is very high for US children overall and nearly universal for some groups of children, due in large part to expansions in public coverage in recent years. The share of children with either public or private coverage is 90 percent or higher for all groups, except Hispanic children of natives (82 percent, see Figure 23). For some groups such as Black and Hispanic children of natives, coverage through Medicaid, Children's Health Insurance Program (CHIP), and other public programs now exceeds coverage through employers and other private sources.

A majority (55 percent) of Black immigrants' children has private insurance coverage, and this rate exceeds the rates for Black children of natives and all Hispanic children regardless of parental nativity. Asian and white children, however, have substantially higher private coverage rates (73 percent and higher). The *public* coverage rate for Black children of immigrants (35 percent) is lower than for Black children of natives and Hispanic children, but considerably higher than for white and Asian children.

Figure 23. Share of Children (from Birth through Age 10) with Public or Private Health Insurance Coverage, by Race, Ethnicity, and Family Immigrant Status

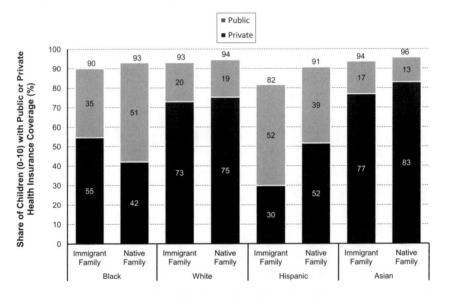

Race, Ethnicity, and Family Immigrant Status

Notes: Analysis includes children living with at least one parent. Due to rounding, percentages may not add up to 100.
Source: Author's analysis of 2005-09 ACS, pooled.

Among children in Black immigrant families, 92 percent of young children with African origins were covered under any form of health insurance, at any time during the year, compared with 88 percent of those with Caribbean origins. There is not that much variation by origin in the share of Black immigrants' children with either public or private insurance coverage. Eighty-nine percent or more of these children have some form of coverage — except for children of Haitian-origin parents, who have somewhat lower coverage (81 percent, see Figure 24). Thus Haitian families represent the parental origin group with the largest share of uninsured children. The lack of insurance in this population

may be due to the large number of Haitian immigrants who are unauthorized — or at least were during the period 2008-09.[22] Unauthorized
children are ineligible for public insurance in most states, and unauthorized parents may fear applying for public coverage for their eligible
US-born children. Moreover, many unauthorized parents work "off the
books" without benefits such as employer-provided coverage.

There is, however, considerable variation in types of coverage for Black
children with immigrant parents from different countries. Children
with Somali parents have the highest public coverage (75 percent),
most likely because many enter as refugees, and refugees are connected with Medicaid and other public benefits immediately upon arrival.
In fact, the high public coverage of children with Somali parents has
resulted in their having the highest overall coverage of any group (96
percent). Black children from two other parental origin groups have
relatively high public coverage: those with parents from the Dominican
Republic (52 percent) and Sudan (51 percent). Sudanese immigrants
also often enter as refugees and receive assistance upon their arrival,
while Dominican immigrants are most likely to settle in New York and
Massachusetts — two states with nearly universal coverage of children
through public insurance programs and other means.

The children of Black immigrants from all other countries are more
likely to have private than public health insurance coverage. The
highest private coverage can be found among children with parental
origins in Nigeria (68 percent), Ghana (65 percent), and Jamaica and
other English-speaking Caribbean countries (63 percent each).

Overall, 52 percent of Black children with African-born parents were
covered by private health insurance at some point during the year, compared to 56 percent with Caribbean-born parents. The rates of public
health insurance coverage (excluding those with any private coverage)
for these groups were 40 percent and 32 percent, respectively.

---

22 More recently, thousands of previously unauthorized Haitian immigrants received Tempo-
    rary Protected Status (TPS), a form of temporary immigration status that allows them to
    work but does not make them eligible for Medicaid in most states. TPS can be awarded to
    immigrant-origin groups already in the United States if they are not able to return to their
    home countries due to natural disasters, armed conflict, or other extraordinary situations;
    it was awarded to Haitians following the January 2010 earthquake in Haiti.

Figure 24. Share of Children (from Birth through Age 10 with Black Immigrant Parents) with Private or Public Health Insurance Coverage, by Parental Country or Region of Origin

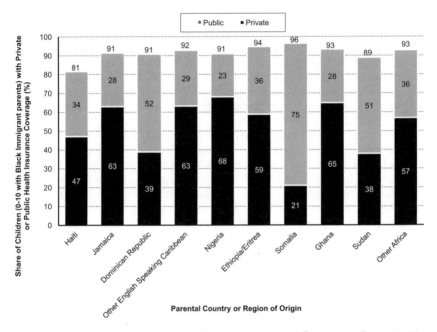

Notes: Analysis includes children living with at least one parent. Due to rounding, percentages may not add up to 100.
Source: Author's analysis of 2005-09 ACS, pooled.

These results suggest the importance of access to public programs for refugee children and those with refugee parents, as well as those from other parental origin groups with limited private insurance coverage.

VI. Conclusions and Implications for Public Policy

Rapid immigration has led to the diversification of the Black child population in the United States, even as it has the overall child population. Black immigrant parents come from countries spread across Africa, the Caribbean, and other world regions — with no single country accounting for more than one-fifth of the total. These parents' diverse origins make it difficult to generate sweeping conclusions about the well-being of Black immigrants' children, since well-being indicators vary greatly by parental country of origin.

In general, the children of Black immigrants fall in the middle of multiple well-being indicators. Black children of natives (i.e., African Americans) and Hispanic children — whether the parents are immigrants or US born — tend to fare worse on most indicators, while Asian and white children fare better. Children with parents from Africa tend to fare about as well as children with parents from the Caribbean.

Children with parents from English-speaking countries that have a long history of immigration to the United States tend to fare the best; these countries include Nigeria and Ghana in Africa along with Jamaica, Trinidad, and several smaller West Indian countries in the Caribbean. The most at risk are children with parents from countries with shorter immigration histories, where English is not a common language, and with substantial refugee flows. Refugees are involuntary migrants and have often experienced trauma and persecution in their home countries or refugee camps; many recent refugees have comparatively low levels of formal education. As a result, children with parents born in the African refugee-sending countries of Somalia, Sudan, and Ethiopia/Eritrea face many risks to their successful development, as do children with parents born in Haiti and the Dominican Republic — the two largest Caribbean origins of Black immigrants who do not speak English as their primary language.

A. *Protective Factors for Black Children of Immigrants*

Family structure and work patterns are key strengths of Black immigrant families, but these strengths vary in nature between African and Caribbean families. Black African families are more likely to have two parents in the home, and Black immigrant fathers generally exhibit high rates of employment. Black Caribbean families are more likely to be headed by single parents, but the mothers in these families have among the highest employment rates of any demographic group. Black Caribbean families are also more likely to have a grandparent in the home and to have two working parents when both parents are in the home. High rates of work among parents and the presence of multiple adults in the home provide important economic resources for children in most Black immigrant families.

Paternal employment is universally high among Black children of immigrants, and only Black immigrant mothers with origins in Somalia and Sudan exhibit low rates of employment — these are countries most associated with recent refugee flows.

Black children of immigrants are more likely than Hispanic children of immigrants to have parents who are US citizens and less likely to have parents who are unauthorized. Two-thirds of Black children of immigrants have at least one US-citizen parent, and 46 percent have at least one US-born parent, signaling a relatively high level of intermarriage with the US-born population. High levels of citizenship promote Black immigrant parents' integration and facilitate access to public benefits and services. Somali and Sudanese parents are the least likely to be US citizens since they arrived in the United States more recently than other Black immigrant groups. A high share came as refugees and therefore retains access to public benefits and services. While Haitian parents have high naturalization rates, many are unauthorized or hold Temporary Protected Status (TPS), barring their use of public benefits.

Parental education and English language fluency also protect children in Black immigrant families. Eighty percent of Black immigrants' children have a parent who speaks English fluently or exclusively, about twice the rate for Hispanic children of immigrants. Black immigrant parents have higher college graduation rates than Black native-born parents or Hispanic parents, and they are about a third as likely as Hispanic immigrant parents to lack a high school education. Here there are some important exceptions, as parents born in Haiti, the Dominican Republic, Sudan, and Somalia have much lower educational attainment and English proficiency rates than Black immigrant parents with other origins. There are also significant gender variations, as Black African fathers tend to be much better educated than Black African mothers, while educational attainment rates among Caribbeans do not vary much by gender. In fact, Jamaican mothers are slightly better educated than Jamaican fathers.

Access to public benefits and services represents a fourth set of protective factors for Black children of immigrants. These children are more likely than any major nativity/race-ethnic group to be enrolled in prekindergarten at ages 3-4. They also have relatively high rates of health insurance coverage, especially through Medicaid and other public programs. Concentration in states along the East Coast with relatively high preschool enrollment and strong social safety nets (for instance, New York) may partly explain why Black children's preschool enrollment and Medicaid participation rates are higher than other children of immigrants.[23] The relatively small share with unauthorized parents and large share with parents who entered as refugees may be another explanation.

B. Risk Factors

Despite relatively high parental educational attainment and employment, children of Black immigrants are still at risk for poverty and associated difficulties because their parents have relatively low earnings. Black immigrant fathers earn wages similar to African American fathers, trailing those of white and Asian fathers. Poverty rates track the pattern of wages, with children in Black immigrant families twice as likely to live in poverty as white or Asian children — though African

---

23 William O'Hare, Mark Mather, and Genevieve Dupuis, *Analyzing State Differences in Child Well-Being* (New York: Foundation for Child Development, 2012), http://fcd-us.org/sites/default/files/Analyzing%20State%20Differences%20in%20Child%20Well-Being_0.pdf.

American and Hispanic children's poverty rates are higher. Only Black children with parents born in Nigeria have a poverty rate as low as that of white children.

Children of Black immigrants are about as likely to live in owned homes as children of Hispanic immigrants, and their families' housing cost burdens are nearly as high. They also have the second-highest rate of overcrowded housing behind children of Hispanic immigrants. High housing costs and crowding may be associated with residence in more expensive states on the East Coast, particularly in New York and particularly in the Haitian population.

Finally, Black children with parents from some refugee-origin countries — particularly Somalia and Sudan — often live in very large families that include five or more children. Resources to promote children's well-being are attenuated in larger families. Most children in Black immigrant families, however, tend to have family sizes that are near the average for all US children.

C. Policy Implications

Public policies are critical to the well-being of many children. Despite the important role that policies play, however, many children are not covered by health insurance and are not attending prekindergarten, particularly if they live in families with limited economic resources. This is especially true for children with Black immigrant parents from a range of African and Caribbean origins. It is essential that policies be expanded and improved to include these children, to ensure they have the same opportunities for success as other US children.

A few states, particularly along the East Coast, account for large shares of children in Black immigrant families. Some of these states — such as New York, Massachusetts, New Jersey, and Maryland — have comparatively strong public policies and programs to promote immigrant integration and to provide health care and early childhood education to many low-income residents, including immigrants.[24] Sustaining these initiatives in the current budget climate will remain a challenge.

The high levels of disadvantage among Black children in refugee families suggest a need for sustained assistance to these families. US refugee resettlement programs focus primarily on initial resettlement — defined as the first several months after arrival — and on the English language proficiency and employment of refugee adults. The federal government does not provide substantial resources to help refugee children with adjustment, integration, or school performance. Yet, refugee children from origins such as Somalia, Sudan, and

---

24 Among these states, New Jersey has a comparatively lower proportion of children overall covered by health insurance; see O'Hare, Mather, and Dupuis, *Analyzing State Differences in Child Well-Being.*

Ethiopia/Eritrea are likely to need prolonged support due to their relatively high poverty rates, crowded housing conditions, and other risk factors associated with socioeconomic disadvantage.

Refugee status incurs some benefits for Black children from refugee backgrounds — for instance, access to health insurance coverage through Medicaid, CHIP, and similar public programs. Expansions in these programs in the wake of the 1996 welfare reforms have provided an important safety net for Black children of immigrants, just as they have for many other low-income children.

Black children in Haitian immigrant families are the one major origin group with a high rate of exclusion from public benefits such as Medicaid and CHIP. As a result, they are significantly less likely to have health insurance than other Black children of immigrants. Their exclusion results from the high share of both Haitian parents and children who are unauthorized or have TPS, a temporary immigration status that does not confer public benefits eligibility in most states. TPS was extended to some Haitian immigrants already in the United States on account of recent natural disasters in Haiti, and Haiti remains the poorest nation in the Western Hemisphere. Developing more permanent forms of legal status and extending basic health benefits eligibility to TPS recipients could represent an important strategy for protecting children in this vulnerable population. ⤳

Works Cited

Blake, Judith. 1981. Family Size and the Quality of Children, *Demography* 18, 321-42.

_____. 1985. Number of Siblings and Educational Mobility. *American Sociological Review* 50: 84-94.

_____. 1987. Differential Parental Investment: Its Effects on Child Quality and Status Attainment. In *Parenting Across the Life Span: Biosocial Dimensions*, eds. Jane B. Lancaster, Jeanne Altmann, Alice S. Rossi, and Lonnie R. Sherrod. New York: Alsine de Gruyter: 351-75.

_____. 1989. *Family Size and Achievement.* Berkeley, CA: University of California Press.

Blau, Peter M. and Otis Dudley Duncan. 1967. *The American Occupational Structure.* New York: Wiley.

Capps, Randy, Genevieve Kenny, and Michael Fix. 2003. Health Insurance Coverage of Children in Mixed-Status Immigrant Families. In *Snapshots of America's Families III*, No. 12. Washington, DC: The Urban Institute.

Capps, Randy, Kristen McCabe, and Michael Fix. 2012. New Streams: Black African Migration to the United States. In *Young Children of Black Immigrants in America: Changing Flows, Changing Faces,* eds. Randy Capps and Michael Fix. Washington, DC: Migration Policy Institute.

Cherlin, Andrew J. 1999. Going to Extremes: Family Structure, Children's Well-Being, and Social Sciences. *Demography* 36 (4): 421–28.

Duncan, Greg J. and Jeanne Brooks-Gunn, eds. 1997. *Consequences of Growing Up Poor.* New York: Russell Sage Foundation.

Edwards, John N., Theodore D. Fuller, Santhat Sermsri, and Sairudee Vorakitphokatorn. 1994. *Household Crowding and Its Consequences.* Boulder, CO: Westview Press.

Evans, Gary W., Susan Saegert, and Rebecca Harris. 2001. Residential Density and Psychological Health among Children in Low-Income Families. *Environment and Behavior* 33 (2): 165–80.

Evans, Gary W., Stephen J. Lepore, B. R. Shejwal, and M. N. Palsane. 1998. Chronic Residential Crowding and Children's Well Being. *Child Development* 69, no. 6: 1514–23.

Evans, Gary W., Henry N. Ricciuti, Steven Hope, Ingrid Schoon, Robert H. Bradley, Robert F. Corwyn, and Cindy Hazan. 2010. Crowding and Cognitive Development: The Mediating Role of Maternal Responsiveness among 36-Month-Old Children. *Environment and Behavior* 42 (1): 135–48.

Featherman, David L. and Robert Mason Hauser. 1978. *Opportunity and Change.* New York: Academic Press.

Fix, Michael, ed. 2009. *Immigrants and Welfare.* New York: Russell Sage Foundation.

Fix, Michael and Jeffrey S. Passel. 1999. *Trends in Noncitizens' and Citizens' Use of Public Benefits Following Welfare Reform: 1994–97.* Washington, DC: The Urban Institute. www.urban.org/publications/408086.html.

Fix, Michael and Wendy Zimmerman. 1995. When Should Immigrants Receive Benefits? *In Welfare Reform: An Analysis of the Issues*, ed. Isabelle V. Sawhill. Washington, DC: The Urban Institute.

Gormley, William T. 2007. Early Childhood Care and Education: Lessons and Puzzles. *Journal of Policy Analysis and Management* 26 (3): 633–71.

____. 2008. The Effect of Oklahoma's Pre-K Program on Hispanic Children. *Social Science Quarterly* 89 (4): 916–36.

Gormley, William T. and Ted Gayer. 2005. Promoting School Readiness in Oklahoma: An Evaluation of Tulsa's Pre-K Program. *Journal of Human Resources* 40 (3): 533–58.

Gormley, W. T., Ted Gayer, Deborah Phillips, and Brittany Dawson. 2005. The Effects of Universal Pre-K on Cognitive Development. *Developmental Psychology* 41 (6): 872–84.

Hernandez, Donald J. and Evan Charney, eds. 1998. *From Generation to Generation: The Health and Well-Being of Children in Immigrant Families.* Washington, DC: National Academy Press. www.nap.edu/catalog.php?record_id=6164#toc.

____. 2011. *Indicators of Characteristics and Circumstances of Children Ages 0-17 in Immigrant Families by Country of Origin and in Native-Born Families by Race-Ethnicity.* www.albany.edu/csda/children.

Kao, Grace. 1999. Psychological Well-Being and Educational Achievement among Immigrant Youth. In *Children of Immigrants: Health, Adjustment, And Public Assistance*, ed. D. J. Hernandez. Washington, DC: National Academy Press.

McLanahan, Sara and Gary Sandefur. 1994. *Growing Up with a Single Parent: What Hurts, What Helps.* Cambridge, MA: Harvard University Press.

McLoyd, Vonnie. 1998. Socioeconomic Disadvantage and Child Development. *American Psychologist* 53 (2): 185–204.

O'Hare, William, Mark Mather, and Genevieve Dupuis. 2012. *Analyzing State Differences in Child Well-Being.* New York: Foundation for Child Development. http://fcd-us.org/sites/default/files/Analyzing%20State%20Differences%20in%20Child%20Well-Being_0.pdf.

Ruggles, Steven, J. Trent Alexander, Katie Genadek, Ronald Goeken, Matthew B. Schroeder, and Matthew Sobek. *Integrated Public Use Microdata Series: Version 5.0* [Machine-readable database]. Minneapolis: University of Minnesota, 2010. http://usa.ipums.org/usa/index.shtml.

Rumbaut, Rubén. G. 1999. Passages to Adulthood: The Adaptation of Children of Immigrants in Southern California. In *Children of Immigrants: Health, Adjustment, and Public Assistance*, ed. D. J. Hernandez, 478–545. Washington, DC: National Academy Press.

Sewell, William H. and Robert M. Hauser. 1975. *Education, Occupation and Earnings.* New York: Academic Press.

Sewell, William H., Robert M. Hauser, and Wendy C. Wolf. 1980. Sex, Schooling, and Occupational Status. *American Journal of Sociology* 83 (3): 551–83.

US Census Bureau. 1994. *Housing of Lower-Income Households.* Statistical Brief No. sb/94/18. Washington, DC: US Census Bureau. www.census.gov/apsd/www/statbrief/sb94_18.pdf.

Zimmermann, Wendy and Karen Tumlin. 1999. Patchwork Policies: State Assistance for Immigrants under Welfare Reform. Occasional Paper No. 24. The Urban Institute, Washington, DC. www.urban.org/publications/309007.html.

PART TWO

FAMILY CIRCUMSTANCES, EARLY CHILDHOOD OUTCOMES, AND SCHOOL READINESS

CHAPTER 4

BLACK AND IMMIGRANT: EXPLORING THE EFFECTS OF ETHNICITY AND FOREIGN-BORN STATUS ON INFANT HEALTH

Tiffany L. Green

Virginia Commonwealth University

Introduction

Poor infant health results in large economic costs to both individuals and to society. One estimate placed the costs of preterm birth at $6 billion in 2001,[1] and there is a wealth of evidence demonstrating that low birth weight[2] is related to adverse health, educational, and labor outcomes from childhood through adulthood.[3] Black[4] children disproportionately experience adverse health outcomes at birth; they are more likely to be born prematurely, have higher rates of low birth weight, and die within the first year of life.[5]

---

1   Rebecca B. Russell, Nancy S. Green, Claudia A. Steiner, Susan Meikle, Jennifer L. Howse, Karalee Poschman, Todd Dias, Lisa Potetz, Michael J. Davidoff, Karla Damus, and Joann R. Petrini, "Cost of Hospitalization for Preterm and Low Birth Weight Infants in the United States," *Pediatrics* 120, No. 1 (2007): e1–e9.

2   Low birth weight is defined as weighing less than 2,500 grams at birth.

3   Sandra E. Black, Paul J. Devereau, and Kjell G. Salvanes, "From the Cradle to the Labor Market? The Effect of Birth Weight on Adult Outcomes," *Quarterly Journal of Economics* 122, No. 1 (2007): 409–39; Rucker C. Johnson and Robert F. Schoeni, "The Influence of Early Life Events on Human Capital, Health Status, and Labor Market Outcomes over the Life Course," *The B.E. Journal of Economic Analysis and Policy: Advances* 11, No. 3 (2011): 1-55.

4   The chapter refers to non-Hispanic Black natives (i.e., African Americans) and non-Hispanic Black immigrants as "Black," when describing racial/ethnic categories examined using 2000-03 Vital Statistics Natality Files. Similarly, the study designates non-Hispanic Asians as "Asian" and non-Hispanic whites as "white;"and interchangeably uses "Hispanic" or "Latino."

5   T.J. Mathews and Marian F. MacDorman, "Infant Mortality Statistics from the 2004 Period Linked Birth/Infant Death Data Set" (National Vital Statistics Reports, 55 No. 14, National Center for Health Statistics, Hyattsville, MD, revised June 13, 2007), www.cdc.gov/nchs/data/nvsr/nvsr55/nvsr55_14.pdf.

Over recent years, researchers have noted superior birth outcomes among immigrant mothers compared to those who are native born, regardless of racial/ethnic background. While the literature has mainly focused on infant health outcomes among Mexican-born immigrant mothers,[6] the birth outcomes of Black immigrant mothers have received comparatively little attention. This oversight is problematic, given the increasing proportion of Black immigrants in the US Black population[7] and the fact that foreign-born Black adults tend to have better health outcomes than do their US-born peers.[8]

The existing infant health research on Black immigrant mothers finds that women from Africa and the Caribbean have birth outcomes superior to those of US-born Black mothers.[9] However, one major limitation of this literature is that most researchers examine only within-group differences among Blacks[10] or differences between native- and foreign-born mothers,[11] making it difficult to understand how Black immigrants compare to native- and foreign-born non-Blacks. Such points of comparison are crucial if we are to understand whether the birth outcomes of Black immigrant mothers are truly unique, or whether the infant health disparities observed between native-born Blacks and whites are replicated among immigrant populations. While there are suggestive findings that infants born to Black immigrant mothers are still at a relative health disadvantage to non-Black immigrant and US-born mothers, this evidence is based on studies that are limited for various reasons, whether in geographic scope and/or generalizability[12] or because they examine a limited set of infant health outcomes.[13] Lastly, the majority of this liter-

---

6   Robert Hummer, Daniel Powers, Starling Pullum, G. Gossman, and W. Frisbie, "Paradox Found (Again): Infant Mortality among the Mexican-origin Population in the United States," *Demography* 44 (2007): 441–57.

7   Mary Mederios Kent, "Immigration and America's Black Population," *Population Bulletin* 62, No. 4 (2007): 3-15, www.prb.org/pdf07/62.4immigration.pdf.

8   Gopal K. Singh and Mohammad Siahpush, "All-cause and Cause-specific Mortality of Immigrants and Native Born in the United States," *American Journal of Public Health* 91, No. 3 (2001): 392–99.

9   Richard J. David and James W. Collins, "Differing Birth Weight among Infants of U.S.-born Blacks, African-born Blacks, and U.S.-born Whites," *New England Journal of Medicine* 337, No. 17 (1997): 1209–14; Eugenia K. Pallotto, Jr., James W. Collins, and Richard J. David, "Enigma of Maternal Race and Infant Birth Weight: A Population-based Study of US-born and Caribbean-born Black Women," *American Journal of Epidemiology* 151 (2000): 1080–85.

10   Ibid.

11   Gopal K. Singh and Stella M. Yu, "Adverse Pregnancy Outcomes: Differences Between US- and Foreign-born Women in Major US Racial and Ethnic Groups," *American Journal of Public Health* 86 (1996): 837-43.

12   Arturo Cervantes, Louis Keith, and Grace Wyshak, "Adverse Birth Outcomes among Native-born and Immigrant Women: Replicating National Evidence regarding Mexicans at the Local Level," *Maternal and Child Health Journal* 3, No. 2 (1999): 99–109.

13   Dolores Acevedo-Garcia, Mah-J. Soobader, and Lisa F. Berkman, "The Differential Effect of Foreign-born Status on Low Birth Weight by Race/Ethnicity and Education," *Pediatrics* 115, No. 1 (2005): e20-30.

ature fails to empirically explore the possibility that prenatal behaviors (such as smoking and use of prenatal care) can systematically differ by nativity, race, and ethnicity — and that these differences may contribute to differences in infant health outcomes.

The purpose of this chapter is to address each of these shortcomings in the literature. Using the vital statistics natality files of the National Center for Health Statistics (NCHS),[14] I analyze data from the states and district containing the primary East Coast Metropolitan Statistical Areas (MSAs) where black immigrants resided over the period 2000-03. [15] In doing so, I explore two questions: First, are there any differences in first-trimester prenatal-care initiation or smoking incidence among Black immigrants compared to other native- or foreign-born women? Second, are Black immigrants more or less likely than other foreign-born or US-born women to experience adverse infant-health outcomes?

This study is among the few to directly compare the birth outcomes of Black foreign-born mothers to those of both (1) their US-born Black counterparts and (2) foreign- and US-born non-Black mothers. Moreover, while low birth weight is the most typical marker of poor infant health, other measures of infant health, may better predict poor health outcomes later in childhood. To further develop the literature on the health of Black immigrant children, this chapter examines preterm birth, low birth weight, and small for gestational age.

The findings from this study suggest that any existing Black health advantage associated with foreign-born status (i.e., nativity) is limited in scope. That is, compared to Black native-born mothers, Black immigrant mothers have lower rates of low-birth-weight children. However, Black foreign-born mothers experience higher rates of preterm birth and are more likely to give birth to children who are small for their gestational age than nearly all other non-Black foreign-born groups.

There is also suggestive evidence that Black foreign-born women may make different choices than native-born Black (and other non-Black) mothers during the prenatal period. For example, Black immigrant mothers have a very low smoking rate — lower than native-born mothers of all races and white foreign-born mothers — which may help to explain why their birth outcomes are better than those of native-born Blacks. However, Black immigrant mothers are the least likely of any group of mothers, native- or foreign-born, to initiate prenatal care during the first trimester of pregnancy — which may lead to a higher incidence of adverse birth outcomes.

---

14 Center for Disease Control and Prevention, National Center for Health Statistics (NCHS), "Vital Statistics Data Available Online," www.cdc.gov/nchs/data_access/Vitalstatsonline. htm.

15 Kent, "Immigration and America's Black Population." The states include Delaware, Florida, Maryland, Massachusetts, New Hampshire, New Jersey, New York, Pennsylvania, and Virginia; the District of Columbia is also included.

This study will proceed as follows: Section I provides an overview of the literature on immigrant mothers and infant health. Section II describes the data and estimation sample, and Section III contains a discussion of the empirical findings. Section IV concludes with further discussion of the implications of the empirical findings, limitations, and plans for future work.

I. Background

A. Birth Outcomes

Over the past few decades, researchers have observed that the birth outcomes found among immigrant mothers in the United States are often superior to those found among their native-born counterparts.[16] Much of the research on immigrant infant-health outcomes has focused on the so-called Mexican paradox. This refers to the observation that Mexican immigrant women typically have superior outcomes to US-born women of Mexican heritage and US-born whites in spite of possessing socioeconomic profiles typically correlated with poor infant health. Many of these socioeconomic indicators, including low educational attainment, low health insurance coverage, and lengthier prenatal-care delay are similar to those found among US-born Blacks.[17]

Comparatively few researchers have studied the birth outcomes of Black immigrants in the United States. While Black immigrant mothers appear to have advantageous health outcomes compared to US-born Blacks, there is little evidence for the existence of a "Black immigrant paradox" analogous to that found among Mexican mothers. In one of the best-known studies examining the birth outcomes of US- and foreign-born Blacks, Richard David and James Collins analyze a data set containing all Illinois births in 1980-95 to US-born non-Hispanic whites and Blacks, as well as to immigrants from sub-Saharan Africa.[18] The authors find that after adjustment for prenatal care, smoking, drug use, and other socioeconomic factors, the African-born women had a birth-weight distribution similar to that of US-born white women. They

---

16 It is important to note that this was not always the case. Infant and child mortality among white immigrants, for example, was far higher than among native-born whites during the late 18th and early 19th centuries. See Jacqueline H. Wolf, "Low Breastfeeding Rates and Public Health in the United States," *American Journal of Public Health* 93, No. 12 (2003): 2000–10; Jeffrey P. Brosco, "The Early History of the Infant Mortality Rate in America: A Reflection upon the Past and a Prophecy of the Future," *Pediatrics* 103, No. 2 (1999): 478–85. See also Nancy S. Landale, Salvador R. Oropesa, and Brenda K. Gorman, *Immigration and Infant Health: Birth Outcomes of Immigrant and Native-Born Women* (Washington, DC: National Academies Press, 1999).

17 D. E. Bender and D. Castro, "Explaining the Birth Weight Paradox: Latina Immigrants' Perceptions of Resilience and Risk," *Journal of Immigrant Health* 2, No. 3 (2000): 155-73; Hummer et al., "Paradox Found (Again)."

18 David and Collins, "Differing Birth Weight among Infants."

also report that the rates of low birth weight among African immigrant women were higher than those among US whites, but lower than those of native-born Blacks. Other work has found a persistent infant health advantage among specific groups of Black immigrants, such as those from Ethiopia, compared to US-born Black women.[19]

Several studies have also focused their attention on geographic areas with relatively large populations of Black immigrants, including New York City. David Howard et al. explore the relationships among race, foreign-born status, and infant health outcomes in their study of US-born white and Black women and foreign-born women who gave birth in New York City in 1998-2002.[20] The authors find that US-born Black mothers generally had a higher risk of low birth weight and preterm birth than US-born whites and foreign-born Blacks. However, they find the strongest nativity effects among Blacks from South and Central America; mothers who emigrated from these regions had a much lower risk of preterm delivery or low birth weight.

Black immigrant mothers also may have an infant mortality advantage in non-singleton births. Hamisu Salihu et al. find that the twins of US-born Black mothers had a much higher likelihood of dying within the neonatal period than the twins of their foreign-born counterparts.[21] The authors also report that even within the sample of twins (already more likely to be born preterm and at lower birth weights), the children of US-born mothers were more likely to have adverse health outcomes such as low and very low birth weight.

However, other work suggests that the children of Black immigrant women only have an advantage in certain segments of the birth weight distribution. Eugenia Pallotto et al. find that while Caribbean-born Black women have lesser rates of low birth weight than US-born Black women, both groups have equivalent rates of very low birth weight.[22] David and Collins find similar results in a comparison study of African- and US-born Blacks.[23]

Furthermore, there is suggestive evidence that the birth outcomes for Black immigrant women may compare unfavorably to those for non-Black immigrants and some non-Black US-born women. Data from the 2004 US vital statistics natality files suggest that Black foreign-born

---

19 H. Wasse, V. L. Holt, and J. R. Daling, "Pregnancy Risk Factors and Birth Outcomes in Washington State: A Comparison of Ethiopian-born and US-born Women," *American Journal of Public Health* 84 (1994): 1505-07.

20 David L. Howard, Susan S. Marshall, S. Jay, P. Kaufman, and David A. Savitz, "Variations in Low Birth Weight and Preterm Delivery among Blacks in Relation to Ancestry and Nativity: New York City, 1998-2002," *Pediatrics* 118 (2006): e1399–e1405.

21 Hamisu M. Salihu, W. S. Mardenbrough-Gumbs, Muktar H. Aliyu, J. E. Sedjro, B. J. Pierre-Louis, R. S. Kirby, and G. R. Alexander, "The Influence of Nativity on Neonatal Survival of Black Twins in the United States," *Ethnicity and Disease* 15, No. 2 (2005): 276–82.

22 Pallotto, Collins, and David, "Enigma of Maternal Race and Infant Birth Weight."

23 David and Collins, "Differing Birth Weight among Infants."

women have the highest infant mortality rates of all immigrant women, though these statistics do not take into account differences in socio-economic status, maternal health, or health behaviors.[24] Arturo Cervantes et al. are among the few to directly compare outcomes among native-born and immigrant women.[25] Using a linked data set of Chicago births in 1994, the authors find suggestive evidence that although Black immigrant women are less likely to have low-birth-weight or preterm infants than Black native-born women, *both* groups still have worse outcomes than native- and foreign-born Latino and non-Hispanic white women. Extending this work, Dolores Acevedo-Garcia et al. use the 1998 vital statistics natality data to compare differences in birth weight across all native- and foreign-born mothers.[26] In contrast to Cervantes et al., they reach the unique conclusion that white immigrant women do not appear to have an immigrant health advantage, but that foreign-born status has the greatest association with better infant health for non-Hispanic Black women, followed by Hispanic women.

B. Prenatal Behaviors

While genetics, maternal health, and the environment play a large part in determining infant health outcomes such as preterm birth and low birth weight, prenatal behaviors and maternal health during pregnancy, including smoking, prenatal care utilization, and stress can also play an important role. The deleterious effects of smoking on infant health outcomes are well established. Both active and passive (i.e., second-hand) smoking during pregnancy are associated with decreased birth weight and higher rates of preterm birth and infant mortality.[27]

Differences in smoking behavior may help, in part, to explain why Black immigrant women tend to have better birth outcomes than their native-born counterparts. Irma Elo and Jennifer Culhane find in a Philadelphia-based study of pregnant Black women that foreign-born women are less likely to report prenatal smoking, drinking, or marijuana use, even after controlling for a number of socioeconomic factors and stressors.[28] Foreign-born mothers were also more likely

24 T.J Mathews and M.F. MacDorman, "Infant Mortality Statistics from the 2004 Period Linked Birth/Infant Death Data Set," *National Vital Statistics Report* 55, No. 14 (2007): 1-32, www.cdc.gov/nchs/data/nvsr/nvsr55/nvsr55_14.pdf.
25 Cervantes, Keith, and Wyshak, "Adverse Birth Outcomes among Native-born and Immigrant Women."
26 Acevedo-Garcia, Soobader, and Berkman, "The Differential Effect of Foreign-born Status."
27 Vincent W. Jaddoe, E.J. W. Troe, Albert Hofman, Johan Mackenbach, Henriëtte A. Moll, E. A. Steegers, and J. C. Witteman, "Active and Passive Maternal Smoking during Pregnancy and the Risks of Low Birth Weight and Preterm Birth: The Generation R Study," *Pediatric and Perinatal Epidemiology* 22 (2008): 162–71; Gopal K. Singh and Michael D. Kogan, "Persistent Socioeconomic Disparities in Infant, Neonatal, and Postneonatal Mortality Rates in the United States, 1969-2001," *Pediatrics* 119, No. 4 (2005): e928-e939.
28 Irma T. Elo and Jennifer Culhane, "Variations in Health and Health Behaviors by Nativity among Pregnant Black Women in Philadelphia," *American Journal of Public Health* 100, No. 11 (2010): 2185-92.

to report better physical and mental health. The authors suggest that the African-born women in the sample were more likely to have better prenatal health behaviors and health statuses than the Caribbean-born women, but note that the relatively small sample sizes prevented more definitive conclusions in this regard. Howard Cabral et al. also reach similar conclusions in a Boston-based study of US- and foreign-born Black women.[29] The foreign-born Black women in this study were more socioeconomically advantaged and also less likely than their native-born peers to smoke, drink alcohol, or use illicit drugs.

Another potentially important prenatal behavior is use of prenatal care. Policymakers have identified prenatal care, one of the most widely used forms of preventive health care, as a key policy strategy to improve infant-health outcomes in the United States.[30] However, the impact of prenatal care on infant health is somewhat more ambiguous than that of smoking. Researchers have questioned the effectiveness of prenatal care on improving infant-health outcomes, in part because the observed associations between prenatal care and infant-health evidence are often correlated with maternal characteristics. For example, mothers who know that they may have a potentially problematic pregnancy may be more likely to have more prenatal-care visits, leading to a positive statistical association between more frequent prenatal care and lower birth weight.[31] However, there is evidence that suggests that prenatal care may reduce the risk of intrauterine-growth restrictions and that estimates of the "mean" effect of prenatal care can hide more important effects at various points in the birth-weight distribution.[32]

Studies suggest that health insurance coverage is a strong determinant of prenatal care utilization and that non-white and foreign-born women are both less likely to have any prenatal coverage and less likely to initiate early prenatal care.[33] Moreover, the evidence regarding differences in prenatal-care utilization among Black women is extremely

---

29 Howard Cabral, Laurence E. Fried, Suzette Levenson, Hortensia Amaro, and Barry Zuckerman, "Foreign-born and US-born Black Women: Differences in Health Behaviors and Birth Outcomes," *American Journal of Public Health* 80 (1990): 70–2.

30 Greg R. Alexander and Milton Kotelchuck, "Assessing the Role and Effectiveness of Prenatal Care: History, Challenges, and Directions for Future Research," *Public Health Rep* 116, No. 4 (2001): 306–16.

31 Theodore Joyce, "Self-Selection, Prenatal-Care, and Birth-Weight among Blacks, Whites, and Hispanics in New-York-City," *Journal of Human Resources* 29, No. 3 (1994): 762–94; Mark R. Rosenzweig and Paul T. Schultz, "Estimating a Household Production Function: Heterogeneity, the Demand for Health Inputs, and their Effects on Birth Weight," *The Journal of Political Economy* 91, No. 5 (1983): 723–46.

32 George L. Wehby, Jeffrey C. Murray, Eduardo E. Castilla, Jorge S. Lopez-Camelo, and Robert L. Ohsfeldt, "Quantile Effects of Prenatal Care Utilization on Birth Weight in Argentina," *Health Economics* 18 (2009): 1307-21; K. S. Conway and P. Deb, "Is Prenatal Care Really Ineffective? Or, is the 'Devil' in the Distribution?" *Health Economics* 24 (2005): 489–513.

33 V. Cokkinides, "Health insurance coverage-enrollment and adequacy of prenatal care utilization," *J Health Care Poor Underserved* 12 (4) (2001): 461-73; Kathryn Pitkin Derose, Jose J. Escarce, and Nicole Lurie, "Immigrants and Health Care: Sources of Vulnerability," *Health Affairs* 26, No. 5 (2007):1258-68.

sparse and reaches mixed conclusions. Cabral et al. note that US- and foreign-born Black mothers have similar patterns of prenatal-care initiation and delay.[34] However, Salihu et al. report that Black immigrant mothers tend to have lower levels of adequate prenatal care than US-born Black women.[35]

Finally, a handful of studies have attempted to quantify differences in stress or exposure to stress that may explain infant-health-outcome differentials between US- and foreign-born Blacks. While few researchers have connected direct, individual-level measures of financial or emotional stress to infant-health outcomes, Elo and Culhane[36] estimate the relationships between material support, objective stress, and prenatal behaviors. The authors find that material support (i.e., social support) is related to improved prenatal behaviors and maternal health — and that foreign-born Black women are less likely than native-born Black women to have access to material support.[37] However, the inclusion of these and other socioeconomic factors fails to explain the better prenatal behaviors and health among Black immigrant women compared to Black native-born women.

Other stress-related literature on Black immigrant mothers uses residential segregation as a proxy for environmental or psychosocial stressors. For example, Sue Grady and Sara McLafferty use 2000 New York City vital statistics data to analyze the relationships between segregation and low-birth-weight risk.[38] In their models, high levels of residential segregation are correlated with a higher risk of low birth weight for all Black women. However, when the authors include controls for country of origin, the association between racial segregation and birth weight disappeared for foreign-born women. The authors hypothesize that immigrant Black women may not have resided in poor or highly segregated areas long enough to experience worsened health and that immigrant cultural traits may have served as a buffer against these adverse conditions.

This study builds and improves upon prior work in this area by comparing the prenatal behaviors and birth outcomes of Black immigrants to both their native-born and non-Black immigrant counterparts, using birth data from the East Coast receiving areas where most Black immigrants reside. In addition to estimating models of low birth weight, I

---

34 Cabral et al., "Foreign-born and US-born Black Women."
35 Salihu et al., "The Influence of Nativity on Neonatal Survival."
36 Elo and Culhane, "Variations in Health and Health Behaviors."
37 Elo and Culhane rate levels of material support based on the number of "yes" responses to the following set of questions: "Do you know someone who (1) would take you to the doctor? (2) would loan you $100? (3) would help you with daily chores if you were sick? (4) you could talk to about problems? and (5) would watch your children?" The more "yes" responses, the higher the level of material support recorded. See Elo and Culhane, "Variations in Health and Health Behaviors."
38 Sue C. Grady and Sara McLafferty, "Segregation, Nativity, and Health: Reproductive Health Inequalities for Immigrant- and Native-born Black Women in New York City," *Urban Geography* 28, No. 4 (2007): 377-97.

also look at preterm birth and infants that are small for their gestational age (a measure that can proxy for intrauterine-growth restriction).[39]

II. Description of Data and Analytical Methods

A. Data

For the empirical analyses, this study employs 2000-03 vital statistics natality files from the National Center for Health Statistics.[40] The federal natality files represent the largest available data on Black immigrant births because they provide annual data on every live birth in the United States.[41] The files include information on infant health outcomes, maternal characteristics, and prenatal behaviors.[42] For the purposes of this study, I restrict the sample to the states and district containing the East Coast metropolitan statistical areas that are home to the most Black (African and Caribbean) immigrants.[43]

Appendix Tables A-1 and A-2 contain descriptive statistics summarizing the key characteristics of the native-born and foreign-born mothers in the sample, by ethnic group. The summary statistics are presented in panels associated with the birth outcomes of interest, prenatal behavior and pregnancy history, maternal characteristics, and year of birth.

---

39 P. Clayton, S. Cianfarani, P. Czernichow, G. Johannsson, R. Rapaport, and A. Rogol, "Management of the Child Born Small for Gestational Age through to Adulthood: A Consensus Statement of the International Societies of Pediatric Endocrinology and the Growth Hormone Research Society," *The Journal of Clinical Endocrinology & Metabolism* 92, No. 3 (2007): 804–10.

40 Geographic identifiers are unavailable in public natality files after 2004.

41 NCHS, "Vital Statistics Data Available Online."

42 I employed the following exclusion criteria when deriving the final estimation sample. First, I excluded all multiple births (n=184,833), those observations without valid values for gender (n=149) and dependent birth outcomes of interest, including birth weight (n=5,510) and gestational age (n=137,515). I also excluded all observations without maternal prenatal behaviors of interest, including prenatal care (n=67,568) and smoking behavior (n=7,435). I also excluded all mothers who failed to report their race/ethnicity (n=51,459) or reported their race/ethnicity as Native American/Pacific Islander mothers, given that they comprised an extremely small proportion (of the sample (n=9,093). Lastly, I excluded mothers with missing information on marital status (n=119) and age (n=839). The final sample, N=3,985,589 is approximately 78 percent of the original sample of all births in the nine states/district mentioned above.

43 Top metropolitan areas of residence for Black immigrants are derived from analysis of 2005 American Community Survey (see Kent, "Immigration and America's Black Population") and include: New York–Northern New Jersey–Long Island (NY-NJ-PA), Miami–Fort Lauderdale–Miami Beach (FL), Washington–Arlington–Alexandria (DC-VA-MD-WV), Boston-Cambridge-Quincy (MA-NH), Philadelphia-Camden-Wilmington (PA-NJ-DE-MD), Orlando-Kissimmee (FL), and Baltimore-Towson (MD). West Virginia is excluded from the analyses, given the very small number of Black immigrants/immigrant births in the state.

This study measures the following infant-health outcomes: preterm birth, low birth weight, and small for gestational age. Compared to infant mortality, these birth outcomes are both more common and vary more substantially across groups, facilitating richer analyses. A preterm infant is any infant born with fewer than 37 weeks of gestation. An infant is classified as low birth weight if she or he weighs less than 2,500 grams at birth. Small-for-gestational-age infants are born at a birth weight below the 10th percentile for their gestational age and gender.[44]

There is substantial variation in the incidence of preterm birth across populations of US- and foreign-born mothers. Overall, foreign-born mothers have lower rates of preterm birth than US-born mothers, 7 percent versus 9 percent (see Table A-1). However, Black immigrant mothers have the highest rates of preterm birth of all foreign-born mothers: 10 percent. In contrast, white immigrant mothers have the lowest rates of preterm birth (5 percent), and Asian and Latino mothers have rates that fall in the middle (7 percent and 6 percent, respectively). Black immigrant women also have roughly equivalent or higher rates of preterm birth than US-born mothers, with the exception of US-born Black mothers, who have the highest rates of preterm birth of any group (12 percent). Among US-born women, white mothers have the lowest rates of preterm birth (7 percent), while Asian and Latino mothers have slightly higher rates of preterm birth (8 percent and 9 percent, respectively).

While the average low-birth-weight rate is nearly equivalent between immigrant and native-born mothers, there are considerable within-in-group differences in both the native- and foreign-born samples. Among US-born mothers, Black women have the highest incidence of low birth weight in the sample (11 percent), followed by Latino and Asian mothers (7 percent), and white mothers (5 percent). These patterns are repeated in the foreign-born sample. While foreign-born Black mothers have lower rates of low birth weight than US-born Black women (8 percent versus 11 percent), they nonetheless have the highest rates of low birth weight in the immigrant sample.

The rate of small-for-gestational-age births is also nearly equivalent in both samples (11 percent versus 10 percent in the foreign- and native-born samples, respectively). Among children born to US-born mothers, Black infants are twice as likely to be classified as small for gestational age compared to non-Hispanic whites (16 percent versus 8 percent), with Hispanic and Asian infants falling in between. Among children born to foreign-born mothers, Black infants are more likely to be small for their gestational age than non-Hispanic white or Hispanic infants (13 percent, 10 percent, and 9 percent, respectively) but Asian immigrant mothers have the highest rate of small-for-gestational-age infants (14 percent).

---

44 Clayton et al., "Management of the Child Born Small for Gestational Age through to Adulthood;" Russell et al., "Cost of Hospitalization for Preterm and Low Birth Weight Infants."

Prenatal behaviors measured in this study include whether or not the mother ever smoked during pregnancy and whether or not she initiated prenatal care during the first trimester. Unsurprisingly, US-born mothers have much higher smoking rates than foreign-born mothers (9 percent versus 6 percent). White mothers have the highest smoking rates overall (13 percent and 4 percent in the US- and foreign-born samples, respectively). While US-born Black mothers have lower smoking rates than US-born white mothers, they still have higher smoking rates than those of US-born Latino and Asian mothers. In contrast, Black immigrant mothers (along with Asian mothers) have the lowest prenatal smoking rates in the entire sample (1 percent), followed by Latino mothers (2 percent).

I define a mother as having initiated first trimester prenatal care if she visited a health-care provider within the first three months of pregnancy. Consistent with previous literature,[45] immigrant mothers tend to delay prenatal care more than native-born mothers: 83 percent of US-born mothers initiate care in the first trimester compared to 81 percent of foreign-born mothers. Moreover, regardless of nativity, Black mothers are the least likely to initiate care in the first trimester (approximately 75 percent), followed by Latino mothers (approximately 81 percent). White Non-Hispanic mothers, both native and foreign born, are the most likely to initiate care in the first trimester (90 percent and 85 percent, respectively).

Maternal characteristics measured in this study include maternal race/ethnicity and foreign-born status, maternal age, whether a mother has given birth previously, marital status, and educational attainment. Following existing practices in the social sciences literature, each child's race/ethnicity and nativity are based on those of the mother.[46] All children are classified as either second-generation immigrants (mother born outside of the United States) or third- or higher-generation immigrants (native born). Maternal race and ethnicity are divided into eight categories: non-Hispanic white immigrant/native, non-Hispanic Black immigrant/native, Hispanic immigrant/native, and non-Hispanic Asian immigrant/native.

Among the native born, Black and Latino mothers tend to be slightly younger and less well educated than white and Asian mothers and are more likely to be unmarried. Notably, native-born Black mothers have similar levels of schooling as Latino immigrants. While Black immigrant mothers are more likely to be married and have attained higher levels of education than US-born Blacks, they still have lower rates of upper-level schooling (16+ years) and are less likely to be married than white and Asian immigrants. I also include indicator variables for the year of birth;

---

45   Cervantes, Keith, and Wyshak, "Adverse Birth Outcomes among Native-born and Immigrant Women."

46   Because this study is based on US birth records, it by necessity excludes first-generation immigrant children born abroad.

state and county of residence; whether a mother gave birth in an area with a population below 100,000; and the season of birth.[47]

B. *Empirical Approach*

While the descriptive statistics suggest that any Black immigrant infant-health advantage may exist only in comparison to US-born Blacks, a number of factors — including the maternal characteristics and geographic variables above — are also associated with birth outcomes. I employ regression-based analyses to explore systematically the associations among race/ethnicity, nativity, prenatal behaviors, and birth outcomes. Each of the prenatal behaviors (smoking, prenatal care) and birth outcomes (preterm, low birth weight, small for gestational age) is a binary outcome, which is estimated using logit regression models.[48]

III. Results

This section discusses the estimated associations among race/ethnicity, nativity, prenatal behaviors, and birth outcomes, with a particular focus on Black immigrants. To offer a more intuitive interpretation of the regression analyses, I generate model-based predictions of each prenatal behavior and birth outcome for each racial/ethnic group, by nativity.

A. *Prenatal Behaviors*

I. Smoking

Black, Latino, and Asian mothers are less likely to smoke than white

---

47   Variables for state, county, and state/county population size are not included in the summary regression tables presented in this chapter but are available upon request.

48   Smoking and first-trimester care are binary (0/1) variables. I estimated both smoking and first-trimester care initiation as logit models. Independent covariates included: first birth, mother's age, mother's race/ethnicity, immigrant status, mother's race/ethnicity multiplied by mother's immigrant status, 9-11 years schooling, 12 years schooling, 13-15 years schooling, 16+ years schooling, education missing, 2000 birth, 2001 birth, 2002 birth, and 2003 birth. Similarly, preterm birth, low birth weight, and small for gestational age (all binary variables) were estimated using logit models. These models also included the prenatal behaviors as "independent" variables: prenatal care, smoked, first birth, mother's age, mother's race/ethnicity, immigrant status, mother's race/ethnicity multiplied by mother's immigrant status, 9-11 years schooling, 12 years schooling, 13-15 years schooling, 16+ years schooling, education missing, 2000 birth, 2001 birth, 2002 birth, and 2003 birth. The reference categories for these variables in the regression analyses were: mother white, mother white immigrant, less than nine years of schooling, 2004 birth, winter birth, lived in area with population above 100,000, lived in Virginia, and 2003 birth year.

mothers (see Table 1).[49] Immigrant mothers also have substantially lower smoking rates than US-born mothers.

Black immigrant mothers have the *lowest* predicted rates of smoking of all women, 0.8 percent, closely followed by Latino and Asian immigrants (1.0 percent and 1.4 percent, respectively). In contrast, non-Hispanic white US-born mothers are predicted to have the highest smoking rates (16.2 percent). White non-Hispanic immigrant mothers have about half the predicted smoking rates of their native-born counterparts, 7.2 percent, but this rate is still higher than any other racial or immigrant category with the exception of Asian native-born mothers (8.5 percent). Black native-born mothers have the lowest predicted smoking rates of any group of native-born women (6.0 percent). In summary, all Blacks have among the lowest predicted rates of prenatal smoking (a behavior connected with poor infant health outcomes), but smoking abstention is most pronounced among foreign-born Blacks.

Table 1. Predicted Rates of Smoking and First-Trimester Prenatal-Care Initiation by Race/Ethnicity and Nativity, 2000-03 (N=3,985,589)

	Smoking		Prenatal Care	
	Marginal Effect	Standard Error	Marginal Effect	Standard Error
White Native-Born, NH	0.162***	(0.000)	0.881	(0.000)
White Immigrant, NH	0.072***	(0.001)	0.803	(0.001)
Black Native, Native-Born NH	0.060***	(0.000)	0.817	(0.000)
Black Immigrant, NH	0.008***	(0.000)	0.754	(0.001)
Latino, Native-Born	0.050***	(0.000)	0.857	(0.001)
Latino, Immigrant	0.010***	(0.000)	0.812	(0.001)
Asian Native-Born, NH	0.085***	(0.003)	0.826	(0.003)
Asian Immigrant, NH	0.014***	(0.000)	0.767	(0.001)

Notes: NH=Non-Hispanic.
*** indicates significance at the 1 percent level; ** at the 5 percent level, and * at the 10 percent level.
Source: Author's analysis of 2000-03 natality files, National Center for Health Statistics, "Vital Statistics Data Available Online," www.cdc.gov/nchs/data_access/VitalStatsOnline.htm.

---

49 Table A-3 in the appendix reports average marginal effects of race/ethnicity, immigrant status, and other factors on smoking and first-trimester prenatal-care initiation. These marginal effects and the predicated outcomes shown in Table 1 are taken from logistic regressions. Average marginal effects reflect the association between a 1-unit change in an independent variable and a 1-unit change in an outcome variable (for example, the impact of having a Black mother on low birth weight.) However, from an empirical standpoint, it is impossible to report the average marginal effect of Black immigrant status because Black immigrant status has two components (Black and immigrant). I report complete estimation results in the form of average marginal effects but to facilitate understanding of the implications of the model, I present predicted probabilities of prenatal behaviors and infant health outcomes, by race/ethnicity and immigrant status, within the body of the chapter and in Table 1.

2. Prenatal-Care Initiation during the First Trimester

While Black immigrant women have the lowest predicted smoking rates of all groups of mothers — a positive prenatal behavior — they also have the lowest rates of prenatal-care initiation during the first three months of their pregnancy. Indeed, though all immigrants are less likely to initiate care during the first trimester than the native born, Black women are still less likely than white, Latino, and Asian immigrant women to initiate early prenatal care (see Table 1).

Black immigrant mothers have the lowest predicted rate of first-trimester prenatal-care initiation (75.4 percent). Asian immigrants also have a comparably low rate of early prenatal-care initiation (76.7 percent). Latino immigrants have the highest predicted rate of first-trimester care initiation (81.2 percent), followed by non-Hispanic white immigrants (80.3 percent). Although US-born Black mothers have a higher predicted rate of early prenatal-care initiation than foreign-born Blacks (81.7 percent), they are still the least likely of all US-born mothers to initiate early care. White non-Hispanic mothers born in the United States have the highest predicted rate of first-trimester care initiation (88.1 percent), followed by Latino and Asian mothers (85.7 percent and 82.6 percent, respectively). In contrast to smoking behavior, Black mothers tend to fare worse than other mothers with respect to prenatal-care initiation. Since prenatal-care use can be associated with worse birth outcomes (because mothers expecting worse outcomes tend to seek prenatal care), the degree to which lack of early prenatal care is a risk factor for poor birth outcomes among Black immigrant mothers is unclear.

B. Birth Outcomes

1. Preterm Birth

While foreign-born Black women are less likely to give birth to preterm infants than US-born Black women, they are much more likely to do so than non-Black women (see Table 2).[50] Black immigrant women have a lower predicted preterm birth-rate than US-born Blacks (11.2 percent vs. 9.2 percent). However, white immigrants have the lowest predicted rate (5.7 percent), slightly below Latino and Asian immigrants (approximately 6.7 percent and 6.8 percent, respectively). Black immigrant women also have a higher predicted preterm-birth rate than nearly all other US-born mothers, including white, Hispanic, and Asian women (whose preterm-birth rates are 6.9 percent, 8.7 percent, and 8.5 percent, respectively).

2. Low Birth Weight

Foreign-born Black women are less likely than US-born Black women to give birth to low-birth-weight infants. However, regardless of

---

50 For the marginal effects of race/ethnicity, immigrant status, and other factors on birth outcomes, see Table A-4 in the Appendix.

nativity, Black women have the highest incidence of low birth weight of any racial/ethnic group. Infants born to Black immigrants have the highest predicted rate of low birth weight of all children of immigrants: 8.2 percent. Only US-born Blacks have a higher rate (10.2 percent). Children of Black immigrants are more likely to be low birth weight than children of non-Hispanic white immigrants (4.4 percent), Hispanic immigrants (5.2 percent), and Asian immigrants (6.8 percent). US-born Black mothers have higher rates of predicted low birth weight than all other groups of native-born non-Blacks.

3. Small for Gestational Age

Finally, birth-outcome patterns change somewhat when looking at rates of infants born small for their gestational age. Asian and Black babies, regardless of the mother's nativity, have relatively high rates of small-for-gestational age. Babies born to non-Hispanic Black immigrant women have a relatively high predicted small-for-gestational age rate of 13.6 percent; only children born to Asian immigrant mothers and Black US-born mothers have higher rates (16.0 percent and 14.9 percent, respectively). Children born to Latino and white mothers fare better on these measures than either Black or Asian children.

Table 2. Predicted Birth Outcomes by Race/Ethnicity and Nativity, 2000-03 (N=3,985,589)

	Preterm Birth (< 37 weeks)		Low Birth Weight (<2500 grams)		Small for Gestational Age (10th percentile)	
	Predicted Rate	Standard Error	Predicted Rate	Standard Error	Predicted Rate	Standard Error
White Native-Born, NH	0.069***	(0.000)	0.047***	(0.000)	0.080***	(0.000)
White Immigrant, NH	0.057***	(0.001)	0.046***	(0.001)	0.095***	(0.001)
Black Native-Born NH	0.115***	(0.000)	0.103***	(0.000)	0.149***	(0.001)
Black Immigrant, NH	0.092***	(0.001)	0.082***	(0.001)	0.137***	(0.001)
Latino, Native-Born	0.087***	(0.001)	0.066***	(0.001)	0.106***	(0.001)
Latino, Immigrant	0.067***	(0.000)	0.052***	(0.000)	0.103***	(0.001)
Asian Native-Born, NH	0.085***	(0.002)	0.073***	(0.002)	0.131***	(0.003)
Asian Immigrant, NH	0.068***	(0.001)	0.068***	(0.001)	0.160***	(0.001)

Notes: Notes: NH=Non-Hispanic.

*** indicates significance at the 1 percent level; ** at the 5 percent level, and * at the 10 percent level.

Source: Author's analysis of 2000-03 natality files, National Center for Health Statistics, "Vital Statistics Data Available Online."

IV. Conclusion and Discussion

The findings in this chapter imply that although Black immigrant mothers tend to have more favorable birth outcomes than their native-born Black counterparts, their birth outcomes are less favorable when compared with those of other racial/ethnic groups — both foreign- and native-born. While disparities in the incidence of preterm birth and low birth weight are largest between Black and white US-born mothers, the differences between Black and white immigrant mothers are nearly as large, particularly in the case of preterm births. These differences are non-trivial. Not only is low birth weight associated with adverse health and human development outcomes,[51] it is the leading correlate of infant mortality among non-Hispanic Black mothers.[52]

I find that the predicted rates of small for gestational age are lowest among the infants of native- and foreign-born non-Hispanic white mothers, followed by Latino mothers. The rates of small for gestational age are higher for Black and Asian immigrants. However, a Sweden-based study comparing the rates of small-for-gestational-age infants born to native-born Swedes with those born to immigrants finds that although African and Asian immigrants have higher rates of small-for-gestational-age babies, they do not consequently experience higher rates of mortality.[53] Similarly, a Canadian-based study finds that small-for-gestational-age standards may need to be modified for those of East Asian and Southeast Asian ancestry.[54] A US-based study of non-Hispanic whites and US- and foreign-born Blacks has a contrasting finding: that a single standard measure of small-for-gestational-age is more highly correlated with infant mortality than ethnic-specific measures.[55] Regardless, in the United States, the rates of infant mortality among Black immigrants are at least twice those of Asian immigrants.[56] Thus, an important next step is to extend this work to include both general and race- and ethnicity-specific measures of small for gestational age in models of infant mortality.

Prenatal smoking is also a potentially important reason for variation in birth outcomes between foreign- and native-born Blacks. I find that Black immigrant women often have substantially different pre-

---

51 Black, Devereau, and Salvanes, "From the Cradle to the Labor Market?"; Johnson and Schoeni, "The Influence of Early Life Events."
52 Matthews and MacDorman, *Infant Mortality Statistics from the 2004 Period.*
53 Finn Rasmussen, Claes Erik Oldenburg, Andres Ericson, and Jan Gunnarskog, "Preterm Birth and Low Birthweight among Children of Swedish and Immigrant Women between 1978 and 1990," *Paediatric and Perinatal Epidemiology* 9, No. 4 (1995): 441-54
54 Joel G. Ray, Depeng Jiang, Michael Sgro, Rajiv Shah, Gita Singh, and Muhammad M. Mamdani, "Thresholds for Small for Gestational Age among Newborns of East Asian and South Asian Ancestry," *Journal of Obstetrics and Gynaecology Canada* 31, No. 4 (2009): 322–30.
55 Michael S. Kramer, Cande V. Ananth, Robert W. Platt, and K. S. Joseph, "US Black Vs White Disparities in Foetal Growth: Physiological or Pathological?" *International Journal of Epidemiology* 35, No. 5 (2006): 1187–95.
56 Mathews and MacDorman, *Infant Mortality Statistics from the 2004 Period.*

natal-care-behavior patterns than both their US-born and non-Black foreign-born counterparts. Black immigrant women are much less likely to smoke than US-born Black women. Given the strong relationships between smoking and birth weight, this may explain, in part, why the rates of low birth weight (and to a lesser extent, very low birth weight and small for gestational age) are lower for non-Hispanic Black immigrant women. In contrast, Black women — particularly those who are foreign born — also tend to delay prenatal care, which may lead to more adverse pregnancy outcomes in comparison to non-Black mothers. However, while simulations predict that earlier prenatal-care initiation is associated with improved birth outcomes among all mothers,[57] these improvements are very small.

In any case, neither smoking nor prenatal-care initiation fully explains the greater rates of adverse birth outcomes among Black mothers, regardless of nativity. Many researchers have hypothesized that the Black-white infant health gap may be related to stressors that disproportionately affect Black women. For example, the weathering hypothesis[58] suggests that stressors related to poverty and discrimination may result in health deterioration and adverse birth outcomes among Black women, compared to white women. In addition, racial disparities in infant health widen with increasing maternal age. However, there is still a need for biological evidence in support of the weathering hypothesis as an explanation for poor Black-infant-health outcomes,[59] and its salience for Black immigrants remains an open question.

It is important to note that public vital statistics data do not include mother's origin countries except Mexico and Canada. Lack of origin-country identifiers represents a weakness in the federal vital statistics data as there are important differences across origin countries with regard to parental health and educational attainment, characteristics that may also influence birth outcomes.[60] Also, while vital statistics data are useful for examining broad trends across groups, they contain limited information on prenatal behaviors, stressors, or other environmental factors that may affect pregnancy outcomes. Finally, the included measures of prenatal behavior (smoking and prenatal-care utilization) are often strongly correlated with maternal characteristics that also influence pregnancy outcomes — making any discussion of these behaviors descriptive, rather than causal. However, the main

---

57 Results from smoking and prenatal-care simulations available upon request.

58 Arline T. Geronimus, "The Weathering Hypothesis and the Health of African-American Women and Infants: Evidence and Speculations," *Ethnicity and Disease* 2, No. 3 (2011): 207–21.

59 Tiffany Green, "Weathering," in *Encyclopedia of Race and Racism,* 2nd edition (Chicago, IL: American Library Association, forthcoming 2012).

60 Tod Hamilton and Robert Hummer, "Immigration and the Health of U.S. Black Adults: Does Country of Origin Matter?" *Social Science and Medicine* 73, No. 10 (2011): 1551-60.

findings of this chapter remain unchanged when measures of smoking and prenatal-care initiation are excluded from infant-health models.[61]

The results of this study provide important evidence that the Black immigrant birth advantage generally occurs only in comparison with Black natives. Meanwhile, second-generation Black immigrant infants are at a health disadvantage compared to non-Black immigrant and non-Black US-born infants. What is particularly telling is that the Black-white infant-health gap observed among US-born Black and non-Hispanic white mothers is also apparent between non-Hispanic Black and white immigrants. Thus, the health and well-being of the children born to Black immigrant mothers has implications for the US Black population. Understanding the socioeconomic mechanisms behind these infant-health disparities remains a topic for further research. ⤴

---

61 Results from models that exclude smoking and prenatal-care measures available upon request.

Appendices

Table A-1. Birth Outcomes, Prenatal Behaviors, and Maternal Characteristics of Native-Born Women, 2000-03 (N=2,882,426)

	White, NH (n=2,097,612)	Black, NH (n=566,157)	Latino (n=199,552)	Asian, NH (n=19,105)	All
Birth Outcomes					
Preterm Birth (<37 weeks)	0.07	0.12	0.09	0.08	0.09
Low Birth Weight (<2500 grams)	0.05	0.11	0.07	0.07	0.08
Small for Gestational Age (<10th percentile)	0.08	0.16	0.11	0.12	0.12
Child Male	0.51	0.51	0.51	0.51	0.52
Prenatal Behaviors					
First-Trimester Prenatal-Care Initiation	0.90	0.74	0.80	0.87	0.83
Mother Smoked	0.13	0.10	0.08	0.05	0.09
Maternal Characteristics					
First Birth	0.43	0.40	0.45	0.55	0.46
Mother's Age	29.21	25.27	25.33	28.80	27.15
Non-Hispanic White	---	---	---	---	0.73
Non-Hispanic Black	---	---	---	---	0.19
Latino	---	---	---	---	0.07
Non-Hispanic Asian	---	---	---	---	0.01
Married	0.78	0.28	0.45	0.80	0.58
Schooling					
0 to 8 years	0.01	0.02	0.03	0.01	0.02
9 to 11 years	0.08	0.22	0.25	0.07	0.15
12 years	0.28	0.40	0.31	0.15	0.29
13 to 15 years	0.23	0.23	0.24	0.18	0.22
16+ years	0.39	0.13	0.15	0.58	0.31
Education Missing	0.01	0.01	0.01	0.01	0.01
Year of Birth					
2000	0.26	0.25	0.23	0.23	0.24
2001	0.26	0.25	0.25	0.24	0.25
2002	0.26	0.25	0.25	0.26	0.26
2003	0.22	0.24	0.26	0.26	0.25

Notes: NH=Non-Hispanic. All variables expressed as means.

Source: Author's analysis of 2000-03 natality files, National Center for Health Statistics, "Vital Statistics Data Available Online."

Table A-2. Birth Outcomes, Prenatal Behaviors, and Maternal Characteristics of Foreign-Born Women, 2000-03 (N=1,103,161)

	White, NH (n=207,146)	Black, NH (n=188,671)	Latino (n=485,700)	Asian, NH (n=221,644)	All
Birth Outcomes					
Preterm Birth (<37 weeks)	0.05	0.10	0.07	0.06	0.07
Low Birth Weight (<2500 grams)	0.04	0.08	0.05	0.06	0.06
Small for Gestational Age (<10th percentile)	0.09	0.13	0.10	0.14	0.12
Child Male	0.51	0.51	0.51	0.51	0.51
Prenatal Behaviors					
First-Trimester Prenatal-Care Initiation	0.85	0.75	0.81	0.82	0.81
Mother Smoked	0.04	0.01	0.02	0.01	0.02
Maternal Characteristics					
First Birth	0.45	0.39	0.40	0.49	0.43
Mother's Age	30.24	29.54	27.27	30.10	29.29
Non-Hispanic White	---	---	---	---	0.19
Non-Hispanic Black	---	---	---	---	0.17
Latino	---	---	---	---	0.45
Non-Hispanic Asian	---	---	---	---	0.19
Married	0.88	0.55	0.51	0.89	0.71
Schooling					
0 to 8 years	0.03	0.05	0.22	0.05	0.09
9 to 11 years	0.05	0.11	0.19	0.07	0.11
12 years	0.27	0.37	0.32	0.22	0.30
13 to 15 years	0.21	0.24	0.15	0.17	0.19
16+ years	0.43	0.22	0.13	0.47	0.31
Education Missing	0.01	0.02	0.02	0.01	0.02
Year of Birth					
2000	0.24	0.24	0.23	0.24	0.24
2001	0.25	0.25	0.25	0.24	0.25
2002	0.26	0.25	0.26	0.26	0.26
2003	0.25	0.26	0.26	0.26	0.26

Notes: NH=Non-Hispanic, All variables expressed in means.

Source: Author's analysis of 2000-03 natality files, National Center for Health Statistics, "Vital Statistics Data Available Online."

Table A-3. Marginal Effects of Nativity and Race/Ethnicity on Smoking and First-Trimester Prenatal-Care Initiation, 2000-03 (N=3,985,589)

	Smoked		First-Trimester Prenatal-Care Initiation	
	Marginal Effect	Standard Error	Marginal Effect	Standard Error
Maternal Characteristics				
First Birth	-0.028***	(0.000)	0.050***	(0.000)
Mother's Age	0.002***	(0.000)	0.006***	(0.000)
Mother Black, NH	-0.094***	(0.000)	-0.059***	(0.001)
Mother Latino	-0.100***	(0.000)	-0.014***	(0.001)
Mother Asian, NH	-0.073***	(0.002)	-0.050***	(0.002)
Mother Immigrant	-0.070***	(0.000)	-0.066***	(0.001)
Mother Married	-0.087***	(0.000)	0.068***	(0.000)
Schooling				
9-11 years schooling	0.034***	(0.001)	0.042***	(0.001)
12 years schooling	-0.021***	(0.001)	0.079***	(0.001)
13-15 years schooling	-0.063***	(0.001)	0.113***	(0.001)
16 years+ schooling	-0.171***	(0.001)	0.157***	(0.001)
Education Missing	-0.012***	(0.002)	0.030***	(0.002)
Year of Birth				
2000	0.010***	(0.000)	-0.016***	(0.001)
2001	0.009***	(0.000)	-0.018***	(0.001)
2002	0.004***	(0.000)	-0.013***	(0.001)

Notes: NH=Non-Hispanic.

*** indicates significance at the 1 percent level; ** at the 5 percent level, and * at the 10 percent level.

Source: Author's analysis of 2000-03 natality files, National Center for Health Statistics, "Vital Statistics Data Available Online."

Table A-4. Marginal Effects of Nativity and Race/Ethnicity on Birth Outcomes, 2000-03 Natality Files, (N=3,985,589)

	Preterm Birth (<37 weeks)		Low Birth Weight (<2500 grams)		Small for Gestational Age (<10th percentile)	
	Marginal Effect	Standard Error	Marginal Effect	Standard Error	Marginal Effect	Standard Error
Child Male	0.007***	(0.000)	-0.009***	(0.000)	0.003***	(0.000)
Prenatal Behaviors						
First-Trimester Prenatal-Care Initiation	-0.005***	(0.000)	-0.003***	(0.000)	-0.008***	(0.000)
Mother Smoked	0.024***	(0.001)	0.047***	(0.001)	0.084***	(0.001)
Maternal Characteristics						
First Birth	0.017***	(0.000)	0.025***	(0.000)	0.045***	(0.000)
Mother's age	0.002***	(0.000)	0.001***	(0.000)	0.000***	(0.000)
Black, NH	0.043***	(0.000)	0.051***	(0.000)	0.063***	(0.001)
Latino	0.016***	(0.001)	0.016***	(0.001)	0.022***	(0.001)
Asian, NH	0.015***	(0.002)	0.025***	(0.002)	0.055***	(0.002)
Immigrant	-0.016***	(0.000)	-0.008***	(0.000)	0.007***	(0.001)
Married	-0.012***	(0.000)	-0.013***	(0.000)	-0.013***	(0.000)
Schooling						
9 to 11 years	0.007***	(0.001)	0.005***	(0.001)	0.000	(0.001)
12 years	0.000	(0.001)	-0.002**	(0.001)	-0.008***	(0.001)
13 to 15 years	-0.005***	(0.001)	-0.009***	(0.001)	-0.02***	(0.001)
16+ years	-0.018***	(0.001)	-0.02***	(0.001)	-0.029***	(0.001)
Education Missing	0.009***	(0.001)	0.005***	(0.001)	-0.008***	(0.002)
Year/Season of Birth						
Spring	-0.003***	(0.001)	-0.002***	(0.001)	-0.001	(0.001)
Summer	-0.001	(0.001)	0.000	(0.001)	-0.002*	(0.001)
Fall	-0.004***	(0.001)	-0.002***	(0.001)	-0.001	(0.001)
2000	-0.005***	(0.001)	-0.004***	(0.001)	-0.005***	(0.001)
2001	-0.005***	(0.001)	-0.004***	(0.001)	-0.001	(0.001)
2002	-0.004***	(0.001)	-0.002***	(0.001)	-0.001	(0.001)

Notes: NH=Non-Hispanic.

*** indicates significance at the 1 percent level; ** at the 5 percent level, and * at the 10 percent level.

Source: Author's analysis of 2000-03 natality files, National Center for Health Statistics, "Vital Statistics Data Available Online."

Works Cited

Acevedo-Garcia, Dolores, Mah-J. Soobader, and Lisa F. Berkman. 2005. The Differential Effect of Foreign-born Status on Low Birth Weight by Race/Ethnicity and Education. *Pediatrics* 115(1): e20-e30.

Alexander, Greg R. and Milton Kotelchuck. 2001. Assessing the Role and Effectiveness of Prenatal Care: History, Challenges, and Directions for Future Research. *Public Health Rep* 116 (44): 306–16.

Bender, D. E. and D. Castro. 2000. Explaining the Birth Weight Paradox: Latina Immigrants' Perceptions of Resilience and Risk. *Journal of Immigrant Health* 2 (3): 155–73.

Black, Sandra E., Paul J. Devereau, and Kjell G. Salvanes. 2007. From the Cradle to the Labor Market? The Effect of Birth Weight on Adult Outcomes. *Quarterly Journal of Economics* 122 (1): 409–39.

Brosco, Jeffrey P. 1999. The Early History of the Infant Mortality Rate in America: A Reflection upon the Past and a Prophecy of the Future. *Pediatrics* 103 (2): 478–85.

Cabral, Howard, Laurence E. Fried, Suzette Levenson, Hortensia Amaro, and Barry Zuckerman. 1990. Foreign-born and US-born Black Women: Differences in Health Behaviors and Birth Outcomes. *American Journal of Public Health* 80: 70–2.

Center for Disease Control and Prevention, National Center for Health Statistics (NCHS). Undated. Vital Statistics Data Available Online. www.cdc.gov/nchs/data_access/Vitalstatsonline.htm.

Cervantes, Arturo, Louis Keith, and Grace Wyshak. 1999. Adverse Birth Outcomes among Native-born and Immigrant Women: Replicating National Evidence regarding Mexicans at the Local Level. *Maternal and Child Health Journal* 3 (2): 99–109.

Clayton, P., S. Cianfarani, P. Czernichow, G. Johannsson, R. Rapaport, and A. Rogol. 2007. Management of the Child Born Small for Gestational Age through to Adulthood: A Consensus Statement of the International Societies of Pediatric Endocrinology and the Growth Hormone Research Society. *J Clin Endocrinol Metab* 92 (3): 804–10.

Cokkinides V. 2001. Health Insurance Coverage-Enrollment and Adequacy of Prenatal Care Utilization. *J Health Care Poor Underserved* 12 (4): 461-73.

Conway, K. S. and P. Deb. 2005. Is Prenatal Care Really Ineffective? Or, is the "Devil" in the Distribution? *Health Economics* 24: 489–513.

David, Richard J. and James W. Collins. 1997. Differing Birth Weight among Infants of U.S.-born Blacks, African-born Blacks, and U.S.-born Whites. *New England Journal of Medicine* 337(17): 1209–14.

Derose, Kathryn Pitkin, Jose J. Escarce, and Nicole Lurie. 2007. Immigrants and Health Care: Sources of Vulnerability. *Health Affairs* 26 (5):1258-68.

Elo, Irma T. and Jennifer Culhane. 2010. Variations in Health and Health Behaviors by Nativity among Pregnant Black Women in Philadelphia. *American Journal of Public Health* 100 (11): 2185-92.

Geronimus, Arline T. 2011. The Weathering Hypothesis and the Health of African-American Women and Infants: Evidence and Speculations. *Ethnicity and Disease* 2 (3): 207–21.

Grady, Sue C. and Sara McLafferty. 2007. Segregation, Nativity, and Health: Reproductive Health Inequalities for Immigrant and Native-born Black Women in New York City. *Urban Geography* 28 (4): 377-97.

Green, Tiffany L. 2011. Infant Feeding and Asthma: Is Breast Milk Best? *Review of Economics of Household*, 9(4): 487-504.

_____. 2012 forthcoming. Weathering. In *Encyclopedia of Race and Racism*, 2nd edition. Chicago, IL: American Library Association.

Hamilton, Tod and Robert Hummer. 2011. Immigration and the health of U.S. black adults: Does country of origin matter? *Social Science and Medicine* 73(10): 1551-60.

Howard, David L., Susan S. Marshall, S. Jay, P. Kaufman, and David A. Savitz. 2006. Variations in Low Birth Weight and Preterm Delivery among Blacks in Relation to Ancestry and Nativity: New York City, 1998-2002. *Pediatrics* 118: e1399–e1405.

Hummer, Robert, Daniel Powers, Starling Pullum, G. Gossman, and W. Frisbie. 2007. Paradox Found (Again): Infant Mortality among the Mexican-origin Population in the United States. *Demography* 44: 441–57.

Jaddoe, Vincent W., E.-J. W. Troe, Albert Hofman, Johan Mackenbach, Henriëtte A. Moll, E. A. Steegers, and J. C. Witteman. 2008. Active and Passive Maternal Smoking during Pregnancy and the Risks of Low Birth Weight and Preterm Birth: The Generation R Study. *Pediatric and Perinatal Epidemiology* 22: 162–71.

Johnson, Rucker C. and Robert Schoeni. 2011. The Influence of Early Life Events on Human Capital, Health Status, and Labor Market Outcomes over the Life Course. *B.E. Journal of Economic Analysis and Policy: Advances* 11 (3): 1-55.

Joyce, Theodore. 1994. Self-Selection, Prenatal-Care, and Birth-Weight among Blacks, Whites, and Hispanics in New-York-City. *Journal of Human Resources* 29 (3): 762–94.

Kent, Mary Mederios. 2007. Immigration and America's Black Population. *Population Bulletin* 62 (4): 3-15. www.prb.org/pdf07/62.4immigration.pdf.

Kramer, Michael S., Cande V. Ananth, Robert W. Platt, and K. S. Joseph. 2006. US Black vs White Disparities in Foetal Growth: Physiological or Pathological? *Int. J. Epidemiol* 35 (5):1187–95.

Landale, Nancy S., Salvador R. Oropesa, and Brenda K. Gorman. 1999. *Immigration and Infant Health: Birth Outcomes of Immigrant and Native-Born Women*. National Academies Press. Washington, DC.

Mathews, T. J. and Marian F. MacDorman. 2007. Infant Mortality Statistics from the 2004 Period Linked Birth/Infant Death Data Set. *National Vital Statistics Report* 55(14): 1-32. www.cdc.gov/nchs/data/nvsr/nvsr55/nvsr55_14.pdf.

Pallotto, Eugenia K., James W. Collins Jr., and Richard J. David. 2000. Enigma of Maternal Race and Infant Birth Weight: A Population-based Study of US-born and Caribbean-born Black Women. *American Journal of Epidemiology* 151: 1080–85.

Rasmussen, Finn, Claes Erik Oldenburg, Andres Ericson, and Jan Gunnarskog. 1995. Preterm Birth and Low Birthweight among Children of Swedish and Immigrant Women between 1978 and 1990. *Paediatric and Perinatal Epidemiology* 9(4): 441-54.

Ray, Joel G., Depeng Jiang, Michael Sgro, Rajiv Shah, Gita Singh, and Muhammad M. Mamdani. 2009. Thresholds for Small for Gestational Age among Newborns of East Asian and South Asian Ancestry. *Journal of Obstetrics and Gynaecology Canada* 31 (4): 322–30.

Rosenzweig, Mark R. and Schultz, T. Paul. 1983. Estimating a Household Production Function: Heterogeneity, the Demand for Health Inputs, and their Effects on Birth Weight. *The Journal of Political Economy* 91 (5): 723–46.

Russell, Rebecca B., Nancy S. Green, Claudia A. Steiner, Susan Meikle, Jennifer L. Howse, Karalee Poschman, Todd Dias, Lisa Potetz, Michael J. Davidoff, Karla Damus, and Joann R. Petrini. 2007. Cost of Hospitalization for Preterm and Low Birth Weight Infants in the United States. *Pediatrics* 120 (1): e1–e9.

Salihu, Hamisu M., W. S. Mardenbrough-Gumbs, Muktar H. Aliyu, J. E. Sedjro, B. J. Pierre-Louis, R. S. Kirby, and G. R. Alexander. 2005. The Influence of Nativity on Neonatal Survival of Black Twins in the United States. *Ethnicity and Disease* 15 (2): 276–82.

Singh, Gopal K. and Stella M. Yu. 1996. Adverse Pregnancy Outcomes: Differences between US- and Foreign-born Women in Major US Racial and Ethnic Groups. *American Journal of Public Health* 86(6): 837-43.

Singh, Gopal K. and Mohammad Siahpush. 2001. All-cause and Cause-specific Mortality of Immigrants and Native Born in the United States. *American Journal of Public Health* 91 (3): 392–99.

Singh, Gopal K. and Michael D. Kogan. 2005. Persistent Socioeconomic Disparities in Infant, Neonatal, and Postneonatal Mortality Rates in the United States, 1969-2001. *Pediatrics* 119 (4): e928-e939.

Wasse, H., V. L. Holt, and J. R. Daling. 1994. Pregnancy Risk Factors and Birth Outcomes in Washington State: A Comparison of Ethiopian-born and US-born Women. *American Journal of Public Health* 84 (9): 1505-07.

Wehby, George L., Jeffrey C. Murray, Eduardo E. Castilla, Jorge S. Lopez-Camelo, and Robert L. Ohsfeldt. 2009. Quantile Effects of Prenatal Care Utilization on Birth Weight in Argentina. *Health Economics* 18 (11): 1307-21.

Wolf, Jacqueline H. 2003. Low Breastfeeding Rates and Public Health in the United States. *American Journal of Public Health* 93 (12): 2000–10.

CHAPTER 5

PARENTING BEHAVIOR, HEALTH, AND COGNITIVE DEVELOPMENT AMONG CHILDREN IN BLACK IMMIGRANT FAMILIES: COMPARING THE UNITED STATES AND UNITED KINGDOM

Margot Jackson

Brown University

Introduction

In the United States, racial disparities in child development are striking, with a particularly pronounced disadvantage among Black children. They are more likely than both their white and nonwhite peers to be born with a low birth weight, to have asthma and other chronic physical health conditions, to demonstrate symptoms of certain behavioral disorders such as attention deficit hyperactivity disorder (ADHD), and to be overweight or obese.[1] There are also strong racial disparities in school readiness and academic achievement, with Black children demonstrating weaker cognitive development and academic

---

1   Janet Currie, "Health Disparities and Gaps in School Readiness," *Future of Children* 15 (2005): 117–38; Michael C. Lu and Neil Halfon, "Racial and Ethnic Disparities in Birth Outcomes: A Life-Course Perspective," *Maternal and Child Health Journal* 7 (2003): 13–30; Marla McDaniel, Christina Paxson, and Jane Waldfogel, "Racial Disparities in Childhood Asthma in the United States: Evidence from the National Health Interview Survey, 1997 to 2003," *Pediatrics* 117 (May 2006): e868–77.

achievement in early childhood and during the school years.[2] In fact, some research suggests that part of the racial disparity in academic performance may be driven by disparities in health.[3]

Racial inequalities in health and cognitive development are more ambiguous among children in immigrant families, who often experience more favorable developmental outcomes than would be expected on the basis of their families' socioeconomic resources.[4] Most research on the development of children in immigrant families has focused on Latin American and Asian populations, who comprise the majority of US immigrants. Yet a sharp increase in the number of Black immigrant families in the United States in recent decades — 11 percent of Black children in the United States are the children of immigrants — makes it important to measure race in a more complex way that accounts for many families' recent immigration histories.

A primary goal of this chapter is to compare children in the United States to those in the United Kingdom, where there is a large Black immigrant population (about 22 percent of foreign-born adults and 12 percent of children in immigrant families) but a notably different context with respect to immigration policy, health care, and social welfare provision. Existing research using UK data has established racial disparities in children's health and academic achievement, with Black children experiencing poorer health and academic achievement than their peers in other racial and ethnic groups.[5] Research examining children with immigrant parents, however — especially children in Black immigrant families — has been largely limited until recently because of a lack of survey data allowing for the identification of these children.

Using data from national samples in the United States and the United Kingdom that include Black African and Caribbean mothers, this chapter examines parental behaviors that might affect children's early health and cognitive development (from birth to age 5), as well

---

2   Charles T. Clotfelter, Helen F. Ladd, and Jacob L. Vigdor, "The Academic Achievement Gap in Grades 3 to 8," *Review of Economics and Statistics* 91 (2009): 398–419; Christopher Jencks and Meredith P. Phillips, eds., *The Black-White Test Score Gap* (Washington, DC: Brookings Institution, 1998).

3   Currie, "Health Disparities and Gaps in School Readiness."

4   Ana Abraido-Lanza, Maria T. Chao, and Karen R. Florez, "Do Healthy Behaviors Decline with Greater Acculturation? Implications for the Latino Mortality Paradox," *Social Science and Medicine* 61(6) (2006): 1243-255.

5   Lorraine Dearden and Luke Sibieta, "Ethnic Inequalities in Child Outcomes," in *Children of the 21st Century (Volume 2): The First Five Years,* eds., Kirstine Hansen, Heather Joshi, and Shirley Dex (Bristol, UK: Policy Press, 2010), 169–85; Yvonne Kelly, Amanda Sacker, Ron Gray, John Kelly, Dieter Wolke, and Maria A. Quigley, "Light Drinking in Pregnancy, a Risk for Behavioural Problems and Cognitive Deficits at 3 Years of Age?" *International Journal of Epidemiology* 38(1) (2009): 129-40; Julien O. Teitler, Nancy E. Reichman, Lenna Nepomnyaschy, and Melissa Martinson, "A Cross-National Comparison of Racial and Ethnic Disparities in Low Birth Weight in the United States and England," *Pediatrics* 120 (November 2007): e1182.

as later health and cognitive outcomes. Concern for the welfare of young children in immigrant families is motivated by several factors, including recent evidence of the enduring impact of early environments on children's brain development[6] and well-being into adulthood.[7] An important part of this investigation is its cross-national focus, which offers insight into Black immigrant families' integration in both the United States and the United Kingdom, where varying policy structures may create differences in the context of reception.

I. Background

A. *Racial Differences in Children's Health and Cognitive Development*

There is a strong correlation between socioeconomic status and health in many industrialized nations: the higher the education and income, the better the health.[8] While much of the work on this connection has centered on adults, a growing body of research suggests that it also exists among children.[9] The lower socioeconomic status of many racial and ethnic minorities, on average, is an important reason why Black children are more likely to be in poorer health than their non-Black peers. However, abundant evidence documents poorer health among Black children, even after accounting for differences in socioeconomic resources. At all age groups and socioeconomic levels, for example, Black children are more likely to be obese or overweight than non-Latino whites.[10] Life expectancy at birth is generally about six years lower

6   Eric I. Knudsen, "Sensitive Periods in the Development of the Brain and Behavior," *Journal of Cognitive Neuroscience* 16 (2004): 1412–25.

7   Margot I. Jackson, "A Life Course Perspective on Child Health, Cognition and Occupational Skill Qualifications in Adulthood: Evidence from a British Cohort," *Social Forces* 89 (2010): 89–116; Ingrid Schoon, John Bynner, Heather Joshi, Samantha Parsons, Richard D. Wiggins, and Amanda Sacker, "The Influence of Context, Timing, and Duration of Risk Experiences for the Passage from Childhood to Mid-adulthood," *Child Development* 73 (2002): 1486–504.

8   Michael G. Marmot, G. Davey Smith, S. Stansfeld, C. Patel, F. North, J. Head, I. White, Eric J. Brunner, and A. Feeney, "Health Inequalities among British Civil Servants: The Whitehall II Study," *Lancet* 337 (1991): 1387–93; Scott M. Lynch, "Cohort and Life-Course Patterns in the Relationship between Education and Health: A Hierarchical Approach," *Demography* 40 (2003): 309-31; James P. Smith, "The Impact of Socioeconomic Status on Health over the Life-Course," *Journal of Human Resources* XLII (2007): 739–64.

9   Anne Case, Darren Lubotsky, and Christina Paxson, "Economic Status and Health in Childhood: The Origins of the Gradient," *American Economic Review* 92 (2002): 1308–34; Brian K. Finch, "Early Origins of the Gradient: The Relationship between Socioeconomic Status and Infant Mortality in the United States," *Demography* 40 (2003): 675–99.

10 National Center for Health Statistics, *Health, United States, 2004, with Chartbook on Trends in the Health of Americans* (Hyattsville, MD: National Center for Health Statistics, 2004), 241–45.

for Blacks than for whites, at 72 years versus 78 years, respectively.[11] Black children are also more likely than whites to have low birth weight and to struggle with asthma, ADHD, nutrient deficiencies, impaired glucose tolerance predictive of diabetes, and even elevated blood pressure and higher total cholesterol.[12] Thus, on several key health indicators, Black children fare worse than white children in the United States.

Disparities in cognitive development between Blacks and their non-Black peers are equally pronounced. Black children do not perform as well as their non-Black peers on assessments of cognitive development and academic achievement in early childhood and during the school years.[13] Some, but not all, of the disparity between Black children and their peers is explained by differences in parents' socioeconomic resources.[14] There is also evidence that the Black achievement disadvantage is particularly persistent as children age, compared to other groups.

Charles Clotfelter, Helen Ladd, and Jacob Vigdor[15] find consistently lower performance among Black students between grades three to eight, compared to declining achievement gaps between Latinos and Asians as compared to non-Latino whites. Though the bodies of research on racial disparities in child health and academic achievement rarely overlap, there is some speculation that racial inequalities in children's health may explain part of the strong racial disparity in academic performance.[16]

B.   The Complicating Role of Immigration

Relative disadvantage in child health and academic achievement is much less pronounced among Latinos and Asians, the other two large ethnic and racial minority groups in the United States. In fact, despite their greater likelihood of social and economic disadvantage, Latinos exhibit the "Latino paradox"— that is, they experience lower rates of many diseases than non-Latino whites, lower rates of infant mortality,

---

11   Ibid., 143.
12   Currie, "Health Disparities and Gaps in School Readiness;" Lu and Halfon, "Racial and Ethnic Disparities in Birth Outcomes;" McDaniel, Paxson, and Waldfogel, "Racial Disparities in Childhood Asthma in the United States;" National Center for Health Statistics, *Health, United States, 2004, with Chartbook on Trends in the Health of Americans.*
13   Jencks and Phillips, *The Black-White Test Score Gap.*
14   Roland G. Fryer and Steven D. Levitt, "The Black-White Test Score Gap through Third Grade," *American Law and Economics Review* 8 (2006): 249–81; Richard J. Murnane, John B. Willett, Kristen L. Bub, Kathleen McCartney, Eric Hanushek, and Rebecca Maynard, "Understanding Trends in the Black-White Achievement Gaps during the First Years of School [with Comments]," *Brookings-Wharton Papers on Urban Affairs* (2006): 97–135.
15   Clotfelter, Ladd, and Vigdor, "The Academic Achievement Gap in Grades 3 to 8."
16   Currie, "Health Disparities and Gaps in School Readiness."

and higher life expectancy.[17] In trying to understand this pattern, it is important to consider the role of immigration. A large body of research, carried out mostly in the United States, documents an immigrant advantage in mothers' health behaviors and in children's birth outcomes. This research shows that foreign-born mothers are more likely than native-born mothers to fully immunize and breastfeed their children,[18] less likely to smoke and drink during pregnancy,[19] and less likely to have babies with a low birth weight.[20]

Evidence of academic achievement is more mixed, with both relative advantage and disadvantage in cognitive development documented among children with foreign-born parents, depending on the population and age group examined. While some research exposes an immigrant advantage in parenting behaviors related to analytic and verbal development among Filipino, Chinese, Mexican, and Central and South American youth in immigrant families,[21] other studies find a disadvantage in the cognitive development of children in some of the same ethnic groups. In addition, some immigrant parents may be less likely to practice parenting behaviors rewarded by host-country educational norms, such as reading to children and participating in school activities.[22]

---

17 Ana F. Abraido-Lanza, Bruce P. Dohrenwend, Daisy S. Ng-Mak, and J. Blake Turner, "The Latino Mortality Paradox: A Test of the Salmon Bias and Healthy Migrant Hypotheses," *American Journal of Public Health* 89 (1999): 1543–48, www.ncbi.nlm.nih.gov/pmc/articles/PMC1508801/4pdf; Nancy S. Landale, R. S. Oropesa, and Bridget K. Gorman, "Migration and Infant Death: Assimilation or Selective Migration among Puerto Ricans?" *American Sociological Review* 65 (2000): 888–909.

18 Laurie M. Anderson, D. L. Wood, and Cathy D. Sherbourne, "Maternal Acculturation and Childhood Immunization Levels among Children in Latino Families in Los Angeles," *American Journal of Public Health* 87 (1997): 2018–21; Rachel T. Kimbro, Scott M. Lynch, and Sara McLanahan, "The Influence of Acculturation on Breastfeeding Initiation and Duration for Mexican-Americans," *Population Research and Policy Review* 27 (2008): 183.

19 Kim Harley and Brenda Eskenazi, "Time in the United States, Social Support and Health Behaviors during Pregnancy among Women of Mexican Descent," *Social Science and Medicine* 62 (2006): 3048–61; Landale, Oropesa, and Gorman, "Migration and Infant Death."

20 Robert A. Hummer, Monique Biegler, Peter B. D. Turk, Douglas Forbes, W. P. Frisbie, Ying Hong, and Starling G. Pullum, "Race/Ethnicity, Nativity, and Infant Mortality in the United States," *Social Forces* 77 (1999): 1083–117; Martha S. Wingate and Greg R. Alexander, "The Healthy Migrant Theory: Variations in Pregnancy Outcomes among US-Born Migrants," *Social Science and Medicine* 62 (2006): 491–98.

21 Andrew J. Fuligni, "The Academic Achievement of Adolescents from Immigrant Families: The Roles of Family Background, Attitudes, and Behavior," *Child Development* 68 (1997): 351–63; Andrew J. Fuligni, Vivian Tseng, and May Lam, "Attitudes toward Family Obligations among American Adolescents with Asian, Latin American, and European Backgrounds," *Child Development* 70 (1999): 1030–44; Tama Leventhal, Yange Xue, and Jeanne Brooks-Gunn, "Immigrant Differences in School-Age Children's Verbal Trajectories: A Look at Four Racial/Ethnic Groups," *Child Development* 77 (2006): 1359–74.

22 Robert Crosnoe, *Mexican Roots, American Schools: Helping Mexican Immigrant Children Succeed* (Stanford: Stanford University Press, 2006); Jennifer E. Glick, Littisha Bates, and Scott T. Yabiku, "Mother's Age at Arrival in the United States and Early Cognitive Development," *Early Childhood Research Quarterly* 24 (2009): 367–80.

C. Where Do Children in Black Immigrant Families Fit In?

As children with immigrant parents make up an increasingly significant share of Black children, it is useful to consider race alongside
factors — such as parental nativity — that may strongly influence a
child's development. In recent decades, the number of Black immigrant
families in the United States has increased dramatically. While about
25 percent of US children have at least one foreign-born parent, 8
percent (about 1.3 million) of these children are Black, with the majority of parents born in African or Caribbean nations.[23] Between 2000 and
2008 alone, there was a 63 percent increase in the US African immigrant population.

Yet the majority of research on the development of children in immigrant families has focused on children with parents from Latin America
and Asia, the two sending regions that account for the majority of US
immigrants. As a result, it is difficult to know whether the development
of Black children in immigrant families more closely resembles that
of their Black peers with native-born parents, or whether they share
the immigrant advantage observed among their peers in some other
racial and ethnic groups. The small number of studies examining
children in Black immigrant families has shown that these children
are less likely to have a low birth weight[24] and asthma[25] than their
peers in Black native families, but that they also perform more poorly
than their white, Asian, and sometimes Latino peers on assessments
of school readiness and academic performance in early childhood.[26] A
slightly larger body of research on older youth and adults from Black
immigrant families suggests that, despite any earlier performance disadvantage, they are ultimately more likely than their Black peers with
native-born parents to attain finish high school and attend two- and
four-year colleges.[27] These findings suggest that educational progress
may occur with age.

---

23 Karina Fortuny and Ajay Chaudry, "Children of Immigrants: Immigration Trends" (Urban
    Institute Fact Sheet No. 1, Urban Institute, Washington, DC, October 2009): 1–5, www.
    urban.org/publications/901292.html.

24 James W. Collins, Shou-Yien Wu, and Richard J. David, "Differing Intergenerational Birth
    Weights among the Descendants of US-Born and Foreign-Born Whites and African Ameri-
    cans in Illinois," *American Journal of Epidemiology* 155 (2002): 210–16.

25 Doug Brugge, Mark Woodin, T. J. Schuch, Fatima L. Salas, Acheson Bennett, and Neal-Dra
    Osgood, "Community-Level Data Suggest that Asthma Prevalence Varies between U.S. and
    Foreign-Born Black Subpopulations," *Journal of Asthma* 45 (2008): 785–9.

26 Jessica J. De Feyter and Adam Winsler, "The Early Developmental Competencies and School
    Readiness of Low-Income, Immigrant Children: Influences of Generation, Race/Ethnicity,
    and National Origins," *Early Childhood Research Quarterly* 24 (2009): 411–31.

27 Philip Kasinitz, John Mollenkopf, Mary Waters, and Jennifer Holdaway, *Inheriting the City:
    The Children of Immigrants Come of Age* (New York: Russell Sage Foundation, 2008); Xue L.
    Rong and Frank Brown, "The Effects of Immigrant Generation and Ethnicity on Education-
    al Attainment among Young African and Caribbean Blacks in the United States," *Harvard
    Educational Review* 71 (2001): 536–66; Kevin J. A. Thomas, "Parental Characteristics and
    the Schooling Progress of the Children of Immigrant and U.S.-Born Blacks," *Demography* 46
    (2009): 513–34.

Straight-line models of immigrant families' assimilation would predict a gradual decline in the health of immigrant families with increasing time in the host country, as they change their behaviors, language and cultural practices, social networks, and residential context.[28] In this framework of unhealthy acculturation, healthier outcomes among Black immigrant families would fade as immigrants increasingly resemble their native-born peers with comparable residential and socioeconomic conditions. Consistent with this hypothesis, most empirical evidence shows that health advantages are more pronounced among recent immigrants.[29] Studies that examine immigrant-native differences using longitudinal data, however, have not found evidence for convergence between immigrant and native-born youth as they age,[30] suggesting that the children of immigrants may retain some degree of health advantage over time.

Critics of straight-line depictions of assimilation argue that the integration of immigrant families may not be uniform, but may instead follow a degree of segmentation that varies according to parents' levels of education, the quality of children's schooling, the reasons for migration, and phenotype, among other factors.[31] This is particularly relevant for the Black immigrant population, which — regardless of country of origin — experiences a strong degree of residential segregation and racialization. Residential segregation between Blacks and other racial and ethnic groups remains high despite declines in recent decades.[32] Accompanying residential segregation is more restricted access to the

---

28   E. Arcia, M. Skinner, D. Bailey, and Vivian Correa, "Models of Acculturation and Health Behaviors among Latino Immigrants to the US," *Social Science and Medicine* 53 (2001): 41–53; Milton M. Gordon, *Assimilation in American Life: The Role of Race, Religion, and National Origins* (New York: Oxford University Press, 1964); Maya D. Guendelman, Sapna Cheryan, and Benoît Monin, "Fitting In but Getting Fat: Identity Threat and Dietary Choices among U.S. Immigrants," *Psychological Science* 22(7) (2011): 959-67.

29   Harley and Eskenazi, "Time in the United States, Social Support and Health Behaviors;" Summer S. Hawkins, Kate Lamb, Tim J. Cole, Catherine Law, and the Millennium Cohort Study Child Health Group, "Influence of Moving to the UK on Maternal Health Behaviours: Prospective Cohort Study," *British Medical Journal* 336 (2008): 1052–55.

30   Kelly S. Balistreri and Jennifer Van Hook, "Socioeconomic Status and Body Mass Index among Hispanic Children of Immigrants and Children of Natives," *American Journal of Public Health* 99 (2009): 2238–46; Kathleen M. Harris, Krista M. Perreira, and Dohoon Lee, "Obesity in the Transition to Adulthood: Predictions across Race/Ethnicity, Immigrant Generation, and Sex," *Archives of Pediatrics Adolescent Medicine* 163 (2009): 1022–28; Margot Jackson, "Nativity Differences in Youths' Weight Trajectories: Foreign-Born Integration during the Transition to Adulthood," *Social Science Research* 40(5): 1419–33.

31   Richard Alba and Victor Nee, *Remaking the American Mainstream: Assimilation and Contemporary Immigration* (Cambridge: Harvard University Press, 2003); Min Zhou, "Segmented Assimilation: Issues, Controversies, and Recent Research on the New Second Generation," *International Migration Review* 31 (1997): 975–1008.

32   John R. Logan, Brian J. Stults, and Reynolds Farley, "Segregation of Minorities in the Metropolis: Two Decades of Change," *Demography* 41 (2004): 1–22; Domenico Parisi, Daniel T. Lichter, and Michael C. Taquino, "Multi-Scale Residential Segregation: Black Exceptionalism and America's Changing Color Line," *Social Forces* 89 (2011): 829–52; Rima Wilkes and John Iceland, "Hypersegregation in the Twenty-First Century," *Demography* 41 (2004): 23–36.

highest-quality schools, to employment opportunities, and a closer proximity to health hazards.[33] Foreign-born Blacks, despite possessing greater educational and economic resources than their native-born Black peers, on average, often find it more difficult than their non-Black immigrant peers to avoid lower-resource neighborhoods and to escape racial discrimination.[34] Evidence of weaker academic performance among the children of Black immigrants, therefore, is consistent with "segmented" models of integration,[35] though more favorable educational outcomes later in adolescence suggest that youth may learn to offset a disadvantaged environment with support networks within their families and communities.[36]

D. A Cross-National Consideration

For the most part, research on nativity-based inequalities in child development has been conducted in the United States. This study examines the United States alongside the United Kingdom, which provides a useful comparison for two important reasons.

First, the comparison permits examination of nativity differences in a country with a history of receiving immigrants and a Black foreign-born population comparable to the United States. In 2009 British statistics showed that 11 percent of the population was foreign born; in the same year, 25 percent of children and adolescents were either foreign born or had at least one foreign-born parent.[37] About 22 percent of foreign-born UK adults were born in either the Caribbean (5 percent) or Africa (17 percent). Among immigrants overall, 12 percent self-identified as Black[38] — largely from Africa and the Caribbean — and about 12 percent of the children of immigrants between ages 0 and 18 were Black. In the United States, 23 percent of young children (birth through age 17) have at least one foreign-born parent, and about 8 percent of these children are Black.[39]

A second motivation for extending analysis to the United Kingdom is that existing alongside Black immigrant populations of comparable proportions are notably different health care and social welfare

---

33 Ted Mouw, "Job Relocation and the Racial Gap in Unemployment in Detroit and Chicago, 1980 to 1990," *American Sociological Review* 65 (2000): 730–53; David R. Williams and Chiquita Collins, "Racial Residential Segregation: A Fundamental Cause of Racial Disparities in Health," *Public Health Reports* 116 (2001): 404–16.

34 John Iceland and Melissa Scopilliti, "Immigrant Residential Segregation in U.S. Metropolitan Areas, 1990–2000," *Demography* 45 (2008): 79–94; Kasinitz et al., *Inheriting the City.*

35 De Feyter and Winsler, "The Early Developmental Competencies and School Readiness of Low-Income, Immigrant Children."

36 Kasinitz et al., *Inheriting the City.*

37 British Office for National Statistics, *Migration Statistics 2008*, Annual Report (Newport, South Wales: United Kingdom Office of National Statistics, 2009).

38 Michael Rendall and John Salt, "The Foreign-Born Population," in *Focus on People and Migration: 2005*, ed., Roma Chappell (London: Palgrave Macmillan, 2005), 132–51.

39 Fortuny and Chaudry, "Children of Immigrants."

systems, which provide a different context of reception for immigrants and their children. The United Kingdom provides more universal health services than the United States, including health care through the British National Health Service, home visits for new mothers, priority in scheduling medical appointments for children, and child centers with integrated child-care services. Welfare-state policies in the United Kingdom are also more generous than those in the United States with respect to family cash assistance, social housing, and child care.[40] By contrast, the United States provides cash and housing assistance to few low-income families, has a hybrid system of public and private insurance that leaves many low-income children without access to health care, and lacks universal child care except for 3- and 4-year-olds in a handful of states. The multitude of policy differences between the two countries could produce cross-national variation in the integration of the children of Black immigrants. While evidence of similar patterns across countries would be noteworthy, it is difficult to attribute any differences to a particular source.

Despite the established body of research on UK migrant integration,[41] research examining children with immigrant parents has been largely limited because survey data allowing for the identification of these children have only recently become available.[42] Existing research using UK data has established sizeable ethnic disparities in children's health and academic achievement. For example, Black children in families of African or Caribbean descent (without separating children by generational groups) are more likely to have a low birth weight[43] but more likely to be breastfed[44] than white children. Black African and Caribbean children (again, not separating by generation) also perform more poorly than white children on cognitive assessments.[45]

40   Janet C. Gornick and Marcia K. Meyers, *Families that Work: Policies for Reconciling Parenthood and Employment* (New York: Russell Sage Foundation, 2005); John Hills, "Ends and Means: The Future Roles of Social Housing in England" (Centre for Analysis of Social Exclusion Report 34, London School of Economics, 2007), http://sticerd.lse.ac.uk/dps/case/cr/CASEreport34.pdf.
41   Michael Marmot, "Changing Places, Changing Risks: The Study of Migrants," *Public Health Reviews* 21 (1993): 185–95.
42   Hawkins et al., "Influence of Moving to the UK on Maternal Health Behaviours;" Lidia Panico, Mel Bartley, Michael Marmot, James Y. Nazroo, Amanda Sacker, and Yvonne J. Kelly, "Ethnic Variation in Childhood Asthma and Wheezing Illnesses: Findings from the Millennium Cohort Study," *International Journal of Epidemiology* 36(5) (2007): 1093-102.
43   Kelly et al., "Light Drinking in Pregnancy;" Teitler et al., "A Cross-National Comparison of Racial and Ethnic Disparities."
44   Lucy J. Griffiths, A. R. Tate, Carol Dezateux, and the Millennium Cohort Study Child Health Group, "The Contribution of Parental and Community Ethnicity to Breastfeeding Practices: Evidence from the Millennium Cohort Study," *International Journal of Epidemiology* 34 (December 2005): 1378–86.
45   Dearden and Sibieta, "Ethnic Inequalities in Child Outcomes."

II. Data

The scarcity of research on children in Black immigrant families can be attributed to the historically small size of this population (which has grown only recently, albeit rapidly). As a result, survey data meant to be representative of the national population have often not included enough children born to Black immigrants to be analyzed as a distinct group.

Data for this research come from the US Fragile Families and Child Wellbeing Study (FFS) and the UK Millennium Cohort Study (MCS). Both studies represent national populations, contain rich longitudinal information on families' and children's health, and oversample racial and ethnic minority families.

The FFS follows approximately 5,000 children born in large US cities between 1998 and 2000, including a large oversample of children born to unmarried parents. When weighted, these data are representative of births in cities with populations over 200,000. Mothers, and most fathers, were interviewed in the hospital soon after birth, with additional interviews at ages 1, 3, and 5; ninth-year interview data are forthcoming. The MCS is the fourth of Britain's national birth cohort studies. The first wave (2001-02) included 18,818 UK children (in 18,552 families) born between September 2000 and January 2002. Information was first collected from parents when the children were 9 months old, with follow-up interviews with the main caregiver (usually the mother) at ages 3, 5, and 7. Data here are used through age 5 to maximize comparability with the FFS. The sample design included an overrepresentation of families living in areas with high proportions of child poverty or ethnic minority populations.

III. Measures and Descriptive Findings

A. Nativity, Race, and Ethnicity

Because the FFS and MCS are samples of children born in US and UK hospitals, respectively, they exclude first-generation children — those born outside these countries. This leaves samples of second-generation children (those born in either the United States or United Kingdom with at least one immigrant parent) and of third-generation children (those with parents born in the United States or United Kingdom). In both samples, mothers identify both their region of birth and their race, making identification of Black children of immigrants and Black children of natives possible.

In the United States, this report distinguishes among Black, non-Black Hispanic, and non-Black non-Hispanic foreign-born mothers.[46] In the United Kingdom, it distinguishes among Black (African or Caribbean), South Asian (Indian, Pakistani, Bangladeshi), white, and other foreign-born mothers. Statistical tests that permit comparison between subgroups (Wald and likelihood ratio tests) indicate that Black Africans and Caribbeans in the British sample do not significantly differ in their relationships to the outcomes.[47] Overall, racial and ethnic categories among native-born mothers separate non-Hispanic white, non-Black Hispanic, Black, and other mothers in the United States, and Black (African or Caribbean), South Asian (Indian, Pakistani, Bangladeshi), other, and white mothers in the United Kingdom. Nativity categories include foreign-born Black, Hispanic and non-Hispanic mothers in the United States, and foreign-born white, South Asian, Black and other mothers in the United Kingdom. Though the reference category in both samples is made up of (non-Hispanic) white natives, the children of Black immigrants are compared to other racial and ethnic groups.

Table 1 presents weighted (i.e., representative) sample characteristics by nativity. The distribution of foreign-born mothers matches national figures in each survey: 28 percent in the United States (representative of large US cities) and 10 percent in the United Kingdom. The FFS includes about 120 Black immigrant mothers — about 2 percent of the sample; 90 percent of these mothers were born in African or Caribbean countries. About 11 percent of mothers are foreign-born, non-Hispanic (predominantly Asian), and 15 percent are foreign born and Hispanic. The MCS includes about 250 Black African or Caribbean immigrant mothers, about 1 percent of all mothers. Four percent of UK mothers in the sample are white immigrants; 3 percent are South Asian immigrants, and another 1 percent of the sample is foreign born and identifies as another ethnicity. UK white immigrant mothers (who constitute 30 percent of immigrant mothers) mainly come from Western Europe (61 percent), with smaller populations from Eastern Europe (8 percent), Australia, New Zealand, the United States, and Canada (12 percent). The remaining 19 percent come from Asian, African, South American, and Caribbean countries.

---

46 Small sample sizes prevent further separation by ethnicity; about 60 percent of foreign-born Hispanic mothers identify as Mexican; among other Hispanic ethnicities, Puerto Ricans and Cubans are notable.

47 In the UK Millenium Cohort Study (MCS), nativity and country-of-origin information was obtained at age 3; the sample is therefore limited to mothers present at age 3.

Table 1. Weighted Characteristics of US FFS and UK MCS Samples

US FFS

Variable	For. Born Black (N=111)	For. Born Non-Hisp (N=168)	For. Born Hispanic (N=552)	US Born (N=4,066)	Total (N=4,897)
Nativity	2	11	15	72	100
Race/Ethnicity					
Hispanic	0	0	100	21	32
Black	100	22	0	27	23
NHW	0	16	0	49	37
Other	0	62	0	3	8
Child Development					
Physical Health					
Breastfed	91	87	80	60	66
Prenatal Care in 1st Trimester	88	84	82	79	80
Birth weight	7.264	7.191	7.428	7.227	7.256
Asthma	16	10	10	15	14
Mental Health					
4 + Warm Parenting Behaviors	40	67	80	79	78
Spanks Child Sometimes/Often	51	10	9	17	16
Mean Internalizing Z-Score	0.497	-0.22	0.32	-0.039	0.014
Mean Externalizing Z-Score	0.287	-0.243	-0.238	-0.002	-0.046

UK MCS

Variable	For. Born Black (N=259)	For. Born White (N=565)	For. Born South As. (N=867)	For. Born Other (N=250)	UK Born (N=13,119)	Total (N=15,060)
Nativity	1	4	3	2	90	100
Race/Ethnicity						
Black African or Caribbean	100	0	0	0	2	3
South Asian (Ind., Pak., Bang.)	0	0	100	0	2	5
Other	0	0	0	100	1	2
White	0	100	0	0	95	90
Child Development						
Physical Health						
Breastfed	97	88	83	96	72	73
Prenatal Care in 1st Trimester	73	81	76	78	78	77
Birth weight	7.501	7.567	6.813	7.25	7.443	7.43
Asthma	9	13	11	14	15	14
Mental Health						
4 + Warm Parenting Behaviors	90	93	71	80	94	93
Spanks Child Sometimes/Often	32	11	17	19	11	11
Mean Internalizing Z-Score	0.169	-0.056	0.423	0.104	-0.06	-0.047
Mean Externalizing Z-Score	0.021	-0.2	0.024	-0.305	-0.055	-0.058

US FFS

Variable	For. Born Black (N=111)	For. Born, Non-Hisp (N=168)	For. Born Hispanic (N=552)	US Born (N=4,066)	Total (N=4,897)
Cognitive Development					
Mean Reading to Child	5.862	5.157	3.862	5.147	4.973
Mean PPVT Z-Score	-1.103	0.691	-0.702	0.287	0.137
Parental Resources					
Mother Some College or Higher	33	70	11	45	41
HH Poverty Ratio in top 30%, Birth	37	59	13	48	44
HH Poverty Ratio in top 30%, Age 5	41	68	14	46	43
Mother Married to Bio. Father, Birth	40	69	61	56	60
Mother Married, Age 5	51	77	56	56	57
Child Male	67	55	52	55	55
Maternal Age at Birth	27.2	29	27.5	26.7	27

UK MCS

Variable	For. Born Black (N=259)	For. Born White (N=565)	For. Born South As. (N=867)	For. Born Other (N=250).	UK Born (N=13,119)	Total (N=15,060)
Cognitive Development						
Mean Reading to Child	4.19	4.3	3.79	4.03	4.28	4.26
Mean Naming Z-Score	-0.5	0.231	-0.949	-0.341	0.152	0.117
Parental Resources						
A-levels or Higher Education	50	69	32	54	51	51
HH Poverty Ratio in top 30%, 9 Mon.	22	49	16	27	35	35
HH Poverty Ratio in top 30%, Age 5	16	49	12	34	37	36
Mother Married to Bio. Father, Birth	46	72	94	78	51	63
Mother Married, Age 5	50	74	92	82	63	65
Child Male	50	51	49	45	51	51
Maternal Age at Birth	31.3	30.8	27.9	30.8	29.2	29.3

Notes: Cells show percentages unless otherwise indicated. NHW=Non-Hispanic white.

Sources: Princeton University, "The Fragile Families and Child Well-Being Study," www.fragilefamilies.princeton.edu/; Centre for Longitudinal Studies, "Millennium Cohort Study," www.cls.ioe.ac.uk/Default.aspx.

B. Child Development

Using both surveys permits examination of two dimensions of children's development at age 5 that have lasting consequences for social and economic attainment later in life: health (physical and mental) and cognitive development. This chapter also examines indicators of mothers' parenting behaviors that are known to be associated with child well-being in each of these domains, focusing on measures that are comparable across the two data sources.

Measures of **physical health** include mothers' breastfeeding initiation (yes/no), early prenatal care (first trimester), as well as children's birth weight (pounds) and asthma history (diagnosed or not). Maternal smoking during pregnancy is not analyzed because, in both surveys, almost no Black immigrant mothers reported smoking. Mothers' breastfeeding behavior and the quality of prenatal medical care are strongly related to children's physical, behavioral, and cognitive development.[48] Although it may seem that the greater likelihood of socioeconomic disadvantage in the FFS would make these mothers more likely than those in the larger population to benefit from prenatal-care assistance, identical findings persist when the sample is weighted to be representative of all births in large US cities.

Measures of **mental health** include children's frequency of internalizing and externalizing behavior problems. Particular behaviors were grouped together to create scales of internalizing (withdrawn, sad) and externalizing (aggressive, angry) behaviors. This chapter also analyzes two parenting measures known to be associated with children's psychological well-being: interviewers' observations of mothers' warmth toward children, and mothers' reported frequency of spanking.[49] In each sample, interviewers recorded whether they observed the following interactions between mothers and children during the interview: positive speaking toward the child; conversing at least twice with the child; answering the child's questions verbally; praising the child spon-

---

48 Greg R. Alexander and Carol C. Korenbrot, "The Role of Prenatal Care in Preventing Low Birth Weight," *The Future of Children* 5 (1995): 103–20; Katriina Heikkilä, Amanda Sacker, Yvonne Kelly, Mary J. Renfrew, and Maria A. Quigley, "Breast Feeding and Child Behaviour in the Millennium Cohort Study," *Archives of Disease in Childhood* 96(7) (2011): 635-43; Sandra J. Kelly, Nancy Day, and Ann P. Streissguth, "Effects of Prenatal Alcohol Exposure on Social Behavior in Humans and Other Species," *Neurotoxicology and Teratology* 22 (2000): 143–49; Wendy H. Oddy, Garth E. Kendall, Eve Blair, Nicholas H. De Klerk, Fiona J. Stanley, Louis I. Landau, S. Silburn, and Stephen Zubrick, "Breast Feeding and Cognitive Development in Childhood: A Prospective Birth Cohort Study," *Paediatric and Perinatal Epidemiology* 17 (2003): 81–90; Lauren S. Wakschlag, Kate E. Pickett, Edwin Cook Jr., Neal L. Benowitz, and Bennett L. Leventhal, "Maternal Smoking during Pregnancy and Severe Antisocial Behavior in Offspring: A Review," *American Journal of Public Health* 92 (2002): 966–74.

49 Using interviewers' observations of mothers' behavior is useful in that it reduces the possibility that mothers' reports of warmth reflect solely cultural norms about appropriate parenting styles.

taneously; and caressing and kissing the child.[50] These are summed up to create a dichotomous measure indicating whether mothers engage in more than three warm behaviors. To measure spanking, an indicator of harsh parenting, in the United States this study uses use mothers' reports of whether and how often they have spanked the child because of misbehaving or acting up. In the United Kingdom, mothers report how often they smack children when they are acting naughty. For both samples mothers who report this behavior sometimes or often are separated from those who report that they spank rarely or never.

Finally, to measure children's *cognitive development*, children's verbal development, measured by performance on the Peabody Picture Vocabulary Test (PPVT) in the FFS and the British Ability Scales Naming Vocabulary test in the MCS, is analyzed. Both tests measure children's spoken vocabulary, with emphasis on noun identification from pictures, as well as the ability to attach verbal labels to pictures. Scores are standardized to age- and sex-specific reference populations. In order to provide a relative assessment, z-scores in both samples of children are analyzed — a z-score indicates a child's deviation from the sample average, also referred to as a standard deviation. Finally, a measure of parenting behavior relevant to cognitive development is worth examining: mothers' frequency of reading to children, measured in days per week in the United States (0 to 7) and on a five-point scale in the United Kingdom (not at all, a few times/month, a few times/week, several days/week, every day).

Table 1 displays descriptive differences in health and cognitive development between the children of Black immigrants and their peers. With respect to parenting behaviors related to physical health, US Black immigrant mothers are much more likely than US-born mothers to breastfeed (91 percent versus 60 percent), as are immigrant mothers from other ethnic groups. Black UK immigrant mothers are also more likely to breastfeed than UK-born mothers and than their white and South Asian immigrant peers. In both countries there are very small differences in immigrant versus native-born mothers' use of early prenatal care, suggesting that the United States largely succeeds at providing health-care access to pregnant mothers and children, despite a health-care system that offers less universal access than in the United Kingdom. These advantageous parenting behaviors, however, do not necessarily produce healthier physical health outcomes.

In both countries, the children of Black immigrants have a healthy birth weight, on average, but in the United States they are as likely as their native-born peers to have been diagnosed with asthma by age 5. The children of Black UK immigrants are slightly less likely than the chil-

---

50 Interviewers' observations are only available at age 3 in the MCS. For this measure the author includes contemporaneous measures of parental resources and sociodemographic factors. Analyzing age-3 warmth measures in the FFS does not change the within- or cross-country findings.

dren of natives to have asthma by age 5 (9 percent versus 15 percent). With respect to parenting and development related to mental health, in both countries the children of Black immigrants demonstrate above-average numbers of internalizing (anxious, depressed) and externalizing (aggressive) behaviors, respectively. In both countries there is also descriptive evidence of more frequent spanking in Black immigrant families, and in the United States, fewer warm parenting behaviors among this group.

With respect to cognitive development, the children of Black immigrants are at a clear disadvantage in both countries. Though Black immigrant mothers read to their children most days of the week, on average, their children perform substantially lower than their peers on verbal achievement assessments. This disadvantage is over a full standard deviation below average in the United States, and a half of a standard deviation in the United Kingdom. Large standard deviations indicate a sizeable difference from the average child in the sample. In contrast, the children of native-born mothers have above-average performance in both countries, as do the children of some immigrant groups, including US non-Hispanic (largely East Asian) and UK white immigrants.

C. Sociodemographic Characteristics

Several characteristics related to both nativity and mothers' behaviors are examined here. In the United States, **maternal education** separates mothers with less than a high school education or a high school diploma from those with some college or a college diploma/higher. In the United Kingdom a comparable measure can be used, separating mothers with no qualifications from those completing A-level college entrance exams and vocational equivalents, or with a university degree. **Family income** is measured using household poverty ratios (adjusted for household size and the number of children) — in each sample a distinction is made between ratios in the top 30 percent versus below. **Family structure** measures differentiate between two groups of mothers — those married to the biological father versus those who are single, cohabiting with the biological father, or coresiding (married or cohabiting) with a nonbiological father. Mothers' age at birth and children's sex are also measured.

Table 1 shows that nativity groups vary dramatically in terms of parental education and family income. Thirty-three percent of US Black immigrant mothers have completed at least some college at the time of children's birth, compared to 70 percent of other non-Hispanic immigrant mothers, 41 percent of the total sample and just 11 percent of Hispanic immigrant mothers. Black immigrant families are also slightly less likely to have a household poverty ratio in the top 30 percent (37 percent) than native-born families (48 percent) when children are born, but more likely than Hispanic immigrant families (13 percent). In the United Kingdom, Black immigrant mothers are about as likely to have postsecondary education as their native-born peers (50 percent versus 51 percent), but less likely than white immigrant mothers (69 percent). South Asian immigrant mothers are disproportionately poorly educated, with only 32 percent having some postsecondary schooling. However, these mothers are only slightly less likely to live in high earning households than Black immigrant mothers. Finally, in both countries Black immigrant mothers are the least likely to be married to their child's biological father around the time of birth — a troubling finding given a vast literature in both countries documenting the disadvantages faced by children who grow up in households without continuously married parents because of a decline in the quantity and quality of resources available to children.[51]

IV. Multivariate Findings

Taken together, the descriptive findings indicate, first, that the children of Black immigrants are more likely than their peers to be exposed to physically healthy parenting behaviors (especially in the United States), but also more likely to be exposed to harsh parenting in the form of spanking; and that they experience a clear disadvantage in cognitive development when compared to their peers. Moreover, it appears that these patterns are largely similar across the United States and United Kingdom. To examine these patterns more rigorously, this analysis uses ordinary least squares and binary logistic regression models to predict children's outcomes and mothers' parenting behaviors around birth and age 5, controlling for the sociodemographic factors described above. To ease interpretation, the author calculates adjusted predicted values from the estimates to compare across nativity groups, ethnic groups, and countries.

A. Parenting Behavior

Tables A-1 and A-2 (see Appendices) show estimates from multivariate regression models of nativity differences in parenting behaviors related to children's physical health, mental health, and cognitive development, adjusted for sociodemographic factors. Multivariate regression models provide a way of controlling for differences between children that may be related to their parents' immigration status, such as education, income, and household composition. One type of multivariate model is the logistic regression model, which expresses relationships in

---

51 For example, Kathleen Kiernan and John Hobcraft, "Parental Divorce during Childhood: Age at First Intercourse, Partnership and Parenthood," *Population Studies* 51 (1997): 41-55; Wendy Sigle-Rushton and Sara McLanahan, "Father Absence and Child Wellbeing: A Critical Review," in *The Future of the Family*, eds., Daniel P. Moynihan, Lee Rainwater, and Timothy Smeeding (New York: Russell Sage Foundation, 2004).

the form of odds ratios. An odds ratio larger than 1 indicates a greater chance of the outcome, whereas an odds ratio smaller than 1 indicates a lower chance of the outcome. An odds ratio of 1 indicates no difference in the outcome between people with and without a particular characteristic.

Table A-1 displays the US findings from the FFS. Each column contains estimates for a different outcome and each table describes differences between the children of Black immigrants and several comparison groups: native-born whites (the reference category), native-born Blacks, foreign-born Hispanics, and other foreign-born non-Hispanics (who are largely East Asian). Consistent with the descriptive evidence presented in Table 1, there are few differences in mothers' receipt of prenatal care. Black immigrant mothers are not significantly more or less likely to use early prenatal care than native-born whites, native-born Blacks, or their immigrant peers in other racial and ethnic groups. However, they are significantly more likely to breastfeed than native-born whites, Blacks, and Hispanics. The odds of breastfeeding are almost six times higher among Black immigrant mothers than among non-Hispanic white natives, after adjusting for social and demographic differences between these groups. Black immigrant mothers are also significantly more likely than native-born Blacks to breastfeed, as shown in the test at the bottom of Table A-1. There is no meaningful difference between the breastfeeding behavior of immigrant Blacks and their Hispanic or other non-Hispanic counterparts. These differences are better understood graphically: Figure 1 displays the probability of early prenatal care and breastfeeding in the United States for each foreign-born and native-born ethnic group, adjusted for social and demographic differences between children. The graph shows few differences in mothers' use of prenatal care, but sharp differences in breastfeeding behavior between Black immigrant mothers and their native-born Black and non-Hispanic white peers.

Figure 1. Probability of Maternal Behaviors: United States

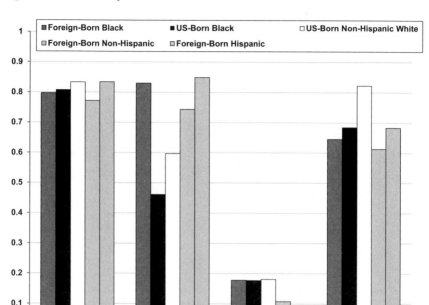

Note: All other variables are held constant at their means.

Source: Princeton University, "The Fragile Families and Child Well-Being Study."

Turning to parenting behaviors related to mental health, there is little evidence of differences between Black immigrant mothers and their peers. After adjusting for differences in parents' socioeconomic resources and family structure, Black immigrant mothers are no more likely to spank their children regularly than their peers in other ethnic and nativity groups. Nor are they less likely to demonstrate a high frequency of warm parenting behaviors — though non-Hispanic white native mothers are the most likely to practice regular warm parenting, this finding is not statistically different from that observed in other groups. Caution should be exercised in interpreting these findings, as the small number of Black immigrant mothers with a positive value on the spanking and warmth variables (N~20) reduces the precision of estimates. Finally, with respect to mothers' frequency of reading to children, most mothers read often to their children, regardless of nativity or ethnicity. Figure 2 shows that an average Black immigrant mother is predicted to read to her children about the same amount as an average non-Hispanic white, native-born mother (five days a week), and slightly more than an average native-born Black mother.

Figure 2. Frequency of Reading to Child, Age 5: United States

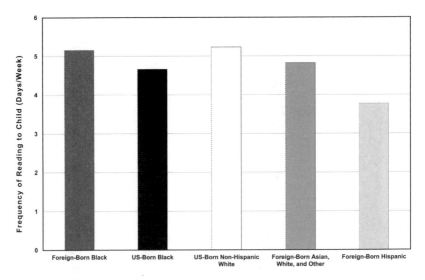

Note: All other variables are held constant at their means.
Source: Princeton University, "The Fragile Families and Child Well-Being Study."

Table A-2 reveals both similarities and differences among UK mothers. Black immigrant mothers are more likely to breastfeed than white natives, or than white immigrant mothers and UK-born Blacks. As in the United States, there is little evidence of immigrant-native differences in early prenatal care. These patterns are reinforced in Figure 3, which shows that Black immigrant mothers are 30 percent more likely to breastfeed than UK-born whites. Also in line with the US findings, examining spanking reveals no meaningful differences in mothers' behavior. In contrast to US patterns, however, Black immigrant mothers are significantly less likely to engage in frequent warm parenting behaviors than both native whites and Blacks. Immigrant mothers in ethnic groups are also less likely to practice warm parenting, as shown graphically in Figure 3.

Figure 3. Probability of Maternal Behaviors: United Kingdom

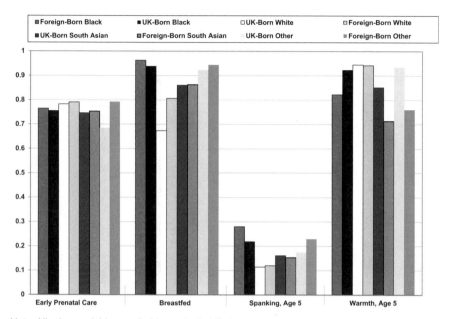

Note: All other variables are held constant at their means.
Source: Centre for Longitudinal Studies, "Millennium Cohort Study."

Finally, Black immigrant mothers read to their children significantly less than native-born white and Black mothers, on average, as do all other foreign-born mothers except for whites. Figure 4 compares the predicted reading frequency for all UK mothers. There is little cross-national variation in Black immigrant mothers' reading behavior, with mothers in both countries reading to their children most days of the week, on average.

Figure 4. Frequency of Reading to Child, Age 5: United Kingdom

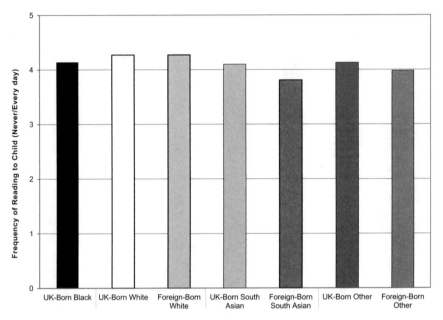

Note: All other variables are held constant at their means.
Source: Centre for Longitudinal Studies, "Millennium Cohort Study."

Overall, examining differences in parenting behavior in Black immigrant families reveals both advantages and disadvantages relative to other groups, as well as some variation across settings. In both countries, there is clear evidence of favorable breastfeeding patterns among Black immigrant mothers, and high usage of early prenatal care among all mothers. Patterns for spanking and warm parenting are less clear, with little multivariate evidence of group differences in the United States — and, in fact, some evidence of warmer parenting among Black immigrant families than among Black natives — but a lower likelihood of warm parenting among Black UK immigrant families, as well as among other immigrant mothers.

B. Children's Health and Cognitive Development

Tables A-3 and A-4 (see Appendices) examine whether the findings observed for parenting behavior extend to children's physical health (asthma), mental health (internalizing and externalizing behaviors), and cognitive development (verbal development). Table A-3, which displays the US findings, shows that children of Black immigrant mothers have a slightly higher birth weight than both native-born Blacks and non-Hispanic whites. Table A-5 shows that this difference is relatively large — almost 0.5 pounds — compared to the predicted birth weight of an average child in a native-born Black family. Later in childhood, at age 5, there is no evidence of an asthma advantage among children in Black immigrant families, in contrast to the substantially lower asthma risk experienced by white and Hispanic children, regardless of parental nativity. There is also little evidence of meaningful differences in children's mental health, as measured by the frequency of internalizing and externalizing behaviors. Finally, Table A-3 and Figure A-1A (see Appendices) show that children in all Black families lag substantially behind children in white families in cognitive development. There is marginally statistically significant evidence that this disadvantage is stronger for children in Black immigrant families than those in native-born families. Children in Hispanic immigrant families experience the largest cognitive disadvantage, which is only slightly reduced after controlling for mothers' English language ability.

Turning to children's physical health in the United Kingdom, Tables A-4 and A-5 show that UK children in Black immigrant families also have a birth weight equivalent to or higher than their peers in native-born families and in other ethnic groups, on average. The US asthma disadvantage, however, is not observed — instead, UK children in Black immigrant families are significantly less likely to have asthma by age 5 than children in all other nativity and ethnic groups. Table A-5 demonstrates this difference: the probability of an asthma diagnosis by age 5 is about 1 percent for the children of Black immigrants, compared to almost 18 percent and 15 percent for the children of UK-born Blacks and whites, respectively. There are few strong differences in the frequency of children's behaviors related to anxiety, depression, and aggression. As in the United States, there is a pattern of more frequent internalizing behaviors among children in Black immigrant families, but this is not statistically significant.

Finally, there is a clear disadvantage in Black children's cognitive development in the United Kingdom, and this disadvantage is stronger among children whose mothers are immigrants. Black children with foreign-born mothers have significantly poorer verbal development than children of native-born whites — Figure A-1B shows that this predicted disadvantage is about 0.7 of a standard deviation for an average child, and that children in Black immigrant families are also predicted to perform about 0.3 of a standard deviation lower than Black children of native-born mothers. The greatest gap in verbal development, however, is between children of Asian immigrant parents and native-born whites: over a full standard deviation. Controlling for the primary use of a language other than English in the home reduces the gap in cognitive development between Black immigrants' children and the children of native-born whites by only about 5 percent.

V. Conclusions

Identifying, explaining, and addressing nativity-based inequalities in child development at an early age is essential for ensuring the smooth social integration of children from immigrant families. It is difficult to predict whether the children of Black immigrants, who constitute an increasingly large fraction of the children of immigrants in the United States, will integrate toward the mainstream of non-Hispanic white America or whether their development will more closely resemble that of Black children with native-born parents.[52] On the one hand, some research has established favorable health outcomes and academic achievement for children of immigrants from Latin America and Asia, suggesting that the cultural and environmental circumstances of some immigrant families are protective for children. On the other hand, racial inequalities in children's development are large and persistent: Black children experience a disproportionate burden of chronic illness and perform more poorly on cognitive assessments than their peers, on average. Black children are also more likely to live in highly segregated neighborhoods, and are therefore more likely to attend under-re-sourced schools and to be exposed to health hazards and crime.

The analyses in this chapter are intended to describe the integration of children in Black immigrant families across two developmental domains — health (physical and mental) and cognitive. A primary goal of the chapter is to study children in both the United States and the United Kingdom, where there are large Black immigrant populations but notably different contexts with respect to immigration policy, health care, and social welfare provision. Using two national samples of mothers and children, this analysis compares children in Black immigrant families to the mainstream of non-Hispanic whites, as well as to Black children of native-born mothers and to children of other immigrant families.

The findings presented here should be interpreted cautiously in light of the small sample sizes available in the data sources analyzed. Though the Black immigrant population has grown rapidly in both the United States and United Kingdom, and both surveys oversample ethnic minority samples, the data include a total of about 120 US children in Black immigrant families, and about 250 UK children. This limits the scope of health markers that can be studied, the ability to separately analyze diverse Black ethnic groups, and the precision with which multivariate regression models can be estimated. For example, in the US data there are too few Black immigrant mothers who smoke while pregnant to analyze disparities in this outcome using multivariate techniques. Similarly, this analysis is forced to combine families from

---

52   Demographic projections suggest that the non-Hispanic white population in the United
     States is growing at the slowest rate, suggesting that the definition of mainstream will
     evolve.

disparate regions of the world — Africa and the Caribbean — despite the possibility that families' behaviors and children's development varies greatly not only by race, but also by region and country of origin.

The limitations imposed by small sample sizes, however, should be balanced against the benefits of using data sources that are representative of national populations, as well as by the cross-national perspective afforded by using two samples. The findings suggest that the development of children in Black immigrant families exhibits both favorable and disadvantaged patterns, depending on the marker under consideration. In both countries, there is clear evidence of favorable breastfeeding patterns among Black immigrant mothers, and high usage of early prenatal care among all mothers. Black immigrant mothers' healthy parenting behavior is paralleled by the healthy birth weight of their children and, in the United Kingdom, by their lower asthma risk at age 5. There is little multivariate evidence of differences in parenting and outcomes related to children's mental health. There is some evidence of warmer parenting among US Black immigrant families than among Black natives, but a lower likelihood of warm parenting among Black UK immigrant families, as well as among other UK immigrant families. These differences do not translate into large disparities in the frequency of children's internalizing and externalizing behaviors, however. In both countries, children of Black immigrant families have more frequent internalizing behaviors than those of white families, though these patterns are not statistically significant. Finally, Black children perform more poorly on cognitive assessments of verbal development, and in the United Kingdom, this disadvantage is particularly pronounced among children whose mothers are immigrants.

The direction and magnitude of parenting and developmental differences between Black children in immigrant families and their peers is largely similar across policy contexts. These similarities are notable: policies related to immigration, health care, parenting support, and social services would suggest that there should be substantial cross-country variation related to the differential context of reception. For example, the availability of federally funded health visits for new mothers in the United Kingdom would suggest that there should be fewer differences in parenting behaviors in that context than in the United States. There are some important exceptions to the fairly similar patterns across countries, however. In the United Kingdom, children of Black immigrant families have a particularly strong cognitive disadvantage (even after controlling for the language spoken at home), though the direction of this relationship is similar in the United States. At the same time, however, these children are less likely to have asthma than their peers in other ethnic and nativity groups. One interpretation is that children in Black UK immigrant families are less likely to be diagnosed than their peers, but no less likely to have asthma. Though there is evidence of racial and ethnic disparities in health-care usage and diagnosis patterns, this possibility would seem more plausible in the United States, where health care is less accessible than in the United Kingdom. A policy-driven interpretation would suggest that Black immigrant families in the United Kingdom are better able to access preventive health care for their children, and better able to afford housing that does not expose children to health risks. The potential benefit of social housing policy does not extend to children's cognitive development, however, and differences in mothers' reading behavior do not explain the lower performance of children in Black immigrant families.

Though it is tempting to explain differences between immigrant and native families by the context of reception, there is a potentially equally important role played by selective migration. In many countries, some people are more likely to migrate than others, producing differences in the host country that reflect not only new circumstances, but also pre-existing characteristics and resources. Existing research, for example, suggests that the average immigrant to the United States has a higher education than an average member of his or her population of origin,[53] and that migrants from some countries are the healthiest of their native population.[54] This selection pattern may be particularly pronounced among the Black immigrant population, which is highly educated relative to the populations in their countries of origin.[55] Variation in migrants' characteristics may contribute to cross-national differences in parents' behaviors and children's development. This variation may also help to explain the *similarity* of many patterns across countries, such as the fairly universal pattern of prevalent breastfeeding and healthy birth weight among Black immigrant families, if parents import healthy behavioral norms from their native countries.

Surely, Black migrants' cultural practices, the resources they bring with them, and the policies available to them contribute to the extent to which they mirror or contrast with their peers in the host country. In the absence of additional data, it is not possible to go beyond speculation in understanding what drives the relative advantages and disadvantages faced by Black immigrant families. These analyses provide a first and necessary step toward that larger question by describing group differences. The findings suggest that Black immigrant families' behaviors are both beneficial and detrimental to their children's development, and that children's integration is neither wholly toward the non-Hispanic white "mainstream" nor "segmented" toward the patterns of Black children in native-born families. An important next

---

53 Cynthia Feliciano, "Educational Selectivity in U.S. Immigration: How Do Immigrants Compare to those Left Behind?" *Demography* 42 (2005): 131–52.

54 Landale, Oropesa, and Gorman, "Migration and Infant Death;" Luis N. Rubalcava, Graciela M. Teruel, Duncan Thomas, and Noreen Goldman, "The Healthy Migrant Effect: New Findings from the Mexican Family Life Survey," *American Journal of Public Health* 98 (2008): 78–84.

55 Randy Capps, Kristen McCabe, and Michael Fix, *New Streams: Black African Migration to the United States* (Washington, DC: Migration Policy Institute, 2011), www.migrationpolicy.org/pubs/AfricanMigrationUS.pdf.

step will be to understand how nativity-based inequalities in child development evolve over time, and how the shape and magnitude of children's developmental trajectories are sensitive to positive and negative changes in their families' social resources and relationships. It is clear that neither children's adaptation to their parents' new society, nor the extent to which parents can use their resources to facilitate smooth developmental pathways, is unidimensional. Philip Kasinitz et al.[56] in their study of several ethnic groups of second-generation youth in New York City (including those in Black immigrant families) argue that youth selectively adopt behaviors and norms of both their country and their parents' country, and that this selective adaptation ultimately increases their ability to achieve productive lives. In this vein, in future work it will be important to understand the changing family, neighborhood, social, and economic arrangements experienced by immigrant children over time, in order to understand whether and how parents and children are able to maximize the favorable aspects of their environments, and minimize those that may be risk inducing. ⫛

---

56 Kasinitz et al., *Inheriting the City.*

Appendices

Table A-1. Regression of Nativity and Ethnic Differences in Maternal Behaviors, US

	Physical Health		Mental Health		Cognitive Development
	Early Prenatal Care	Breastfeeding	Spanking	Warmth	Reading to Child
Foreign Born	-0.304	0.918**	-0.588	-0.677	-0.128
Black	-0.161	-0.560**	-0.012	-0.738**	-0.563**
Black, Foreign Born	0.23	0.822*	0.583	0.499	0.619†
Hispanic	-0.308*	-0.199†	-0.543**	-0.411†	-0.433**
Hispanic, Foreign Born	-0.710*	0.866*	0.158	0.716	-0.614*
Mother More than HS	0.489**	0.886**	-0.007	0.159	0.240**
High HH Poverty Ratio	0.626**	0.185*	-0.045	0.385**	0.126
Married at Birth	0.760**	0.618**	0.082	0.239	0.0241
Cohabiting at Birth	0.272*	0.131†	-0.129	0.143	-0.163*
Child Male	0.129†	-0.0489	0.270**	-0.087	-0.086
Intercept	0.954**	0.202	-0.352	0.583*	5.509**
Tests of Coefficient Equality					
FB Black vs. NB Black					
x2 (1)	0.89	8.36	1.29	3.86	10.18
p>x2	0.35	0	0.26	0.05	0
FB Black vs. FB Hispanic					
x2 (1)	2.63	0.02	1.19	0.34	20.31
p>x2	0.1	0.88	0.28	0.56	0
FB Black vs. FB Non-Hispanic					
x2 (1)	0.73	0.02	1.99	1.31	1.82
p>x2	0.39	0.89	0.16	0.25	0.17
Model Type	L	L	L	L	OLS
N	4897	4897	4139	3023	4139

Notes: All covariates measured contemporaneously. Models also mother's age at birth. Reference categories are as follows: for nativity, native-born non-Hispanics; for race/ethnicity, non-Hispanic white, mother HS or less, HH poverty ratio not in top 30 percent. FB = foreign born; HH = household; HS = high school; L = binary logit regression; NB = native born; OLS = ordinary least squares regression.
†<.10; * p<.05 ; ** p <.01.
Source: Princeton University, "The Fragile Families and Child Well-Being Study."

Table A-2. Regression of Nativity and Ethnic Differences in Maternal Behaviors, UK

	Physical Health		Mental Health		Cognitive Development
	Early Prenatal Care	Breastfeeding	Spanking	Warmth	Reading to Child
Foreign Born	0.0947	0.734**	0.137	-0.359*	-0.0207
Black	-0.247	2.063**	0.789**	-0.505*	-0.167**
Black, Foreign Born	0.0603	0.141	0.0145	-1.104**	-0.227**
South Asian	-0.012	1.007**	0.424**	-1.168**	-0.230**
South Asian, Foreign Born	-0.0112	-0.671**	-0.145	-0.482*	-0.262**
Other	-0.502*	1.778**	0.573*	-0.203	-0.0923
Other, Foreign Born	0.531	-0.381	-0.0599	-1.561**	-0.276*
More than High School	0.075†	0.976**	-0.0549	0.621**	0.272**
HH Pov. Ratio Top 30%	0.179**	0.539**	-0.214**	0.282**	0.151**
Child Male	0.051	-0.058	-0.363**	0.0773	0.031†
Married at Birth	0.552**	0.600**	0.247**	0.447**	0.074**
Cohabiting at Birth	0.362**	0.432**	0.298**	0.334**	-0.061*
Intercept	0.571**	-1.165**	-0.962**	0.944**	4.122**
Tests of Coefficient Equality					
FB Black vs. NB Black					
x2 (1)	0.15	17.48	3.62	0.7	0.07
p>x2	0.7	0	0.05	0.4	0.79
FB Black vs. FB White					
x2 (1)	1.17	27.51	8.4	0.16	3.49
p>x2	0.28	0	0	0.69	0.06
Model Type	L	L	L	L	OLS
N	**15060**	**15060**	**13381**	**13381**	**13381**

Note: All covariates measured contemporaneously. Models also control for mother's age at birth. Reference categories are as follows: native-born white, mother no qualifications or O-levels only, HH poverty ratio not in top 30%. FB = foreign born; HH = household; HS = high school; L = binary logit regression; NB = native born; OLS = ordinary least squares regression.
†<.10; * p<.05 ; ** p <.01.
Source: Centre for Longitudinal Studies, "Millennium Cohort Study."

Table A-3. Regression of Nativity and Ethnic Differences in Child Development, Age 5, US

	Physical Health		Mental Health		Cognitive Development
	Birth Weight (lbs.)	Asthma	Externalizing Behaviors	Internalizing Behaviors	PPVT Z-Score
Foreign Born	-0.215	-0.473	-0.189	-0.032	-0.0561
Black	-0.398**	0.540**	-0.121*	-0.134**	-0.557**
Black, Foreign Born	0.636**	0.506	0.014	0.245	-0.0693
Hispanic	-0.03	0.678**	-0.101	0.088	-0.511**
Hispanic, Foreign Born	0.508**	-0.224	-0.022	0.201	-0.445**
Mother More than HS	0.151**	0.056	-0.137**	-0.199**	0.423**
High HH Poverty Ratio	0.051	-0.248**	-0.154**	-0.161**	0.247**
Married at Birth	0.304**	-0.430**	-0.235**	-0.182**	0.0576
Child Male	0.203**	0.438**	0.122**	0.042	-0.127**
Intercept	7.135**	-1.764**	0.400**	0.212*	0.289**
Tests of Coefficient Equality					
FB Black vs. NB Black					
χ2 (1)	23.58	0	0.38	3	2.65
p>χ2	0	0.95	0.55	0.08	0.09
FB Black vs. FB HIspanic					
χ2 (1)	0.68	4.72	0.05	0.08	3.27
p>χ2	0.41	0.03	0.83	0.78	0.07
FB Black vs. FB Non-Hispanic					
χ2 (1)	7.25	1.44	0.38	0.67	0
p>χ2	0	0.23	0.54	0.41	0.97
Model Type	OLS	L	L	L	OLS
N	**4987**	**4139**	**3023**	**3023**	**3023**

Notes: All covariates measured contemporaneously. Models also control for mother's age at birth. Reference categories are as follows: for nativity, native-born non-Hispanics; for race/ethnicity, non-Hispanic white, mother HS or less, HH poverty ratio not in top 30%. FB = foreign born; HH =household; HS = high school; L = binary logit regression; NB = native born; OLS = ordinary least squares regression.
†<.10; * p<.05 ; ** p <.01
Source: Princeton University, "The Fragile Families and Child Well-Being Study."

Table A-4. Regression of Nativity and Ethnic Differences in Child Development, Age 5, UK

	Physical Health		Mental Health		Cognitive Development
	Birth Weight (lbs.)	Asthma	Externalizing Behaviors	Internalizing Behaviors	PPVT Z-Score
Foreign Born	0.087	-0.0805	0.035	0.164*	-0.0857†
Black	-0.375**	0.366*	0.0784	0.005	-0.402**
Black, Foreign Born	0.199	-0.839**	-0.247	0.122	-0.318*
South Asian	-0.780**	0.0785	0.199	0.263**	-0.785**
South Asian, Foreign Born	0.01	-0.367*	-0.0939	0.189	-0.256**
Other	-0.569**	-1.154*	0.0091	0.115	-0.449**
Other, Foreign Born	0.011	1.304	-0.0389	0.0729	-0.228
Mother A-levels or higher	0.127**	-0.200**	-0.786**	-0.204**	0.315**
High HH Poverty Ratio	0.04	-0.234**	-0.462**	-0.123**	0.225**
Child Male	-0.271**	-0.401**	-0.291**	-0.044*	0.0563**
Married at Birth	0.271**	-0.194**	-0.298**	-0.231**	0.127**
Intercept	7.576**	-0.224	1.170**	0.517**	-0.423**
Tests of Coefficient Equality					
FB Black vs. NB Black					
$x2$ (1)	5.32	7.49	0.44	0.06	0.23
$p > x2$	0.02	0.01	0.51	0.8	0.63
FB Black vs. FB White					
$x2$ (1)	15.39	3.49	0	0.06	14.27
$p > x2$	0	0.06	0.98	0.82	0
Model Type	OLS	L	OLS	OLS	OLS
N	13381	13381	13381	13381	13381

Notes: All covariates measured contemporaneously. Models also control for mother's age at birth. Reference categories are as follows: native-born white, mother no qualifications or O-levels only, HH poverty ratio not in top 30%. FB = foreign born; HH = household; HS = high school; L = binary logit regression; NB = native born; OLS = ordinary least squares regression.
†<.10; * p<.05 ; ** p <.01
Source: Centre for Longitudinal Studies, "Millennium Cohort Study."

Figure A-1A. Predicted Z-Scores: United States

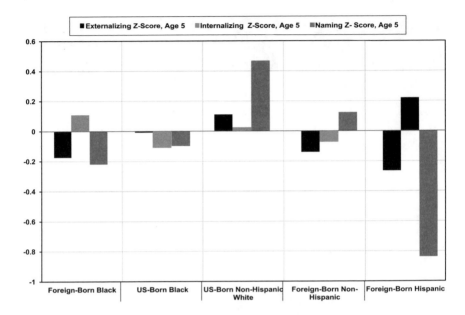

Note: All other variables in Table 4 are held constant at their means.

Source: Princeton University, "The Fragile Families and Child Well-Being Study."

Table A-5. Predicted Child Outcomes, by Nativity and Race/Ethnicity, US and UK*

US	Birth Weight (lbs.)	Asthma
US-Born Black	6.854	0.226
Foreign-Born Black	7.274	0.231
US-Born Non-Hispanic White	7.257	0.144
Foreign-Born Non-Hispanic	6.847	0.121
Foreign-Born Hispanic	7.325	0.178
UK	Birth Weight (lbs.)	Asthma
UK-Born Black	7.085	0.189
Foreign-Born Black	7.371	0.01
UK-Born White	7.461	0.145
Foreign-Born White	7.548	0.145
UK-Born South Asian	6.681	0.15
Foreign-Born South Asian	6.777	0.101
UK-Born Other	6.892	0.048
Foreign-Born Other	6.989	0.2

Note: *Probabilities computed from parameters shown in Tables A-3 and A-4. All other covariates held constant at their means.

Source: Princeton University, "The Fragile Families and Child Well-Being Study;" Centre for Longitudinal Studies, "Millennium Cohort Study."

Figure A-1B. Predicted Z-Scores, United Kingdom

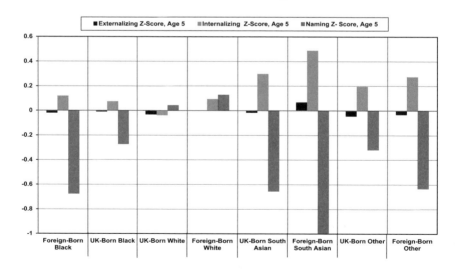

Note: All other variables are held constant at their means.

Source: Centre for Longitudinal Studies, "Millennium Cohort Study."

Works Cited

Abraido-Lanza, Ana F., Bruce P. Dohrenwend, Daisy S. Ng-Mak, and J. Blake Turner. 1999. The Latino Mortality Paradox: A Test of the Salmon Bias and Healthy Migrant Hypotheses. *American Journal of Public Health* 89: 1543–48. www.ncbi.nlm.nih.gov/pmc/articles/PMC1508801/4pdf.

Abraido-Lanza, Ana F., Maria T. Chao, and Karen R. Florez. 2006. Do Healthy Behaviors Decline with Greater Acculturation? Implications for the Latino Mortality Paradox. *Social Science and Medicine* 61(6): 1243-55.

Alba, Richard and Victor Nee. 2003. *Remaking the American Mainstream: Assimilation and Contemporary Immigration.* Cambridge: Harvard University Press.

Alexander, Greg R. and Carol C. Korenbrot. 1995. The Role of Prenatal Care in Preventing Low Birth Weight. *The Future of Children* 5: 103–20.

Anderson, Laurie M., D. L. Wood, and Cathy D. Sherbourne. 1997. Maternal Acculturation and Childhood Immunization Levels among Children in Latino Families in Los Angeles. *American Journal of Public Health* 87: 2018–21.

Arcia, E., M. Skinner, D. Bailey, and Vivian Correa. 2001. Models of Acculturation and Health Behaviors among Latino Immigrants to the US. *Social Science and Medicine* 53: 41–53.

Balistreri, Kelly S. and Jennifer Van Hook. 2009. Socioeconomic Status and Body Mass Index among Hispanic Children of Immigrants and Children of Natives. *American Journal of Public Health* 99: 2238–46.

British Office for National Statistics. 2009. *Migration Statistics 2008.* Annual Report. Newport, South Wales: United Kingdom Office of National Statistics.

Brugge, Doug, Mark Woodin, T. J. Schuch, Fatima L. Salas, Acheson Bennett, and Neal-Dra Osgood. 2008. Community-Level Data Suggest that Asthma Prevalence Varies between U.S. and Foreign-Born Black Subpopulations. *Journal of Asthma* 45: 785–9.

Case, Anne, Darren Lubotsky, and Christina Paxson. 2002. Economic Status and Health in Childhood: The Origins of the Gradient. *American Economic Review* 92: 1308–34.

Capps, Randy, Kristen McCabe, and Michael Fix. 2011. *New Streams: Black African Migration to the United States.* Washington, DC: Migration Policy Institute. www.migrationpolicy.org/pubs/AfricanMigrationUS.pdf.

Centre for Longitudinal Studies. The Millenium Cohort Study. www.cls.ioe.ac.uk/page.aspx?&sitesectionid=851&sitesectiontitle=Welcome+to+the+Millennium+Cohort+Study.

Clotfelter, Charles T., Helen F. Ladd, and Jacob L. Vigdor. 2009. The Academic Achievement Gap in Grades 3 to 8. *Review of Economics and Statistics* 91: 398–419.

Collins, James W., Shou-Yien Wu, and Richard J. David. 2002. Differing Intergenerational Birth Weights among the Descendants of US-Born and Foreign-Born Whites and African Americans in Illinois. *American Journal of Epidemiology* 155: 210–16.

Crosnoe, Robert. 2006. *Mexican Roots, American Schools: Helping Mexican Immigrant Children Succeed.* Stanford: Stanford University Press.

Currie, Janet. 2005. Health Disparities and Gaps in School Readiness. *Future of Children* 15: 117–38.

De Feyter, Jessica J. and Adam Winsler. 2009. The Early Developmental Competencies and School Readiness of Low-Income, Immigrant Children: Influences of Generation, Race/Ethnicity, and National Origins. *Early Childhood Research Quarterly* 24: 411–31.

Dearden, Lorraine and Luke Sibieta. 2010. Ethnic Inequalities in Child Outcomes. In *Children of the 21st Century (Volume 2): The First Five Years,* eds., Kirstine Hansen, Heather Joshi, and Shirley Dex, 169–85. Bristol, UK: Policy Press.

Feliciano, Cynthia. 2005. Educational Selectivity in U.S. Immigration: How do Immigrants Compare to those Left Behind? *Demography* 42: 131–52.

Finch, Brian K. 2003. Early Origins of the Gradient: The Relationship between Socio-economic Status and Infant Mortality in the United States. *Demography* 40: 675–99.

Fortuny, Karina and Ajay Chaudry. 2009. Children of Immigrants: Immigration Trends. Urban Institute Fact Sheet No. 1: 1–5. Washington, DC: Urban Institute. www.urban.org/publications/901292.html.

Fryer, Roland G. and Steven D. Levitt. 2006. The Black-White Test Score Gap through Third Grade. *American Law and Economics Review* 8: 249–81.

Fuligni, Andrew J. 1997. The Academic Achievement of Adolescents from Immigrant Families: The Roles of Family Background, Attitudes, and Behavior. *Child Development* 68: 351–63.

Fuligni, Andrew J., Vivian Tseng, and May Lam. 1999. Attitudes toward Family Obligations among American Adolescents with Asian, Latin American, and European Backgrounds. *Child Development* 70: 1030–44.

Glick, Jennifer E., Littisha Bates, and Scott T. Yabiku. 2009. Mother's Age at Arrival in the United States and Early Cognitive Development. *Early Childhood Research Quarterly* 24: 367–80.

Gordon, Milton M. 1964. *Assimilation in American Life: The Role of Race, Religion, and National Origins.* New York: Oxford University Press.

Gornick, Janet C. and Marcia K. Meyers. 2005. *Families that Work: Policies for Reconciling Parenthood and Employment.* New York: Russell Sage Foundation.

Griffiths, Lucy J., A. R. Tate, Carol Dezateux, and the Millennium Cohort Study Child Health Group. 2005. The Contribution of Parental and Community Ethnicity to Breastfeeding Practices: Evidence from the Millennium Cohort Study. *International Journal of Epidemiology* 34: 1378–86.

Guendelman, Maya D., Sapna Cheryan, and Benoît Monin. 2011. Fitting In but Getting Fat: Identity Threat and Dietary Choices among U.S. Immigrant Groups. *Psychological Science* 22(7): 959-67.

Harley, Kim and Brenda Eskenazi. 2006. Time in the United States, Social Support and Health Behaviors during Pregnancy among Women of Mexican Descent. *Social Science and Medicine* 62: 3048–61.

Harris, Kathleen M., Krista M. Perreira, and Dohoon Lee. 2009. Obesity in the Transition to Adulthood: Predictions across Race/Ethnicity, Immigrant Generation, and Sex. *Archives of Pediatrics Adolescent Medicine* 163: 1022–28.

Hawkins, Summer S., Kate Lamb, Tim J. Cole, Catherine Law, and the Millennium Cohort Study Child Health Group. 2008. Influence of Moving to the UK on Maternal Health Behaviours: Prospective Cohort Study. *British Medical Journal* 336: 1052–55.

Heikkilä, Katriina, Amanda Sacker, Yvonne Kelly, Mary J. Renfrew, and Maria A. Quigley. 2011. Breast Feeding and Child Behaviour in the Millennium Cohort Study. *Archives of Disease in Childhood* 96(7): 635-42.

Hills, John. 2007. Ends and Means: The Future Roles of Social Housing in England. *Centre for Analysis of Social Exclusion Report* 34. London: London School of Economics. http://sticerd.lse.ac.uk/dps/case/cr/CASEreport34.pdf.

Hummer, Robert A., Monique Biegler, Peter B. D. Turk, Douglas Forbes, W. P. Frisbie, Ying Hong, and Starling G. Pullum. 1999. Race/Ethnicity, Nativity, and Infant Mortality in the United States. *Social Forces* 77: 1083–117.

Iceland, John and Melissa Scopilliti. 2008. Immigrant Residential Segregation in U.S. Metropolitan Areas, 1990–2000. *Demography* 45: 79–94.

Jackson, Margot I. 2010. A Life Course Perspective on Child Health, Cognition and Occupational Skill Qualifications in Adulthood: Evidence from a British Cohort. *Social Forces* 89: 89–116.

_____. 2011. Nativity Differences in Youths' Weight Trajectories: Foreign-Born Integration during the Transition to Adulthood. *Social Science Research* 40(5): 1419-33.

Jencks, Christopher and Meredith P. Phillips, eds. 1998. *The Black-White Test Score Gap*. Washington, DC: Brookings Institution.

Kasinitz, Philip, John Mollenkopf, Mary Waters, and Jennifer Holdaway. 2008. *Inheriting the City: The Children of Immigrants Come of Age.* New York: Russell Sage Foundation.

Kelly, Sandra J., Nancy Day, and Ann P. Streissguth. 2000. Effects of Prenatal Alcohol Exposure on Social Behavior in Humans and Other Species. *Neurotoxicology and Teratology* 22: 143–49.

Kelly, Yvonne, Amanda Sacker, Ron Gray, John Kelly, Dieter Wolke, and Maria A. Quigley. 2009. Light Drinking in Pregnancy, a Risk for Behavioural Problems and Cognitive Deficits at 3 Years of Age? *International Journal of Epidemiology* 38(1): 129-40.

Kiernan, Kathleen and John Hobcraft. 1997. Parental Divorce during Childhood: Age at First Intercourse, Partnership and Parenthood. *Population Studies* 51: 41-55.

Kimbro, Rachel T., Scott M. Lynch, and Sara McLanahan. 2008. The Influence of Acculturation on Breastfeeding Initiation and Duration for Mexican-Americans. *Population Research and Policy Review* 27: 183.

Knudsen, Eric I. 2004. Sensitive Periods in the Development of the Brain and Behavior. *Journal of Cognitive Neuroscience* 16: 1412–25.

Landale, Nancy S., R. S. Oropesa, and Bridget K. Gorman. 2000. Migration and Infant Death: Assimilation or Selective Migration among Puerto Ricans? *American Sociological Review* 65: 888–909.

Leventhal, Tama, Yange Xue, and Jeanne Brooks-Gunn. 2006. Immigrant Differences in School-Age Children's Verbal Trajectories: A Look at Four Racial/Ethnic Groups. *Child Development* 77: 1359–74.

Logan, John R., Brian J. Stults, and Reynolds Farley. 2004. Segregation of Minorities in the Metropolis: Two Decades of Change. *Demography* 41: 1–22.

Lu, Michael C. and Neil Halfon. 2003. Racial and Ethnic Disparities in Birth Outcomes: A Life-Course Perspective. *Maternal and Child Health Journal* 7: 13–30.

Lynch, Scott M. 2003. Cohort and Life-Course Patterns in the Relationship between Education and Health: A Hierarchical Approach. *Demography* 40:309-31.

Marmot, Michael G., G. Davey Smith, S. Stansfeld, C. Patel, F. North, J. Head, I. White, Eric J. Brunner, and A. Feeney. 1991. Health Inequalities among British Civil Servants: The Whitehall II Study. *Lancet* 337: 1387–93.

Marmot, Michael. 1993. Changing Places, Changing Risks: The Study of Migrants. *Public Health Reviews* 21: 185–95.

McDaniel, Marla, Christina Paxson, and Jane Waldfogel. May 2006. Racial Disparities in Childhood Asthma in the United States: Evidence from the National Health Interview Survey, 1997 to 2003. *Pediatrics* 117: e868–77.

Mouw, Ted. 2000. Job Relocation and the Racial Gap in Unemployment in Detroit and Chicago, 1980 to 1990. *American Sociological Review* 65: 730–53.

Murnane, Richard J., John B. Willett, Kristen L. Bub, Kathleen McCartney, Eric Hanushek, and Rebecca Maynard. 2006. Understanding Trends in the Black-White Achievement Gaps during the First Years of School [with Comments]. *Brookings-Wharton Papers on Urban Affairs:* 97–135.

National Center for Health Statistics. 2004. *Health, United States, 2004, with Chartbook on Trends in the Health of Americans.* Hyattsville, MD: National Center for Health Statistics.

Oddy, Wendy H., Garth E. Kendall, Eve Blair, Nicholas H. De Klerk, Fiona J. Stanley, Louis I. Landau, S. Silburn, and Stephen Zubrick. 2003. Breast Feeding and Cognitive Development in Childhood: A Prospective Birth Cohort Study. *Paediatric and Perinatal Epidemiology* 17: 81–90.

Panico, Lidia, Mel Bartley, Michael Marmot, James Y. Nazroo, Amanda Sacker, and Yvonne J. Kelly. 2007. Ethnic Variation in Childhood Asthma and Wheezing Illnesses: Findings from the Millennium Cohort Study. *International Journal of Epidemiology* 36(5): 1093-102.

Parisi, Domenico, Daniel T. Lichter, and Michael C. Taquino. 2011. Multi-Scale Residential Segregation: Black Exceptionalism and America's Changing Color Line. *Social Forces* 89: 829–52.

Princeton University. The Fragile Families and Child Well-Being Study. www.fragilefamilies.princeton.edu/.

Rendall, Michael and John Salt. 2005. The Foreign-Born Population. In *Focus on People and Migration: 2005*, Roma Chappell, ed. 132–51. London: Palgrave Macmillan.

Rong, Xue L. and Frank Brown. 2001. The Effects of Immigrant Generation and Ethnicity on Educational Attainment among Young African and Caribbean Blacks in the United States. *Harvard Educational Review* 71: 536–66.

Rubalcava, Luis N., Graciela M. Teruel, Duncan Thomas, and Noreen Goldman. 2008. The Healthy Migrant Effect: New Findings from the Mexican Family Life Survey. *American Journal of Public Health* 98: 78–84.

Schoon, Ingrid, John Bynner, Heather Joshi, Samantha Parsons, Richard D. Wiggins, and Amanda Sacker. 2002. The Influence of Context, Timing, and Duration of Risk Experiences for the Passage from Childhood to Mid-adulthood. *Child Development* 73: 1486–504.

Sigle-Rushton, Wendy and Sara McLanahan. 2004. Father Absence and Child Wellbeing: A Critical Review. In *The Future of the Family*, Daniel P. Moynihan, Lee Rainwater, and Timothy Smeeding, eds. New York: Russell Sage Foundation.

Smith, James P. 2007. The Impact of Socioeconomic Status on Health over the Life-Course. *Journal of Human Resources* XLII: 739–64.

Teitler, Julien O., Nancy E. Reichman, Lenna Nepomnyaschy, and Melissa Martinson. 2007. A Cross-National Comparison of Racial and Ethnic Disparities in Low Birth Weight in the United States and England. *Pediatrics* 120: e1182–89.

Thomas, Kevin J. A. 2009. Parental Characteristics and the Schooling Progress of the Children of Immigrant and U.S.-Born Blacks. *Demography* 46: 513–34.

Wakschlag, Lauren S., Kate E. Pickett, Edwin Cook Jr., Neal L. Benowitz, and Bennett L. Leventhal. 2002. Maternal Smoking during Pregnancy and Severe Antisocial Behavior in Offspring: A Review. *American Journal of Public Health* 92: 966–74.

Wilkes, Rima and John Iceland. 2004. Hypersegregation in the Twenty-First Century. *Demography* 41: 23–36.

Williams, David R. and Chiquita Collins. 2001. Racial Residential Segregation: A Fundamental Cause of Racial Disparities in Health. *Public Health Reports* 116: 404–16.

Wingate, Martha S. and Greg R. Alexander. 2006. The Healthy Migrant Theory: Variations in Pregnancy Outcomes among US-Born Migrants. *Social Science and Medicine* 62: 491–98.

Zhou, Min. 1997. Segmented Assimilation: Issues, Controversies, and Recent Research on the New Second Generation. *International Migration Review* 31: 975–1008.

CHAPTER 6

PATTERNS AND PREDICTORS OF SCHOOL READINESS AND EARLY CHILDHOOD SUCCESS AMONG YOUNG CHILDREN IN BLACK IMMIGRANT FAMILIES

Danielle A. Crosby and Angel S. Dunbar

University of North Carolina at Greensboro

Introduction

Policy and academic interest in young children has grown substantially in recent years, prompted in part by advancements in the scientific understanding of early childhood and mounting evidence of the importance of early experiences for later development. Of particular concern is the finding that achievement disparities among different racial, ethnic, and socioeconomic groups emerge before children begin school and often persist long term.

Over the past decade, there has been a marked increase in the number of studies focused on the antecedents of early school success that aim to inform policy and practice, and ultimately improve outcomes for children. Within this body of literature, children in immigrant families have begun to garner attention because of their sizable and growing share of the US child population. Between 1990 and 2010, the immigrant child population doubled, from 4 million to 8 million, accounting for all of the growth in the US population aged 8 or younger during that period. It is estimated that one out of every four young children has at least one parent who was born outside of the United States.[1] Significant changes over the past few decades in demographic trends and immigration flows have meant that a majority of these families have origins outside of Europe and Canada, making the broader context of racial and ethnic stratification in the United States a more salient consideration in understanding their experiences.[2]

Much of the existing work on early development and school readiness among immigrants' children has focused on Hispanic (and to some extent Asian) children, who comprise the largest segments of this population. As a result, information about the experiences of young children of immigrants in other racial/ethnic groups is lacking. Although 12 percent of all Black children living in the United States are first- or second-generation immigrants (from Africa, the Caribbean, Latin America, or other origins), comparatively little research exists regarding their health and development, especially during early childhood.

This chapter seeks to address this gap by providing information about the patterns and predictors of school readiness and early academic success of children in Black immigrant families. Drawing on a unique data set that follows a nationally representative cohort of children from birth to school entry, we describe the early childhood experiences and outcomes of children in Black immigrant families relative to their peers and test to what extent group differences in emergent academic skills are related to sociodemographic characteristics, the home learning environment, and participation in early education programs. While existing studies have generally compared children of Black immigrants to children of Black US-born parents (as we do here), we also examine how this group fares in comparison to their non-Black peers from both immigrant and nonimmigrant families. In making these comparisons, we are interested in identifying not only areas of relative disadvantage, but areas of relative advantage.

I. Background

It has become increasingly clear that children's educational experiences in the years leading up to school entry — both at home and in out-of-

---

1   Donald J. Hernandez, Nancy Denton, and Suzanne E. Macartney, "Children in Immigrant Families: Looking to America's Future," *Social Policy Report* 23, No. 3 (2008): 3–23; Karina Fortuny, Randolph Capps, Margaret Simms, and Ajay Chaudry, *Children of Immigrants: National and State Characteristics* (Washington, DC: Urban Institute, 2009), www.urban.org/publications/411939.html.
2   Karen R. Humes, Nicholas A. Jones, and Roberto R. Ramirez, "Overview of Race and Hispanic Origin: 2010" (2010 Census Briefs C201BR-02, US Census Bureau, Washington, DC, March 2011), www.census.gov/prod/cen2010/briefs/c2010br-02.pdf; Mary Mederios Kent, "Immigration and America's Black Population," *Population Bulletin* 62, No. 4 (2007): 3–16,
www.prb.org/pdf07/62.4immigration.pdf.

home settings — are linked to their long-term academic trajectories.[3] A large body of research has identified warm, responsive interactions with adults; rich language environments; and the availability of developmentally stimulating materials and activities as particularly important for promoting early cognitive development and establishing the foundations for academic success.[4] Also well established in the literature is the idea that children from different social and economic backgrounds enter school with different odds of success. For example, as much as half of the Black-white gap in high school test scores is believed to exist at kindergarten entry.[5] Children's differential access to early learning experiences, mainly due to family socioeconomic circumstances, may be a key contributor to such gaps. Indeed, disparities in early academic skills by race, ethnicity, and income have been linked to group differences in the prevalence of home literacy activities and materials,[6] responsive adult-child interactions,[7] and participation in early care and education programs.[8]

A. School Readiness and Early School Success among Children of Immigrants

Broadly speaking, children of immigrants are often characterized as a vulnerable population academically because of low average levels of parent education, family income, and exposure to English.[9] Immigrant families also tend to face unique challenges associated with adjusting to a new society and community, and a potentially unfamiliar education system. Despite these potential areas of risk, the literature also

---

3   Katherine A. Magnuson, Marcia K. Meyers, Christopher J. Ruhm, and Jane Waldfogel, "Inequality in Preschool Education and School Readiness," *American Educational Research Journal* 41 (2004): 115–57; Michaella Sektnan, Megan McClelland, Alan Acock, and Fred Morrison, "Relations between Early Family Risk, Children's Behavioral Regulation, and Academic Achievement," *Early Childhood Research Quarterly* 25 (2010): 464–79.

4   National Research Council and Institute of Medicine, *From Neurons to Neighborhoods: The Science of Early Childhood Development* (Washington, DC: National Academies Press, 2000).

5   Meredith Phillips, James Crouse, and John Ralph, "Does the Black-White Test Score Gap Widen after Children Enter School?" in *The Black-White Test Score Gap*, eds. C. Jencks and M. Phillips (Washington, DC: The Brookings Institution, 1998).

6   Valerie E. Lee and David T. Burkam, *Inequality at the Starting Gate: Social Background Differences in Achievement as Children Begin School* (Washington, DC: Economic Policy Institute, 2002); Christine Winquist Nord, Jean Lennon, Baiming Liu, and Kathryn Chandler, *Home Literacy Activities and Signs of Children's Emerging Literacy, 1993 and 1999*, NCES 2000-02rev (Washington, DC: National Center for Education Statistics, 1999), http://nces. ed.gov/pubs2000/2000026.pdf; Amy Rathbun and Jerry West, *From Kindergarten through Third Grade: Children's Beginning School Experiences*, NCES 2004–007 (Washington, DC: US Government Printing Office, 2004), http://nces.ed.gov/pubsearch/pubsinfo.asp?pubid=2004007.

7   Jeanne Brooks-Gunn and Lisa B. Markman, "The Contribution of Parenting to Ethnic and Racial Gaps in School Readiness," *Future of Children* 15, No. 1 (2005): 139–68.

8   Katherine Magnuson and Jane Waldfogel, "Early Childhood Care and Education: Effects on Ethnic and Racial Gaps in School Readiness," *Future of Children* 15, No. 1 (2005): 169–96.

9   Lee and Burkam, *Inequality at the Starting Gate.*

suggests several protective mechanisms that may operate for children in immigrant families. These include positive selection factors associated with migration: individuals who successfully migrate are often healthier and more resourceful or skilled than those who remain in the home country.[10] As a group, immigrant parents tend to have high rates of marriage and employment,[11] low rates of maternal depression,[12] and high levels of commitment to educational opportunities for their children.[13] These characteristics are likely to benefit children's development.

The scientific literature on the transition to school for young children in immigrant families is still emerging. Many school readiness studies examine disparities by family income level, race/ethnicity, and language use; fewer pay attention to parents' nativity and its intersection with other "gaps." At the same time, research on the academic trajectories of immigrant children has focused primarily on middle childhood and adolescence, rather than early childhood. The available evidence for younger children suggests that children of immigrants begin school at an academic disadvantage relative to their peers with US-born parents.[14] Furthermore, such disparities may emerge quite early in life — recent national data indicate that by 24 months of age, children with immigrant parents score significantly lower on standardized assessments of cognitive development than those with US-born parents.[15]

Yet, broad comparisons of children in immigrant and native families often obscure the significant heterogeneity that exists within these

10 Cynthia Feliciano, "Educational Selectivity in US Immigration: How Do Immigrants Compare to Those Left Behind?" *Demography* 42, no. 1 (2005): 131–52.

11 Donald J. Hernandez, "Demographic Change and the Life Circumstances of Immigrants," *Future of Children* 14, no. 2 (2004): 16–47; Jane Reardon-Anderson, Randolph Capps, and Michael E. Fix, "The Health and Well-Being of Children in Immigrant Families" (New Federalism: National Survey of America's Families Policy Brief B-52, Urban Institute, Washington, DC, November 2002), www.urban.org/publications/310584.html.

12 Rashmita S. Mistry, Jeremy C. Biesanz, Nina Chien, Carolee Howes, and Aprile D. Benner, "Socioeconomic Status, Parental Investments, and the Cognitive and Behavioral Outcomes of Low-Income Children from Immigrant and Native Households," *Early Childhood Research Quarterly* 23 (2008): 193–212.

13 Tama Leventhal, Yange Xue, and Jeanne Brooks-Gunn, "Immigrant Differences in School-Age Children's Verbal Trajectories: A Look at Four Racial/Ethnic Groups," *Child Development* 77, No. 5 (2006): 1359–74; India Ornelas, Krista Perreira, Linda Beeber, and Lauren Maxwell, "Challenges and Strategies to Maintaining Emotional Health: Qualitative Perspectives of Mexican Immigrant Mothers," *Journal of Family Issues*, 30 (2009): 1556-75.

14 Robert Crosnoe, "Health and the Education of Children from Race/Ethnic Minority and Immigrant Families," *Journal of Health and Social Behavior* 47, No. 1 (2006): 77-93; Wen Jui Han, "The Academic Trajectories of Children of Immigrants and Their School Environments," *Developmental Psychology* 44, No. 6 (2008): 1572–90; Katherine Magnuson, Claudia Lahaie, and Jane Waldfogel, "Preschool and School Readiness of Children of Immigrants," *Social Science Quarterly* 87 (2006): 1241–62.

15 Bruce Fuller, Margaret Bridges, Edward Bein, Heeju Jang, Sunyoung Jung, Sophia Rabe-Hesketh, Neal Halfon, and Alice Kuo, "The Health and Cognitive Growth of Latino Toddlers: At Risk or Immigrant Paradox?" *Maternal and Child Health* 13 (2009): 755–68.

populations.[16] Educational outcomes for immigrants have been shown to vary by generation, immigration status, country and region of origin, age at arrival, time in the United States, language, skin color, religion, and even gender. Moreover, much of this research has focused on Latino and Asian children as the two largest segments of the immigrant population, leaving many unanswered questions about other immigrant groups.[17]

B. The Early Developmental Experiences and Outcomes of Black Children of Immigrants

Studies providing information about the early childhood experiences of children in Black immigrant families are rare. Relatively more data are available regarding the educational progress of older children and adolescents, who are much more likely than younger children to be first generation (i.e., foreign born) rather than second generation (i.e., US born with foreign-born parents). This generational difference has important implications for comparing results across studies of different age groups, as discussed in more detail below.

The work on older children's academic performance suggests an immigrant advantage (at times referred to as the "immigrant paradox"), such that immigrant youth have better-than-expected outcomes given their family's socioeconomic status. Put another way, immigrant youth in middle and high school have been found to outperform native youth from similar socioeconomic backgrounds on standardized academic achievement tests.[18] This advantage appears to pertain to Black immigrant youth as well, who score higher on achievement measures, and are more likely to finish high school and pursue postsecondary education than Black children in native families.[19] Comparisons in this literature across different immigrant populations indicate that children of Black immigrants academically surpass some groups (e.g., children of Hispanic immigrants) while lagging behind others (e.g., white and

---

16 Donald J. Hernandez, Nancy Denton, and Suzanne E. Macartney, "Children in Immigrant Families: Looking to America's Future," *Social Policy Report* 23, No. 3 (2008): 3–23.

17 Susan K. Brown and Frank D. Bean, "Assimilation Models, Old and New: Explaining a Long-Term Process," *Migration Information Source* special issue on the second generation, October 2006, www.migrationinformation.org/USfocus/display.cfm?ID=442; Robert Crosnoe and Ruth López Turley, "K-12 Educational Outcomes of Immigrant Youth," *Future of Children* 21 (2011): 129–52; Magnuson, Lahaie, and Waldfogel, "Preschool and School Readiness of Children of Immigrants."

18 See review by Crosnoe and Turley, "K-12 Educational Outcomes of Immigrant Youth," 129–52; Natalia Palacios, Katarina Guttmannova, and Lindsay P. Chase-Lansdale, "Early Reading Achievement of Children in Immigrant Families: Is There an Immigrant Paradox?" *Developmental Psychology* 44 (2008): 1381–95.

19 Kevin J. A. Thomas, "Poverty among Young Children in Black Immigrant, US-Born Black, and Non-Black Immigrant Families: The Role of Familial Contexts" (Discussion Paper Series DP 2010-02, University of Kentucky Center for Poverty Research, 2010).

Asian immigrants), a pattern that aligns closely, but not entirely, with intergroup differences in socioeconomic status.[20] For example, Black immigrant families experience lower poverty rates than (non-Black) Hispanic immigrants, but higher rates than white and Asian immigrant families.[21]

At the same time, existing studies of early academic skills among young children of immigrants (the vast majority of whom are US born), do not suggest as clear an advantage. A recent study of low-income 4-year-olds found that children of immigrants score lower on measures of school readiness than their co-ethnic peers in nonimmigrant families.[22] More specifically, the Black children of immigrant parents in this sample displayed weaker cognitive and language skills than Black children of native parents, even when controlling for child and family characteristics. In another large study, children of immigrants scored higher on an assessment of kindergarten math than their co-ethnic peers in native families, but this advantage was evident only after socioeconomic and home language characteristics were taken into account.[23] Moreover, this advantage did not exist for children of Caribbean immigrants, who were one of the lowest-scoring groups along with children in Black native and American Indian families.

Taken together, this set of findings provides tentative evidence that children of Black immigrants enter school at an academic disadvantage compared to many of their peers in non-Black immigrant and native families; however, it appears they may make significant gains during the elementary years, as they outperform their native peers in middle and high school. As we note above, though, studies of secondary education tend to focus on first-generation immigrant youth, whereas studies of school readiness focus primarily on second-generation immigrant children (given that more than 90 percent of this age group was born in the United States). It is therefore unclear whether the more positive outcomes observed for later versus early schooling among children of Black immigrants reflect an upward academic trajectory, changes in relative status compared to other children (e.g., children of Black natives), or differences associated with generational status.

An important backdrop for understanding the experiences of immi-

20 Crosnoe, "Health and the Education of Children from Race/Ethnic Minority and Immigrant Families." Andrew J. Fuligni, "The Academic Achievement of Adolescents from Immigrant Families: The Roles of Family Background, Attitudes, and Behavior," *Child Development* 68 (1997): 351–63.
21 Thomas, "Poverty among Young Children in Black Immigrant, US-Born Black, and Non-Black Immigrant Families."
22 Jessica De Feyter and Adam Winsler, "The Early Developmental Competencies and School Readiness of Low-Income, Immigrant Children: Influences of Generation, Race/Ethnicity, and National Origins," *Early Childhood Research Quarterly* 24 (2009): 411–31.
23 Jennifer Glick and Bryndl Hohmann-Marriott, "Academic Performance of Young Children in Immigrant Families: The Significance of Race, Ethnicity, and National Origin," *International Migration Review* 41, No. 2 (2007): 371–402.

grant children and families is the existing racial and ethnic stratification of the United States. Black immigrants may share similar
experiences of prejudice and discrimination with US-born Blacks,
which may undercut some of the advantages described above. Indeed,
evidence suggests that discrimination may operate in educational
settings for young children. In their study of elementary school outcomes, Robert Crosnoe and Ruth Turley observe that compared to other
immigrant groups Black immigrant children, "did not demonstrate
this pattern of immigrant advantages in teacher-rated socioemotional
school readiness, suggesting that the well-documented tendency for
teachers to view black children's behavior in school as problematic
may trump the more positive views they tend to have of immigrant
children."[24]

In general, higher levels of parental education and employment are
associated with better developmental outcomes for children; however,
recent evidence suggests that these resources may have less "payoff"
for children in Black immigrant families compared to other groups.[25]
Their lower incomes may be due in part to the limited employment
options for educated Black immigrants who often work in low-wage,
unskilled jobs — a phenomenon referred to as "brain waste."[26] The
extent to which children benefit from higher levels of parent education
when it does not translate into better employment conditions and
economic resources remains an open question. Higher levels of human
capital presumably lead to upward mobility over time, but the fact that
Black immigrant families are likely to be disadvantaged during their
initial years in the United States, when they are also likely to have
young children, is worrying.

II. Using National Longitudinal Data to Examine the Early Development of Children in Black Immigrant Families

The goal of this chapter is to contribute to the limited literature that
exists about the early development of children in Black immigrant
families. We use rich longitudinal data from a recent national study of
early childhood to provide new information about the patterns and predictors of early academic skills for this understudied, yet demograph-
ically significant, group. In the broader literature on school readiness,
gaps between native and immigrant children have been linked to group

---

24 Crosnoe and Turley, "K-12 Educational Outcomes of Immigrant Youth," 140.
25 Thomas, "Poverty among Young Children in Black Immigrant, US-Born Black, and Non-
    Black Immigrant Families."
26 Jeanne Batalova and Michael Fix, *Uneven Progress: The Employment Pathways of Skilled
    Immigrants in the United States* (Washington, DC: Migration Policy Institute, 2008), www.
    migrationpolicy.org/pubs/BrainWasteOct08.pdf.

differences in family socioeconomic status, home learning environments, parental practices, and enrollment in early childhood education programs; however, little is known about the role these factors play for children in Black immigrant families.[27] Moreover, studies have tended to aggregate children of African, Caribbean, and Latin American descent, despite differences among these regional populations that may have important implications for children.[28]

The data available for this study not only allow us to explore some of the mechanisms underlying disparities at the intersection of race/ethnicity and nativity, but can also help identify particular areas of strength for Black immigrant families. A better understanding of both the needs and competencies of this growing population can inform policy and practice.

Our specific aims are as follows:

- To describe the early childhood (birth to school entry) outcomes and experiences of second-generation (i.e., US-born) children in Black immigrant families in comparison to their peers in native and non-Black immigrant families

- To test whether a variety of demographic and family process variables (including early learning environments in the home and in early education programs) account for any observed differences in early academic skills between children of Black immigrants and children of other racial/ethnic backgrounds

- To examine which factors are most predictive of early school success among young children of Black immigrants, considering potential differences between children of African and Caribbean descent

By including children from multiple racial and ethnic backgrounds, we extend previous work, which has tended to focus on comparisons between Black children in immigrant and nonimmigrant families. In addition, with the available data we are able to disaggregate immigrant families based on parents' region of origin; we are particularly interested in distinctions between children of African and Caribbean heritage.

---

27 Crosnoe and Turley, "K-12 Educational Outcomes of Immigrant Youth," 129–52; Jennifer E. Glick, Littisha Bates, and Scott T. Yabiku, "Mother's Age at Arrival in the United States and Early Cognitive Development," *Early Childhood Research Quarterly* 24 (2009): 367–80; Kevin J. A. Thomas, "Parental Characteristics and the Schooling Progress of the Children of Immigrant and US-Born Blacks," *Demography* 46 (2009): 513–34, www.ncbi.nlm.nih.gov/pmc/articles/PMC2831345/.

28 Thomas, "Poverty among Young Children in Black Immigrant, US-Born Black, and Non-Black Immigrant Families."

Our primary focus in this chapter is children's early reading and math skills (at age 4 and in kindergarten) as indicators of their academic functioning during the transition to school. However, we also examine several aspects of children's health and behavior given evidence that intellectual, social, emotional, and physical domains of development are interrelated, especially during the early years of life.[29]

III. Data, Sample, and Measures

A. The Early Childhood Longitudinal Study, Birth Cohort

With the arrival of the new millennium, the US Department of Education launched a new research initiative designed to assess "the way America raises, nurtures, and prepares its children for school."[30] The Early Childhood Longitudinal Study, Birth Cohort (ECLS-B) follows a nationally representative cohort of children from birth until school entry, collecting extensive information about their health, development, and experiences across multiple contexts. Drawn from birth certificates using a clustered, list frame sampling design, the ECLS-B includes nearly 10,700 children within 9,850 families and is representative of the nearly 4 million children born in the United States in 2001.[31] Four major data collections — involving home visits, parent interviews, child assessments, child-care observations, and teacher surveys — were conducted when children were approximately 9 months, 2 years, 4 years, and 5 to 6 years of age (entering kindergarten).

The strengths of the ECLS-B for addressing this study's guiding questions include in-depth measures of the ecology of early childhood; established, developmentally informed measures of child functioning; substantial samples of children in immigrant families from several racial/ethnic groups; and extensive information about family characteristics such as country of origin, age at arrival, time in the United States, and various aspects of language use. Importantly, accommodations were made to include families whose primary language is not English.

---

29 Anne Case, Darren Lubotsky, and Christina Paxson, "Economic Status and Health in Childhood: The Origins of the Gradient," *American Economic Review* 92, No. 5 (2002): 1308–34; Daniel P. Keating and Sharon Z. Simonton, "Health Effects of Human Development Policies," in *Making Americans Healthier: Social and Economic Policy as Health Policy*, eds. James House, Robert Schoeni, Harold Pollack, and George Kaplan (New York: Russell Sage, 2008), 61–94.

30 Kristen Flanagan and Jerry West, *Children Born in 2001: First Results from the Base Year of the Early Childhood Longitudinal Study, Birth Cohort*, NCES 2005–036 (Washington, DC: US Department of Education, National Center for Education Statistics, 2004), 1, http://nces.ed.gov/pubs2005/children/.

31 Excluded from the study were children born to young mothers (under 15 years), and those who died or were adopted prior to the nine-month survey.

B. Analysis Sample

The information presented in this study is based on the nearly 10,000 children in the ECLS-B with valid information about parents' nativity status, country of origin, and child outcome data at the 9-month (n=9100), 2-year (n=8900), 4-year (n=7600), and kindergarten wave (n=6450).[32] Following standard conventions, we define children of immigrants as those with at least one parent born outside of the United States or its territories. Mirroring other national estimates, the ECLS-B data indicate that 24 percent of children born in the United States in 2001 have at least one foreign-born parent.[33]

Immigrant parents in the ECLS-B sample come from more than 100 countries. For analysis purposes, we categorize children of immigrants into eight groups based on parents' region of origin: Africa, the Caribbean, Latin America, East Asia, India/South Asia, Southeast Asia, the Middle East, and Europe (see Table 1). Given our focus on children of Black immigrants, we limit our African and Caribbean samples to families in which the parent identifies the child's race as Black (singularly or in combination with another racial category).[34] For children of natives (i.e., those with two US-born parents), we rely on broad racial/ethnic categories to create six comparison groups: non-Hispanic Black, non-Hispanic white, Hispanic, Asian/Pacific Islander, American Indian/Native Alaskan, and multiracial/other. Because the last three groups have small samples and are not the central focus of this analysis, we display results only for Black, white, and Hispanic children of natives.

---

32 All unweighted sample sizes are rounded to the nearest 50 to comply with National Center for Education Statistics (NCES) regulations regarding restricted-use data.

33 Hernandez, Denton, and Macartney, "Children in Immigrant Families."

34 Two groups (approximately 50 cases) were excluded from the analysis because of small sample sizes and questions about sensible groupings. First, 12 percent of parents from Africa (e.g., of European heritage in South Africa) and the Caribbean (e.g., of Indian heritage in Guyana) did not identify as Black and were therefore excluded from our Black African and Caribbean samples. Second, 10 percent of Black immigrant parents were born in a country outside of Africa or the Caribbean; with only 1 or 2 individuals from any one country, it was difficult to categorize these families in a meaningful way.

Table 1. Race/Ethnicity and Parental Birthplace for Children Born in the United States in 2001

Race/Ethnic Groups Based on Parents' Region of Origin	Countries Represented	Share of All Children
African immigrant	Algeria, Burkina, Cape Verde, Chad, Egypt, Ethiopia, Ghana*, Kenya, Liberia, Morocco, Nigeria*, Rwanda, Senegal, Somalia*, Sudan, Toga, Uganda, Zaire, Zambia	0.8%
Caribbean immigrant	Antigua, Bahamas, Cuba*, Dominican Republic*, Guyana, Haiti*, Jamaica*, Santo Domingo, Trinidad & Tobago, West Indies	1.9%
Hispanic immigrant	Argentina, Bolivia, Brazil, Chile, Columbia, Costa Rica, Ecuador, El Salvador, Guatemala, Honduras, Mexico*, Nicaragua, Panama, Peru, Venezuela, Uruguay	14.3%
East Asian immigrant	China*, Hong Kong, Korea*, Japan, Taiwan*	1.1%
Indian Asian immigrant	India*, Bangladesh, Nepal, Pakistan*, Sri Lanka	0.8%
Southeast Asian immigrant	Burma, Cambodia, Indonesia, Laos, Malaysia, Marshall Islands, Micronesia, New Guinea, Pacific Islands, Philippines*, Singapore, Solomon Islands, Thailand, Vietnam*	1.3%
Middle Eastern immigrant	Afghanistan, Armenia, Iraq, Iran, Israel*, Jordan, Kuwait, Lebanon, Saudi Arabia, Syria, Yemen	0.8%
European immigrant	Australia, Belgium, Canada*, Czech Republic, Denmark, Finland, France, Germany*, Hungary, Ireland, Italy, Lithuania, the Netherlands, New Zealand, Poland, Portugal, Romania, Russia, Serbia, Spain, Switzerland, Ukraine, Uzbekistan, Yugoslavia	2.3%
Black native		11.9%
White native		50.1%
Hispanic native		10.0%
Asian/Pacific Islander native		0.3%
American Indian/ Native Alaskan		0.5%
Multiracial native		3.4%

Notes: n = 10,600; all unweighted sample sizes are rounded to nearest 50 per NCES restricted-use data regulations. Countries denoted with an "*" account for at least 10 percent of the respondents in that region of origin category.

Source: Author calculations using the Early Childhood Longitudinal Study-Birth Cohort, 9-month—Kindergarten 2007 Restricted Use Data File, National Center for Education Statistics (NCES), US Department of Education.

C. Measures

1. Sociodemographic Variables

As mentioned, the ECLS-B collected extensive information about multiple aspects of young children's lives. We begin our analysis by describing the circumstances of Black immigrant families with young US-born children relative to other families with young children in terms of family structure, parents' educational attainment and employment status, and multiple indicators of household economic conditions (e.g., poverty rates, the ratio of household income to the poverty level, home and car ownership, and the experience of food insecurity). For all of the immigrant groups, we also present information about parents' age at arrival in the United States, citizenship status, and English use and fluency.

2. Child Outcome Variables

Our second set of analyses describes how children of Black immigrants fare relative to other children on several key indicators of health and development, including the following:

- *Mothers' prenatal/perinatal health practices.* As important predictors of children's health and development, we include indicators of whether mothers received prenatal care in their first trimester; whether mothers smoked cigarettes, drank alcohol, or used drugs during pregnancy; and whether infants were breastfed.

- *Birth outcomes.* Health records and parent reports provided information about whether their child had low birth weight (<2,500 grams), was part of a multiple birth, required an extended stay in the hospital post-birth, or was born with a disability or chronic health issue.

- *General child health.* At each time point, parents rated their child's overall health on a scale from 1 ("poor") to 5 ("excellent"). Research suggests that parent ratings of child health status are a reliable predictor of health outcomes and needs.

- *Child weight status.* During the 4-year and kindergarten home visit, children's height and weight were assessed and used to calculate their Body Mass Index (BMI). Growth charts (by age and gender) were used to identify children with a BMI above the 85th (i.e., overweight) and 95th (i.e., obese) percentile.

- *Early cognitive development.* During the 9-month and 2-year home visits, trained research staff conducted a standardized assessment of children's early mental skills. Children were observed in play and given a series of age-appropriate tasks.

Assessors rated children on their level of exploration, problem-solving skills (e.g., finding a hidden toy), verbalizations and language comprehension, and early matching and counting skills.

- *Early academic skills.* At age 4 and in kindergarten, children were tested on their early reading and math abilities. Trained research staff conducted assessments during the home visit. We used percentile scores (1–100) on these tests to indicate how children compared to their same-age peers on school readiness skills.

- *Social behavior in the classroom.* Although our primary focus is on children's academic skills, we include information about children's behavior in classroom settings, as this can be an important predictor of successful transitions to school. At age 4, teachers rated how often children exhibited positive behaviors (e.g., cooperating with other children) and negative behaviors (e.g., aggression). Values on these two scales ranged from 1 ("never") to 5 ("very often").

3. Mediating Variables

In our third set of analyses, we investigate the extent to which intergroup differences in child outcomes can be explained not only by sociodemographic factors but also by children's experiences of warm and supportive parenting, access to developmentally stimulating materials (e.g., books, puzzles) and activities (e.g., reading, singing, visiting a museum), and their parents' beliefs and expectations regarding education. In addition, we consider the role of different care and education settings that serve young children. Children's primary care arrangements at age 4 are categorized into parental care only, home-based child care (by someone other than a parent), and center-based child care. We also calculate rates of participation in Head Start, a center-based program designed specifically to promote children's development for which many immigrant families are eligible. (Additional details about the study data and variables are available in the Appendix).

IV. Results

A. Demographic Snapshot of Black Immigrant Families with Young US-Born Children

Our first set of findings provides a descriptive snapshot of the life circumstances of young children in Black immigrant families relative to children in other major native and immigrant groups identified in the ECLS-B data (see Table 2).[35] Throughout, we note dimensions on which children in African versus Caribbean immigrant families differ significantly; however, in the absence of statistically significant differences, we describe Black children of immigrants as one group.

Table 2. Parent and Family Characteristics (First Year of Life) of Children Born in the United States in 2001, by Nativity, Race/Ethnicity, and Region

	Children of Black Immigrants		Children of Other Immigrants						Children of US-Born Parents		
	African	Caribbean	Hispanic	East Asian	Indian Asian	Southeast Asian	Middle Eastern	European	Non-Hispanic Black	Non-Hispanic White	Hispanic
Primary caregiver's marital status											
Married	86%	61%[a]	62%[c]	97%[d]	98%[d]	83%[d]	100%[b]	93%[d]	24%[b]	79%	49%[c]
Cohabiting	2%	18% [a]	28%[b]	1%[d]	1%[d]	9%[b]	0%[d]	6%[d]	14%[c]	10%[c]	21%[c]
Single	12%	21%	10%	2%[b]	1%[b]	8%[b]	0%[b]	1%[b]	61%[b]	10%	30%
Highest level of parent education:											
Less than a high school degree	9%	11%	32%[b]	3%	3%[b]	10%	5%	0%[b]	23%[b]	6%	19%
High school degree/ equivalent	20%	34% [a]	35%	6%[d]	3%[d]	21%	10%	10%	36%[c]	20%	33%
Post-secondary education	70%	55%	33%[b]	91%[b]	94%[b]	69%	85%[b]	90%[d]	40%[b]	74%	48%

---

35 All analyses presented here incorporate NCES-computed sample weights to adjust for disproportionate sampling, survey nonresponse, and noncoverage of the target population; for additional details, see Christine Nord, Brad Edwards, Carol Andreassen, James L. Green, Kathleen Wallner-Allen, *Early Childhood Longitudinal Study, Birth Cohort, (ECLS-B), User's Manual for the ECLS-B Longitudinal 9-Month–2-Year Data File and Electronic Codebook*, NCES 2006-046 (Washington, DC: US Department of Education, National Center for Education Statistics, 2006). Reported standard errors account for the complex survey design of the ECLS-B.

	Children of Black Immigrants		Children of Other Immigrants						Children of US-Born Parents		
	African	Caribbean	Hispanic	East Asian	Indian Asian	Southeast Asian	Middle Eastern	European	Non-Hispanic Black	Non-Hispanic White	Hispanic
Mother employed at 9-month survey	55%	67%	48%[b]	47%[b]	34%[b]	58%	26%[b]	66%	74%	60%	65%
Employed spouse/ partner	72%	69%	84%[b]	95%[b]	98%[b]	84%[b]	97%[b]	97%[b]	35%[b]	86%[b]	66%
Parent occupational prestige (Scale from 0 to 100)	45	40	37[b]	50[b]	52[b]	43	45	47[b]	40	44	40
Household income											
Ratio of income to federal poverty level	2.16	2.40	1.38[b]	4.58[b]	4.49[b]	2.55	3.63	4.06[b]	1.35[b]	3.34[b]	1.97
Income below the poverty level	26%	22%	42%[b]	6%[b]	9%[b]	19%	16%	5%[b]	50%[b]	13%	31%
Income below twice the poverty level	64%	56%	82%[b]	24%[b]	26%[b]	51%	36%	25%[b]	78%[b]	37%[b]	63%
Household is food insecure	7%	18% [a]	19%[c]	5%[d]	5%[d]	10%	7%	8%	18%[c]	8%	12%
Family owns home	28%	35%	28%	57% [b]	50%	45%	52%	66%[b]	23%	65%[b]	28%
Family owns car	90%	86%	82%	97%[b]	92%	93%	95%	92%	68%[b]	96%[b]	86%

Notes: [a] indicates significant difference between children of Black African and children of Black Caribbean parents at p < 0.1 or better. [B] indicates significant difference between other groups of children versus children of Black Immigrants overall at p < 0.1 or better. [c] indicates significant difference between other groups of children and children of Black African immigrants only, at p < 0.1 or better. [D] Indicates significant difference between other groups of children versus children of Black Caribbean immigrants only, at p < 0.1 or better.

Source: Author calculations using the Early Childhood Longitudinal Study-Birth Cohort, 9-month—Kindergarten 2007 Restricted Use Data File, NCES.

1. Family Structure

Consistent with other data sources, we find that Black immigrant parents in the ECLS-B have relatively high marriage rates, although this is one area of particular difference between parents of African and Caribbean origin. At 86 percent, children of African immigrant parents are significantly more likely to have married parents than all children of natives, as well as children of Hispanic immigrants. Caribbean and

Hispanic immigrants are the immigrant parents least likely to be married, but they are more likely to be married than Black native-born parents.

2. Parental Education, Employment, and Income

Turning to indicators of human capital and financial resources, we find that Black immigrant families generally rank in the middle, relative to the other immigrant and native groups included in this study. While they tend to be more advantaged than Hispanic and South East Asian immigrant families and several native groups (most notably Black natives), they are consistently less advantaged than native and immigrant parents of either Asian or European descent.

Roughly two-thirds of children in Black immigrant families have at least one parent with more than a high school education, a significantly higher share than children in Hispanic immigrant and Black native families, but lower than those in Asian, Middle Eastern, and European immigrant families. Notably, Black immigrant parents have education levels that are on par with those of white native parents.

In terms of attachment to the labor force, we, like other researchers, find that immigrant parents in general are very likely to be employed. Interestingly, mothers in Black immigrant families are more likely to be employed within their infant's first year than mothers in several other immigrant groups (including Hispanic, Indian Asian, Middle Eastern, and European). While extensive employment on the part of Black immigrant mothers may mean additional resources for their families, its impact on parent and child well-being will depend on families' options for infant care and their ability to meet their preferences for balancing work and the transition to parenthood. We also note that Black immigrant households are less likely than other immigrant households to include an employed spouse or partner. Given the high marriage rates already noted for this group, this statistic may indicate that Black immigrant fathers are more likely than fathers in other immigrant groups to be unemployed. For example, 86 percent of African immigrant parents report being married, but only 72 percent of mothers indicate that they have a spouse (or partner) who is employed. Nonetheless, Black immigrant households are still nearly twice as likely as Black native households to include an employed spouse or partner.

Group differences in occupational prestige generally follow differences in parent education. On average, Black immigrant parents tend to work in less prestigious jobs than parents from East Asia, India, and Europe but in more prestigious jobs than Hispanic immigrant parents. On average, Black immigrant parents' occupations are of a similar prestige level as native-born parents (regardless of race/ethnicity).

When it comes to financial resources and economic hardship, Black immigrant families again rank somewhere in the middle of the distribution. With income levels slightly above twice the federal poverty threshold (which is based on income adjusted for family size), Black immigrant families are more advantaged than Hispanic immigrant and Black native families, but they are not as advantaged as East Asian, Indian Asian, and European immigrants. They also have less household income (and are less likely to own a home or a car) than white native families, despite similar levels of parent education and occupational prestige. The relatively low incomes of Black immigrant families may reflect lower employment rates among Black immigrant versus white native fathers, but are also likely to be due to lower wages for Black immigrant parents.

Although African and Caribbean immigrant families appear to have similar levels of resources (at least as measured here), we find that Caribbean parents are more than twice as likely (18 percent versus 7 percent) to report experiencing household food insecurity during their child's first year. The reason for this difference is unclear from the data examined here and requires further investigation; potential factors include differences in dietary practices and food costs in settlement communities. The risk faced by Caribbean immigrant families in lacking consistent access to adequate amounts of food is similar to that experienced by Hispanic immigrant and Black native families, but higher than for most of the other groups examined in this analysis.

3. Citizenship and Language Use

In comparison to other immigrant groups, Black immigrant families have some advantages regarding citizenship status and English language proficiency (see Table 3). Approximately 40 percent of children in Black immigrant families have at least one parent who is a US citizen (either because of naturalization or the presence of a US-born parent), much higher than the rate for children in Hispanic immigrant families (25 percent). Black immigrant families are also more likely than Hispanic, East Asian, and Indian Asian immigrant families to report English as their primary language. Moreover, among those who do not consider English their primary language, a majority (two-thirds) rate themselves as fluent in reading, writing, and speaking English. Similar rates of parental English fluency were found for the other immigrant groups, with the exception of Hispanic immigrant families, who reported lower levels of English fluency. Roughly 20 percent of Black immigrant families are multilingual, speaking their heritage language at home but having strong abilities in English as well.

African and Caribbean parents tend to differ on the length of time they have spent in the United States. African parents tend to arrive at older ages and have spent less time in the country than most other immigrant groups. In 2002–03 when these data were collected, 42 percent of African immigrant parents had been in the United States five years or less; the average age of immigration for this group is 24 years. In contrast, Caribbean immigrant parents have been in the United States much longer on average: 28 percent came as a child younger than age 10.

Table 3. Parent and Family Characteristics for Children Born in the United States to Immigrant Parents in 2001, by Race/Ethnicity and Region

	Children of Black Immigrants		Children of Other Immigrants					
	African	Caribbean	Hispanic	East Asian	Indian Asian	Southeast Asian	Middle Eastern	European
At least one US citizen parent	42%	47%	24%ª	53%	38%	57%	63%	46%
Mother/primary caregiver migration characteristics*								
Age at US arrival	24	17ª	18ᶜ	20ᶜ	22ᵈ	18ᶜ	20	18ᶜ
Immigrated as child (less than 10 years old)	7%	28%ª	17%	21%ᶜ	10%	22%	21%	30%ᶜ
Residing in US for less than 6 years	42%	22%ª	32%	25%	53%ᵈ	23%	31%	25%
Residing in US for 6 to 10 years	7%	24%ª	19%ᶜ	17%	15%	18%ᶜ	15%	11%
Residing in US for more than 10 years	51%	54%	49%	59%	31%ᵈ	59%	54%	65%
Primary household language is English	45%	53%	17%ᵇ	34%ᵇ	15%ᵇ	43%	42%	72%ᵇ
Mother/primary caregiver is fluent in English*	62%	72%	39%ᵇ	57%	60%	63%	56%	81%

Notes: ª indicates significant difference between children of Black African and children of Black Caribbean parents at p < 0.1 or better. ᵇ indicates significant difference between other groups of children versus children of Black Immigrants overall at p < 0.1 or better. ᶜ indicates significant difference between other groups of children and children of Black African immigrants only, at p < 0.1 or better. ᵈ indicates significant difference between other groups of children versus children of Black Caribbean immigrants only, at p < 0.1 or better.

Source: Author calculations using the Early Childhood Longitudinal Study-Birth Cohort, 9-month—Kindergarten 2007 Restricted Use Data File, NCES.

B. *The Health and Developmental Status of Young Children in Black Immigrant Families*

1. Infant and Child Health

Parental and child health indicators suggest several advantages for children of Black immigrants (see Table 4). Black immigrant mothers are much less likely to smoke or use alcohol or drugs during pregnancy. They are also more likely to breastfeed their infants than US-born mothers across various racial/ethnic groups. African mothers report especially high rates of breastfeeding. Children of Black immigrants are less likely than children of Black US-born parents to be born with low birth weights and are less likely than multiracial native children to be born with a congenital anomaly or chronic health condition.

Table 4. Indicators of Health and Development (Birth to Kindergarten) for Children Born in the United States in 2001, by Nativity, Race/Ethnicity, and Region

	Children of Black Immigrants		Children of Other Immigrants						Children of US-Born Parents		
	African	Caribbean	Hispanic	East Asian	Indian Asian	Southeast Asian	Middle Eastern	European	Non-Hispanic Black	Non-Hispanic White	Hispanic
Prenatal/perinatal health											
Mother received prenatal care in first trimester of pregnancy	84%	87%	88%	93%	91%	89%	92%	95%	85%	93%	87%
Mother smoked or used alcohol or drugs in last trimester of pregnancy	4%	4%	2%	4%	2%	2%	0%	18%[b]	10%[b]	18%[b]	13%[b]
Moderate or very low birth weight	7%	8%	6%	6%	9%	9%	5%	5%	13%[b]	6%	8%
Child had extended stay in hospital post-birth	4%	15%[a]	13%[c]	12%	14%[c]	10%	6%	11%	16%[c]	12%	12%
Born with chronic health condition	2%	3%	5%	5%	7%	4%	15%	5%	7%	7%	7%
Child ever breastfed	93%	80%[a]	81%[c]	87%	90%	72%[c]	92%	88%	44%[c]	69%[c]	66%[c]
General child health status (1=poor; 5=excellent)											
At 9 months of age	4.7	4.5[a]	4.3[c]	4.6	4.3[c]	4.4[c]	4.5	4.6	4.4[c]	4.6[c]	4.5[c]
At 2 years of age	4.5	4.4	4.2[b]	4.5	4.3	4.3	4.3	4.5	4.4	4.6	4.5
At 4 years of age	4.4	4.2	4.1	4.4	4.1	4.2	4.3	4.6[b]	4.3	4.5	4.3
During the kindergarten year	4.3	4.3	4.1[b]	4.2	4.2	4.1	4.3	4.6[b]	4.3	4.5	4.4
Child weight status											
Overweight at age 4	36%	39%	46%[b]	26%	22%[b]	35%	30%	35%	38%	33%	36%
Obese at age 4	20%	18%	28%[b]	15%	15%	17%	18%	15%	21%	16%	18%
Overweight in kindergarten	42%	38%	46%[b]	26%	23%	28%	47%	31%	42%	30%	37%
Obese in kindergarten	20%	17%	28%[b]	12%	9%	12%	25%	5%[b]	21%	13%	20%

	Children of Black Immigrants		Children of Other Immigrants						Children of US-Born Parents		
	African	Caribbean	Hispanic	East Asian	Indian Asian	Southeast Asian	Middle Eastern	European	Non-Hispanic Black	Non-Hispanic White	Hispanic
Cognitive and academic skills (percentile scores)											
Mental skills at 9 months	52	49	48	46	49	44	44	50	49	52	52
Mental skills at 2 years	35	40	35	57[b]	48	41	41	61[b]	43	58[b]	45
Early reading skills at 4 years	57	50	32[b]	70[b]	72[b]	54	54	65[b]	42[b]	57	43[b]
Early math skills at 4 years	52	51	38[b]	74[b]	68[b]	56	57	67[b]	41[b]	56	43
Early reading skills in kindergarten	60	56	37[b]	69[b]	77[b]	53	56	66	43[b]	55	47[b]
Early math skills in kindergarten	59	50	36[b]	73[b]	70[b]	54	59	66[b]	38[b]	57	44
Social behavior (preschool teacher rating) (1 = never, 5 = very often)											
Positive behaviors	3.7	3.8	3.8	3.9	3.9	3.8	3.6	3.8	3.8	3.9	3.8
Problem behaviors	1.8	2.1[a]	2.1	1.8	1.7[d]	2.0	2.1	2.0	2.2[c]	2.1	2.2

Notes: [a] indicates significant difference between children of Black African and children of Black Caribbean parents at p < 0.1 or better. [b] indicates significant difference between other groups of children versus children of Black Immigrants overall at p < 0.1 or better. [c] indicates significant difference between other groups of children and children of Black African immigrants only, at p < 0.1 or better. [d] indicates significant difference between other groups of children versus children of Black Caribbean Immigrants only, at p < 0.1 or better.

Source: Author calculations using the Early Childhood Longitudinal Study-Birth Cohort, 9-month—Kindergarten 2007 Restricted Use Data File, NCES.

African immigrant mothers tend to rate their children as being in very good to excellent health at nine months of age and are more likely to do so than most other groups of mothers. Caribbean mothers also report fairly positive levels of child health, on par with most other groups and significantly more positive than Hispanic immigrant mothers. The parent-reported health advantage of children in Black immigrant versus Hispanic immigrant families is generally maintained through kindergarten entry. Only European immigrant mothers report significantly and consistently better child health.

But on more objective measures of child weight, children of Black immigrants do not fare as well. Data on obesity and overweight status — based on BMI measurements — reveal alarmingly high rates of unhealthy weight among children of Black immigrants. A full third of Black immigrant children are categorized as overweight at age 4 and nearly 40 percent are overweight at kindergarten entry. Obesity rates are close to 20 percent at both time points. On these indicators, children of Black immigrants fare better than only their peers in Hispanic immigrant families.

2. Early Cognitive and Academic Skills

We find that group differences in children's cognitive skills (by families' region of origin and race/ethnicity) emerge by 24 months and persist through kindergarten entry. In general, the pattern of differences we observe suggests that children of Black immigrants make gains over time relative to some of their peers, particularly those in Hispanic immigrant and Black native-born families.

As infants, children of Black immigrants score at the 50th percentile on a measure of early mental abilities, a level similar to their peers in each of the other region-of-origin and race/ethnicity groups (see Table 4). By 24 months, however, children of African and Caribbean immigrants score in the 35th and 40th percentile respectively, falling behind children in East Asian, Indian Asian, and European immigrant families, as well as white native families. In preschool and kindergarten, East Asian, European, and Indian Asian immigrants maintain an advantage in terms of reading and math skills over children of Black immigrants on the order of 10 to 15 percentile points. At the same time, it is notable that children of Black immigrants do not score significantly lower than children in any of the native groups. In fact, with average percentile scores above 50, children of Black immigrants score higher on measures of early reading skills (in preschool and kindergarten) than children in Hispanic immigrant, Black native, and Hispanic native families. With respect to early math skills, children of Black immigrants hold a similar advantage relative to these groups (with the exception of Hispanic children of natives, who have comparable math scores).

3. Social Behavior in the Classroom

Other studies have shown that young children of immigrants often compare favorably to their peers with native-born parents in terms of social behavior. We find evidence of this for children of Black immigrants but primarily for those of African rather than Caribbean origin. Based on reports by their preschool teachers, children in African immigrant families displayed fewer problem behaviors than children in almost any other immigrant or native group. Although teachers rated children in Caribbean immigrant families as having more problematic behaviors than those in African immigrant families, problematic behavior levels for children in Caribbean families were on par with those for children in white native families. These generally positive findings for preschool-age children in Black immigrant families contrasts somewhat with those reported in a national study of school-age children, which found that kindergarten teachers rated the behavior of children of Black immigrants less positively than children in other immigrant groups.[36]

C. Children's Early Learning Experiences at Home and in Child Care

Our next set of results about the early childhood experiences of young children in Black immigrant families focuses on several factors that may play a role in promoting school readiness skills and may help explain racial/ethnic and nativity group differences in child outcomes. These variables include family economic well-being, the home learning environment, and children's participation in early education programs.

As noted earlier, Black immigrant families tend to have higher incomes during their child's first year than Hispanic immigrant families and Black native families but lower incomes than East Asian, Indian Asian, and European immigrant families and white native families. This general pattern appears to persist over time (see Table 5). Average family income levels over the first four years of the child's life indicate the same intergroup differences. At the same time, it is important to note that one-third of Black immigrant households report experiencing food insecurity at some point during their child's first four years. Many other immigrant and native groups experience similar levels of food insecurity. Two differences of note are that Black immigrant families face significantly more risk of food insecurity than East Asian or Indian immigrant families but less risk than Black native families.

While Black immigrant families fall in the middle of the distribution in terms of their financial and material resources, the parents rank high on measures of orientation toward education for their young children. Black immigrant parents report higher expectations for children's eventual educational attainment than every other group of parents except East Asian and Indian Asian immigrant parents. Caribbean immigrant parents are also more likely than other parents (with the exception of Black native parents) to say that preparing their child for kindergarten is a very important consideration in the decisions they make about child care. At the time of the 4-year survey, about 15 percent of Black immigrant parents expressed concerns that their child was not ready for kindergarten. This is a slightly lower percentage than reported in other native and immigrant groups, but the difference is not statistically significant.

---

36 Crosnoe and Turley, "K-12 Educational Outcomes of Immigrant Youth," 140.

Table 5. Family Economic Conditions, Parenting Practices, and Early Learning Experiences of Children Born in the United States in 2001, by Nativity, Race/Ethnicity, and Region

	Children of Black Immigrants		Children of Other Immigrants						Children of US-Born Parents		
	African	Caribbean	Hispanic	East Asian	Indian Asian	Southeast Asian	Middle Eastern	European	Non-Hispanic Black	Non-Hispanic White	Hispanic
Average family income-to-needs ratio, birth to age 4	2.3	2.3	1.5[b]	5.0[b]	4.4[b]	2.6	3.9	4.3[b]	1.4[b]	3.4[b]	2.1
Family experienced any food insecurity, birth to age 4	29%	36%	50%	11%[b]	9%[b]	31%	15%	15%	53%[b]	24%	39%
Parent educational expectations at 4-year survey (ranges from 1-6)	5.2	4.9	4.6[b]	4.8	5.2	4.5[b]	5.1	4.5[b]	4.2[b]	3.9[b]	4.1[b]
Parent considers kindergarten preparation very important in selecting child care for their 4-year old	83%	98%[a]	89%[d]	76%[d]	81%[d]	84%[d]	74%[d]	79%[d]	91%	81%[d]	87%[d]
Parent is concerned that their 4-year old child is not ready for kindergarten	13%	15%	20%	21%	13%	26%	21%	13%	16%	17%	20%
Primary child care arrangement during year prior to kindergarten											
Parental care	16%	3%[a]	27%[b]	9%	12%[d]	21%[d]	15%[d]	9%	13%[d]	16%[d]	18%[d]
Home-based care (non-parental)	13%	11%	17%	14%	10%	25%[b]	11%	13%	19%	20%[b]	25%[b]
Center-based care	71%	87%	57%[b]	77%	77%	53%[b]	74%	78%	68%[b]	64%[b]	57%[b]
Number of years in center care, age 2 to kindergarten	1.6	1.8	1.1[b]	1.7	1.6	1.1[b]	1.6	1.6	1.5	1.4[b]	1.2[b]
Preschool caregiver's level of education (ranges from 0-22)	17.2	17.0	14.6[b]	17.4	17.2	16.7	17.5	17.3	16.3	16.5	15.4
Child has participated in Head Start by age 4	21%	36%	29%	5%[b]	10%[b]	13%[b]	10%[b]	11%[b]	40%	10%[b]	24%
Average rating of warm, supportive parenting behavior, birth to age 4 (z-score with mean of 0)	-0.42	-0.37	-0.55	0.16[b]	0.01[b]	-0.22	-0.28	0.45[b]	-0.23	0.25[b]	-0.01[b]
Average level of developmentally stimulating activities and materials available in the home, birth to age 4 (ranges from 1-4)	2.4	2.4	2.3[b]	2.8[b]	2.6[b]	2.5	2.6	2.9[b]	2.4	2.9[b]	2.6[b]

Notes: [a] indicates significant difference between children of Black African and children of Black Caribbean parents at $p < 0.1$ or better. [b] indicates significant difference between other groups of children versus children of Black Immigrants overall at $p < 0.1$ or better. [c] indicates significant difference between other groups of children and children of Black African immigrants only, at p < 0.1 or better. ^d indicates significant difference between other groups of children versus children of Black Caribbean mmigrants only, at p < 0.1 or better.

Source: Author calculations using the Early Childhood Longitudinal Study-Birth Cohort, 9-month—Kindergarten 2007 Restricted Use Data File, NCES.

When it comes to early childhood education settings, children of Black immigrants are more likely than their peers in most other native and immigrant groups to attend center-based programs in the year prior to kindergarten.[37] Indeed, center enrollment rates are higher for 4-year-olds in Black immigrant families (particularly those from the Caribbean) than for children in all of the native-born groups, as well as for those in Hispanic immigrant families. The fact that children of Black immigrants experience more years of center-based care between the ages of 2 and 5 than children in other immigrant families and white native families suggests that they enter center-based settings at an earlier age. High rates of center-based care enrollment among Black children of immigrants may represent an important advantage in their early development. For preschool-aged children, especially those in low-income families, center-based programs tend to provide higher-quality learning environments than home-based programs.[38] Few differences are observed in preschool teachers' educational qualifications, although children of Black immigrants have teachers with higher levels of education than children in Hispanic immigrant families.[39]

The relative advantage of Black immigrant parents with respect to children's education is less evident when we examine early learning experiences in the home environment (at least as measured in the ECLS-B data we employed). Black immigrant parents tend to display fewer supportive parenting behaviors and provide fewer developmentally stimulating materials and activities to young children than East Asian, Indian Asian, and European immigrant parents and white and Hispanic native parents. On the other hand, children of Black immigrants appear to have greater access to learning materials at home than children of Hispanic immigrants.

D. What Factors Help Explain Early Academic Skill Differences between Children of Black Immigrants and Their Peers?

To better understand observed differences in the early academic skills

---

37 Center enrollment is used as a broad indicator of exposure to early childhood education; however, it is important to note that center-based settings vary widely in their structure, mission, and quality.

38 See, for example, Susanna Loeb, Margaret Bridges, Daphna Bassok, Bruce Fuller, and Russ W. Rumberger, "How Much is Too Much? The Influence of Preschool Centers on Children's Social and Cognitive Development," *Economics of Education Review* 26 (2007): 52–66; Magnuson et al., "Inequality in Preschool Education and School Readiness,"115–57.

39 Observations of program quality were conducted for only a subsample of ECLS-B participants, which includes very few children of Black immigrants. We use providers' education as a rough proxy of quality.

of children of Black immigrants relative to their peers, we conducted a series of regression analyses that examine the extent to which different variables can explain (or are associated with) group disparities in children's academic scores.[40]

I. Explaining Group Differences in Preschool Academic Skills

Black children of immigrants show higher preschool reading skills than Hispanic children — both those with immigrant parents and those with native-born parents — even when controlling for a variety of demographic, immigration, health, home environment, and child-care characteristics.[41] In other words, differences between Black children of immigrants and Hispanic children in reading ability persist even after accounting for intergroup differences in socioeconomic status, parenting practices, the home learning environment, early education settings, and the use of English language in the home. Black children of immigrants also show higher preschool reading skills than Black children of natives, but these differences are entirely accounted for by demographic and socioeconomic factors.

Black children of immigrants show lower reading skills than white and Asian children (in both immigrant and native families), but these differences disappear after controlling for socioeconomic factors. In other words, disadvantages in early reading for Black immigrants' children relative to other groups of children are due primarily to socioeconomic factors.

A similar pattern appears for preschool math skills, with Black children of immigrants showing significantly higher skill levels than Hispanic

---

40 Analyses were conducted using multiple regression techniques to predict children's skill scores from indicators of their race/ethnicity and parents' region of origin, as well as the various family, home, and child care variables that might contribute to group differences in skills.

41 For each of the four primary outcomes we analyze (reading and math skills in preschool and kindergarten), we begin with a baseline model (Model 1) that predicts children's early academic skills from their membership in a particular race/ethnic and nativity group. Model 2 takes into account several child and family demographic characteristics that are typically associated with child well-being (child age and gender, household size and structure, parent education and employment, and family income). Model 3 adds indicators of children's health and development in infancy (low birth weight, congenital anomalies, chronic health issues, and early mental skills), providing some indication of whether school readiness originates early in life or emerges over time. In Model 4 we introduce longitudinal measures of the home environment, including family economic well-being over time, parental warmth and support in interactions with children, and developmentally stimulating materials and activities. In Model 5 we add two indicators of children's exposure to early childhood education, namely, the number of years they participated in center-based care in the two to three years prior to kindergarten and whether they ever participated in Head Start. Finally, in Model 6 we add a measure of the primary caregiver's self-reported fluency in English to evaluate whether group differences in language use are associated with differences in children's academic skills, particularly for children in immigrant families. Tables with the regression results are available in the Appendix as Tables A-1, A-2, A-3, A-4, A-5 and A-6.

children even when controlling for socioeconomic status, home environment, parenting, early education settings, and home language. Once again, Black children of immigrants show lower preschool math skills than their peers in East Asian, Indian Asian, and European immigrant families, but their lower skills appear to be largely associated with differences in family demographic and socioeconomic characteristics. However, children of East Asian heritage maintain an advantage that changes little across the remaining models — even those that account for early education settings and parenting practices. Finally, differences between children of Black immigrants and children in white and Black native families diminish greatly when family socioeconomic status and other demographic variables are taken into account.

2. Explaining Group Differences in Kindergarten Academic Skills

Reading skills diverge somewhat among the various populations of children at the kindergarten level, relative to the preschool level. Black children of immigrants continue to show higher reading skill levels than Hispanic children (in both immigrant and native families) even when controlling for demographic and socioeconomic factors, the home environment, parenting practices, early education settings, and home language. Moreover, Black children of immigrants outperform both Black and white children of natives once socioeconomic controls are included. Thus, by kindergarten, children of Black immigrants appear to show a significant advantage in reading skills over the three largest demographic groups of children: Hispanic, Black, and white children of natives. Only children of Asian Indian immigrants display consistently higher reading scores than children of Black immigrants that cannot be fully explained by the variables we tested.

More of the differences in kindergarten math skills observed between children of Black immigrants and their peers appear to be related to basic socioeconomic and demographic characteristics than is the case for reading skills. Black children of immigrants have higher math scores than Black children in native families as well as Hispanic children in both native and immigrant families. But their advantage over Black and Hispanic natives' children seems to be related mostly to socioeconomic and demographic factors. After controlling for these factors, Black children of immigrants perform better on math only when compared with Hispanic children of immigrants.

Similarly, the lower math scores of Black immigrants' children relative to children in Indian Asian immigrant, European immigrant, and white native families are largely accounted for by sociodemographic differences among these groups. Only children of East Asian immigrants maintain a small advantage in kindergarten math scores once the full range of demographic, socioeconomic, family environment, and childcare factors are taken into account.

The regression models described here establish that most of the differences between children in Black immigrant families and other children in terms of reading and math scores in prekindergarten and kindergarten are related to demographic and socioeconomic factors. Once these factors are controlled for, children of Black immigrants perform on par with Black and white native-born parents and most other immigrant groups, with only a few exceptions. Children in East Asian or Asian Indian immigrant families are the two top scoring groups, and in some cases they perform better than Black children of immigrants even after demographic and socioeconomic characteristics, as well as aspects of the family environment and child care, are taken into account. At the same time, Black children of immigrants score consistently higher than Hispanic children of immigrants even when all of these factors are controlled.

3. Predictors of School Readiness among Children of Black Immigrants

We also examine differences between children in Black African and Caribbean families on these academic performance measures.[42] These analyses also show that children of African immigrants tend to outperform children of Caribbean immigrants, particularly on preschool assessments of reading skills. The gap in preschool reading between children of African versus Caribbean immigrants emerges when controlling for children's participation in center-based programs, suggesting that the high rate of center use by Caribbean parents helps to narrow the reading score gap between Caribbean and African children.

V. Final Thoughts

Using national longitudinal data for a birth cohort of American children, this study aims to describe the early childhood experiences of second-generation African and Caribbean immigrants and to examine the link between these experiences and children's early academic skills during the transition to school. Throughout, we compare the children of Black immigrant parents to their peers in other racial/ethnic groups (by parents' region of origin), identifying areas of relative advantage and disadvantage.

We find several areas of strength for Black immigrant families that are likely to support positive outcomes for their children. Like other researchers, we find that Black immigrant parents have relatively high

---

42 Because the sample of Black immigrant families is relatively small in the ECLS-B (n=150), we examine a reduced list of variables, including family income, food insecurity, supportive parenting practices, the home learning environment, and participation in center-based care. These factors have generally been associated with school readiness in other populations of children, and we find here that they predict preschool and kindergarten reading skills — but not math skills — among children of Black immigrants as well.

rates of marriage and employment and are more likely than many other immigrant groups to be fluent in English. Black immigrant mothers also report good health practices around the time of their child's birth. Compared to US-born mothers, they are much less likely to use alcohol, tobacco, or drugs during pregnancy and much more likely to breast-feed. Breastfeeding rates are higher for African immigrants than for any of the other immigrant groups we examined. It is not surprising then that Black children of immigrants appear to enjoy relatively good health during early childhood. They face less risk of low birth weight than children of Black US-born parents and fewer birth complications than children of Hispanic immigrants. Black immigrant parents consistently report that their children are in good overall health and are more likely to do so than Hispanic immigrant parents.

Beyond making investments in health, Black immigrant parents are also strongly oriented toward education for their children. Relative to some immigrant groups (e.g., Hispanic and Southeast Asian) and all of the major native groups, Black immigrant parents report high educational expectations for their children and are very likely to enroll them in center-based care during their preschool year. Center care use is particularly high among Caribbean immigrant families, who specifically identify preparation for kindergarten as a reason for selecting this type of child care.

Our descriptive analysis also reveals potential areas of disadvantage for young children in Black immigrant families. On most indicators of economic well-being, Black immigrant families fare better than Hispanic immigrants and Black natives but still experience more disadvantage than Asian and European immigrants and white natives. More than half are poor or near poor, with annual incomes below twice the federal poverty level. In terms of child outcomes, although many advantages are observed for children of Black immigrants in the health domain, approximately 40 percent are overweight (and nearly 20 percent are considered obese) by age 4. In this sense, children of Black immigrants compare unfavorably to children in most other immigrant groups (with the exception of Hispanics) and experience similar levels of risk for obesity as Black and Hispanic children with US-born parents.

A. Understanding Differences in School Readiness Skills between Children of Black Immigrants and Their Peers

Similar to other studies, ours finds evidence that developmental disparities across different groups defined by race/ethnicity and immigrant status begin early in life.[43] At age 2, children of Black immigrants score lower on a cognitive assessment than many of their peers in other groups (especially Asian and European immigrants, and white native families). However, by kindergarten, children of Black immigrants are

---

43 Fuller et al., "The Health and Cognitive Growth of Latino Toddlers."

doing relatively well in reading and math, outperforming Hispanic children in immigrant and native families as well as Black children in native families. Moreover, any disadvantage they face vis-à-vis other groups (with the potential exceptions of children in East Asian and Asian Indian immigrant families) can be largely accounted for by family socioeconomic status. When socioeconomic variables are controlled for, children of Black immigrants actually do better on reading assessments than several other groups, including white children in native families. Moreover, they fare consistently better than Hispanic immigrants' children, the largest group of children of immigrants.

Despite relatively high levels of parent education and employment, Black immigrant households often face considerable economic challenges.[44] Our findings suggest that efforts to reduce socioeconomic disadvantage in Black immigrant populations may serve as an investment in children's educational success. Another implication of this work is that strategies to promote positive outcomes among children of Black immigrants should build on identified areas of strength. For example, if recognized as a resource, children's language and literacy skills could be used to help support their development in other domains. In addition, the fact that so many Black immigrant families — a much higher percentage than has been observed for other immigrant groups — participate in early care and education programs should prompt a closer look at the quality and effectiveness of these settings for children of Black immigrants. Such programs might also serve as a valuable means of engaging with parents.

B. Understanding Variation in School Readiness Skills among Children of Black Immigrants

While our analysis of how academic skill differences across groups narrow or widen with the consideration of various factors is informative, it does not provide specific information about the extent to which certain experiences matter more for some groups than for others. In particular, more information is needed about the characteristics, resources, and practices that promote school success among children of Black immigrants, a population that has received much less research attention than other, more populous immigrant groups (e.g., Hispanic and Asian).

Within-group analyses conducted for this study suggest that Black children in immigrant families transition into kindergarten with better reading skills if their families have more income and if they experience warm and supportive parent-child interactions, have access to stimulating materials and activities at home, and attend center-based programs during their preschool years. Above and beyond these variables, having a parent of African versus Caribbean origin is associated with

---

44 Hernandez, Denton, and Macartney, "Children in Immigrant Families."

better reading scores in preschool; however, by kindergarten we find no significant differences by parental region of origin. This set of findings about the importance of early learning experiences in children's home and care environments is consistent with the broader school readiness literature, and suggests that general efforts to help parents provide these opportunities may benefit children of Black immigrants.

It is noteworthy, however, that even when we account for an extensive set of variables (including child and family characteristics, household resources, and aspects of the home and care environment), our analytic models explain only 10 to 20 percent of the variation in children's reading and math scores. This implies that factors beyond those examined here play a role and should be investigated. As just one example, the ECLS-B did not collect information about families' cultural beliefs and practices, but these may be important while considering children's development and academic progress.

C. Study Strengths and Limitations

The ECLS-B is a unique data source that offers several strengths with respect to the aims of this study. Using a variety of methods (e.g., parent, caregiver, and teacher surveys; observations and direct child assessments), it provides rich longitudinal data on multiple aspects of early childhood, including information about children's experiences across multiple contexts and their functioning across multiple developmental domains. Its collection of information about parents' country of origin, age at arrival, time in the United States, and several aspects of language use allow for the study of between-group and within-group diversity among immigrant families from several regions of the world.

Despite some advantages over other data sets, the ECLS-B lacks in-depth information about experiences particularly (or uniquely) relevant for immigrants — for example, parents' experiences in their country of origin and with the migration process, acculturation and families' efforts to maintain cultural beliefs and practices, and characteristics of receiving communities, such as available resources and public attitudes. These factors are likely to shape young children's experiences and opportunities, yet their inclusion in studies of educational outcomes among children of immigrants has been almost entirely limited to older children and adolescents.

Several caveats apply to the results presented in this chapter. First, our findings pertain only to second-generation African and Caribbean immigrant children (as a birth cohort study, the ECLS-B contains information only about children born in the United States). It is unclear how similar or different the pattern of results would be for children who immigrate to the United States with their parents at a very young age. That said, more than 90 percent of children younger than age 6 living in immigrant households are US citizens by birth.[45] Second, the nonexperimental nature of the data precludes us from making strong statements about causality. Our analytic models include a rich set of covariates, but our ability to conduct more sophisticated analyses to address causal questions is limited by small sample sizes, especially for our key group — Black children of immigrants. So although we find clear associations among family characteristics, early learning environments, and the development of academic skills, additional work is needed to identify the causal mechanisms that explain these links.

Future studies should intentionally include larger samples of children in Black immigrant families, which would permit more refined statistical analyses and also make it possible to identify important sources of heterogeneity (e.g., country of origin, parent education, refugee and immigration status) within this population.[46] Furthermore, longitudinal designs capturing development from early childhood through adolescence are needed to investigate whether the advantages observed for young children of Black immigrants are sustained over time, or if early gains are lost as children progress through school. One potentially important factor to consider is the extent to which Black children of immigrants encounter biased perceptions by their peers and teachers.

Finally, we note that discussions of school readiness have tended to focus heavily on the skills and abilities of children and the family role in contributing to these. However, another important component of school readiness is the extent to which schools and communities are ready to effectively serve and support all children. Although the current study is of the former type, we hope that the information it provides can contribute to discussions of the latter. ⤴

---

45 Karina Fortuny, Donald J. Hernandez, and Ajay Chaudry, *Young Children of Immigrants: The Leading Edge of America's Future* (Washington, DC: Urban Institute, 2010), www.urban.org/publications/412203.html.

46 See, for example, Donald J. Hernandez, *Changing Demography and Circumstances for Young Black Children in African and Caribbean Immigrant Families* (Washington, DC: Migration Policy Institute, 2012), www.migrationpolicy.org/pubs/CBI-Hernandez.pdf.

Appendix: Methodological Details

A. *Data Source*

Data for this project come from the Early Childhood Longitudinal Study-Birth Cohort (ECLS-B), a national prospective study of development for a sample of 14,000 children. Using a clustered, list-frame sampling design based on birth certificate data, the ECLS-B provides nationally representative information for the nearly 4 million infants born in the United States between January and December 2001. Several populations largely absent from other longitudinal studies of early childhood were oversampled in the ECLS-B, including children with low or very low birth weight, twins, and children of American Indian/ Native Alaskan, Asian/Pacific Islander, and Chinese heritage. Excluded from the sample were children with mothers younger than age 15, as well as those who died or were adopted prior to the initial data collection.

Through home visits, parent and caregiver interviews, child assessments, and child-care observations, the ECLS–B collected in-depth information about children's experiences from birth until kindergarten entry, across multiple contexts of development. The first data collection occurred approximately 9 months after birth, with subsequent surveys conducted at ages 2, 4, and 5 years (kindergarten entry for most). An additional data collection occurred in 2007–08 to capture kindergarten year information for the subsample of children who entered school at age 6. Overall response rates for the five data collections were 74 percent, 93 percent, 91 percent, 92 percent, and 93 percent, respectively. The ECLS-B — and its companion study the Early Childhood Longitudinal Study-Kindergarten Cohort (ECLS-K), which follows a cohort of children from Kindergarten to fifth grade — are being conducted by the National Center for Education Statistics (NCES) and the Institute of Education Sciences (IES), in collaboration with numerous federal health, education, and human service agencies. Detailed information about the ECLS datasets is available on the NCES Web site: http://nces. ed.gov/ecls/index.asp.

B. *Study Measures*

Family and household characteristics. Unless otherwise noted, these measures reflect data from the 9-month parent survey (i.e., the first wave in which data were collected) and provide a picture of family circumstances during children's first year of life including indicators of family structure (whether the primary caregiver is married, cohabiting, or single).

We also include the highest level of education completed by either resident parent in our analysis and educational attainment of both parents in the descriptive work. Parents' employment behavior is captured by indicators of whether the mother was employed in the year prior to the child's birth, is employed at the time of the 9-month interview, and whether there is an employed spouse or partner in the household at 9 months. We also include the ratio of family income to the federal poverty level, which is adjusted for household size; a dichotomous indicator of household food insecurity based on items and methods outlined in the US Department of Agriculture *Guide to Measuring Household Food Security*; and indicators of home and car ownership.[47] To capture household economic conditions over time, we also create two summary variables — the *average* ratio of income to the poverty level across the first three waves of the study (9 months, 2 years, and 4 years) and a dichotomous variable indicating whether the family experienced any food insecurity across the first three waves.

Characteristics of immigrant households. In addition to information about parents' country of origin, the ECLS-B collected information about their age at arrival in the United States, citizenship status, and multiple questions about their language use. Our analysis of these characteristics reflects information for the primary caregiver (mother in the majority of cases). For families where the primary caregiver was US born, information for the other (foreign-born) parent was used. The two language variables we focus on are whether or not the caregiver's primary language is English and whether the caregiver is fluent in English (based on an average self-rating of "good" or "excellent" in speaking, reading, and writing English). The second variable accounts for the fact that some parents may primarily speak their heritage language at home and with family, but also have some level of fluency in English.

Birth outcomes and indicators of child health. To assess family health behaviors we included indicators of whether mothers received prenatal care in their first trimester; whether mothers smoked cigarettes, drank alcohol, or used drugs during pregnancy; and whether infants were breastfed. In terms of child health, we include indicators of low birth weight (<2,500 grams), a multiple birth, extended stay in the hospital following birth, the presence of chronic health or medical conditions at birth, and parent ratings of overall child health at 9 months, 2 years, 4 years, and in kindergarten (1=poor, 5=excellent). Finally, we also examine group differences in children's weight at age 4 and the kindergarten year, given growing concerns about this aspect of health and its implications for development and well-being. Direct assessments of children's height and weight during the home visit were used to calculate their Body Mass Index (BMI). Using growth charts (by gender and age) and guidelines provided by the Centers for Disease Control, chil-

---

47 Gary Bickel, Mark Nord, Cristofer Price, William Hamilton, and John Cook, *Guide to Measuring Household Food Security, Revised 2000* (Alexandria, VA: US Department of Agriculture, Food and Nutrition Service, 2000), www.fns.usda.gov/fsec/FILES/FSGuide.pdf.

dren with BMI above the 85th percentile were identified as overweight, and those above the 95th percentile were identified as obese.

Children's early cognitive development. The Bayley Short Form-Research Edition (BSF-R) was designed specifically for the ECLS-B and retains all of the psychometric properties of the Bayley Scales of Infant Development-II (BSID-II).[48] The mental scale of the BSF-R measures early cognitive and language development, as evidenced by memory, expressive and receptive vocabulary, reasoning, problem solving, and concept attainment (NCES 2005). The majority of children were assessed in English, although home languages were used whenever possible.

Home learning environment. To measure the early learning environment, we focus on three ways by which parents and family members might influence young children's development — their direct interactions with children, the provision of developmentally stimulating materials and activities, and the emphasis they place on education.

As part of the 9-month, 2-year, and 4-year home visits, parents were given an age-appropriate "teaching" task to complete with their child. Parent-child interactions during this activity were videotaped and later coded by trained research staff for their level of sensitivity, positive and negative regard, and cognitive stimulation. To create a composite variable of positive parenting behaviors across the three time points, we standardized the scores on each measure and then computed an average score for *warm and supportive parenting* (M=0, SD=1).

Parents were asked about children's access to developmentally stimulating materials (e.g., children's books, puzzles) and their engagement in developmentally supportive activities with children (i.e., reading, telling stories, singing, and visiting the library, museums, or the zoo) at 9 months, 2 years, and 4 years. For the analyses presented here, we created a composite score on *developmentally stimulating materials and activities* across these three time points

A third aspect of the home learning environment that may influence children's academic outcomes is parents' beliefs and expectations regarding education. In the 4-year old survey, parents reported how far in school they expected their child to go, and how important preparation for kindergarten (as one of a list of features) was to them in selecting care for their child.

---

48   Carol Andreassen and Philip Fletcher, *Early Childhood Longitudinal Study, Birth Cohort (ECLS-B) Methodology Report for the Nine-Month Data Collection (2001–02), Volume 1: Psychometric Characteristics*, NCES 2005–100 (Washington, DC: US Department of Education, National Center for Education Statistics, 2005); Mark Nord, Margaret Andrews, and Steven Carlson, *Household Food Security In The United States, 2003* (Food Assistance and Nutrition Research Reports 33835, US Department of Agriculture, Economic Research Service, Washington, DC, 2004).

Early care and education experiences. At each survey wave, parents provided details about the nonparental care arrangements that children experienced on a regular basis, including information about type, hours in care, and cost. Based on these data, we create an indicator variable for whether or not children are attending a center-based program in the year before they enter kindergarten (at approximately age 4 or 5, depending on year of school entry) and the number of years of center-based care between age 2 and kindergarten entry. Descriptively, we also note whether children have ever participated in Head Start, as one of the largest federal early intervention programs which serves a large proportion of ethnic and language minority children.

Children's academic skills at the transition to school. Children's emergent reading and mathematic skills were assessed during the preschool and kindergarten data collections using cognitive batteries from the ECLS-K.[49] We standardize assessment scores by child age and then convert them to percentile scores ranging from 1 to 100 to provide information about where children's abilities rank relative to their same age peers.

Children's behavior at the transition to school. Although our primary focus is on children's academic skills in preschool and kindergarten, we include descriptive information about children's social behavior at these two time points, as this is an important predictor of the likelihood that children will make a successful transition to school. During the preschool year, mothers and early care and education providers rated children's behavior using a subset of items from the *Preschool and Kindergarten Behavioral Scales — Second Edition* (PKBS-2) and *Social Skills Rating System.*[50] In addition, during the kindergarten year, teachers answered a similar set of questions about children's behavior. Two variables were constructed for the frequencies of positive behaviors and problem behaviors — both scaled from 1 ("never") to 5 ("very often").

---

49 NCES, *Early Childhood Longitudinal Study, Kindergarten Class of 1998–99 (ECLS-K).* See Donald A. Rock and Judith M. Pollack, *Early Childhood Longitudinal Study — Kindergarten Class of 1998-99 (ECLS-K), Psychometric Report for Kindergarten Though First Grade* (Publication No. NCES 2002-05, NCES, Washington, DC, 2002), http://nces.ed.gov/pubs2002/200205.pdf.
50 Kenneth Merrell, *Preschool and Kindergarten Behavior Scales — Second Edition* (Austin, TX: PRO-ED, 2003); Frank M. Gresham and Stephen N. Elliot, *Social Skills Rating System* (Circle Pines, MN: American Guidance Service, 1990).

C. Multivariate Regression Results

Table A-1. OLS Regressions Predicting Preschool Reading Skills for Children of Black Immigrants Relative to Their Peers Born in the United States in 2001

	Preschool Reading Skills					
	Model 1: No covariates	Model 2: M1+basic demographics[a]	Model 3: M2+child developmental status at 9 months[b]	Model 4: M3+home environment, birth-PK[c]	Model 5: M4+early care and education[d]	Model 6: M5+language use[e]
Children of Black immigrants	omitted, comparison group					
Children of Hispanic immigrants	-21.44***	-15.44***	-16.22***	-16.02***	-15.00***	-15.60***
Children of East Asian immigrants	18.06***	2.403	2.015	0.0452	1.171	1.082
Children of Indian Asian immigrants	19.58***	4.576	3.741	4.367	5.318	5.308
Children of Southeast Asian immigrants	2.371	0.0188	0.510	0.244	1.776	1.702
Children of Middle Eastern immigrants	2.246	-9.954+	-9.224+	-10.14+	-9.071	-9.110
Children of European immigrants	12.90**	1.457	0.425	-3.881	-2.902	-2.700
Children of Non-Hispanic Black natives	-10.39***	-4.163	-4.470	-5.418+	-4.739	-4.305
Children of Non-Hispanic White natives	4.377+	-0.866	-1.230	-5.761*	-4.382	-3.995
Children of Hispanic natives	-8.921**	-6.487*	-6.873*	-9.688**	-8.473**	-8.103*
Children of Asian/Pacific Islander natives	3.652	4.352	5.640	1.845	4.124	4.512
Children of American Indian/Alaskan natives	-19.68***	-13.81***	-15.06***	-15.88***	-15.27***	-14.82***
Children of multiracial natives	-2.354	-2.334	-2.650	-5.154	-3.939	-3.528
Constant	52.20***	4.502	2.991	-10.09	-12.87*	-9.793
R2	0.110	0.280	0.288	0.327	0.331	0.331

Notes: Estimates are weighted by W3C0 to account for sampling design. Standard deviations appear in parentheses.

[a] Demographic variables included in the model are child age (in months), child is a boy, mother is single, household size, highest level of parent education, mother employed at 9 months, spouse/partner employed at 9 months, income-to-needs ratio (based on federal poverty threshold, adjusted for family size). [b] Measures of infant developmental status include an indicator of low birth weight, an indicator of chronic health condition at birth, and the child's score on the Bayley scales of mental development, administered at the 9-month visit. [c] Home environment variables include an average income-to-needs ratio across Time 1 (9 months), Time 2 (2 years) and Time 3 (4 years); a dichotomous indicator of any household food insecurity across T1-T3; a composite of positive parenting interactions, T1-T3; and a composite score for developmentally stimulating materials and activities, T1-T3. [d] Children's experiences in early care and education programs are captured by number of years in center-based care T2-T3. [e] Measures of the child's language environment include whether the primary home language is English and the primary caregiver's fluency in spoken and written English.

Source: Author calculations using the Early Childhood Longitudinal Study-Birth Cohort, 9-month—Kindergarten 2007 Restricted Use Data File, National Center for Education Statistics, US Department of Education.

Table A-2. OLS Regressions Predicting Preschool Math Skills for Children of Black Immigrants Relative to Their Peers Born in the United States in 2001

	Preschool Math Skills					
	Model 1: No covariates	Model 2: M1+basic demographics[a]	Model 3: M2+child developmental status at 9 months[b]	Model 4: M3+home environment, birth-PK[c]	Model 5: M4+early care and education[d]	Model 6: M5+language use[e]
Children of Black immigrants	omitted, comparison group					
Children of Hispanic immigrants	-13.81***	-7.849**	-8.534**	-7.873**	-6.780*	-8.819**
Children of East Asian immigrants	23.08***	7.742*	8.395*	7.019*	8.045*	7.765*
Children of Indian Asian immigrants	16.65***	2.326	2.772	4.036	5.129	5.085
Children of Southeast Asian immigrants	4.624	2.241	3.959	4.018	5.445	5.157
Children of Middle Eastern immigrants	6.092	-4.756	-4.307	-5.186	-4.296	-4.594
Children of European immigrants	16.29***	4.922	5.094	2.100	2.970	3.625
Children of Non-Hispanic Black natives	-9.893***	-3.863	-4.063	-4.559	-3.843	-2.386
Children of Non-Hispanic White natives	4.576+	-0.534	-0.545	-3.750	-2.495	-1.198
Children of Hispanic natives	-7.837*	-5.608+	-6.160*	-8.119*	-6.980*	-5.733+
Children of Asian/Pacific Islander natives	5.310	5.556	7.454	4.315	6.574	7.877
Children of American Indian/Alaskan natives	-21.29***	-14.43***	-14.84***	-14.89***	-14.03***	-12.49***
Children of multiracial natives	-4.582	-4.482	-4.533	-6.533+	-5.342	-3.958
Constant	51.05***	-3.791	-4.350	-12.92+	-15.40*	-5.107
R2	0.082	0.245	0.255	0.283	0.287	0.289

Notes: Estimates are weighted by W3C0 to account for sampling design. Standard deviations appear in parentheses.

[a] Demographic variables included in the model are child age (in months), child is a boy, mother is single, household size, highest level of parent education, mother employed at 9 months, spouse/partner employed at 9 months, income-to-needs ratio (based on federal poverty threshold, adjusted for family size). [b] Measures of child developmental status at 9 months of age include an indicator of low birth weight, an indicator of chronic health condition at birth, and the child's score on the Bayley scales of mental development, administered at the 9-month visit. [c] Home environment variables include an average income-to-needs ratio across Time 1 (9 months), Time 2 (2 years), and Time 3 (4 years); a dichotomous indicator of any household food insecurity across T1-T3; a composite of positive parenting interactions, T1-T3; and a composite score for developmentally stimulating materials and activities, T1-T3. [d] Children's experiences in early care and education programs are captured number of years in center-based care, T2-T3.

e Measures of the child's language environment include whether the primary home language is English and the primary caregiver's fluency in spoken and written English.
+ p<0.1 * p<0.05 ** p<0.01 *** p<0.001
Source: Author calculations using the Early Childhood Longitudinal Study-Birth Cohort, 9-month—Kindergarten 2007 Restricted Use Data File, NCES.

Table A-3. OLS Regressions Predicting Kindergarten Reading Skills for Children of Black Immigrants Relative to Their Peers Born in the United States in 2001

	Kindergarten Reading Skills					
	Model 1: No covariates	Model 2: M1+basic demographics[a]	Model 3: M2+child developmental status at 9 months[b]	Model 4: M3+home environment, birth-PK[c]	Model 5: M4+early care and education[d]	Model 6: M5+language use[e]
Children of Black immigrants	omitted, comparison group					
Children of Hispanic immigrants	-19.40***	-12.90***	-12.35***	-11.92***	-11.13**	-11.55**
Children of East Asian immigrants	12.71***	0.360	2.581	0.877	1.301	1.228
Children of Indian Asian immigrants	20.08***	8.071+	8.807*	9.179*	9.713*	9.701*
Children of Southeast Asian immigrants	-3.348	-4.695	-3.290	-3.392	-2.437	-2.509
Children of Middle Eastern immigrants	-1.246	-9.417	-5.617	-5.732	-5.454	-5.582
Children of European immigrants	9.077*	-2.493	-2.562	-6.399	-5.881	-5.759
Children of Non-Hispanic Black natives	-13.90***	-7.963*	-6.918*	-7.680*	-7.173*	-6.914*
Children of Non-Hispanic White natives	-1.876	-7.281*	-6.717*	-10.10**	-9.498**	-9.279**
Children of Hispanic natives	-10.20***	-7.066*	-7.249*	-9.261**	-8.529*	-8.309*
Children of Asian/Pacific Islander natives	-4.677	-6.905	-7.701	-11.14	-9.372	-9.150
Children of American Indian/Alaskan natives	-22.43***	-15.96***	-15.25***	-16.22***	-14.96***	-14.69***
Children of multiracial natives	-7.708+	-9.295+	-8.575*	-11.13*	-10.49*	-10.26*
Constant	56.78***	6.498	1.477	-4.120	-3.011	-1.595
R2	0.071	0.201	0.215	0.234	0.239	0.239

Notes: Estimates are weighted by WK1C0 to account for sampling design. Standard deviations appear in parentheses.
[a] Demographic variables included in the model are child age (in months), child is a boy, mother is single, household size, highest level of parent education, mother employed at 9 months, spouse/partner employed at 9 months, income-to-needs ratio (based on federal poverty threshold, adjusted for family size). [b] Measures of child developmental status at 9 months of age include an indicator of low birth weight, an indicator of chronic health condition at birth, and the child's score on the Bayley scales of mental development, administered at the 9-month visit. [c] Home environment variables include an average income-to-needs ratio

across Time 1 (9 months), Time 2 (2 years), and Time 3 (4 years); a dichotomous indicator of any household food insecurity across T1-T3; a composite of positive parenting interactions, T1-T3; and a composite score for developmentally stimulating materials and activities, T1-T3. [d] Children's experiences in early care and education programs are captured number of years in center-based care, T2-T3. [e] Measures of the child's language environment include whether the primary home language is English and the primary caregiver's fluency in spoken and written English.
+ p<0.1 * p<0.05 ** p<0.01 *** p<0.001
Source: Author calculations using the Early Childhood Longitudinal Study-Birth Cohort, 9-month—Kindergarten 2007 Restricted Use Data File, NCES.

Table A-4. OLS Regressions Predicting Kindergarten Math Skills for Children of Black Immigrants Relative to Their Peers Born in the United States in 2001

	Kindergarten Math Skills					
	Model 1: No covariates	Model 2: M1+basic demographics[a]	Model 3: M2+child developmental status at 9 months[b]	Model 4: M3+home environment, birth-PK[c]	Model 5: M4+early care and education[d]	Model 6: M5+language use[e]
Children of Black immigrants	omitted, comparison group					
Children of Hispanic immigrants	-16.42***	-10.29**	-9.629**	-8.430*	-8.181*	-10.05**
Children of East Asian immigrants	20.09***	6.726	9.650*	8.201+	8.244+	7.922+
Children of Indian Asian immigrants	18.01***	5.014	5.685	6.384	6.119	6.069
Children of Southeast Asian immigrants	1.694	-0.387	2.305	3.388	3.631	3.318
Children of Middle Eastern immigrants	6.265	-1.954	0.314	0.944	0.897	0.326
Children of European immigrants	13.91**	2.037	3.880	1.149	1.212	1.763
Children of Non-Hispanic Black natives	-14.13***	-8.128*	-7.027*	-7.086*	-6.905+	-5.743
Children of Non-Hispanic White natives	4.755+	-1.069	-0.0931	-3.138	-3.043	-2.059
Children of Hispanic natives	-8.208**	-5.646	-5.256	-6.673+	-6.478+	-5.489
Children of Asian/Pacific Islander natives	0.778	-1.638	-0.370	-3.902	-3.434	-2.429
Children of American Indian/Alaskan natives	-19.52***	-13.29***	-12.22**	-12.39***	-11.81**	-10.62**
Children of multiracial natives	-4.130	-5.634	-5.196	-7.462+	-7.298+	-6.265
Constant	52.44***	-9.447	-18.40*	-26.67**	-25.66**	-19.28+
R2	0.108	0.243	0.261	0.286	0.287	0.288

Notes: Estimates are weighted by WK1C0 to account for sampling design. Standard deviations appear in parentheses.
[a] Demographic variables included in the model are child age (in months), child is a boy, mother is single, household size, highest level of parent education, mother employed at 9 months, spouse/partner employed at 9 months, income-to-needs ratio (based on federal poverty threshold, adjusted for family size). [b] Measures of child developmental status at 9

months of age include an indicator of low birth weight, an indicator of chronic health condition at birth, and the child's score on the Bayley scales of mental development, administered at the 9-month visit. ᶜ Home environment variables include an average income-to-needs ratio across Time 1 (9 months), Time 2 (2 years), and Time 3 (4 years); a dichotomous indicator of any household food insecurity across T1-T3; a composite of positive parenting interactions, T1-T3; and a composite score for developmentally stimulating materials and activities, T1-T3. ᵈ Children's experiences in early care and education programs are captured number of years in center-based care, T2-T3. ᵉ Measures of the child's language environment include whether the primary home language is English and the primary caregiver's fluency in spoken and written English.

+ p<0.1 * p<0.05 ** p<0.01 *** p<0.001

Source: Author calculations using the Early Childhood Longitudinal Study-Birth Cohort, 9-month—Kindergarten 2007 Restricted Use Data File, NCES.

Table A-5. Regression Analysis of Predictors of Pre-Kindergarten Academic Skills Among Children of Black Immigrants Born in the United States in 2001

	Preschool Reading Skills			Preschool Math Skills		
	(1)	(2)	(3)	(4)	(5)	(6)
Children of African immigrant parents	omitted, comparison group			omitted, comparison group		
Children of Caribbean immigrant parents	-8.782	-9.243	-12.12*	-3.755	-4.025	-4.809
Child age at time of assessment (in months)	0.677	0.914	1.004+	1.427***	1.570***	1.622***
Bayley mental skills score at 9 months (percentile score)	0.166	0.142	0.0682	0.204*	0.192*	0.158
Average income-to-needs ratio, T1-T3		3.656***	2.082*		1.844*	1.753
Any experience of household food insecurity, T1-T3		-4.619	-4.101		-3.978	-2.410
Warm, supportive parenting composite score, T1-T3			8.741*			3.918
Developmentally stimulating activities composite score, T1-T3			2.236			-4.603
Number of years in center-based care, T2-T4			4.047+			2.251
Constant	14.91	-3.535	-7.794	-31.64	-41.71+	-33.88
R²	0.051	0.147	0.230	0.086	0.114	0.122
F for change in R²	3.57*	13.18***	4.42**	3.97**	2.14	0.80

Notes: Estimates are weighted by W3C0 to account for sampling design. Coefficients shown are unstandardized. Robust standard errors (estimated using jackknife method) appear in parentheses.

+ p<0.10 * p<0.05 ** p<0.01 *** p<0.001

Source: Author calculations using the Early Childhood Longitudinal Study-Birth Cohort, 9-month—Kindergarten 2007 Restricted Use Data File, NCES.

Table A-6. Regression Analysis of Predictors of Kindergarten Academic Skills Among Children of Black Immigrants Born in the United States in 2001

	Kindergarten Reading Skills			Kindergarten Math Skills		
	(1)	(2)	(3)	(4)	(5)	(6)
Children of African immigrant parents	omitted, comparison group			omitted, comparison group		
Children of Caribbean immigrant parents	-5.895	-4.494	-4.785	-3.755	-4.025	-4.809
Child age at time of assessment (in months)	0.886	0.958	1.094	1.427***	1.570***	1.622***
Bayley mental skills score at 9 months (percentile score)	0.179+	0.144	0.122	0.204*	0.192*	0.158
Average income-to-needs ratio, T1-T3		2.015*	0.565		1.844*	1.753
Any experience of household food insecurity, T1-T3		-6.772	-6.632		-3.978	-2.410
Warm, supportive parenting composite score, T1-T3			0.931			3.918
Developmentally stimulating activities composite score, T1-T3			12.82+			-4.603
Number of years in center-based care, T2-T4			0.0814			2.251
Constant	-8.973	-15.95	-50.74	-31.64	-41.71+	-33.88
R^2	0.056	0.103	0.147	0.086	0.114	0.122
F for change in R^2	1.73	3.83*	1.01	4.37**	3.93*	0.24

Notes: Estimates are weighted by WK1C0 to account for sampling design. Coefficients shown are unstandardized. Robust standard errors (estimated using jackknife method) appear in parentheses.

+ $p<0.1$ * $p<0.05$ ** $p<0.01$ *** $p<0.001$

Source: Author calculations using the Early Childhood Longitudinal Study-Birth Cohort, 9-month—Kindergarten 2007 Restricted Use Data File, NCES.

Works Cited

Andreassen, Carol and Philip Fletcher. 2005. *Early Childhood Longitudinal Study, Birth Cohort* (ECLS-B) *Methodology Report for the Nine-Month Data Collection* (2001–02), Volume 1: Psychometric Characteristics, NCES 2005–100. Washington, DC: US Department of Education, National Center for Education Statistics.

Batalova, Jeanne and Michael Fix. 2008. *Uneven Progress: The Employment Pathways of Skilled Immigrants in the United States.* Washington, DC: Migration Policy Institute. www.migrationpolicy.org/pubs/BrainWasteOct08.pdf.

Bickel, Gary, Mark Nord, Cristofer Price, William Hamilton, and John Cook. 2000. *Guide to Measuring Household Food Security, Revised 2000.* Alexandria, VA: US Department of Agriculture, Food and Nutrition Service. www.fns.usda.gov/fsec/FILES/FSGuide.pdf.

Brooks-Gunn, Jeanne and Lisa B. Markman. 2005. The Contribution of Parenting to Ethnic and Racial Gaps in School Readiness. *Future of Children* 15 (1): 139–68.

Brown, Susan K. and Frank D. Bean. 2006. Assimilation Models, Old and New: Explaining a Long- Term Process. *Migration Information Source* special issue on the second generation, October 2006. www.migrationinformation.org/USfocus/display.cfm?ID=442.

Case, Anne, Darren Lubotsky, and Christina Paxson. 2002. Economic Status and Health in Childhood: The Origins of the Gradient. *American Economic Review* 92 (5): 1308–34.

Crosnoe, Robert. 2006. Health and the Education of Children from Race/Ethnic Minority and Immigrant Families. *Journal of Health and Social Behavior* 47 (1): 77-93.

Crosnoe, Robert and Ruth López Turley. 2011. K-12 Educational Outcomes of Immigrant Youth. *Future of Children* 21: 129–52.

De Feyter, Jessica and Adam Winsler. 2009. The Early Developmental Competencies and School Readiness of Low-Income, Immigrant Children: Influences of Generation, Race/Ethnicity, and National Origins. *Early Childhood Research Quarterly* 24: 411–31.

Feliciano, Cynthia. 2005. Educational Selectivity in US Immigration: How Do Immigrants Compare to Those Left Behind? *Demography* 42 (1): 131–52.

Flanagan, Kristen and Jerry West. 2004. *Children Born in 2001: First Results from the Base Year of the Early Childhood Longitudinal Study, Birth Cohort*, NCES 2005–036. Washington, DC: US Department of Education, National Center for Education Statistics. http://nces.ed.gov/pubs2005/children/.

Fortuny, Karina, Donald J. Hernandez, and Ajay Chaudry. 2010. *Young Children of Immigrants: The Leading Edge of America's Future.* Washington, DC: Urban Institute. www.urban.org/publications/412203.html.

Fortuny, Karina, Randolph Capps, Margaret Simms, and Ajay Chaudry. 2009. *Children of Immigrants: National and State Characteristics.* Washington, DC: Urban Institute. www.urban.org/publications/411939.html.

Fuligni, Andrew J. 1997. The Academic Achievement of Adolescents from Immigrant Families: The Roles of Family Background, Attitudes, and Behavior. *Child Development* 68: 351–63.

Fuller, Bruce, Margaret Bridges, Edward Bein, Heeju Jang, Sunyoung Jung, Sophia Rabe-Hesketh, Neal Halfon, and Alice Kuo. 2009. The Health and Cognitive Growth of Latino Toddlers: At Risk or Immigrant Paradox? *Maternal and Child Health* 13: 755–68.

Gresham, Frank M. and Stephen N. Elliot. *Social Skills Rating System.* 1990. Circle Pines, MN: American Guidance Service.

Glick, Jennifer E. and Bryndl Hohmann-Marriott. 2007. Academic Performance of Young Children in Immigrant Families: The Significance of Race, Ethnicity, and National Origin. *International Migration Review* 41: 371–402.

Glick, Jennifer E., Littisha Bates, and Scott T. Yabiku. 2009. Mother's Age at Arrival in the United States and Early Cognitive Development. *Early Childhood Research Quarterly* 24: 367–80.

Han, Wen Jui. 2008. The Academic Trajectories of Children of Immigrants and Their School Environments. *Developmental Psychology* 44 (6): 1572–90.

Hernandez, Donald J. 2004. Demographic Change and the Life Circumstances of Immigrants. *Future of Children* 14 (2): 16–47.

_____. 2012. *Changing Demography and Circumstances for Young Black Children in African and Caribbean Immigrant Families.* Washington, DC: Migration Policy Institute. www.migrationpolicy.org/pubs/CBI-Hernandez.pdf.

Hernandez, Donald J., Nancy Denton, and Suzanne E. Macartney. 2008. Children in Immigrant Families: Looking to America's Future. *Social Policy Report* 23 (3): 3–23.

Humes, Karen R., Nicholas A. Jones, and Roberto R. Ramirez. 2011. *Overview of Race and Hispanic Origin: 2010.* 2010 Census Briefs C201BR-02, US Census Bureau, Washington, DC. www.census.gov/prod/cen2010/briefs/c2010br-02.pdf.

Keating, Daniel P. and Sharon Z. Simonton. 2008. Health Effects of Human Development Policies. In *Making Americans Healthier: Social and Economic Policy as Health Policy*, eds. James House, Robert Schoeni, Harold Pollack, and George Kaplan. New York: Russell Sage.

Kent, Mary Mederios. 2007. Immigration and America's Black Population. *Population Bulletin* 62: 3–16. www.prb.org/pdf07/62.4immigration.pdf.

Lee, Valerie E. and David T. Burkam. 2002. *Inequality at the Starting Gate: Social Background Differences in Achievement as Children Begin School.* Washington, DC: Economic Policy Institute.

Leventhal, Tama, Yange Xue, and Jeanne Brooks-Gunn. 2006. Immigrant Differences in School-Age Children's Verbal Trajectories: A Look at Four Racial/Ethnic Groups. *Child Development* 77 (5): 1359–74.

Loeb, Susanna, Margaret Bridges, Daphna Bassok, Bruce Fuller, and Russ W. Rumberger. 2007. How Much is Too Much? The Influence of Preschool Centers on Children's Social and Cognitive Development. *Economics of Education Review* 26: 52–66.

Magnuson, Katherine and Jane Waldfogel. 2005. Early Childhood Care and Education: Effects on Ethnic and Racial Gaps in School Readiness. *Future of Children* 15 (1): 169–96.

Magnuson, Katherine, Claudia Lahaie, and Jane Waldfogel. 2006. Preschool and School Readiness of Children of Immigrants. *Social Science Quarterly* 87: 1241–62.

Magnuson, Katherine A., Marcia K. Meyers, M., Christopher J. Ruhm, and Jane Waldfogel. 2004. Inequality in Preschool Education and School Readiness. *American Educational Research Journal* 41: 115–57.

Merrell, Kenneth. 2003. *Preschool and Kindergarten Behavior Scales — Second Edition*. Austin, TX: PRO-ED.

Mistry, Rashmita S., Jeremy C. Biesanz, Nina Chien, Carolee Howes, and Aprile D. Benner. 2008. Socioeconomic Status, Parental Investments, and the Cognitive and Behavioral Outcomes of Low-Income Children from Immigrant and Native Households. *Early Childhood Research Quarterly* 23: 193–212.

National Research Council and Institute of Medicine. 2000. *From Neurons to Neighborhoods: The Science of Early Childhood Development.* Washington, DC: National Academies Press.

Nord, Christine Winquist, Jean Lennon, Baiming Liu, and Kathryn Chandler. 1999. *Home Literacy Activities and Signs of Children's Emerging Literacy, 1993 and 1999*, NCES 2000-02rev. Washington, DC: National Center for Education Statistics. http://nces.ed.gov/pubs2000/2000026.pdf.

Nord, Mark, Margaret Andrews, and Steven Carlson. 2004. *Household Food Security in The United States, 2003.* Food Assistance and Nutrition Research Reports 33835, US Department of Agriculture, Economic Research Service, Washington, DC.

Nord, Christine, Brad Edwards, Carol Andreassen, James L. Green, and Kathleen Wallner-Allen. 2006. *Early Childhood Longitudinal Study, Birth Cohort, (ECLS-B), User's Manual for the ECLS-B Longitudinal 9-Month–2-Year Data File and Electronic Codebook*, NCES 2006-046. Washington, DC: US Department of Education, National Center for Education Statistics.

Ornelas, India, Krista Perreira, Linda Beeber, and Lauren Maxwell. 2009. Challenges and Strategies to Maintaining Emotional Health: Qualitative Perspectives of Mexican Immigrant Mothers. *Journal of Family Issues* 30: 1556-75.

Palacios, Natalia, Katarina Guttmannova, and Lindsay P. Chase-Lansdale. 2008. Early Reading Achievement of Children in Immigrant Families: Is There an Immigrant Paradox? *Developmental Psychology* 44: 1381–95.

Phillips, Meredith, James Crouse, and John Ralph. 1998. Does the Black-White Test Score Gap Widen after Children Enter School? In *The Black-White Test Score Gap*, eds. Christopher Jencks and Meredith Phillips. Washington, DC: The Brookings Institution.

Rathbun, Amy and Jerry West. 2004. *From Kindergarten through Third Grade: Children's Beginning School Experiences*, NCES 2004–007. Washington, DC: US Government Printing Office. http://nces.ed.gov/pubsearch/pubsinfo.asp?pubid=2004007.

Reardon-Anderson, Jane, Randolph Capps, and Michael E. Fix. 2002. The Health and Well-Being of Children in Immigrant Families. New Federalism: National Survey of America's Families Policy Brief B-52. Washington, DC: Urban Institute. www.urban.org/publications/310584.html.

Rock, Donald A. and Judith M. Pollack. 2002. *Early Childhood Longitudinal Study — Kindergarten Class of 1998-99 (ECLS-K), Psychometric Report for Kindergarten Though First Grade*, NCES 2002-05. Washington, DC: US Department of Education, National Center for Education Statistics. http://nces.ed.gov/pubs2002/200205.pdf.

Sektnan, Michaella, Megan McClelland, Alan Acock, and Fred Morrison. 2010. Relations between Early Family Risk, Children's Behavioral Regulation, and Academic Achievement. *Early Childhood Research Quarterly* 25: 464–79.

Thomas, Kevin J. A. 2009. Parental Characteristics and the Schooling Progress of the Children of Immigrant and US-Born Blacks. *Demography* 46: 513–34. www.ncbi.nlm.nih.gov/pmc/articles/PMC2831345/.

_____. 2010. Poverty among Young Children in Black Immigrant, US-Born Black, and Non-Black Immigrant Families: The Role of Familial Contexts. Discussion Paper Series DP 2010-02, University of Kentucky Center for Poverty Research.

CHAPTER 7

CIRCUMSTANCES AND OUTCOMES AMONG BLACK IMMIGRANT MOTHERS AND THEIR YOUNG CHILDREN: EVIDENCE FROM PALM BEACH COUNTY, FLORIDA

Lauren Rich, Julie Spielberger, Angela Valdovinos D'Angelo

Chapin Hall at the University of Chicago

Introduction

Immigration contributed to one-fifth of Black population growth in the United States between 2001 and 2006.[1] Between 1980 and 2005, the number of Haitians quadrupled amid a generally rising number of Black immigrants from around the world.[2] Yet, despite this growth in the population of Black immigrants, there has been relatively little research exploring their demographic characteristics, their incorporation into the US mainstream, or how well their young children are faring in terms of their health, development, and school readiness.[3] Furthermore, while there is some knowledge of the circumstances of children in Black immigrant families growing up in populous, ethnic, urban centers, little is known about the lives of families and children

1   Mary Mederios Kent, "Immigration and America's Black Population" (*Population Bulletin* 62, No. 4, Population Reference Bureau, Washington, DC, December 2007): 1-20, www.prb.org/pdf07/62.4immigration.pdf.
2   Ibid.
3   There is some evidence that the young adult children (ages 25-39) of Black immigrants fare well in terms of educational attainment when compared to third-generation whites, although they do not fare as well as Asians. In contrast, second-generation Mexicans and Puerto Ricans achieve fewer years of education than both second-generation Blacks and third-generation whites. See Jeffery G. Reitz, Heather Zhang, and Naoko Hawkins, "Comparisons of the Success of Racial Minority Immigrant Offspring in the United States, Canada and Australia," *Social Science Research* 40 (2011): 1051–66.

who reside in smaller urban and rural locations. As a step toward filling this gap, we analyze survey and administrative data collected through Chapin Hall's six-year longitudinal study of a birth cohort in Palm Beach County, FL. This study affords a unique opportunity to examine Black immigrant mothers' demographic characteristics, access to social services and other resources, parenting practices, and other variables that affect the life chances of their children. We also examine the early development of these children, and compare their outcomes to the children of Black US-born and Latina immigrant mothers.

Located on the southeast Atlantic coast of Florida just north of Miami, Palm Beach is the largest county in the state in terms of land area and the third most populous, with an estimated population of more than 1.3 million according to the 2010 US Census. Palm Beach County is ethnically diverse, with more than 100 languages spoken by the families of children in the county's school district.[4] Although it is the wealthiest county in the state, Palm Beach County includes large pockets of poverty. The county's population growth of nearly 17 percent from 2000 to 2010 was largely fueled by immigration. The foreign-born share of the county's population increased from 17 percent to 21 percent over the decade; by comparison, the immigrant share of the population in Florida and the United States in 2010 was 19 percent and 12 percent, respectively.

Historically, most immigrant groups typically settle in predictable patterns into well-known urban settings.[5] California, New York, and Florida — in particular the major cities within them — are the most popular destinations for the 12 largest US immigrant groups. Not surprisingly, as of 2002, Los Angeles was a common settling community for Mexican immigrants, while Dominicans dominated New York City, and Miami was a traditional receiving community for Cubans.[6] However, recent research shows that immigrants are increasingly settling into new destinations. Between 2000 and 2009, 14 states experienced growth in the immigrant population of 49 percent or more.[7] These new destination states are mainly located in the southern and central regions of the United States, and include places such as South Carolina, Tennessee, and Alabama.[8]

Palm Beach can be thought of as a new destination county for immigrants within Florida. While the state of Florida has a long history of

---

4   According to the Palm Beach County school district, 141 different languages and dialects are represented in the 2010-11 school population; School District of Palm Beach County, "About Us," accessed September 8, 2012, www.palmbeachschools.org/Community/AboutUs.asp.

5   Alejandro Portes and Ruben G. Rumbaut, *Immigrant America: A Portrait*, 3rd edition (Berkeley, CA: University of California Press, 2006).

6   Ibid: 51.

7   Aaron Terrazas, "Immigrants in New-Destination States," *Migration Information Source*, February 2011, migrationinformation.org/USFocus/display.cfm?ID=826.

8   Ibid.

receiving immigrants, Palm Beach County has only recently experienced a large influx. The county attracts a diverse population of immigrants, perhaps reflecting the county's varied geography of rural as well as urban communities, and its relatively short history of settlement by large immigrant groups. The immigrant parents in the county represent a diverse array of Latin American and Caribbean countries, with the seven largest in terms of population being (in order) Haiti, Mexico, Cuba, Jamaica, Guatemala, Colombia, and Honduras. Compared to immigrants in traditional receiving communities, the Palm Beach groups tend to be smaller, have less established social networks, and live in areas that are not typically well-settled ethnic enclaves. Immigrants are dispersed across the county, as are Black immigrants, who comprise over 25 percent of the total immigrant population in several subdivisions.

In this report we focus on the early outcomes of the young children of Black, mainly Haitian-born, mothers and the factors that affect these children's development. In addition, we examine how the experiences and outcomes of these children compare to children with Black US-born and Latina immigrant mothers. We have adopted an ecological frame-work, which posits that the developing child is embedded in a family, community, and policy context, and that the relationships between these contexts and individual development change across the lifespan.[9]

This report has three main sections. The first compares Black immi-grant, Latina immigrant, and Black US-born mothers in Palm Beach County with respect to (1) characteristics such as educational attain-ment, employment status, marital status, number of children, and household income; (2) use of social and other services, such as mater-nal and child health services, public income supports, and enrollment in health insurance; and (3) postnatal outcomes such as physical and mental health (e.g., depression and parenting stress), parenting prac-tices, and use of child care. The second section explores differences in the characteristics and development of the children of these mothers, including premature births, birth weight, language and math literacy, socioemotional skills, and school readiness. The final section offers statistical analyses that explore the extent to which the outcomes of children of Black immigrant mothers differ from those of the children of Latina immigrant and Black US-born mothers, after controlling for background characteristics and other variables. For the statistical analyses we focus on mothers' reports of children's socioemotional development and pre-academic skills as well as on measures of kinder-garten readiness obtained from the schools.

Given previous evidence suggesting relatively higher educational attainment among Afro-Caribbean Blacks in the United States,[10] we

---

9   Urie Bronfenbrenner, "Toward an Experimental Ecology of Human Development," *American Psychologist* 32, No. 7 (1977): 513–31.

10   Reitz, Zhang, and Hawkins, "Comparisons of the Success of Racial Minority Immigrant Offspring."

hypothesize that the Black immigrant mothers in our sample might have economic or social advantages over other mothers in the sample, with these advantages potentially translating into better developmental outcomes for their children. Although there is scant research on the early outcomes of the children of Black immigrants, there is some evidence from the Early Childhood Longitudinal Study-Kindergarten Cohort (ECLS-K) that, when compared to third-generation Black children, children of Black immigrants display significantly higher achievement in reading in the spring of their kindergarten year.[11] Our findings do not show an advantage for children of Black immigrant mothers versus children of Black native-born mothers in literacy in the fall of the kindergarten year (after controlling for background and other characteristics). However, we do find an immigrant advantage on a broader test of school readiness that covers academic as well as social and personal skills. When comparing children of Black immigrant mothers with those of Latina immigrant mothers, we find that the children of Black immigrants are significantly more likely to achieve top scores in both a literacy measure and a broader assessment of school readiness, even after controlling for a wide array of background characteristics.

I.   Overview of the Palm Beach County Longitudinal Study

In 2004 the Children's Services Council (CSC) of Palm Beach County provided funding for Chapin Hall at the University of Chicago to conduct a six-year longitudinal study examining the use and potential effectiveness of an array of county services in promoting school readiness and school success among children, and in improving functioning among families most in need of support. The goal of the study was to describe the characteristics and needs of families the service system was intended to serve, how families used the services, and how service use related to child and family outcomes.

We use two main components of the study for these analyses. First, the study team collected Department of Health vital statistics and data on the use of maternal/child health services for approximately 30,000 mothers who gave birth in Palm Beach County during 2004 or 2005. The vital statistics data included information on the mothers' country of origin and other characteristics, birth outcomes, and use of prenatal care and the Special Supplemental Nutrition Program for Women, Infants and Children (WIC). Data on the use of maternal/child health

---

11   It should be noted that these particular findings come from descriptive analyses, and as such do not account for differences in family background and other characteristics between immigrant and nonimmigrant children. See Natalia Palacios, Katarina Guttmannova, and P. Lindsay Chase-Lansdale, "Early Reading Achievement of Children in Immigrant Families: Is There an Immigrant Paradox?" *Developmental Psychology* 44, No. 5 (2008): 1381–95.

services came from the Palm Beach County Maternal Child Health Partnership (MCHP) database, and included information on assessment, home visitation, and the use of coordinated services for families experiencing medical, social, and environmental risks that could affect children's development.

The second part of the study was based on a sample of over 500 mothers who gave birth in the county in 2004 or 2005 (hereafter referred to as "the survey sample"), and who resided in one of four geographic areas targeted by CSC that showed relatively higher levels of poverty, teen pregnancy, crime, and child abuse and neglect. The targeted geographic areas (TGAs) that form the geographic frame for the survey sample were defined by zip code areas and mostly overlapped with four subdivisions of the county.[12]

Mothers were recruited through two maternal health programs in Palm Beach County that were deemed likely to provide the widest access to mothers of newborns in the TGAs. To be selected for the sample, mothers were required to be at least 16 years old; reside in one of the TGAs; and speak English, Spanish, or Haitian Creole.[13]

The survey sample was stratified along two dimensions. First, the sample was selected so that approximately half would be identified as high risk, meaning that the children were at risk for developmental delays and/or their families were at risk for dysfunction.[14] Second, because the Glades TGA was sparsely populated and the immigrants living here were more transitory at the time of the study, the population living in this TGA was oversampled in order to ensure that the subsample was large enough to make reasonable estimates of its

---

12 The four targeted areas were the Glades, Lake Worth/Lantana, Riviera Beach/Lake Park, and West Palm Beach. About the time this study began, 75 to 93 percent of public school students in these targeted communities received free or reduced-cost lunches, the rate of child abuse and neglect was between 4.1 and 6.6 times the county average, and crime rates in the TGAs ranged from 14 to 93 percent above the county rate. See Children's Services Council of Palm Beach (CSC), *State of the Child in Palm Beach County* (Palm Beach County: CSC, 2003).

13 Additional details on the recruitment strategy can be found in Chapin Hall's Year 1 report on the Palm Beach County Longitudinal Study. See Julie Spielberger, John Schuerman, Sandra Lyons, and Thomas Haywood, *The Palm Beach County Family Study: Baseline Report* (Chicago, IL: Chapin Hall at the University of Chicago, 2006).

14 Our determination of risk was based on mothers' scores on a postnatal risk screen developed by the CSC-funded Healthy Start (HS) program and administered in the hospital shortly after birth. The screen included questions about the mother's age, education, race, marital status, prenatal care, and substance use, as well as questions about her child's birth weight, condition at birth, and birth complications. If the postnatal risk screen was not available, we used scores from an in-home assessment by a HS nurse or the HS prenatal risk screen. The prenatal risk screen included the same maternal background questions as the postnatal screen, as well as questions about neighborhood and domestic safety, household hunger, mother's mental health, and feelings concerning the pregnancy. About 3 percent of the sample had no risk screens recorded in the administrative data; these mothers were classified as "not at risk."

characteristics. A total of 703 mothers were recruited for the study, and the final baseline sample was 531 mothers.[15]

The mothers in the survey sample were interviewed in person shortly after the birth of the focal child, and then annually in each of four subsequent years.[16] At the time of the first interview, the focal children ranged in age from a few weeks to 6 months, with a mean age of 2 months.[17]

Data on Child Outcomes

We collected data on child development beginning in the third year of the study (when the children were 2 years old). In this year, mothers were asked a few questions to identify the age at which their children first achieved a list of developmental milestones appropriate for 2-year-olds. In addition, mothers were asked to describe their children's use of language, and to indicate whether or not they had begun toilet training their children.

In the fourth and fifth years of the study, mothers were asked whether their children had demonstrated a variety of behaviors typical of 3- and 4-year-olds in the areas of toilet training, language and communication skills, socioemotional competencies, and preliteracy (e.g., use of books, drawing, writing, and letter recognition).

Focal children who entered kindergarten in the Palm Beach County school district were tested using the Florida Kindergarten Readiness Screen (FLKRS). The FLKRS is administered by teachers and covers seven developmental domains — language and literacy, mathematics, social and personal skills, science, social studies, physical health and fitness, and creative arts. The screening includes two sets of measures. The first is a subset of the Early Childhood Observation System (ECHOS), an observational instrument that is used to monitor children's skills, knowledge, and behaviors in the seven developmental domains listed above. Children's total scores on ECHOS fall into one of

---

15   Additional details on the sampling strategy can be found in Spielberger et al., *The Palm Beach County Family Study.*

16   Sample sizes in years 2 through 5 were 444, 399, 355, and 353, respectively. Attrition analyses conducted in each year showed that the attrition was approximately random.

17   The in-person interviews collected data in the following domains: (1) household composition and demographic characteristics; (2) family economic circumstances; (3) living conditions; (4) maternal and child health status, insurance, and use of prenatal and other health services; (5) mother's use of formal services and income supports; (6) child-care and after-school arrangements; (7) social support; (8) mother's and partner's parenting practices; (9) mother's mental health and substance use; and (10) child development (beginning in year 3). The mothers were also interviewed briefly by telephone approximately six months after each of the annual in-person interviews. The telephone interviews collected data on household composition; family economic circumstances; maternal and child health status, insurance, and use of health services; mother's use of formal services and income supports; child care; mother's parenting practices; and mother's depressive symptoms.

three readiness categories — *not yet demonstrating, emerging/progressing*, or *consistently demonstrating* — with the latter two designated as indicating readiness for school.

The other component of FLKRS is the Florida Assessments for Instruction in Reading (FAIR), which is also teacher administered and screens children's letter naming and phonemic awareness skills. FAIR scores are used to determine the child's probability of reading success, which ranges from 1 percent to 99 percent. FAIR provides two rankings: children with a probability of reading success scored at or above 67 percent are considered ready for kindergarten, while those scoring below 67 are considered not ready.

Of the children who were still part of the study sample at kindergarten entrance, ECHOS data were available for 283 (88 percent) of the children, and FAIR data were available for 293 (90 percent) of the children.

II. Methods

In the first section below we use vital statistics data on the county 2004-05 birth cohort in order to compare the characteristics of Black foreign-born mothers at the time of birth to the characteristics of mothers from other groups. In particular, we focus our analysis on differences and similarities between Black and Latina foreign-born mothers, and on those between Black foreign-born and Black US-born mothers.[18] In addition, because a large proportion of the Black immigrant mothers in both the cohort and survey samples are from Haiti, we consider whether there are any notable differences at the time of delivery between Haitian mothers and those from other countries in Central or South America or the Caribbean. Finally, because our survey sample is drawn exclusively from mothers living in the TGAs, we consider how mothers living in these areas of the county differ from those living in other areas. Taken together, these analyses provide select information on the overall circumstances of mothers who gave birth in Palm Beach County in 2004-05, and how these circumstances vary across race, ethnicity, nativity, and location.

In the second section, we use vital statistics data in order to examine the differences and similarities between our survey sample and the mothers in the county birth cohort. We also use the vital statistics and survey data to compare the characteristics of Black immigrant mothers

18 Because our survey sample consists primarily of Black and Latina mothers, we did not pay close attention to differences between Black foreign-born mothers and those who were non-Black or non-Latina, whether foreign or US born. In addition, because Black foreign-born and Latina US-born mothers differ initially along the two major dimensions of race and nativity, which might lead to very different social, cultural, and other experiences, we felt that a comparison of these two groups would ideally be the subject of a separate paper.

in our survey sample to the characteristics of Latina foreign-born and Black US-born mothers. Finally, we use survey and school district data to compare the characteristics and outcomes of the children of Black foreign-born mothers to the characteristics and outcomes of children from our two comparison groups.

In the third and final section we conduct multivariate regression analyses of four of our child outcome measures: the two maternal reports of a child's socioemotional well-being and pre-academic skills, and the two scores from FLKRS: ECHOS and FAIR. The purpose of these multivariate analyses is to explore how the kindergarten readiness of children of Black immigrant mothers differs from that of children of Latina immigrant mothers and children of Black native-born mothers, when controlling for a range of child, parent, and family characteristics. These characteristics include the child's age and gender (in the first models or the first columns in the tables shown later in this report); additional child, mother, and family socioeconomic characteristics (added to the second models shown in the second columns of the tables); and a set of variables about parent expectations for their children, support for their education, and access to early education (added to the third models and shown in the third columns).[19]

The first of the four child outcomes, socioemotional well-being, was based on maternal reports about how often their children engaged in 14 different behaviors — with responses ranging from 0 (almost never) to 2 (most of the time) — when the children were approximately 4 years old. The maternal reports of these 14 behaviors were averaged to create an overall score for each child. In keeping with standard practice in child development research, we standardized this variable to have a mean of 0 and a standard deviation of 1 (i.e., the average score among all children was set to 0 and the standard deviation of this score was used to measure the deviation from the average for each of the children in the sample).

The second outcome (pre-academic skills) was based on maternal reports regarding the child's ability to recognize/say the names of colors, recognize/say the names of the letters of the alphabet, and count. Responses ranged from 1 to 4, with 4 indicating ability to recognize/say the names of all colors/letters, or to count up to 20 or higher. Similar to the socioemotional skills score, the responses were averaged to create an overall score for each child.

The third outcome is the Palm Beach County school district's general

---

19 The specific variables added to the second set of models were: the mother's educational level, whether the mother was a teenager at the time of the birth, whether the child was underweight at birth, the mother's marital and employment status, whether the household income was at or below poverty level, whether the focal child had special medical needs, the number of negative housing conditions (e.g., overcrowded home), and the mother's scores on a measure of parenting stress and on a depressive symptoms scale.

measure of kindergarten readiness: ECHOS. We analyzed whether children were scored by their teachers as either "emerging/progressing" or "consistently demonstrating" with respect to kindergarten readiness. Then we separately analyzed whether children were scored as "consistently demonstrating" readiness.

The fourth and final outcome we used is the FAIR test of children's prereading skills. We used the county district's cutoff of 67 percent on the test to determine which children were considered ready for kindergarten.

III. Results

A. Maternal and Child Characteristics

Below we provide a descriptive overview of the population used in these analyses. Using data from vital statistics, the Palm Beach County survey, and the county school district, we highlight demographic differences between Black foreign-born, Latina foreign-born, and Black US-born mothers. In addition, to the extent possible, we examine country-of-origin differences within the group of foreign-born Black mothers. These descriptive statistics provide a basis for comparing the survey sample, which is used in the multivariate analyses, to the larger Black foreign-born population in Palm Beach County.

I. Maternal Characteristics for Palm Beach County Birth Cohort

Tables 1 and 2 use vital statistics data collected on all births in the county in 2004-05. These tables focus on the demographic characteristics of the mothers of children born in Palm Beach County and provide breakdowns by race/nativity and country of origin.

Black immigrant mothers versus Latina immigrant and Black native-born mothers. Black foreign-born mothers show certain advantages, including dispersal across the county outside of distressed areas, older average age, a higher marriage rate, and high levels of formal education versus Latina immigrant and Black native-born mothers (see Table 1).

Table 1. Maternal Characteristics by Mother's Race and Nativity, Palm Beach County 2004-05 Birth Cohort

	Black Immigrants	Hispanic Immigrants	Black, US Born	Hispanic, US Born	Other Immigrants	Other, US Born	Total
	n=3,444	n=6,196	n=4,160	n=2,406	n=2,352	n=11,039	N=29,597
Mother's country of origin							
U.S.A.	0	0	100	100	0	100	60
Haiti	69[a]	0	0	0	0	0	8
Mexico	0	28	0	0	0	0	6
Guatemala	0	18	0	0	0	0	4
Other Central/ South American/ Caribbean Country	21	49	0	0	16	0	14
Other Country	10[a]	5	0	0	83	0	9
Unknown	0	0	0	0	1	0	0
TGA residence							
Glades	3	5	16	5	1	1	4
Non-Glades	44	55	54	45	21	22	38
Outside of the TGAs	54[a, b]	40	30	50	79	77	58
Mother is married	57[a, b]	50	21	52	88	77	60
Teen mother at time of focal child's birth	5[a, b]	10	24	18	1	5	9
Mother's age							
Mean (sd)	30.0 (6.2)[a,b]	28.0 (6.1)	24.6 (6.0)	26.4 (6.5)	31.8 (5.1)	30.8 (6.0)	29.0 (6.5)
Mother's education							
High school diploma or more	67[a]	49	69	70	93	92	75
Unknown	4	5	2	2	1	1	3
Father's education[1]							
High school diploma or more	58	42	46	60	90	86	66
Unknown	25	22	41	19	6	9	19
Uses WIC	60[a, b]	53	56	42	12	13	35
Focal child - low birth weight	11[a]	7	15	8	7	6	8

	Black Immigrants	Hispanic Immigrants	Black, US Born	Hispanic, US Born	Other Immigrants	Other, US Born	Total
Prenatal care							
Began prior to pregnancy	1	1	2	3	3	3	2
First trimester	41[a]	37	41	51	63	65	52
Second trimester	29[b]	29	26	18	12	9	19
Third trimester	9[b]	12	6	4	3	2	6
Timing unknown	18	17	23	23	19	19	20
Did not get prenatal care	2	2	3	2	1	1	2
Number of prenatal visits							
Mean (sd)	9.8 (4.1)[a]	9.3 (4.1)	10.0 (4.6)	11.0 (4.5)	11.7 (4.0)	12.4 (4.5)	11.0 (4.5)
Type of insurance coverage							
Medicaid	34[a]	23	62	47	13	19	30
Other	1[b]	1	0	0	1	0	1
Private insurance	28[a]	21	26	41	63	69	45
Self-pay	29[b]	47	4	4	14	4	17
Unknown	8	7	8	8	9	8	8
Mother's pregnancy complications[2]	42[a]	34	39	34	33	35	36
Focal child birth complications[3]	13[a]	10	12	10	8	10	10
Focal child premature	12[a]	10	16	11	9	10	11

Notes: Full Palm Beach County 2004-05 Birth Cohort included; No weights applied.

[a] Denotes z-test of column proportions are statistically significant at $p < .05$ or lower between Black, Foreign-born and Hispanic, Foreign-born.

[b] Denotes z-test of column proportions are statistically significant at $p < .05$ or lower between Black, Foreign-born and Black, US-born.

[1] Significance testing was not conducted on father's education due to the large number of unknowns.

[2] Mother's pregnancy complications include: diabetes, prepregnancy; diabetes, gestational; hypertension, prepregnancy; hypertension, gestational; hypertension; eclampsia; previous preterm birth; previous poor pregnancy outcome; pregnancy result of infertility treatments; previous C-section deliveries; other.

[3] Focal child birth complications include: assisted ventilation required; newborn received antibiotics; significant birth injury; hyaline membrane disease/RDS; NICU admissions; seizures or serious neurologic dysfunction; newborn given surfactant; other.

Source: Palm Beach County Department of Health vital statistics.

Black immigrant mothers are most likely to be from Haiti (69 per-cent),[20] while Latina foreign-born mothers tend to be from Mexico (28 percent) or other Latin American/Caribbean countries (49 percent). Black foreign-born mothers are more likely to live outside of the TGAs (54 percent) than Latina foreign-born (40 percent) and Black US-born mothers (30 percent). Black foreign-born mothers are older and more likely than Latina foreign-born and Black US-born mothers to be married, and are less likely to be teen mothers. Black immigrant mothers are more likely to hold a high school diploma than Latina foreign-born mothers (67 versus 49 percent), and equally as likely to hold a diploma as Black US-born mothers.

Black foreign-born mothers show relatively good access to health care and social services. They have slightly more prenatal visits on average (9.8 visits) than Latina foreign-born mothers (9.3 visits), and about the same as Black US-born mothers (10.0 visits). They are also more likely than Latina foreign-born and Black US-born mothers to use WIC, and more likely than Latina foreign-born mothers to be covered under Medicaid (34 vs. 23 percent). In comparison, Black US-born mothers are more likely to be covered under either Medicaid (62 percent) or private insurance (26 percent), so very few pay for medical services out of pocket (4 percent).

Despite their socioeconomic advantages and relatively strong access to social services, 42 percent of Black foreign-born mothers have a pregnancy complication, 12 percent have a premature child, and 13 percent of their children experience at least one birth complication. These figures are all significantly higher than for Latina foreign-born mothers, but lower than for Black native-born mothers.

Haitian mothers versus other Black immigrant mothers. Among Black foreign-born mothers, Haitian mothers appear to face slightly more risks than Black foreign-born mothers from other countries (see Table 2). Despite the fact that Haitian mothers are more likely than other Black immigrant mothers to be married and live outside the TGAs, they appear to be somewhat disadvantaged on several indicators. For example, only 60 percent of Haitian immigrant mothers have a high school degree or more education, compared to 85 percent of Black foreign-born mothers from other Caribbean and Central and South American countries. Haitian mothers are also more likely to use public benefits such as WIC (71 percent versus 60 percent or less for other Black foreign-born mothers) and Medicaid (38 percent versus 34 percent or less). Haitian mothers make fewer prenatal visits than other Black immigrant mothers, which may be associated with the relatively higher share of Haitian mothers (44 percent) who experience a preg-nancy complication. Haitian mothers do not, however, differ from other

---

20 Foreign-born Black mothers also come from African countries such as Angola, Botswana, Cameroon, Nigeria, and Zimbabwe, as well as from various Caribbean countries such as the Bahamas, Bermuda, Cayman Islands, Trinidad and Tobago, and Turks and Caicos. These countries each represent a very small proportion of all foreign-born Black mothers.

Black immigrant mothers on childbirth outcomes (i.e., low birth weight, prematurity, or childbirth complications).

Table 2. Maternal Characteristics for Black, Foreign-Born Mothers by Country of Origin, Palm Beach County 2004-05 Birth Cohort

	Haiti	Other Central/ South American/ Caribbean Country	Other Country	Total
	n=2,363	n=734	n=347	N=3,444
TGA residence				
Glades	2	3	3	3
Non-Glades	41	52	46	44
Outside of the TGAs	57[a]	45	51	54
Mother is married	60[a]	50	52	57
Teen mother at time of focal child's birth	4	5	6	5
Mother's age				
Mean (sd)	30.2 (6.1)	29.7 (6.4)	29.6 (6.3)	30.0 (6.2)
Mother's education				
High school diploma or more	60[a, b]	85	73	67
Unknown	2	0	22	4
Father's education[1]				
High school diploma or more	56	64	63	58
Unknown	22	28	36	25
Uses WIC	71[a, b]	48	12	60
Focal child - low birth weight	11	10	11	11
Prenatal care				
Began prior to pregnancy	1	1	1	1
First trimester	42[b]	50	13	41
Second trimester	34[a, b]	22	9	29
Third trimester	10[b]	9	2	9
Timing is unknown	11	17	73	18
Did not get prenatal care	2	2	2	2
Number of prenatal visits				
Mean (sd)	9.6 (3.9)[a]	10.2 (4.5)	10.0 (4.5)	9.8 (4.1)
Type of insurance coverage				
Medicaid	38[a, b]	32	12	34
Other	1	1	0	1
Private insurance	26[b]	42	14	28
Self-pay	34[a, b]	24	5	29
Unknown	1	1	68	8

	Haiti	Other Central/ South American/ Caribbean Country	Other Country	Total
Mother's pregnancy complications[2]	44[a]	37	39	42
Focal child birth complications[3]	14	12	10	13
Focal child premature	12	14	13	12

Notes: Full Palm Beach County 2004-05 birth cohort included limiting the sample to only Black, Foreign-born mothers; No weights applied.

[a] Denotes z-test of column proportions are statistically significant at $p< .05$ or lower between Haiti and other Central/South American/Caribbean country.

[b] Denotes z-test of column proportions are statistically significant at $p< .05$ or lower between Haiti and other country.

[1] Significance testing was not conducted on father's education due to the large number of unknowns.

[2] Mother's pregnancy complications include: diabetes, prepregnancy; diabetes, gestational; hypertension, prepregnancy; hypertension, gestational; hypertension; eclampsia; previous preterm birth; previous poor pregnancy outcome; pregnancy result of infertility treatments; previous C-section deliveries; other.

[3] Focal child birth complications include: assisted ventilation required; newborn received antibiotics; significant birth injury; hyaline membrane disease/RDS; NICU admissions; seizures or serious neurologic dysfunction; newborn given surfactant; other.

Source: Palm Beach County Department of Health vital statistics.

Mothers in the TGAs. In analyses not shown, we examined all mothers who gave birth in 2004 or 2005 in Palm Beach County using the vital statistics data and compared mothers residing in the TGAs to those residing elsewhere in the county. Mothers in the TGAs are more likely to be from Mexico (9 percent versus 3 percent elsewhere in the county), Guatemala (7 percent versus 2 percent), and other countries in South/ Central America and the Caribbean (16 percent versus 13 percent). They are less likely to be married (43 percent versus 73 percent), more likely to be a teen mother (14 percent versus 6 percent), and thus younger than mothers living elsewhere in the county (with a mean age of 27 versus 30.4 years). Mothers in the TGAs are also less likely to have a high school diploma (61 percent versus 85 percent), and more likely to use WIC (52 percent versus 23 percent), be covered by Medicaid (41 percent versus 21 percent), and pay out of pocket for medical services (23 percent versus 12 percent). Finally, they have a lower number of prenatal visits (9.9 versus 11.7), are more likely to have a child with low birth weight (9 percent versus 7 percent), and more likely to have a premature child (12 percent versus 10 percent).

2. Maternal and Child Characteristics for the Palm Beach County Survey Sample

The demographic and socioeconomic characteristics obtained from vital statistics for the survey sample are very similar to those countywide for Black immigrant mothers, even though the survey was conducted almost entirely in the distressed TGAs (see Table 3). For instance, in the survey sample two-thirds of all Black immigrant mothers were from Haiti — similar to the proportion in the countywide sample (69 percent). Black immigrant mothers in the survey sample were older than Latina immigrant or US-born Black mothers, and less likely to be teen mothers. Black immigrant mothers were also more likely than US-born Black mothers to be married, and more likely than Latina immigrant mothers to have a high school diploma or higher. However, the average ages and marriage rates for all mothers were lower in the survey sample than the countywide sample, while the teen mother rates were higher.

Table 3. Maternal Characteristics by Mother's Race and Nativity, Palm Beach County Birth Cohort Survey Sample

	Black Immigrant	Hispanic Immigrant	Black, US Born	Hispanic, US Born	Other, US Born	Total
	n=55	n=225	n=156	n=55	n=38	N=529
Mother's country of origin						
U.S.A.	0	0	100	100	100	47
Haiti	66	0	0	0	0	7
Mexico	0	42	0	0	0	18
Guatemala	0	31	0	0	0	13
Other Central/South American/Caribbean Country	29	27	0	0	0	14
Other Country	6a	0	0	0	0	1
TGA residence						
Glades	15	9	47	22	5	22
Non-Glades	84[b]	89	53	75	92	77
Outside of the TGAs	2	2	1	4	3	2
Mother is married	38[b]	29	12	20	26	24
Teen mother at time of focal child's birth						
Teen mother	7[a, b]	15	33	36	11	21
Mother's age						
Mean (sd)	29.1 (6.8)[a, b]	26.2 (5.9)	22.8 (4.9)	23.0 (5.6)	25.8 (5.5)	25.1 (6.0)
Mother's education						
High school diploma or more	55[a]	24	58	44	66	42
Unknown	4	4	2	0	0	3

	Black Immigrant	Hispanic Immigrant	Black, US Born	Hispanic, US Born	Other, US Born	Total
Father's education[1]						
High school diploma or more	44	16	34	33	45	28
Unknown	31	32	47	36	32	37
Uses WIC	80	75	73	75	47	73
Focal child - low birth weight	13	7	15	9	13	11
Prenatal care						
Began prior to pregnancy	9[a]	0	3	2	3	2
First trimester	44	26	43	40	61	37
Second trimester	25	45	28	42	16	36
Third trimester	6	15	10	2	5	10
Timing is unknown	16	12	15	13	16	14
Did not get prenatal care	0	1	2	2	0	1
Number of prenatal visits						
Mean (sd)	9.8 (3.8)	8.7 (3.5)	9.6 (4.6)	10.1 (4.4)	12.2 (6.3)	9.4 (4.3)
Type of insurance coverage						
Medicaid	36[a]	17	76	78	79	47
Other	0	1	0	0	0	0
Private insurance	20[a]	4	19	18	21	13
Self-pay	38[b]	76	2	4	0	37
Unknown	6	2	3	0	0	2
Mother's pregnancy complications[2]	38	31	40	29	34	35
Focal child birth complications[3]	15	8	16	5	13	11
Focal child premature	13	10	17	13	11	13

Notes: Year 1 sample (n=529); No weights applied. Please note that Other, Foreign-born were excluded from the table due to a sample size of n=2.

[a] Denotes z-test of column proportions are statistically significant at $p < .05$ or lower between Black, Foreign-born and Hispanic, Foreign-born.

[b] Denotes z-test of column proportions are statistically significant at $p < .05$ or lower between Black, Foreign-born and Black, US-born.

[1] Significance testing was not conducted on father's education due to the large number of unknowns.

[2] Mother's pregnancy complications include: diabetes, prepregnancy; diabetes, gestational; hypertension, prepregnancy; hypertension, gestational; hypertension; eclampsia; previous preterm birth; previous poor pregnancy outcome; pregnancy result of infertility treatments; previous C-section deliveries; other.

[3] Focal child birth complications include: assisted ventilation required; newborn received antibiotics; significant birth injury; hyaline membrane disease/RDS; NICU admissions; seizures or serious neurologic dysfunction; newborn given surfactant; other.

Source: Palm Beach County Department of Health vital statistics.

The survey conducted in the TGAs also included several indicators not available in the larger, countywide sample; these indicators are central to the analyses around child development and school readiness in the remainder of this report. Overall, Black foreign-born mothers experience some advantages compared to the other two groups (see Table 4). Black foreign-born mothers are more likely than Black US-born mothers to live outside of the Glades subdivision (86 percent versus 53 percent), which is the most isolated and, historically, least connected to services. Black foreign-born mothers are also more likely than the other two groups to be married (36 percent versus 12 percent); however, they are also much more likely than Latina foreign-born mothers to be neither married nor cohabitating (46 percent versus 14 percent). Black foreign-born mothers also exhibit more markers of acculturation than Latina foreign-born mothers; Black foreign-born mothers are far more likely to speak English at home (36 percent versus 3 percent) and to have been interviewed in English (52 percent versus 5 percent). Black foreign-born mothers have also been in the United States on average almost twice as long as Latina immigrant mothers (8.0 years versus 4.6 years).

Table 4. Maternal Characteristics by Mother's Race and Nativity, Survey Data for Palm Beach County Survey Sample

	Black Immigrant	Hispanic Immigrant	Black, US Born	Hispanic, US Born	Other, US Born	Total
Survey data and Survey sample	n=56	n=225	n=156	n=52	n=40	N=529
TGA residence						
Glades	14	9	47	23	5	22
Non-Glades	86[b]	91	53	77	95	78
Years in U.S.A. (immigrant mothers only)						
Mean (sd)	8.0 (6.2)[c]	4.6 (4.4)	—	—	—	5.3 (5.0)
Language spoken at home						
English	36[a]	3	98	59	98	47
Spanish	4	92	0	41	3	44
Haitian Creole	61[b]	0	2	0	0	7
Konjubal	0	3	0	0	0	1
Other	0	2	0	0	0	1
Language the interview was conducted in						
English	52[a]	5	100	81	100	53
Spanish	2	95	0	19	0	42
Haitian Creole	46	0	0	0	0	5
Number of negative housing conditions						
Mean (sd)	1.6 (1.8)	1.3 (1.6)	1.4 (1.8)	1.1 (1.5)	0.50 (0.9)	1.3 (1.7)

	Black Immigrant	Hispanic Immigrant	Black, US Born	Hispanic, US Born	Other, US Born	Total
Marital status and living arrangements						
Married	36[b]	30	12	23	23	24
Cohabitating	18	56	26	40	40	41
Not married/ cohabitating	46[a]	14	62	37	38	36
Mother currently working	20[a]	4	21	25	13	14
Mother's partner currently working	n=40	n=197	n=99	n=37	n=32	n=405
	90[b]	93	65	95	81	85
Number of children						
Mean (sd)	2.0 (1.1)	1.9 (1.0)	2.2 (1.5)	2.0 (1.0)	1.7 (1.0)	2.0 (1.2)
At or below poverty threshold	80	74	76	57	50	72
"Income (income mid-point used as a proxy)"						
Mean (sd)	$13,004.63 ($12,581.01)	$19,082.95 ($11,629.75)	$13,955.59 ($16,530.90)	$21,357.14 ($19,464.78)	$23,256.25 ($17,856.31)	"$17,463.38 ($15,007.27)"
Mother's health "good, very good, or excellent"	84	76	92	81	85	83
Use of Healthy Beginnings Services						
Received either Care Coordination and/or Intensive Care Coordination	86	95	80	65	73	85
Mother has health insurance	43[b]	30	93	75	80	58
Income supports						
Food stamps	21[b]	23	71	48	48	41
Women, Infants, and Children (WIC)	93	90	87	79	73	87
TANF	0	1	19	6	18	8
Rent voucher	0	2	8	6	8	5
SSI	7[b]	0	24	19	15	11
Unemployment insurance	7	4	3	0	13	4
Earned Income Tax Credit	14	9	17	17	33	15
Total areas in which services were used in past year[1]						
Mean (sd)	3.3 (1.7)	3.0 (1.2)	4.1 (2.1)	3.6 (1.9)	4.5 (3.1)	3.5 (1.9)
Depression Score 16 or higher[2]	53[a]	23	50	39	35	36

	Black Immigrant	Hispanic Immigrant	Black, US Born	Hispanic, US Born	Other, US Born	Total
Year 2 Parenting stress (86+)	24	17	21	17	21	19
Overall parenting score[3]						
Mean (sd)	0.80 (.12)[a]	0.71 (.18)	0.80 (.14)	0.80 (.14)	0.80 (.16)	0.76 (.16)
Number of children's books in the home at Year 5						
Mean (sd)	27.3 (41.9)	14.4 (16.9)	25.2 (30.3)	16.4 (21.0)	53.7 (57.5)	22.2 (30.6)
Educational expectations for child						
Year 4						
To receive less than a high school diploma	0	2	0	0	0	1
To graduate from high school	0	12	5	18	5	8
To attend college	10	2	5	6	5	4
To graduate from college	90	85	90	77	90	87
Year 5						
To receive less than a high school diploma	0	1	0	0	0	0
To graduate from high school	0	19	12	16	14	14
To attend college	17	8	12	13	24	12
To graduate from college	83	73	77	71	62	74

Notes: Year 1 sample (N=531) No weights applied. Other, Foreign-born are not included in this table due to a small sample (n=3).

[a] Denotes z-test of column proportions are statistically significant at p< .05 or lower between Black, Foreign-born and Hispanic, Foreign-born.

[b] Denotes z-test of column proportions are statistically significant at p< .05 or lower between Black, Foreign-born and Black, US-born.

[c] Denotes *one way ANOVA* differences are statistically significant at *p*< .001 or lower between Black, Foreign-born and Hispanic, Foreign-born.

[1] Items in this score include meeting the family's basic needs, such as food, clothing, and housing; child care; medical and mental health care; and addressing concerns about their children's health and development. Only those items asked in all five years of the survey are included in this score.

[2] The Center for Epidemiologic Studies Depression Scale (CES-D) scores range from 0 to 60, with higher scores indicating the presence of more depressive symptoms.

[3] The overall parenting score ranges from 0 to 1 with 1 indicating more positive parenting.

Source: Yearly in-person interviews.

Employment levels are generally higher in Black immigrant families than in either Latina immigrant or Black native-born families. Black foreign-born mothers are more likely than Latina foreign-born mothers to be working (20 percent versus 4 percent), perhaps reflecting the fact that they are less likely to have a partner. However, when they do have a partner, he is much more likely to be working than the typical partner of Black US-born mothers (90 percent versus 65 percent). Black foreign-born mothers, on the other hand, are relatively disconnected from public benefits when compared with Black native-born mothers; for instance, they are less likely than Black US-born mothers to have health insurance (43 percent versus 93 percent), use food stamps (21 percent versus 71 percent), or receive Supplemental Security Income (7 percent versus 24 percent).

Other measures of mothers' well-being showed mixed results for Black immigrant mothers versus other groups. For example, Black foreign-born mothers are more than twice as likely as Latina foreign-born mothers to have a depression score of 16 or higher (53 percent versus 23 percent). On the other hand, they have a significantly higher positive parenting score (0.80 versus 0.71).

The survey sample in the TGAs also includes several measures of children's circumstances — including health, health care, and childcare arrangements — not available in the broader countywide sample (see Table 5). There are few differences across the focal race/ethnic and nativity groups, but children of Black immigrant mothers are far more likely than children of Latina immigrant mothers to be in formal, center-based child care at all preschool ages. The gap in center-based care enrollment between children of Black and Latina immigrants increases from 18 percentage points in year 2 of the study (19 percent versus 1 percent) to 40 points in year 5 (67 percent versus 27 percent). Children of Black native-born mothers have similarly high levels of enrollment in center-based care.

Table 5. Child Characteristics by Mother's Race and Nativity, Palm Beach County Survey Sample

	Black Immigrant	Hispanic Immigrant	Black, US Born	Hispanic, US Born	Other, US Born	Total
Survey data and Survey sample	n=56	n=225	n=156	n=52	n=40	n=529
Age of Focal Child in Months [Mean (sd)]						
Year 1	2.1 (1.4)	1.7 (1.1)	1.8 (1.2)	1.8 (0.9)	1.9 (1.2)	1.8 (1.2)
Year 2	15.0 (1.7)	14.4 (1.3)	14.7 (1.7)	14.7 (1.1)	14.8 (1.3)	14.6 (1.5)
Year 3	27.1 (2.2)[a, b]	26.0 (1.3)	26.4 (1.5)	26.5 (1.5)	26.2 (1.3)	26.3 (1.5)
Year 4	39.5 (2.0)	39.0 (1.2)	39.0 (1.4)	40.0 (1.3)	39.0 (1.4)	39.1 (1.4)
Year 5	50.5 (2.2)	50.0 (1.8)	50.3 (1.7)	50.5 (1.4)	50.1 (1.7)	50.2 (1.8)
Focal child is a girl	55	41	40	46	55	44

	Black Immigrant	Hispanic Immigrant	Black, US Born	Hispanic, US Born	Other, US Born	Total
Focal child's general health status						
Year 1						
Good, very good, or excellent	98	85	98	96	95	92
Year 2						
Good, very good, or excellent	100	80	93	83	97	88
Year 3						
Good, very good, or excellent	98	87	98	97	96	93
Year 4						
Good, very good, or excellent	100	85	95	100	100	92
Year 5						
Good, very good, or excellent	100	87	96	97	100	93
Focal child has special medical needs						
Year 2	4[b]	16	29	21	27	20
Year 3	14	15	26	25	25	20
Year 4	10	16	23	6	35	18
Year 5	11	19	27	16	19	21
Focal child's child care						
Year 1						
At home	80	96	67	75	80	82
Relatives, friends, or neighbors	18[a]	4	26	19	8	14
Child-care center, Head Start, prekindergarten, or family child care	2	0	6	2	8	3
Other or multiple arrangements	0	0	2	4	5	1
Year 2						
At home	38	70	32	52	53	52
Relatives, friends, or neighbors	43	28	24	29	30	29
Child-care center, Head Start, prekindergarten, or family child care	19[a]	1	41	19	17	19
Other or multiple arrangements	0	1	2	0	0	1
Year 3						
At home	30	66	26	50	42	46
Relatives, friends, or neighbors	27	22	25	19	29	24

	Black Immigrant	Hispanic Immigrant	Black, US Born	Hispanic, US Born	Other, US Born	Total
Child-care center, Head Start, prekindergarten, or family child care	39[a]	10	43	31	29	27
Other or multiple arrangements	5	2	7	0	0	4
Year 4						
At home	33	63	39	44	55	49
Relatives, friends, or neighbors	28	20	15	18	25	19
Child-care center, Head Start, prekindergarten, or family child care	39[a]	15	45	38	10	30
Other or multiple arrangements	0	2	2	0	10	2
Year 5						
At home	25	53	27	26	43	38
Relatives, friends, or neighbors	8	16	10	26	14	14
Child-care center, Head Start, prekindergarten, or family child care	67[a]	27	54	48	43	44
Other or multiple arrangements	0	4	9	0	0	5

Notes: Year 1 sample (N=531) No weights applied. Other, Foreign-born are not included in this table due to a small sample (n=3).

[a] Denotes z-test of column proportions are statistically significant at $p < .05$ or lower between Black, Foreign-born and Hispanic, Foreign-born.

[b] Denotes z-test of column proportions are statistically significant at $p < .05$ or lower between Black, Foreign-born and Black, US-born.

[1] Items in this score include meeting the family's basic needs, such as food, clothing, and housing; child care; medical and mental health care; and addressing concerns about their children's health and development. Only those items asked in all five years of the survey are included in this score.

[2] The Center for Epidemiologic Studies Depression Scale (CES-D) scores range from 0 to 60, with higher scores indicating the presence of more depressive symptoms.

Source: Yearly in-person interviews.

The children of Black immigrant mothers differ significantly from those of Black native-born mothers in the survey sample in one regard: they are far less likely to have reported health problems. Black foreign-born mothers are significantly less likely than Black US-born mothers to report that their child has special medical needs in year 2 (4 percent versus 29 percent); this pattern continues through year 5 of the survey, but is not statistically significant after year 2.[21]

---

21 Mothers were asked, "Did a doctor or professional ever tell you that your child has any special medical needs?" However, these special needs were not independently verified.

Child outcomes for Palm Beach County survey sample. Children of Black immigrant mothers fare significantly better than those of Latina immigrants on outcome measures reported by their mothers (see Table 6). In year 5 of the study, children of Black immigrants are more likely than children of Latina immigrants to be reported in the top 25 percent for socioemotional well-being (28 percent versus 8 percent) and in the top 25 percent for pre-academic skills (56 percent versus 11 percent). There are no statistically significant differences in these parent-reported outcomes between children of Black immigrant mothers and children of Black native-born mothers.

Table 6. Child Outcomes at Year 5 by Mother's Race and Nativity, Palm Beach County Survey Sample

	Black Immigrant	Hispanic Immigrant	Black, US Born	Hispanic, US Born	Other,US Born	Total
	n=36	n=135	n=128	n=31	n=21	N=351
How does focal child communicate						
Does not talk yet	0	0	0	0	0	0
Mostly talking in one-word sentences	0	3	1	3	5	2
Talking in 2-3 word phrases	0	8	4	3	5	5
Talking in fairly complete, short sentences	31	23	16	13	14	20
Talking in long, complicated sentences	69	66	80	81	76	73
Communication skills in the top 25%	42	19	32	13	48	27
Social-Emotional skills in the top 25%	28[a]	8	34	19	38	22
Use of book skills in the top 25%	81	58	73	74	81	68
Pre-academic skills in the top 25%	56[a]	11	53	29	38	34
Preliteracy skills in the top 25%	47	35	56	39	62	46

Notes: Year 5 sample (N=529) No weights applied. Other, Foreign-born are not included in this table due to a small sample.

[a] Denotes *z*-test of column proportions are statistically significant at *p*< .05 or lower between Black, Foreign-born and Hispanic, Foreign-born.

[b] Denotes *z*-test of column proportions are statistically significant at *p*< .05 or lower between Black, Foreign-born and Black, US-born.

Mother's self-reported responses to the below questions included in the above scales:

Communication Skills: Speaks clearly so that strangers understand; Refers to him/her-self as I; Uses appropriate social greetings; Is a good listener; Waits his/her turn to talk; and If asked, can say his/her first and last name. (Scored on a three-point scale ranging from "almost never" to "sometimes" to "most of the time.")

Social-Emotional Skills: Seems happy; Gets angry easily; Pays attention well; Is eager to learn new things; Is accepted and liked by other children; Adjusts easily to a new situation; Likes to try new things; Helps or cooperates with adults; Likes playing with other children close to his/her age; Worries about things; Is overly active and unable to sit still; Finishes what he/she is asked to do; Is aggressive; and Does things without thinking. (Scored on a three-point scale ranging from "almost never" to "sometimes" to "most of the time.")

Use of Books Skills: Looks at picture books on his/her own; Points to pictures while looking at picture books; Pretends to read the words in a book; Reads the written words in a book; and When looking at a book, can tell what is in each picture. (Scored on a three-point scale ranging from "almost never" to "sometimes" to "most of the time.")

School Readiness Skills: Can point to the colors when you say the names; Can say the names of the colors; Points to the letters of the alphabet when you say the names; Can say the names of the letters of the alphabet; and How high can he/she count. (Scored on a four-point scale ranging from "all of them" to "most of them" to "some of them" to "none of them.")

Preliteracy Skills: Scribbles or draws on paper; Draws pictures of people or objects; Tells you in words about what he/she has drawn; Tries to draw shapes, numbers, or letters; Can draw one or more shapes that you recognize; and Can draw one or more letters that you recognize. (Scored on a two-point scale ranging from "no" to "yes.")

Source: Yearly in-person interviews.

Perhaps most importantly, children of Black immigrants perform better than either children of Latina immigrants or children of Black natives on the county school district's kindergarten readiness assessments (see Table 7). Children of Black immigrant mothers are significantly more likely than those of Latina immigrants to be in the "consistently demonstrating" category on the ECHOS assessment (49 percent versus 13 percent). Children of Black immigrant mothers are also more likely than those of Latina immigrants to score a 67 or more on the FAIR assessment (58 percent versus 30 percent). They are more likely to pass both the ECHOS and FAIR assessments than children of Black native-born mothers, though here the differences in scores are not statistically significant.

Table 7. Focal Child's School Readiness by Mother's Race and Nativity, Survey Sample and County

	Survey Sample						
	Black Immigrant	Hispanic Immigrant	Black, US Born	Hispanic, US Born	Other, US Born	Total	PBC
School Readiness							
ECHOS scores							
Not yet demonstrating	12	32	21	21	15	24	13
Emerging/ Progressing	39	55	55	46	46	52	40
Consistently demonstrating	49[a]	13	25	32	39	24	47
FAIR scores							
66 or less	42	70	63	57	60	63	35
67 or more	58[a]	30	38	43	40	37	65

Notes: [a] Denotes z-test of column proportions are statistically significant at p< .05 or lower between Black, Foreign-born and Hispanic, Foreign-born. [b] Denotes z-test of column proportions are statistically significant at p< .05 or lower between Black, Foreign-born and Black, US-born.
Source: Palm Beach County school district.

Moreover, children of Black immigrant mothers in the distressed TGAs are about as likely as the countywide population of kindergarten entrants to pass the ECHOS assessment (49 percent versus 47 percent) — suggesting that children of Black immigrants in the TGAs experience some protection against the overall pattern of disadvantage in these areas.

B. Regression Analyses of Child Outcomes

Below we show that the children of Black immigrant mothers continue to display an advantage over the children of Latina immigrant mothers on kindergarten readiness measures, even when controlling for socio-economic and other child and family characteristics. The children of Black immigrant mothers also show an advantage relative to those of Black native-born mothers on some measures, but these advantages tend to disappear when we control for child and family characteristics.

I. Socioemotional Behaviors (Maternal Report)

Black immigrant mothers report better behavior for their children than do Latina mothers, and this pattern persists when controlling for socioeconomic and other characteristics (see Appendix Table A-1). When controlling only for child age and gender, the behavior score (as reported by the mother) is over two-thirds of a standard deviate higher (reported in the table as 0.71) for the children of Black immigrants than for the children of Latina immigrants.[22] The behavioral advantage of the children of Black immigrants over those of Latina immigrants in year 5 of the study persists even when controlling for the mother's education, family structure, birth outcomes, poverty-level income, and other characteristics.

Despite reporting comparatively better behavior for their children, Black immigrant mothers report higher parenting stress and depression than Latina immigrant mothers, which are factors generally associated with poorer child behavior. On the other hand, Black immigrant mothers report much higher levels of child-care enrollment than Latina immigrant mothers, a factor associated with better child behavior. Yet neither of these factors significantly influences the strong advantage of Black immigrants' children over Latina immigrant's children in the behavioral domain. At the same time, there do not appear to be significant differences between the children of Black immigrant mothers and those of Black native-born mothers in this domain.

---

22 The standard deviation is used to describe the variability in a set of numbers. In this case, it tells us how much, on average, the individual scores within a given group vary (or deviate) from the average score for the entire group.

2. Pre-Academic Skills (Maternal Report)

Black immigrant mothers also report higher pre-academic skill levels among their children than do Latina immigrant mothers (see Appendix Table A-2). When controlling for age and gender, the pre-academic skills of the children of Black immigrants are more than a standard deviation higher than those of the children of Latina immigrants. After controlling for family and child characteristics, the gap in pre-academic skills is somewhat reduced, but still remains. Children of employed mothers and those with highly educated mothers have significantly higher pre-academic skills scores, and so the relatively high rates of employment and education among Black foreign-born mothers are a partial explanation for their children's relatively high scores. In addition, the effects of parenting stress and maternal depression on pre-academic skills (two indicators on which Black immigrant mothers fare relatively poorly) are much smaller than they are for behavior scores, and they do not reach statistical significance. After accounting for parenting variables and use of center-based child care, all of which are positively and significantly related to pre-academic skills, the size of the advantage that the children of Black foreign-born mothers have compared to those of Latina foreign-born mothers declines, but remains fairly large and highly significant.

3. ECHOS

Analysis of the "consistently demonstrating" category on the ECHOS portion of FLKRS showed a strong advantage for the children of Black immigrant mothers. When controlling only for gender and age, the odds that these children receive a score of "consistently demonstrating" are almost six times those for the children of Latina immigrants (see Appendix Table A-3). In addition, the odds that the children of Black immigrants score "consistently demonstrating" are also over twice as large as they are for the children of Black native-born mothers (not shown in table). Moreover, children of Black immigrants are significantly more likely to score "consistently demonstrating" than either children of Latina immigrants or children of Black natives even *after* controlling for the full range of socioeconomic and other characteristics. Overall, children with less-educated mothers and low birth weight children are less likely than other children to reach the "consistently demonstrating" threshold, while those children with more books in the home are more likely than other children to score above this threshold. Thus two of the factors that favor the children of Black immigrants (higher parental education and books in the home) may partially explain their advantage in kindergarten readiness.[23]

23　We also analyzed the likelihood of children receiving a score of either "consistently demonstrating" or "emerging/progressing" on the ECHOS, since this is how the Palm Beach County school district defines readiness for school. We found that, after controlling for child and family characteristics, Black children of immigrants did *not* have an advantage over other children. In addition, the only variable that showed a strong relationship to the ECHOS score was the number of books in the home.

4. FAIR (67 or above)

Our analysis of the other Palm Beach County school district measure of school readiness — the FAIR kindergarten literacy assessment — shows that the children of Black immigrant mothers fare better than those of Latina immigrants, even when controlling for socioeconomic and other characteristics. When controlling only for gender and age, the odds that the children of Black immigrant mothers pass the FAIR literacy assessment (i.e. achieve a score of 67 or higher) are more than three times those of the children of Latina immigrants (see Appendix Table A-4). As we saw for the results from the ECHOS, birth weight and mother's education are both significantly associated with the likelihood of passing the FAIR. The number of children's books in the home is not significantly associated with passing the FAIR, but enrollment in center-based child care has a strong positive association. Poverty-level income and mother's employment also show significant associations. Once again, these factors favor the children of Black immigrants and may partially — though not entirely — explain their relatively strong performance on the literacy assessment.

IV. Discussion and Conclusion

The results presented here show strong advantages of the children of Black immigrant mothers in early childhood outcomes and school readiness when compared to the children of Latina immigrant mothers. The children of Black immigrants score better than the children of Latina immigrants across the board on both parent-reported measures of well-being and kindergarten readiness assessments, even when controlling for their socioeconomic circumstances, access to early education, mothers' well-being, and other important characteristics. In addition, they fared better than the children of Black native-born mothers on one of the two measures of school readiness (the ECHOS).

Perhaps most significantly, the children of Black immigrants in our sample, who resided in the TGAs, had kindergarten readiness assessment scores comparable to those for the average child entering kindergarten in the Palm Beach County school district. This finding suggests that many Black immigrant families with young children are able to overcome some of the negative environmental factors associated with living in distressed areas, such as higher rates of poverty, teen pregnancy, crime, and child abuse and neglect. The factors that protect Black immigrants' children from these environmental risks appear to include relatively high parental education and employment, as well as access to and utilization of center-based child care and early education. But the survey data we collected do not include variables that adequately explain the relative advantage of Black immigrants' children on these measures; some of that advantage must be related to migrant selectivity, parenting skills, and other factors that are more difficult for surveys generally to measure.

Our analyses show that some of the advantages experienced by the children of Black immigrant mothers are due to their parents' relatively better educational and socioeconomic status. For instance, in the countywide sample we analyzed, Black foreign-born mothers had more formal education than Latina foreign-born mothers and were less likely to be teen mothers. Black immigrant mothers were advantaged relative to Black US-born mothers in terms of marital status, age, and likelihood of being a teen mother. Also, Black foreign-born mothers were less likely than both groups to reside in the TGAs. On the other hand, compared to Latina foreign-born mothers, Black foreign-born mothers had higher rates of pregnancy complications and were somewhat more likely to give birth to a child with low birth weight. Taken together, these factors generally show an advantage for Black immigrant mothers — an advantage that is reflected in better outcomes for their children at least upon entrance to kindergarten.

The more detailed data from our survey of families living in the TGAs reveal additional advantages for Black immigrant mothers compared to Latina immigrant mothers, in terms of number of years living in the United States, employment status, and overall parenting scores. On the other hand, Black foreign-born mothers were significantly less likely than Latina foreign-born mothers to be living with a partner and more likely to be depressed than Latina foreign-born mothers.[24] Thus the picture of Black immigrant advantage in parenting is not entirely clear, as single parenthood and depression are significant risk factors for poorer child behavior and school readiness.

What else might account for the better outcomes of Black immigrants' children, particularly in comparison to Latina immigrants' children? One possibility is that the children of Black immigrant mothers in our sample benefited from the higher English proficiency and longer US residency of their parents.[25] However, supplementary regression analyses conducted for the sample of only the children of Black and

---

24 While there is some evidence that shows Latino immigrants typically have better health and mental health than U.S.-born populations, very little is known about the Black immigrant population. See Javier I. Escobar, "Immigration and Mental Health: Why Are Immigrants Better Off?" *Archives of General Psychiatry* 55, No. 9 (1998): 781; and Jeanne Miranda, Juned Siddique, Thomas R. Belin, and Laura P. Kohn-Wood, "Depression Prevalence in Disadvantaged Young Black Women," *Social Psychiatry and Psychiatric Epidemiology* 40, No. 4 (2005): 253–58.

25 One of the few studies describing prevalence of depression among Black immigrants shows that they have lower levels of depression compared to US-born Blacks, yet the odds of depression increase with each additional year spent in the United States (see Jean Miranda et al., "Depression Prevalence in Disadvantaged Young Black Women"). Black immigrant mothers may become more depressed over time because as they reside in the United States longer they begin to be socially categorized as a "Black American" and therefore are more susceptible to stereotypes, discrimination, and racism that African Americans face. See Teceta Tormala and Kay Deaux, "Black immigrants to the United States: Confronting and constructing ethnicity and race," in *Cultural Psychology of Immigrants*, ed. Ramaswami Mahalingam (Mahwah, NJ: Erlbaum, 2006): 253-258.

Latina immigrants showed that the Black immigrant advantage generally remained after controlling for number of years in the United States, whether English was spoken at home, and whether or not the mother entered the United States before the age of 13. Another possibility is that there are important unobserved characteristics associated with the relatively higher educational levels of Black immigrant mothers.

With respect to policy implications, our analyses support the well-documented association between the use of center-based care and child outcomes, and suggest the need to explore ways to enroll greater numbers of both Black and Latino immigrants' children in high-quality center-based care and preschool. We also found that parents' encouragement of children's literacy, as measured by the number of children's books in the home, was an important factor in the differential outcomes of Latina and Black immigrants' children. This finding suggests a need to better understand early parenting practices that help prepare children for school, as well as a need to increase the availability and quality of interventions designed to bolster such practices, particularly among mothers with lower educational backgrounds or literacy skills, and for whom English is a second language. Finally, consistent with some previous research, we found that low birth weight mattered for later outcomes, suggesting a need to continue to ensure that mothers have access to and utilize prenatal care. Greater attention to these and related issues would not only help build on the positive development of the children of Black immigrants, but might also help to better support the development of the children of other low-income and immigrant groups. ⌐

Appendices

Table A-1. Linear Regression Analysis of Maternal Report of Behavior

	Controlling for Child's Age and Gender			Baseline Variables			Full Model		
	Coeff.	SE	Sig.	Coeff.	SE	Sig.	Coeff.	SE	Sig.
Race/Nativity									
Black, Immigrant	0.71	0.17	***	0.78	0.19	***	0.72	0.20	***
Black, US Born	0.58	0.12	***	0.74	0.15	***	0.64	0.16	***
Hispanic, Immigrant (excluded variable)	—	—	—	—	—	—	—	—	—
Hispanic, US Born	0.56	0.21	**	0.21	0.21	**	0.39	0.22	^
Other	0.69	0.21	***	0.22	0.22	**	0.64	0.24	**
Focal child's age at Year 5	-0.06	0.03	*	-0.05	0.03	NS	-0.04	0.03	NS
Male focal child	-0.29	0.10	**	-0.27	0.10	**	-0.26	0.10	**
Baseline characteristics									
Mother's education									
Less than high school diploma	—	—	—	-0.14	0.15	NS	-0.04	0.16	NS
High school diploma/GED	—	—	—	-0.14	0.16	NS	-0.17	0.16	NS
More than high school diploma (excluded variable)	—	—	—	—	—	—	—	—	—
Teen mother	—	—	—	0.03	0.14	NS	0.01	0.15	NS
Focal child low birth weight	—	—	—	-0.22	0.16	NS	-0.26	0.16	NS
Lives in Glades	—	—	—	-0.13	0.13	NS	-0.11	0.14	NS
Lives with partner	—	—	—	-0.05	0.12	NS	-0.02	0.12	NS
Currently working	—	—	—	0.01	0.16	NS	-0.06	0.16	NS
At/below poverty threshold	—	—	—	-0.28	0.12	*	-0.17	0.12	NS
Focal child has special needs	—	—	—	-0.06	0.17	NS	-0.02	0.17	NS
Number of negative housing conditions	—	—	—	-0.06	0.03	*	-0.04	0.03	NS
Parental stress score[1]									
High parental stress	—	—	—	-0.48	0.14	***	-0.51	0.15	***
Depression: CES-D score > 16	—	—	—	-0.23	0.11	*	-0.25	0.12	*
Year 3 through 5 characteristics									
Overall parenting score	—	—	—	—	—	—	0.20	0.19	NS
Ever received center-based child care	—	—	—	—	—	—	0.23	0.12	*
Year 5 characteristics									
Number of children	—	—	—	—	—	—	-0.06	0.04	^
Number of children's books at home	—	—	—	—	—	—	0.00	0.00	NS
Educational expectations for focal child	—	—	—	—	—	—	0.20	0.15	NS

	Controlling for Child's Age and Gender			Baseline Variables			Full Model		
	Coeff.	SE	Sig.	Coeff.	SE	Sig.	Coeff.	SE	Sig.
Constant	2.67	1.44	^	2.76	1.49	^	2.02	1.58	NS
N	353			326			302		
R-squared	0.12			0.25			0.28		

[1] For the parental stress score, a dummy variable to indicate the score was missing was included in the regression, but is not shown in the table.

Table A-2. Linear Regression Analysis of Maternal Report of Pre-Academic Skills

	Controlling for Child's Age and Gender			Baseline Variables			Full Model		
	Coeff.	SE	Sig.	Coeff.	SE	Sig.	Coeff.	SE	Sig.
Race/Nativity									
Black, Immigrant	1.22	0.16	***	1.07	0.17	***	0.84	0.18	***
Black, US Born	1.09	0.10	***	0.95	0.13	***	0.68	0.14	***
Hispanic, Immigrant (excluded variable)	—	—	—	—	—	—	—	—	—
Hispanic, US Born	0.89	0.19	***	0.73	0.19	***	0.53	0.20	**
Other	0.94	0.19	***	0.75	0.20	***	0.52	0.21	**
Focal child's age at Year 5	0.04	0.03	NS	0.00	0.03	NS	0.00	0.03	NS
Male focal child	-0.08	0.09	NS	-0.05	0.09	NS	-0.01	0.09	NS
Baseline characteristics									
Mother's education									
Less than high school diploma	—	—	—	-0.52	0.14	***	-0.35	0.14	**
High school diploma/GED	—	—	—	-0.34	0.15	*	-0.32	0.14	*
More than high school diploma (excluded variable)	—	—	—	—	—	—	—	—	—
Teen mother	—	—	—	0.04	0.12	NS	0.01	0.13	NS
Focal child low birth weight	—	—	—	-0.06	0.15	NS	-0.10	0.14	NS
Lives in Glades	—	—	—	0.18	0.12	NS	0.20	0.12	^
Lives with partner	—	—	—	0.01	0.11	NS	0.04	0.11	NS
Currently working	—	—	—	0.47	0.14	***	0.38	0.14	**
At/below poverty threshold	—	—	—	-0.23	0.11	*	-0.12	0.11	NS
Focal child has special needs	—	—	—	-0.27	0.15	^	-0.26	0.15	^
Number of negative housing conditions	—	—	—	-0.06	0.03	*	-0.04	0.03	NS
Parental stress score[1]									
High parental stress	—	—	—	-0.05	0.12	NS	-0.06	0.18	NS
Depression: CES-D score > 16	—	—	—	-0.11	0.10	NS	-0.10	-0.10	NS

	Controlling for Child's Age and Gender			Baseline Variables			Full Model		
	Coeff.	SE	Sig.	Coeff.	SE	Sig.	Coeff.	SE	Sig.
Year 3 through 5 characteristics									
Overall parenting score	—	—	—	—	—	—	0.42	0.17	**
Ever received center-based child care	—	—	—	—	—	—	0.39	0.10	***
Year 5 characteristics									
Number of children	—	—	—	—	—	—	-0.07	0.03	*
Number of children's books at home	—	—	—	—	—	—	0.004	0.002	**
Educational expectations for focal child	—	—	—	—	—	—	0.29	0.13	*
Constant	-2.36	1.29	^	0.20	1.35	NS	-1.05	1.38	NS
N	353			326			302		
R-squared	0.29			0.40			0.47		

[1] For the parental stress score, a dummy variable to indicate the score was missing was included in the regression, but is not shown in the table.

Table A-3. Logistic Regression Analysis of ECHOS Test Scores (Consistently Demonstrating)

	Controlling for Child's Age and Gender			Baseline Variables			Full Model		
	Odds Ratio	SE	Sig.	Odds Ratio	SE	Sig.	Odds Ratio	SE	Sig.
Race/Nativity									
Black, Immigrant	5.7	2.57	***	5.3	2.92	**	4.0	2.51	*
Black, US Born	2.2	0.78	*	1.5	0.76	NS	1.1	0.62	NS
Hispanic, Immigrant (excluded variable)	—	—	—	—	—	—	—	—	—
Hispanic, US Born	2.9	1.57	*	1.8	1.19	NS	1.7	1.22	NS
Other	3.8	2.45	*	1.9	1.58	NS	1.2	1.27	NS
Child's age when ECHOS administered	4.5	2.59	**	4.2	2.71	*	7.1	5.22	**
Male focal child	1.0	0.29	NS	1.0	0.34	NS	1.2	0.44	NS
Baseline characteristics									
Mother's education									
Less than high school diploma	—	—	—	0.2	0.09	***	0.2	0.09	**
High school diploma/GED	—	—	—	0.5	0.24	NS	0.3	0.19	^
More than high school diploma (excluded variable)	—	—	—	—	—	—	—	—	—
Teen mother	—	—	—	1.4	0.65	NS	1.7	0.86	NS
Focal child low birth weight	—	—	—	0.1	0.11	*	0.1	0.06	**

	Controlling for Child's Age and Gender			Baseline Variables			Full Model		
	Odds Ratio	SE	Sig.	Odds Ratio	SE	Sig.	Odds Ratio	SE	Sig.
Lives in Glades	—	—	—	0.7	0.28	NS	0.8	0.37	NS
Lives with partner	—	—	—	0.8	0.32	NS	0.7	0.27	NS
Currently working	—	—	—	1.7	0.75	NS	1.9	0.91	NS
At/below poverty threshold	—	—	—	0.9	0.35	NS	1.5	0.69	NS
Focal child has special needs	—	—	—	0.8	0.52	NS	0.8	0.55	NS
Number of negative housing conditions	—	—	—	0.9	0.09	NS	1.0	0.10	NS
Parental stress score[1]									
High parental stress	—	—	—	2.0	0.93	NS	2.6	1.33	^
Depression: CES-D score > 16	—	—	—	0.5	0.20	^	0.5	0.19	^
Year 3 through 5 characteristics									
Overall parenting score	—	—	—	—	—	—	1.0	0.69	NS
Ever received center-based child care	—	—	—	—	—	—	0.8	0.35	NS
Year 5 characteristics									
Number of children	—	—	—	—	—	—	1.0	0.13	NS
Number of children's books at home	—	—	—	—	—	—	1.0	0.01	***
Educational expectations for focal child	—	—	—	—	—	—	1.0	0.56	NS
Constant	283			260			240		
N	25.43			53.24			69.80		
χ^2	0.29			0.40			0.47		

[1] For the parental stress score, a dummy variable to indicate the score was missing was included in the regression, but is not shown in the table.

Table A-4. Logistic Regression Analysis of FAIR Test Scores

	Controlling for Child's Age and Gender			Baseline Variables			Full Model		
	Odds Ratio	SE	Sig.	Odds Ratio	SE	Sig.	Odds Ratio	SE	Sig.
Race/Nativity									
Black, Immigrant	3.2	1.36	**	3.7	1.95	*	3.7	2.18	*
Black, US Born	1.6	0.46	NS	1.8	0.81	NS	1.8	0.90	NS
Hispanic, Immigrant (excluded variable)	—	—	—	—	—	—	—	—	—
Hispanic, US Born	2.2	1.05	^	2.2	1.35	NS	1.5	0.96	NS
Other	1.5	0.85	NS	1.0	0.79	NS	0.7	0.58	NS

	Controlling for Child's Age and Gender			Baseline Variables			Full Model		
	Odds Ratio	SE	Sig.	Odds Ratio	SE	Sig.	Odds Ratio	SE	Sig.
Child's age when ECHOS administered	4.5	2.24	**	3.3	1.92	*	3.6	2.22	*
Male focal child	0.9	0.23	NS	0.9	0.27	NS	1.0	0.32	NS
Baseline characteristics									
Mother's education									
Less than high school diploma	—	—	—	0.3	0.13	**	0.3	0.18	*
High school diploma/GED	—	—	—	0.3	0.14	*	0.3	0.15	*
More than high school diploma (excluded variable)	—	—	—	—	—	—	—	—	—
Teen mother	—	—	—	1.1	0.44	NS	1.0	0.48	NS
Focal child low birth weight	—	—	—	0.2	0.13	**	0.2	0.11	**
Lives in Glades	—	—	—	0.7	0.26	NS	0.5	0.20	^
Lives with partner	—	—	—	0.8	0.29	NS	0.7	0.28	NS
Currently working	—	—	—	3.1	1.42	*	2.9	1.40	*
At/below poverty threshold	—	—	—	0.5	0.15	*	0.5	0.17	*
Focal child has special needs	—	—	—	0.8	0.43	NS	0.9	0.51	NS
Number of negative housing conditions	—	—	—	0.9	0.08	NS	0.8	0.08	*
Parental stress score1									
High parental stress	—	—	—	0.9	0.38	NS	0.9	0.45	NS
Depression: CES-D score > 16	—	—	—	0.5	0.17	*	0.5	0.18	^
Year 3 through 5 characteristics									
Overall parenting score	—	—	—	—	—	—	0.7	0.4	NS
Ever received center-based child care	—	—	—	—	—	—	2.2	0.77	*
Year 5 characteristics									
Number of children	—	—	—	—	—	—	1.0	0.12	NS
Number of children's books at home	—	—	—	—	—	—	1.0	0.01	NS
Educational expectations for focal child	—	—	—	—	—	—	0.6	0.27	NS
Constant	289			265			242		
N	19.15			59.49			64.23		
x^2	0.29			0.40			0.47		

[1] For the parental stress score, a dummy variable to indicate the score was missing was included in the regression, but is not shown in the table.

Works Cited

Bronfenbrenner, Urie. 1977. Toward an Experimental Ecology of Human Development. *American Psychologist* 32 (7): 513–31.

Children's Services Council of Palm Beach County (CSC). 2003. *State of the Child in Palm Beach County.* Palm Beach County, FL: CSC.

Escobar, Javier I. 1998. Immigration and Mental Health: Why Are Immigrants Better Off? *Archives of General Psychiatry* 55 (9): 781.

Kent, Mary Mederios. 2007. Immigration and America's Black Population. *Population Bulletin* 62 (4): 1-20. Washington, DC: Population Reference Bureau. www.prb.org/pdf07/62.4immigration.pdf.

Miranda, Jeanne, Juned Siddique, Thomas R. Belin, and Laura P. Kohn-Wood. 2005. Depression Prevalence in Disadvantaged Young Black Women. *Social Psychiatry and Psychiatric Epidemiology* 40 (4): 253–58.

Palacios, Natalia, Katarina Guttmannova, and P. Lindsay Chase-Lansdale. 2008. Early Reading Achievement of Children in Immigrant Families: Is There an Immigrant Paradox? *Developmental Psychology* 44 (5): 1381–95.

Portes, Alejandro and Ruben G. Rumbaut. 2006. *Immigrant America: A Portrait*, 3rd edition. Berkeley, CA: University of California Press.

Reitz, Jeffery G., Heather Zhang, and Naoko Hawkins. 2011. Comparisons of the Success of Racial Minority Immigrant Offspring in the United States, Canada and Australia. *Social Science Research* 40: 1051–66.

Spielberger, Julie, John Schuerman, Sandra Lyons, and Thomas Haywood. 2006. *The Palm Beach County Family Study: Baseline Report.* Chicago, IL: Chapin Hall at the University of Chicago.

Terrazas, Aaron. 2011. Immigrants in New-Destination States. *Migration Information Source,* February 2011. http://migrationinformation.org/USFocus/display.cfm?ID=826.

Tormala, Teceta and Kay Deaux. 2006. Black immigrants to the United States: Confronting and constructing ethnicity and race. In *Cultural Psychology of Immigrants,* ed. Ramaswami Mahalingam. Mahwah, NJ: Erlbaum.

CHAPTER 8

TRANSNATIONAL PARENTING: CHILD FOSTERING IN GHANAIAN IMMIGRANT FAMILIES

Cati Coe

Rutgers University

Introduction

Today, we are witnessing high, but not unprecedented, rates of migration across national borders and around the globe. It is widely known that this movement holds the potential to influence social and economic conditions in migrant-sending and -receiving countries. What is less commonly recognized is that contemporary flows of migration seem to be generating transnational family arrangements that may influence children's development and well-being. Families are scattered among countries, with spouses separated and children living apart from one or both parents and their siblings for years at a time. Statistics describing the prevalence and structures of transnational families, however, are hard to come by.

One study based on interviews with 385 adolescents born in China, Central America, the Dominican Republic, Haiti, and Mexico living in the United States found that 85 percent had been separated from one or both parents for an extended period.[1] A larger survey of 8,573 US-based immigrants who had just received legal permanent residence (LPR, known as a "green card") and their children found that 15 percent of these immigrants' children had been separated from at least one parent for two years or more. Separation was more common for those children who were born outside the United States: 31 percent had been separat-

---

1   Carola Suárez-Orozco, Irina L. G. Todorova, and Josephine Louie, "Making Up for Lost Time: The Experience of Separation and Reunification among Immigrant Families," *Family Process* 41 no. 4 (2002): 625–43.

ed from a parent.[2] These statistics make it clear that separation is quite common among the children of immigrants in the United States and elsewhere.

Ethnographic research suggests that parent-child separation may be more common among Black immigrants than other immigrants because of parenting traditions that distribute child care through practices known as child fostering, child circulation, or child shifting. These practices have developed in areas of West Africa and the Caribbean that have long traditions of regional migration. This chapter explores the practice of child fostering and its implications for parent-child separation among immigrants from Ghana.

Like many Caribbean immigrants and some West Africans who come from politically stable countries, many Ghanaian immigrants do not raise their young children in the United States. Instead, these children are raised in their country of origin by other family members.[3] Some of these children are "left behind" when a parent migrates; others are born in the United States and later sent to Ghana as infants or adolescents. Ethnographic research shows that the ages of their return to the United States vary: many do so as young adults, others when they are ready for elementary school.

This chapter analyzes the reasons why many Ghanaian immigrants decide to raise their young children in Ghana. It also assesses the informal and formal social resources available to support the well-being of young children of a select group of Black immigrants in the United States.

---

2   Thomas H. Gindling and Sara Poggio, *Family Separation and Reunification as a Factor in the Educational Success of Immigrant Children* (Baltimore, MD: Maryland Institute for Policy Analysis and Research, University of Maryland, Baltimore County, 2008). In the survey, 59 percent came from Latin America, 19 percent from Asia, and 22 percent from other parts of the world.

3   For Burkinabe, see Andy Newman, "Fire Puts a Sad Ending on an Optimistic Immigrant Tale," *New York Times*, February 25, 2006, www.nytimes.com/2006/02/25/nyre-gion/25victims.html?pagewanted=print&_r=0. For Caribbean immigrants, see Karen Fog Olwig, "Narratives of the Children Left Behind: Home and Identity in Globalised Caribbean Families," *Journal of Ethnic and Migration Studies* 25, no. 2 (1999): 267–84; and Andrea Smith, Richard Lalonde, and Simone Johnson, "Serial Migration and Its Implications for the Parent-Child Relationship: A Retrospective Analysis of the Experiences of the Children of Caribbean Immigrants," *Cultural Diversity and Ethnic Minority Psychology* 10, no. 2 (2004): 107–22. For Chinese immigrants in Canada who send their infants back to China, see Yvonne Bohr and Connie Tse, "Satellite Babies in Transnational Families: A Study of Parents' Decisions to Separate from their Infants," *Infant Mental Health Journal* 30, no. 3 (2009): 265–86. For Peruvian "left-behind children," see Jessaca B. Leinaweaver, "Outsourcing Care: How Peruvian Migrants Meet Transnational Family Obligations," *Latin American Perspectives* 37, no. 5 (2010): 67–87.

I. Distributed Care and Fostering in Ghana

Across West Africa, children are often raised by someone other than their parents, in a practice termed "fostering" in the anthropological literature because rights to the children's birth parents are not abrogated, making it more similar to fostering than to adopting as is practiced in the United States and Europe. Ghana's censuses report quite consistently that between 15 to 25 percent of children live with neither their mother nor their father, with the rates slowly declining over the past 40 years.[4] However, fostering is not quite the right word to use, depending as it does on a Western notion of nuclear family life and rights. Rather, it is fairer to say that parenting — entailing child care, training, and launching a child into adulthood — can be distributed widely across many people; birth parents are central, but they are not the only adults who can or are expected to assist in this process.[5] In many ways, distributing care in this way provides a safety net for children in adverse circumstances (for example, those whose parents suffer from mental illness or are disabled) although it is not only such children who are fostered. In the anthropological literature on the Caribbean, these practices are known as "child-shifting," which seems more descriptive of the practice than "fostering" because children easily and informally move among households.[6]

Children in Ghana circulate among households throughout their childhood and adolescence, depending on many factors including the health and wealth of the caregiver and their parents, geographical proximity to schooling, and opportunities to learn skills and habits from the family with which they are living. Although the most common fostering occurs among close family members, with children fostered by an aunt, uncle, or grandparent, it also takes place among more distant kin or

---

4   Elizabeth Ardayfio-Schandorf and Margaret Amissah, "Incidence of Child Fostering among School Children in Ghana," in *The Changing Family in Ghana*, ed. Elizabeth Ardayfio-Schandorf (Accra, Ghana: Ghana Universities Press, 1996); Uche C. Isiugo-Abanihe, "Child Fostering in West Africa," *Population and Development Review* 11, no. 1 (1985): 53–73; Hilary Page, "Childrearing versus Childbearing: Coresidence of Mother and Child in Sub-Saharan Africa," in *Reproduction and Social Organization in Sub-Saharan Africa*, ed. Ron J. Lesthaeghe (Berkeley, CA: University of California Press, 1989).

5   Erdmute Alber, "Denying Biological Parenthood: Fosterage in Northern Benin," *Ethnos* 68, no. 4 (2003): 487–506; Esther Goody, *Parenting and Social Reproduction: Fostering and Occupational Roles in West Africa* (Cambridge, UK: Cambridge University Press, 1982); Ughetta Moscardino, Oge Nwobu, and Giovanna Axia, "Cultural Beliefs and Practices Related to Infant Health and Development among Nigerian Immigrant Mothers in Italy," *Journal of Reproductive and Infant Psychology* 24, no. 3 (2006): 241–55.

6   On "child-shifting" among Caribbean migrants, see Isa Maria Soto, "West Indian Child Fostering: Its Role in Migrant Exchange," in *Caribbean Life in New York City: Sociocultural Dimensions*, eds. Constance R. Sutton and Elsa M. Chaney (Staten Island, NY: Center for Migration Studies of New York, 1987); and Maarit Forde, "Modes of Transnational Relatedness: Caribbean Migrants' Networks of Child Care and Ritual Kinship," in *Everyday Ruptures: Children, Youth, and Migration in Global Perspective*, eds. Cati Coe, Rachel R. Reynolds, Deborah A. Boehm, Julia Meredith Hess, and Heather Rae-Espinoza (Nashville, TN: Vanderbilt University Press, 2011).

non-kin, in which case the child can be treated like a house servant in exchange for his or her continued schooling or trade apprenticeship. Practices of fostering have been critical to rural-urban migration across West Africa, with female urban migrants since the 1970s sending their children to their mothers back in the villages, so they can dedicate themselves to their work. Rural migrants also sent their children to urban relatives so that they could go to school and see more of the world.[7] As West Africans have moved farther afield, including to the United States and Europe, they have used fostering to facilitate their migrations and to ensure their children's well-being, including connections to kin, good schooling, and familiarity with their home language and culture.[8]

Despite certain continuities, international migrants have introduced two changes in fostering practices in comparison to their counterparts who remain in Ghana: (1) the age of the fostered child is younger, and (2) the child is fostered in households that are relatively less wealthy.[9] Ghana's 1998 census reported fostering rates of 23.6 percent for children 10 to 14 years old, 12 percent for those aged 3 to 5, but only 2.6 percent for those under the age of 2.[10] Grandmothers were the most prevalent foster parents for children under the age of 5, with a wider range of caregivers for older children. My research suggests that international migrants, on the other hand, are as likely to foster out babies and young children as teenagers, usually to grandmothers. Furthermore, unlike general patterns in Ghana, where the likelihood of being fostered out increases with age, it is when children of international migrants become young adults that they tend to leave the foster household and move abroad with their birth parents.

The second difference has to do with the wealth of the fostering-in and fostering-out households. Children in Ghana tend to shift from poorer households to wealthier households that are better able to provide them with educational and training opportunities, shelter, and food. Contributing to this trend, urban middle-class families in Ghana prefer to raise their own children to make sure that they can control their training and character, but are willing to foster-in children of their

7   Lynne Brydon, "Women at Work: Some Changes in Family Structure in Amedzofe-Ava-time, Ghana," *Africa* 49, no. 2 (1979): 97–111; Mona Etienne, "Maternité Sociale, Rapports d'Adoption et Pouvoir des Femmes chez les Baoulé (Côte d'Ivoire)," *L'Homme* 19, nos. 3–4 (1979): 63–107.

8   Goody, *Parenting and Social Reproduction*; Bruce Whitehouse, "Transnational Childrearing and the Preservation of Transnational Identity in Brazzaville, Congo," *Global Networks* 9, no. 1 (2009): 82–99.

9   For a more complete discussion see Cati Coe, "How International Migration Has Affect-ed the Distribution of Childcare in Ghana," in *Youth and Identity in Africa*, eds. Abubakar Momoh and Ndiouga Benga (Dakar, Senegal: Council for the Development of Social Science Research in Africa, in press).

10 Ghana Statistical Service, *Ghana Demographic and Health Survey, 1998* (Accra, Ghana: Ghana Statistical Service, 1998).

poorer relatives.[11] Although international migrants are considered to be more wealthy than those living in Ghana and to have access to better educational opportunities abroad, they tend not to raise their own children, much less the children of their siblings, as they might do if they were in Ghana. Instead, the children of international migrants are shifted to relatively poorer households back in Ghana that are dependent on remittances from abroad.

Many Ghanaian parents living in the United States would like to raise their own children but feel unable to do so to their satisfaction; they therefore feel compelled to foster them with relatives in Ghana. It is an imperfect option, but one that is available to them, given their family histories and cultural repertoires. An exploration of the tensions involved in parents' decisions around child fostering gives us an opportunity to see some of the obstacles to their children's well-being in the United States.

II. Ghanaians in the United States

Migration has long characterized West African social and economic life, and migrants and refugees have historically been valued as sources of new knowledge, skills, and resources. In the late 19th and early 20th centuries, skilled craftsmen and traders typically traveled throughout West Africa. During the late colonial and early postcolonial periods in the 1950s and 1960s, elite Ghanaians went abroad — particularly to Britain, the imperial center — for several years for an education that won them high-status civil service positions on their return. Other Ghanaians traveled to the United States for their education, among them the first prime minister, Kwame Nkrumah, who attended Lincoln University in Pennsylvania and the University of Pennsylvania before going to Britain in 1945 for two years. He returned to what was then known as the Gold Coast in 1947 to lead the British colony's movement toward independence, which Ghana achieved in 1957. International migration to the United Kingdom and United States has thus been historically associated with the elite class and high status in Ghana, like in other West African countries.

Ghanaians' international migration increased substantially after structural adjustment programs were instituted by the World Bank during the 1980s, causing civil servants' wages to stagnate even as Ghana began to experience economic growth.[12] In the 1990s Ghanaians began traveling farther afield in greater numbers, including to Dubai, Israel, Jamaica, Japan, and South Africa. Almost 1 million

---

11 Ardayfio-Schandorf and Amissah, "Incidence of Child Fostering among Schoolchildren in Ghana.

12 Kwaku A. Twum-Baah, John S. Nabila, and Andrews F. Aryee, eds., *Migration Research Study in Ghana* (Accra, Ghana: Ghana Statistical Service, 1995).

Ghanaians were estimated to be living outside their country in 2005, representing 4.6 percent of a population of 22 million people. Most of these migrants moved to other West African countries that are part of the Economic Community of West African States (ECOWAS), which made travel between these countries easier.13 The United States and United Kingdom were among the most significant destinations outside of Africa (at 7.3 percent and 5.8 percent respectively); many Ghanaians initially migrated to another African country (such as Togo, Nigeria, Botswana, or Gabon) to enable eventual migration to a higher-income country.14 International migration has become increasingly available to a broader swath of the population, including students, teachers, and lower-level civil servants, and skilled blue-collar workers such as mechanics and electricians. Still, it is primarily those living in southern Ghana's urban areas who can raise the capital and tap into overseas connections to migrate outside of Africa.15

Two changes in US immigration law have enabled more Africans to migrate legally to the United States. The *Immigration Act of 1965* eliminated national-origin quotas that in effect discriminated against those from Asia, Africa, and some parts of Europe. Even more significant was the *Immigration Act of 1990*, which established a green card lottery for nationals of countries with low rates of immigration to the United States. Every year, no more than 55,000 permanent resident visas are made available through this lottery to foreign nationals who met certain educational or basic work experience requirements.[16] Although so-called diversity immigrants account for a small share (4.8 percent in 2010) of legal permanent admissions to the United States, African nationals have received a large share of them (41 percent of the diversity lottery visas in 2010). In 2009 Ghana had the highest number of lottery winners of any country (8,742), although not all of these individuals ultimately received a green card.[17]

---

13 International Organization for Migration (IOM), "Migration in Ghana: A Country Profile, 2009," www.iom.int/jahia/Jahia/about-migration/lang/en.

14 Ibid. While outside the Economic Community of West African States (ECOWAS) zone, Botswana and Gabon are popular destinations for Ghanaian migrants because they are among the wealthier countries in Africa. (Gabon is an oil producer, and Botswana's revenue comes from diamonds.)

15 Kevin J. A. Thomas, "What Explains the Increasing Trend in African Emigration to the US?" *International Migration Review* 45, no. 1 (2011): 3–28; Kwaku Twum-Baah, "Volume and Characteristics of International Ghanaian Migration" in *At Home in the World? International Migration and Development in Contemporary Ghana and West Africa*, ed. Takyiwaa Manuh (Accra, Ghana: Sub-Saharan Publishers, 2005).

16 Winners from the 2010 visa lottery (run between October 2 and December 1, 2008) were selected at random from over 13.6 million qualified entries.

17 US Department of State, "Diversity Visa Lottery 2010 (DV-2010) Results," http://travel.state.gov/visa/immigrants/types/types_4574.html. For instance, in 2008, Ghana had 7,322 lottery winners, but only 1,142 actually received green cards. See Department of Homeland Security (DHS) Office of Immigration Statistics, *2008 Yearbook of Immigration Statistics* (Washington, DC: DHS, 2009), www.dhs.gov/xlibrary/assets/statistics/yearbook/2008/ois_yb_2008.pdf.

Ghanaian immigrants, like other Africans, are primarily new immigrants. Forty-one percent of Black African immigrants in the United States arrived between 2000 and 2005, and three-quarters came in 1990 or later.[18] As of 2007 more than four in ten Black Ghanaians had arrived in the United States in 2000 or later.[19]

Although the Black African immigrant population in the United States is growing rapidly, the number of Black African immigrants remains small in comparison to immigrants of other racial/ethnic backgrounds and origins. In 2009 the number of Black African immigrants living in the United States was estimated to be 1.1 million, or about 3 percent of the total foreign-born population. Among Black African immigrants, 110,000 were Ghanaians (10 percent) and Ghana was the third-most popular country of origin for Black African immigrants, following Nigeria and Ethiopia.[20] In 2007, among metro areas, the New York–northeastern New Jersey metropolitan area and metropolitan Washington, DC were home to the largest numbers of Black Ghanaian immigrants.[21]

Many African immigrants to the United States are highly educated, and Ghanaian immigrants are more likely than immigrants overall and native-born Americans to report a bachelor's degree or more as their highest educational credential.[22] The criteria for the diversity visa lottery favors the more educated, as awardees must have at least a high school education or its equivalent, or two years of work experience in the past five years in an occupation that requires at least two years of training or experience.[23]

According to American Community Survey (ACS) data, in 2007, 91 percent of Ghanaians in the United States had a high school diploma or higher (in comparison to 85 percent among the total US population). More specifically, 20 percent reported a bachelor's degree as their highest educational credential (compared to 17 percent of the overall population), and 14 percent a master's, professional, or doctoral degree (compared to 10 percent of the total population).[24] Strong educational

18 Mary Mederios Kent, "Immigration and America's Black Population" (*Population Bulletin* 62, no. 4, Population Reference Bureau, December 2007), www.prb.org/pdf07/62.4immigration.pdf.
19 Author's analysis of the US Census Bureau's American Community Survey (ACS) 2006-08, pooled. Accessed from Steven Ruggles, J. Trent Alexander, Katie Genadek, Ronald Goeken, Matthew B. Schroeder, and Matthew Sobek, *Integrated Public Use Microdata Series: Version 5.0* [Machine-readable database] (Minneapolis, MN: Minnesota Population Center [producer and distributor, 2010).
20 See Chapter 2 in this volume, Randy Capps, Kristen McCabe, and Michael Fix, *New Streams: Black African Migration to the United States.*
21 Author's analysis of ACS 2006-08, pooled.
22 Capps, McCabe and Fix, *New Streams.*
23 US Department of State, "Instructions for the 2011 Diversity Immigrant Visa Program," www.travel.state.gov/pdf/DV-2011instructions.pdf.
24 Capps, McCabe and Fix, *New Streams.*

credentials are extremely difficult to obtain in Ghana. Space at secondary and tertiary schools is limited, so students have to do very well on a series of exams at different points in their educational careers to progress. In Ghana in 2009, only 36 percent of young people of secondary-school age were in secondary school, while only 6 percent of those ages 18 to 21 years were pursuing higher education.[25] Thus, Ghanaian immigrants are slightly better educated than the overall US population and far better educated than Ghanaians who do not emigrate — suggesting they represent a small group from the elite and middle class among Ghanaians.

However, Ghanaians' educational credentials do not necessarily pay off in the United States. ACS data show that in 2007 median annual earnings among civilian employed Black Ghanaians ages 16 and older were similar to those for Americans overall, despite the higher educational levels of Black Ghanaians.[26] In 2007, 13 percent of civilian employed Ghanaian immigrants ages 16 and older worked in health-care support positions, 11 percent in office and administrative support roles, 10 percent in health-care practitioner and technical occupations, and 9 percent in sales and related occupations. More specifically, 12 percent reported working as "nursing, psychiatric, and home health aides."[27] Median wages for all US workers in this occupational category in 2008 were $11.46 an hour, with an annual median income of $24,010 in May 2010.[28] Half of the home-care workers were so poor they had to depend on food stamps or other public assistance, and were not eligible for overtime pay.[29]

Similar to other immigrants, most Ghanaians enter the country through family reunification: of the 7,429 Ghanaians who obtained legal permanent resident (LPR) status in 2010, 4,393 were the immediate relatives of US citizens and another 527 entered under family-sponsored preferences (therefore, a total of 66 percent obtained LPR status through family relationships). Another 2,086 (28 percent) of Ghanaians who received green cards in 2010 entered through the diversity visa program, 265 (4 percent) through employment-based pathways, and

---

25 United Nations Educational, Scientific and Cultural Organization (UNESCO) Institute for Statistics, "Ghana profile," http://stats.uis.unesco.org.

26 Capps, McCabe and Fix, *New Streams.*

27 Author's analysis of ACS, 2005-09.

28 For hourly wages in 2008, see Bureau of Labor Statistics, "Nursing and Psychiatric Aides," *Occupational Outlook Handbook, 2010-2011 Edition,* www.bls.gov/oco/ocos327.htm; for annual salary figures in 2010, see Bureau of Labor Statistics, "Occupational Employment Statistics: Occupational Employment and Wages, May 2010: Nursing Aides, Orderlies, and Attendants," www.bls.gov/oes/current/oes311012.htm#(2)).

29 Steven Greenhouse, "Justices to Hear Case on Wages of Home Aides," *The New York Times,* March 25, 2007, www.nytimes.com/2007/03/25/nyregion/25aides.html?_r=2&oref=slogin&; Douglas Martin, "Evelyn Coke, Home Care Aide Who Fought Pay Rule, is Dead at 74," *New York Times,* August 9, 2009, www.nytimes.com/2009/08/10/nyregion/10coke.html?scp=1&sq=evelyn%20coke&st=cse.

135 (less than 2 percent) as refugees or asylees.[30] As with other immigrants, it is likely that some Ghanaians live and work in the United States without authorization, although Black African immigrants are generally less likely than immigrants overall to lack legal status.[31]

Given their comparative advantages — relatively advanced educational credentials, high rates of English-language proficiency, and relatively low likelihood of lacking legal status — it is surprising that some Ghanaian immigrants decide to raise their children in Ghana rather than the United States. That they do so provides a window into the difficulties that Black immigrants face in caring for their young children. Some of these challenges are shared by native-born US families; others are particular to immigrants because of immigration laws and policies.

III. Methodology and Sample

A. Methods

Members of the Ghanaian diaspora in the United States who were involved in this study reported that raising one's children back in Ghana is common, but it is difficult to get exact statistics on this phenomenon. In 2008, children under the age of 15 represented only 7 percent of the Ghanaian-born population in the United States, whereas they constituted 20 percent of the total US population and (for 2009) 36 percent of the total population in Ghana.[32] While some of the children of Ghanaian immigrants are US-born and therefore do not show up in estimates of the Ghanaian born, we also know from ethnographic research that there are US-born children sent to be raised in Ghana and Ghanaian-born children who will eventually join their parents in the United States who are not represented in the US figures.

To examine this phenomenon, this analysis uses ethnographic data collected in the United States and Ghana, including participant observation in Ghanaian churches and community celebrations in Philadelphia and New Jersey over three years (2004–07) and in Ghana during four trips that occurred between 2005 and 2009, totaling 12 months. This chapter is primarily based on 38 unstructured interviews conducted with Ghanaian immigrant parents in the United States. This group is not a random sample; it was generated through contacts in Ghanaian communities in the United States and through surveys in schools and a small town in Ghana. Fifteen parents (or 39 percent of all parents interviewed) had children living solely in Ghana, 14 parents (37 percent) had children living only in the United States, and nine parents

---

30 DHS, Office of Immigration Statistics, *2008 Yearbook of Immigration Statistics.*
31 Capps, McCabe, and Fix, *New Streams.*
32 UNESCO Institute for Statistics, "Ghana Profile." The US age data is based on Catherine Andrzejewski's analysis of 2008 ACS data.

(24 percent) had children living in both places; in the latter situation, the most common scenario was a younger child living with one or both parents in the United States and an older one left behind or sent back to Ghana, who was expected to come to the United States in a few years.

Many of the parents with children in Ghana intended to have their children join them in the United States, although a few unauthorized parents simply decided that it would be better for their children to remain in Ghana given their status. Parents and children who were separated because of the wait times imposed by the US immigration system and expense of family sponsorship or naturalization applications tended to be apart for five years or more. This analysis concentrates on the 13 parents who raised their children in Ghana for reasons unrelated to immigration constraints, as well as those parents who were raising their children in the United States. These two groups of parents were grappling with some of the same dilemmas and thought about the resources available to them in Ghana and the United States in similar ways. The numbers involved are not meant to illustrate the prevalence of Ghanaians raising their children in Ghana by choice; rather, they are intended as a source of insight into *why* a parent would do so.

The interviews with parents are supplemented with interviews with nine adolescents and young adults who had come to the United States recently after being raised in Ghana, as well as focus-group discussions in Ghana with 52 children of emigrant parents, some of whom had been sent back to Ghana as teenagers and infants but most of whom had been left behind.[33] This study also draws on a household survey conducted in 2008 by the author in a small town called Akropong in the region of Akuapem in southeastern Ghana to discern the differences in fostering patterns between the children of international migrants and the children of internal migrants. This survey included data on 220 households, interviews with 92 caregivers and 80 children ages 8 to 22, focus-group discussions with 45 of the same children, and interviews with six of their US-based parents. Twelve of these households were fostering children under the age of 8 who had one or both parents abroad. Five other families in three larger cities (Kumasi, Koforidua, and Accra) served as more in-depth case studies, where all parties in the care-giving triad — caregivers, children, and parents — were interviewed.

Because of its focus on Ghanaian immigrants in the United States who chose to foster their children with relatives in Ghana, this study draws primarily on the previously described interviews with parents in the United States, and not the study conducted in southern Ghana. Interviews and conversations were conducted in Twi (Akuapem or Asante Twi) or English, and most took place in person in informants' homes or

---

33 Not all of the parents had migrated to the United States.

public areas that they chose out of convenience and decorum, although a small share took place by phone. Of the 38 interviews with Ghanaian parents in the United States, ten were conducted with both husband and wife (48 people total).

B. *Description of the Study Sample*

Most informants lived on the East Coast of the United States, between Worcester, MA, and northern Virginia, with the largest concentrations in the Philadelphia metropolitan area, where the author conducted participation-observation in Ghanaian churches and community activities (n=15); northern and central New Jersey (n=6); the Washington, DC metropolitan area (n=5); New York City and its northern suburbs (n=4); and metropolitan Chicago (n=3).

The median length of stay in the United States for informants in the United States was six years, with two-thirds having lived ten years or fewer in the United States, with a range of one to 35 years. The informants were therefore somewhat newer to the United States than national surveys suggest is true for Ghanaian immigrants as a whole. The difference may also suggest that newer migrants are more likely to be separated from their children.

Seven study participants (20 percent) had a college degree, a smaller proportion than in national survey data (33 percent). The most common occupation in Ghana was that of a retail market woman or small-scale trader (a common occupation among women in Ghana, n=9); teacher (n=6); or government worker (n=4). A few had not worked in Ghana but came to the United States as young people for further education and found work in the United States subsequently. Of the 32 people whose prior residence in Ghana was known, two-thirds (n=21) lived in a metropolitan area prior to their emigration. Reflecting the prevalence of health-care employment among Ghanaians seen nationally, of the 46 participants whose US employment characteristics were obtained, 14 worked in the health-care field (30 percent), four as nurse's aides, three as home health aides, and the remaining seven in other occupations within the health-care field. Many of those working in health care had not done such work in Ghana but had entered that field because of the availability of jobs and low skill levels required. This allowed them to begin remitting to their families immediately, without needing to undergo extensive retraining, which is often costly and time consuming.

Those interviewed varied in the degree to which their prior experience and training in Ghana aided them in securing employment and earning money in the United States. Those working in skilled jobs involving manual labor tended to experience continuity in their occupations: the two men who had been electricians in Ghana worked as electricians in the United States, and the one man who had been an automobile mechanic in Ghana also worked as a mechanic in the United States. On the other hand, of the six who had been teachers in Ghana, two went through the certification process to become teachers in the United States, one was a student, and of the remaining three one was working as a mental health worker; the second, a home health aide; and the third, a babysitter. Those who were educated in the United States were more successful in obtaining professional employment that matched their educational credentials; their occupations were social worker, accountant, civil servant, radiologist, and teacher.[34] One woman who had worked as an accountant at a bank in Ghana (the equivalent of a certified public accountant) also worked for a bank in the United States but felt she was overqualified. The two informants who reported they lacked legal status worked in the least stable and most poorly remunerated jobs.

There was great variation in the neighborhoods in which the 43 Ghanaians who provided their addresses lived. The average census tract where participants lived had the following characteristics:

- A relatively high (20 percent) foreign-born population, of whom 19 percent were African born

- A relatively diverse racial/ethnic composition of 40 percent white, 44 percent Black, and 15 percent Latino

- Median household income (1999) of $47,833 (near the national average)

- Poverty rate of 12 percent (also near the national average)

- A four-year college completion rate of 25 percent

- A high-school completion rate of 85 percent.

But 12 households lived in census tracts where poverty rates were 18 percent; 17 households lived in census tracts with about average rates of poverty; and 13 households lived in census tracts with low rates of poverty (less than 5 percent). Fifteen lived in areas where whites were the largest group (three in the Midwest, one in the Northeast); ten lived in census tracts in highly segregated Black neighborhoods, where Blacks constituted more than 80 percent of the residents, with varying levels of income; eight lived in majority-Black neighborhoods, three of which were Black, middle-class areas in terms of income and education; six lived in segregated white neighborhoods; and three, all in New York City, lived in majority Latino neighborhoods, with high foreign-born populations and an average high poverty rate, working-poor income, and low educational level.

---

34 For similar findings about the significance of location of education among Asian Americans, see Zhen Zeng and Yu Xie, "Asian-Americans' Earnings Disadvantage Reexamined: The Role of Place in Education," *American Journal of Sociology* 109, no. 5 (2004): 1075–108.

Overall, Ghanaians interviewed as part of the US portion of the study tended to live disproportionately with other immigrants, US-born Blacks, and other Africans, in neighborhoods with slightly lower-than-average household income and average education levels among resident adults. One teenage girl living in Worcester, MA, who had recently come from Ghana to join her father in the United States, expressed surprise at her school and new school friends: she had expected to meet whites in the United States but instead found herself in a diverse school of Central American, South Asian, and African immigrants. In most of the interviews, the Ghanaians compared themselves to US-born Blacks and Latino immigrants — their neighbors and work colleagues — with particular regard to their ways of parenting.

IV. Findings

A. The Difficulties of Combining Work and Child Care: Ghana and the United States

One of the reasons that parents in the study decided to send their young children to Ghana to be raised was because of the difficulties of balancing work and child care. Such a finding is surprising because in Ghana, women of all social classes are expected to work and raise many children. Combining work and family life is therefore not new to Ghanaian women or something to adjust to in the United States, as it is for some other female immigrants.[35]

It is helpful to look at how Ghanaian women have been able to balance high fertility with productive work in Ghana. Many choose work such as trading or farming that generates a steady source of income or food, allowing them to feed their children on a daily basis, even if doing so means reducing their profits or cutting into their business capital.[36] Self-employed, they can control the intensity and duration of their daily work routines, working less when children are small and increasing their workload and profits as children grow older. In some instances, children accompany their mothers to the market or the farm, although some research shows that women would prefer not to take them, as they accomplish much less when children are around.[37] Even women with jobs in the formal sector have more flexibility with infant care than they would in formal employment in the United States. One study found that while many of the occupations that women pursued in

---

35 Elisabetta Zontini, *Transnational Families, Migration, and Gender: Moroccan and Filipino Women in Bologna and Barcelona* (New York: Bergahn Books, 2010).

36 Gracia Clark, "'Nursing Mother Work' in Ghana: Power and Frustration in Akan Market Women's Lives," in *Women Traders in Cross-Cultural Perspective: Mediating Identities, Marketing Wares*, ed. Linda J. Seligmann (Stanford, CA: Stanford University Press, 2001).

37 Ibid; Alma Gottlieb, *The Afterlife Is Where We Come From: The Culture of Infancy in West Africa* (Chicago, IL: University of Chicago Press, 2004).

Ghana were compatible with child care, 30 percent of women working in the formal sector also cared for their children while they worked.[38]

Because bringing children to work may interfere with a woman's productivity, many mothers, according to the author's ethnographic research, rely on a distributive model of caring in which other people help with child care while the mothers work. For instance, an adolescent relative may move into a mother's household to help with the domestic labor, or the children may go to live with another relative so that a mother can work. Mothers usually cultivate long-term relationships and lifelong ties of obligations with these relatives.

For example, a 60-year-old woman in Akropong described how, when she was about 10, she went to help her older sister after her sister married and had a child:

> When I was a little girl, my older sister got married. She was a trader and she took things around to sell, so when she gave birth, I carried — I lived with her and carried her child on my back[39] so she could go to the market. I made food for the children at home.

This scenario was relatively common for women in this town. Some who helped out their older sisters or aunts in this way were rewarded by having their school fees paid for by the mother or being sent to learn a trade, although that was not the case for this particular woman, to her lifelong disappointment.

This practice of circulating relatives is still common today: a mother in Akropong described how a few years before, her sister's daughter, a high school student, came to live with her after she gave birth to twins. Her husband was a high school teacher at a boarding school, and they lived on the campus. It was convenient for her niece to live with them, attend high school as a day student, and help care for the newborns and an older toddler in the early mornings, evenings, and weekends. Occasionally, however, particularly in urban areas, an adolescent girl from a poorer or more rural family may be hired to help care for the children, as younger relatives become unavailable because of their own schooling.

Other women are helped by their mothers. Either the grandmother will temporarily move in with her daughter after her grandchild is born, or her daughter and grandchild will come to live with her for a few months. Akosua, now living in Philadelphia, talked about the support her mother gave her in Ghana after the birth of her first child. She worked as a secretary in a bank, her husband had recently gone abroad,

---

38 Ann K. Blanc and C. B. Lloyd, "Women's Work, Child-Bearing, and Child-Rearing over the Lifecycle in Ghana," in *Gender, Work, and Population in Sub-Saharan Africa*, eds. Aderanti Adepoju and Christine Oppong (London: James Currey, 1994).

39 Gottlieb describes how carrying a child on one's back indexes taking care of a child more generally (see Gottlieb, *The Afterlife is Where We Come From*).

and she was living in a house belonging to her husband's family. When she went back to work, her mother stayed with her for a while, before returning to stay in her own house. However, her mother continued to be helpful, and Akosua took her daughter to her mother's house in the morning before work and picked her up in the evenings. She summarized what this felt like: "My family is there — everybody is there, taking care of me." These and other practices of distributed parenting make infant care manageable (though complicated), even for women who are employed in the formal sector.

However, when Ghanaians have small children in the United States, it is harder to balance work and family life by circulating children among mothers and younger siblings. Women would like to bring over their mother or a relative for a few months or years to help them, but it is difficult to get a tourist visa for them, given the efforts taken by the US Embassy in Ghana to prevent visitors who might overstay their visas from coming to the United States. One woman reported that after the birth of her child her mother was denied a visa because the reason given for the visit — to help with child care — was viewed as a form of work and not allowed on a visitor's visa, even though the work was for a family member and not for wages.

Some do succeed in bringing over relatives. One informant recounted that if the grandmother owns a house in Ghana (a tiny fraction do), she may be viewed as being more likely to return to Ghana and therefore more likely to be granted a visa.

The significance of support to a mother of young children is revealed by Ama's story. A nurse, Ama reported how she made it through the difficult period when her twins were young. She invited her mother over for a year. But even though her mother had a green card and could live in the United States permanently, she did not want to stay more than six months because, as Ama explained, she felt cooped up and lonely in the house. Whereas in Ghana the mother would often visit friends, in the United States her only company was the television, as the other household members were busy with work or school. Like Akosua's mother, who got bored when she was alone in a big house during the day and returned to her own residence, Ama's mother returned to Ghana along with Ama's twins when they were 20 months old. After staying in Ghana for a few years with their grandmother, they returned to live with Ama in the United States.

While legal reasons prevent some parents from bringing over relatives to help with child care, other immigrant parents are challenged financially as a relative can be sponsored for a visa only if one can document sufficient income to support another household member. For example, when one informant tried to bring her mother over to help with her second child, she was told that she did not have the income to support an additional person in her household.

In the absence of family support from Ghana, women rely on family support in the United States. Rita managed the birth of her first baby by sharing a residence with her husband's sister: she took the graveyard shift as a certified nursing assistant and the sister-in-law the day shift. But having given birth again a year later, she was considering sending the children back to Ghana as the burden was too great and she wanted to go back to school to become a nurse. Some women reported that they similarly coordinated their schedules with their husbands, so that there was always someone with the baby. However, relatives and husbands alike are constrained by their own work and continued schooling and cannot always provide as much assistance as new mothers need. Under- and unemployed relatives in Ghana, on the other hand, are often willing and able to provide such help. Rita reported, "I call [my mother in Ghana], I am all the time crying: 'Mummy, it's too much for me to raise the kids and take care of them'." Her mother asked her to bring the children to Ghana.

After the birth of her first child in Ghana, Akosua and her daughter joined her husband in the United States, where she had a son. Unlike in Ghana, where she had family support after her daughter's birth, in the United States her husband was able to take off two weeks after their son's birth but then had to go back to work full-time. All the domestic work fell on Akosua. Even though she had relatives in the United States, she said:

> Nobody is there for you, because everybody is working, the bills are piling [up], the bills you are piling [up], you have to pay this, you have to pay that. If you call out [from work] for one or two days, you lack something.

While Akosua's husband did do some of the housework while she was recovering from her son's birth,[40] neither he nor other relatives who lived in the United States were able to help much, because they had to work many hours to make ends meet. The lack of grandparent support for child care is typical among pioneer immigrants, as most African immigrants are.[41]

Because they are unable to enact the strategies of balancing work and family that they would use in Ghana, Ghanaian mothers in the United States — like many mothers in the United States — must ask fathers and other relations to help out, cut back on work or schooling, and/or rely on day care.

---

40 A woman from Accra, Ghana interestingly describes a similar situation of giving birth when she and her husband lived in Cameroon in the late 1920s and early 1930s: "My husband was also very helpful; he would go for water and sweep the rooms and the compound before going to work every day for the first week after my delivery. After that week I did everything." See Claire C. Robertson, *Sharing the Same Bowl: A Socioeconomic History of Women and Class in Accra, Ghana* (Bloomington, IN: Indiana University Press, 1984): 71.

41 Yoshikawa, *Immigrants Raising Citizens.*

Ghanaian parents reported that fathers in the United States take on more household and child care responsibilities than they would in Ghana, but that of the division of labor is still far from equal, as is the case in most American families.[42] Some couples reported that disagreements over housework, paid work, and child care added tension to married life. Many women worried that these disagreements made divorce more likely in the United States — although divorce also occurs in Ghana. Moreover, disagreements over domestic duties may be a symptom of marital discord rather than the cause of it.[43]

As for work, few Ghanaian migrant women stay home to raise children. Indeed, some report feeling an even greater need to work than their Ghana-based counterparts because they know that relatives back home depend on their remittances. This orientation is reflected in the relatively high rates of employment among Ghanaian women and men in the United States.[44] Migrants with poor relatives back home feel the pressure to work acutely. One woman imagined her parents and siblings in Ghana starving without her remittances. "I have a lot of people over there; all their eyes are on me," she said. The money women contribute also gives them leverage in household and family decisions.[45]

Women are encouraged to use the opportunity of being in the United States to make money. One morning, in the basement of a Ghanaian church in the United States, a young woman compared pay and employment prospects in two major East Coast cities with two older women, as her toddler ran around the tables set up for an event later in the day.[46] The mother complained about having to follow her husband to

---

42 Karine Moe and Dianna Shandy, *Glass Ceilings and 100-Hour Couples: What the Opt-Out Phenomenon Can Teach Us about Work and Family* (Athens, GA: University of Georgia Press, 2010).

43 Clark, "'Nursing Mother Work' in Ghana." For more on conflicts in Ghanaian marriages abroad, see Takiwaa Manuh, "Migrants and Citizens: Economic Crisis in Ghana and the Search for Opportunity in Toronto, Canada" (Ph.D. dissertation, Indiana University, 1998). Cheikh Babou also raises concerns about divorce among the Senegalese diaspora. See Cheikh Anta Babou, "Migration and Cultural Change: Money, 'Caste,' Gender, and Social Status among Senegalese Female Hair Braiders in the United States," *Africa Today* 55, no. 2 (2008): 3–22. For similar transformations in migrant households from Mexico, see Jennifer S. Hirsch, *A Courtship after Marriage: Sexuality and Love in Mexican Transnational Families* (Berkeley, CA: University of California Press, 2003); Pierrette Hondagneu-Sotelo, *Gendered Transitions: Mexican Experiences of Immigration* (Berkeley, CA: University of California Press, 1994); and Robert Courtney Smith, *Mexican New York: Transnational Lives of New Immigrants* (Berkeley, CA: University of California Press, 2006).

44 See Chapter 3 of this volume, Donald J. Hernandez, "Young Children in Black Immigrant Families from Africa and the Caribbean."

45 John A. Arthur, *The African Diaspora in the United States and Europe: The Ghanaian Experience* (Burlington, VT: Ashgate, 2008).

46 A study of African immigrants in Washington, DC, noted that one reason that African immigrants might be drawn to New York City and Washington, DC (as the two metropolitan areas with the most African immigrants) was for their high per capita incomes. See Jill H. Wilson and Shelly Habecker, "The Lure of the Capital City: An Anthro-Geographical Analysis of Recent African Immigration to Washington, DC," *Population, Space, and Place* 14 (2008): 433–48.

a city where wages were lower and job opportunities scarcer, and she shared, somewhat tentatively, that she would soon send her son to live with her sister in Ghana for a few years so that she could work more easily. The older women listening to her reassured her that her plan would work out.

What allows Ghanaian mothers to work in Ghana, therefore, is a combination of limited occupational choices that allow mothers to bring their young children to work and practices of distributed care, wherein relatives share child-rearing responsibilities. In the United States, however, few employers allow mothers to bring their children to work, and distributed parenting is limited by restrictions on visas for relatives who are willing to provide support and the need for relatives, including fathers, who are already in the United States to work as much as possible to pay their own bills and also remit back home. The next section describes why institutional options that distribute care of young children more broadly — namely day care — do not provide a solution to these dilemmas among Ghanaian parents.

B. The Costs and Inconvenience of Formal Child Care in the United States

Day care is an institutional way of distributing parenting responsibilities more widely; it is a more temporary and market-based form of fostering, so to speak. But unlike the long-term and reciprocal relationships that are formed through fostering, the bonds between parents and paid caregivers are often short-term and relatively weak. Although child-care centers vary in quality, as a whole they have been associated with improvements in children's cognitive abilities, such as motor and language skills, in early childhood.[47] However, Ghanaian parents reported finding day care a poor substitute for distributed parenting due to its high cost, inability to accommodate nonstandard work schedules, and varying quality. And because day-care centers cannot care for sick children, parents must often take off from work to do so.[48]

Of these factors, day care's high cost is the most critical. Although Ghanaian immigrants use day care at relatively high rates among immigrants, they would be even more likely to use it if they had greater access to child-care subsidies or affordable day-care options.[49] The Children's Defense Fund reported that in 2008, the annual cost of day care was similar to the annual in-state tuition at public four-year

---

47 Children's Defense Fund, *The State of America's Children: Early Childhood Development* (Washington, DC: Children's Defense Fund, 2010), www.childrensdefense.org/child-research-data-publications/data/the-state-of-americas-children-2010-report-early-childhood-development.pdf.

48 Chinese immigrant parents in Canada also found the cost of day care to be prohibitive (see Bohr and Tse, "Satellite Babies in Transnational Families").

49 Hernandez, "Young Children in Black Immigrant Families."

colleges.[50] The Ghanaians who reported using day care for their young children (and thus were raising their children in the United States) tended to have relatively high earnings; still, day care was one of their largest expenses.[51] The total costs multiplied with each new child; costs were also higher for infants. A couple in northern New Jersey — both teachers — with three children ages 5 to 9 said that their children go to the YMCA for an hour before school and two hours after school. They felt it was a lot of money for that short a period of time — the equivalent of renting an additional two-bedroom apartment. Another couple — he has a PhD in public health and was working for a state agency, she was working for a bank and going to school part-time— reported having three small children in full-time day care, and complained that day care cost more than the mortgage on their Maryland condominium, even though it was subsidized by the mother's school. Many Ghanaians in the study reported that their incomes made formal day care unaffordable. Rita, a mother of two working as a certified nursing aide, complained that she was asked to pay $800 per child per month for day care but felt that all she could afford for child care in her budget was $250 to $300 per month. Given that the average salary of a nurse's aide is $24,010, $1,600 might indeed use up all or most of her post-tax monthly income.[52]

Ghanaian parents also expressed worry about the quality of care among day-care or informal child-care providers.[53] Irene, a home health aide, took her baby back to Ghana to be raised by her family because it gave her peace of mind to know that the baby would be well taken care of — something she worried about in day care. What's more, she said, if her children were in day care while she worked, she would never see them except when she was exhausted and stressed. Finally, she argued that if a child was in day care and became sick, the child would have to stay home or be taken to the emergency room, causing the mother not only to miss a day of work but also to run the risk of losing her job if it happened too frequently. Irene's mention of the emergency room rather than a doctor reveals the absence of health insurance, common among low-income workers and home health aides.[54] It also suggests that

---

50 Children's Defense Fund, *The State of America's Children*.

51 These data support the finding that professional immigrant families in Italy, Finland, France, and Portugal tended to rely more on the delegation of care to institutional and formal forms of care than immigrant families with more modest incomes. See Karin Wall and José São José, "Managing Work and Care: A Difficult Challenge for Immigrant Families," *Social Policy and Administration* 38, no. 6 (2004): 591–621.

52 Bureau of Labor Statistics, Nursing and Psychiatric Aides, *Occupational Outlook Handbook, 2010-2011 Edition* (Washington DC: Bureau of Labor Statistics, 2011), www.bls.gov/oco/ocos327.htm.

53 Moe and Shandy report on the Cost, Quality, and Outcomes study on day care centers, conducted in the mid-1990s, which found that on average, child-care centers were rated about halfway between "minimal" and "good" (Moe and Shandy, *Glass Ceilings and 100-Hour Couples*, 75).

54 Patrice Mareschal, "Innovation and Adaptation: Contrasting Efforts to Organize Home Care Workers in Four States," *Labor Studies Journal* 31 (1): 25–49.

programs that expand health coverage for low-income children do not always reach immigrants' children.[55]

If a child is raised in Ghana, Irene explained, a mother can work double shifts or take a live-in position (as she does) and make more money. She can be sure that her child gets the best medical treatment in Ghana that her remittances can buy. For healthy children, this strategy tends to work well. Likewise, a mother of a son with autism returned with him to Ghana because she could get better and cheaper all-day care for him there than in the United States. Some parents with children with severe medical problems, however, bring them to the United States temporarily for specialized therapy or surgery.

Under these circumstances, many mothers who want to work (particularly in time-intensive and low-wage occupations) but lack assistance for child care foster out their infants temporarily to grandmothers or other trusted relatives in Ghana. They may bring the children back to the United States when they are ready for school and require fewer hours of day care, or as adolescents. In other words, they rely on family networks as they would in Ghana, except that they foster out their children to their family in Ghana, rather than add relatives to their household to help with child care.

C. The Care of Young Children in Ghana

Seven grandmothers who were responsible for caring for children under the age of 5 were interviewed in Ghana: the children's parents were in the United States (four), Britain (two), and South Africa (one). Six of the seven were content with the arrangements. All but two of the grandmothers lived in multigenerational households in their hometowns, in compounds shared by adults (siblings and adult children of the elderly caregiver) and younger and older children. Thus, particularly for the two grandmothers who were frail or disabled through polio, the care of a baby or toddler could be distributed among many people in the household. The adult children and adolescents helped with the laundry, child minding, cooking, and other household work. Other grandchildren, whose parents were elsewhere in Ghana or living in the compound, were playmates to the youngsters, sharing the toys and special foods the fostered children received from abroad.

Grandmothers relied on preschool in addition to family care to help take care of young children. Low-cost government-supported preschool is provided at the age of 3 in Ghana. When parents provided sufficient remittances, some grandmothers took younger children in their house-

---

55 Twice as many immigrant children (16 percent) are uninsured as native-born children (8 percent). See Donald J. Hernandez and Wendy D. Cervantes, *Children in Immigrant Families: Ensuring Opportunity for Every Child in America* (Washington, DC: First Focus, 2011), www.firstfocus.net/library/reports/children-in-immigrant-families-ensuring-opportunity-for-every-child-in-america.

holds (not only the children of emigrants) to private, more expensive day-care centers and crèches. Supported by an extensive network of relatives and some institutional care, many of the grandmothers felt satisfied by the arrangements and were not overwhelmed by the care of the infants and young children.

The only grandmother unhappy with the arrangement was working in a government office in a large city. Living outside her hometown, she did not have access to a large support network. Finding caring for her two grandchildren more onerous than she anticipated, she fostered in three adolescents in exchange for supporting their trade apprenticeships. They transported the grandchildren, ages 4 and 6, to and from school and cared for them after school. However, the grandchildren were picky eaters, accustomed to imported foods and expensive sodas and sweets, and ate nutritious food only when their grandmother fed it to them. They were having difficulty adjusting to life away from their mother, who was an emigrant to South Africa. The grandmother, like Ghanaian mothers in the United States, was having difficulty combining work with child care, although she had mitigated some of the stress by fostering in the adolescents as house servants, which Ghanaian immigrant mothers cannot do.

The young children of Ghanaian immigrants are surrounded by more people in Ghana than they would be in the United States, in part because of greater under- and unemployment among adults. Their status is also bolstered by their connections abroad — that they are US citizens or have parents who are abroad — and so they are given special treatment, including toys and food brought back by their parents and relative freedom from responsibility. Indeed, many migrant parents worried that their children were becoming spoiled, living in greater luxury than they themselves had experienced in Ghana as children or were able to afford in the United States.

In the author's household survey, there are some children, however, who have been abandoned by their migrant parents and left in the care of grandmothers and do not enjoy these benefits and increased status. Most of the children who fit this description were abandoned by their father *prior to* the father's emigration, rather than as a consequence of it. The author did not encounter any children abandoned by a migrant mother. Many of the children abandoned by fathers (migrant or otherwise) were living in poverty with their grandmothers, who were unevenly supported by their other adult children. Some of the children had difficulty continuing their education because of school costs.

Many children who are fostered in Ghana reported that they regularly received gifts and phone calls from their parents, but opinions about whether the separation was painful for them varied widely. Other studies show that the children's emotional pain depends on the culturally based narratives that caregivers and parents tell children about the cause of separation, the degree of intimacy and closeness between the caregiver and child, and the stigmatization of parent-child separation more generally in that community, within the local media, and among state officials.[56] In Ghana, fostering is common, so children may be less likely to feel that separation from parents is abnormal, and caregivers can further normalize the situation by comparing international migrants to urban migrants within Ghana. Furthermore, material forms of caring are treated as important aspects of relationships in Ghana. Children therefore view remittances and gifts as signs of caring rather than as poor substitutes for kisses and "being there," as Honduran children "left behind" do.[57] Children raised by caregivers from a young age reported that they have close relationships with their caregivers and do not miss their parents, while those who were sent back or who were adolescents when their parents migrated are more distressed about the separation. Because children's responses to the separation were so varied, the longer-term implications for children's development are unclear.

V. The Implications for Children's Development

Parents differed in their assessment of whether it was good to foster out their young children, drawing on their own experiences, as well as those of friends in their networks, to evaluate the consequences. Some parents brought their children to the United States when they were ready to begin school in kindergarten or first grade, when the hours and costs of day care were not so onerous. Others delayed bringing their children to the United States until they were in their last few years of high school or ready to begin college. At this point the parents reported being concerned about the quality of or violence in neighborhood schools in Ghana and the possibility that their teenagers might go wayward. The parents also reported that raising older children in the United States was more financially feasible.

Adolescents and preteen children involved in the study consistently reported that they did not have difficulty with the transition to school

---

56 Elspeth Graham and Lucy P. Jordan, "Migrant Parents and the Psychological Well-Being of Left-Behind Children in Southeast Asia," *Journal of Marriage and Family* 73 (2011): 763–87; Olwig, "Narratives of Children Left Behind;" Heather Rae-Espinoza, "The Children of Emigres in Ecuador: Narratives of Cultural Reproduction and Emotion in Transnational Social Fields," in *Everyday Ruptures: Children, Youth, and Migration in Global Perspective*, eds. Cati Coe, Rachel R. Reynolds, Deborah A. Boehm, Julia Meredith Hess, and Heather Rae-Espinoza (Nashville, TN: Vanderbilt University Press, 2011).

57 Leah Schmalzbauer, "Searching for Wages and Mothering from Afar: The Case of Honduran Transnational Families," *Journal of Marriage and Family*, 66 (2004): 1317–31; Cati Coe, "What is Love? The Materiality of Care in Ghanaian Transnational Families," *International Migration* 49 (6): 7–24; Ernestina Tetteh, "Voices of Left Behind Children: A Study of International Families in Accra, Ghana" (master's thesis, Nordic Afrika Institute, 2008).

in the United States, except for a few months during which they grew accustomed to American English, the isolation of their households, and the "rudeness" of their school peers. Surprisingly, many expressed that school in the United States was easier than in Ghana, because of the emphasis on homework rather than examinations and the lack of physical punishment. Perhaps as a result, or because of influence by their peer groups, they tended not to take school very seriously, unaware of the hidden inequalities in American education.[58]

One day in a youth group meeting at a Ghanaian church in the United States that the author attended regularly for two years, the leader, Kwasi, parent of a toddler and infant, talked to the teenagers about how "fortunate" they were to be in the United States. In Ghana, he told them, you had to be the best to continue, but here education was easy. In his secondary school, he was afraid of the teacher and couldn't raise his left hand to answer a question or he would be slapped. Here, Kwasi said, teachers asked you about your problems and gave you lots of help if you didn't understand, so you should make the most of your opportunity in school. One teenage girl who came regularly to church with her mother and had been raised in the United States from birth responded by saying that even if she didn't do her homework, she still passed the class. She also said that though school in the United States was easier than in Ghana, she had learned a lot in her American school. However, in general, Ghanaian parents involved in the study voiced more concern about the character of their children than their scholastic competence, feeling that discipline, hard work, and perseverance were more significant to academic success than prior educational preparation.

Many children experienced warm relationships with those who raised them, particularly if they had lived with them from a young age. Coming to the United States usually involved a transition in their relationship with their parents, even if they had been in regular contact with them through phone calls and occasional visits and associated them fondly with remittances and gifts. The process of reunification with parents, and concomitant separation from a previous caregiver, can be painful for children. One mother reported that her 7-year-old son, Kwaku, joined his parents in the United States when he was 4 years old after staying with his grandmother in Ghana for three years. But they were strangers to him, she said, and for a while Kwaku kept asking for his grandmother and wanting to return to Ghana. Over time he got used to the United States and no longer wants to return. In Ghana, children experience less pain in moving among households because there is more of this type of circulation: children can stay in households temporarily, such as over school holidays, and then move back to their primary home, allowing them to slowly build relationships with multiple caregivers.

---

58 Jonathan Kozol, *The Shame of the Nation: The Restoration of Apartheid Schooling in America* (New York: Crown Publishers, 2005); Alejandro Portes and Rubén G. Rumbaut, *Legacies: The Story of the Immigrant Second Generation* (Berkeley, CA: University of California Press, 2001).

Some parents delay bringing over their children until they are in their teens. At this age, too, tensions may arise. Although teenagers in their bid to join their parents in the United States may promise to contribute to household income and help with child care, many respondents reported that young men tend to strike out on their own after their arrival, establishing independent households maintained by their newfound income. Young women were perceived as more helpful to their parents, residing in the family home, continuing with their education, and contributing to the family by helping with child care and other domestic chores.[59] Many teenagers reported that their affections remained with their caregivers back in Ghana, years after they came to the United States, although they appreciated the opportunities that their migrant parents provided them. For example, one young woman whose education in Ghana had been financed by her migrant father joined him when she was ready for college. She was grateful that he supported her to go to community college to the extent that she did not have to work part- or full-time, as many of her peers did, but she felt a distance between them. Although sad that she did not care as much about her father as many of her college friends did, she seemed to be coping with the emotional distance and respected and appreciated her father in spite of it. Children are raised to live with a variety of people and to control their emotions, and the Ghanaian young people who had recently arrived from Ghana seemed to be living out that legacy in their new circumstances.

Many children and young adults who had been fostered out reported experiencing a lower quality of life in the United States than they did in Ghana: from a larger to a smaller living space, from private to public schooling, and from the freedom to visit a network of friends with a lot of free time to a constriction of public leisure activities because of more private spaces, the busy lives of adults, and concerns about safety. Furthermore, they experience a loss of status — from being considered a wealthy and fortunate child of a migrant abroad (an "American") to being considered an "African," a representative of a continent often portrayed as rife with poverty, disease, and strife. Some respond by shedding their "Africanness" as quickly as possible; others try to maintain their distinctiveness from US-born Blacks, recognizing it as a different kind of stigmatized identity in the United States.

Parents in the United States viewed the higher quality of life in Ghana as a sign that children were "spoiled" by their caregivers or by remittances but reported that their children adapted quite easily to the challenges of US life. For instance, one young man raised first by a family friend and then by his grandmother in Ghana was considered lazy by his parents in the United States because he wasn't working as a

---

59 Smith, Lalonde, and Johnson similarly report that among the children of Caribbean immigrants, boys reunited with their parents reported higher levels of deviance than girls, and were less likely to conform to their parents (see Smith, Lalonde, and Johnson, "Serial Migration and Its Implications for the Parent-Child Relationship").

teenager in Ghana (young people in Ghana who are going to school do not normally work, even part time). He admitted to spending much of their remittances on frivolous items. However, when he arrived in the United States at the age of 18, he adjusted easily to working in a restaurant, happily earning his own wages, which allowed him to become independent of his parents and go to community college part time.

In sum, young people who come to the United States to rejoin their parents tend to experience a loss of pre-existing relationships, a downgrading of status, and a lower quality of life but greater opportunities for autonomy and independent income. But the long-term social, economic, and psychological consequences of fostering on the children of Ghanaian immigrants remain uncertain.

VI. Policy Implications

Like other African immigrants, Ghanaians in the United States are a relatively educated population whose educational credentials from Ghana often do not pay off in terms of their employment and income in the United States.[60] The largest single occupation in which Ghanaians work — as health-care aides — is time intensive, poorly remunerated, and characterized by difficult emotional ties and physical labor. More broadly, the difficulty Ghanaian immigrants experience combining relatively low-paying but time-intensive employment with parenting in the United States may explain why, for those in less-skilled jobs, raising children in Ghana in the care of relatives is particularly attractive. These parents would be more likely to raise their children in the United States if they had access to high-quality, low-cost child care; if relatives could stay with them to help with infant and child care, particularly after birth; if their Ghanaian credentials were more transferrable; and/ or if those working in certain health and mental health professions were paid a family-sustaining wage and given health benefits. These changes would likely improve not only the lives of Ghanaian immigrants and their children, but also those of many other low-income American parents, native born and immigrant alike. But unlike most other low-income parents and many other immigrants, Ghanaians have another option: child fostering in Ghana.

The fostering option may be attractive to Ghanaian immigrant parents for a number of reasons. First, Ghanaians in Ghana have greater access to preschool for 3- and 4-year-olds than those in the United States do.[61]

---

60 Capps, McCabe, and Fix, *New Streams.*

61 In 2008–09, only 25 percent of 4-year-olds and 4 percent of 3-year-olds were in state-funded prekindergarten programs in the United States, in comparison to 35 percent and 18 percent, respectively, in government-funded programs in Ghana in 2002–03. See Children's Defense Fund, *The State of America's Children*; UNESCO, International Bureau of Education, *Ghana: Early Childhood Care and Education (ECCE) Programmes* (Geneva: UNESCO International Bureau of Education, 2006), http://unesdoc.unesco.org/images/0014/001471/147192e.pdf.

Additional effort has gone into expanding preprimary education in Ghana in recent years, with the World Bank estimating that 70 percent of 4- and 5-year-olds were enrolled in preschool in Ghana in 2009.[62]

Children of immigrants in the United States, on the other hand, have especially low rates of prekindergarten enrollment due to socio-economic barriers, lack of awareness about the availability of early childhood education, and confusion about eligibility rules.[63] Low-cost opportunities for early childhood education, such as Head Start, have been expanded by the Obama administration.[64] Still, more could be done, particularly in terms of immigrants' access to Head Start and public child care subsidies that are available to low-income families. Ghanaians tend to live in states that are not among the worst in providing resources and access to early childhood education, but they may still face significant barriers to accessing high-quality, low-cost preschool and day care.[65]

Second, most low-income American parents can rely on unpaid family child care, but Ghanaian immigrants have difficulty doing so. Current US immigration laws make it difficult for Ghanaian immigrants in the United States — especially those with lower incomes or without substantial assets — to bring over parents or other relatives to help raise their children. US immigration laws are unlikely to grant more temporary or permanent visas to these relatives due to concerns about visa overstays. But at the very least, the current immigration categories for extended relatives should be protected, and efforts should be taken to make sure they are made available to immigrants from countries in Africa and elsewhere that rely heavily on diversity admissions and therefore have relatively small co-ethnic communities in the United States.

Third, improving the job prospects and earnings of Ghanaian immigrant workers in the United States would allow them to afford child care outside the home. Given the mismatch between Ghanaian immigrants' qualifications and employment, credentials earned in Ghana

---

62 See World Bank, "World Development Indicators," http://data.worldbank.org/indicator/ SE.PRE.ENRR. The World Bank is a bit suspicious of its own figures, but considers it the best estimate given what districts report, which is closer to 96 percent.

63 Wendy Cervantes, *Improving the Wellbeing of Children of Immigrants: Priorities for the 112th Congress* (Washington, DC: First Focus), www.firstfocus.net/library/fact-sheets/improv- ing-the-wellbeing-of-children-of-immigrants-priorities-for-the-112th-congr.html.

64 Office of Management and Budget, "The Federal Budget, Fiscal Year 2011: Department of Health and Human Services," www.whitehouse.gov/omb/factsheet_department_health/.

65 Ten states have no state-funded prekindergarten for 3- and 4-year-olds: Hawaii, Idaho, Indiana, Mississippi, Montana, New Hampshire, North Dakota, South Dakota, Utah, and Wyoming. An additional 15 states, including Maryland and Virginia, do not serve 3-year- olds in their prekindergarten programs. See Steven W. Barnett, Dale J. Epstein, Megan E. Carolan, Jen Fitzgerald, Debra J. Ackerman, and Allison H. Friedman, *The State of Preschool 2010* (New Brunswick, NJ: National Institute for Early Childhood Research, 2010), http://nieer.org/publications/state-preschool-2010.

might be more easily transferred through reciprocal agreements. Thanks to organizations that review and verify the credentials of foreign-educated nurses and physicians, it is easier for these workers to transfer their credentials to the United States than it is for other professionals to do so.[66] While the review process is expensive and time-consuming, it is preferable to the several years of study that face accountants and teachers, whose prior education counts for little on the path to certification. If the United States begins to face a teaching shortage, reciprocal agreements for teachers from other countries may increase.[67]

Finally, low-income workers in the health and mental health fields — including the many Ghanaians in such jobs — should be paid a family-sustaining wage and receive access to affordable health insurance. Their wages have been kept artificially low by Medicare and Medicaid reimbursement rates. Home-health aides have, in some states, pursued unionization, which has led to higher average wages and health coverage.[68] It is promising that in December 2011 the US Department of Labor's Wage and Hour Division proposed extending federal minimum wage and overtime requirements to certain in-home care workers.[69]

These strategies should be adopted by policymakers interested in promoting the well-being and development of US-born children of Black immigrants, whose successful integration will lead to their making greater social and economic contributions to US society in the long term. Such strategies also apply to working immigrant parents of other origins, as well as working US-born parents. The fostering phenomenon among Ghanaian immigrant parents is a signal that the United States has weak societal and institutional supports for raising young children — supports that some other countries, even those considered middle and low income, provide to a greater extent. ↲

---

66   The Commission on Graduates of Foreign Nursing Schools International is a nonprofit, private organization created in 1977 to evaluate and verify the credentials of foreign nurses (www.cgfns.org/sections/about/); the Educational Commission for Foreign Medical Graduates does the same for physicians (www.ecfmg.org/about/index.html).

67   Jose Katigback, "Pinoy Teachers in US Fight Back," *The Philippine Star*, July 17, 2011; Teresa Watanabe, "Filipino Teachers Exchange Homeland for Jobs in America," *Los Angeles Times*, March 18, 2009.

68   Patrice Mareschal, "Innovation and Adaptation: Contrasting Efforts to Organize Home Care Workers in Four States," *Labor Studies Journal* 31, no. 1 (2006): 25–49.

69   US Department of Labor, Wage and Hour Division, "Notice of Proposed Rulemaking to Amend the Companionship and Live-In Worker Regulations," http://webapps.dol.gov/FederalRegister/HtmlDisplay.aspx?DocId=25639&Month=12&Year=2011; The White House, Office of the Press Secretary, "We Can't Wait: President Obama Will Announce Administrative Action to Provide Minimum Wage and Overtime Protections for Nearly 2 Million In-Home Care Workers," (press release, December 15, 2011), http://www.whitehouse.gov/the-press-office/2011/12/15/we-can-t-wait-president-obama-will-announce-administrative-action-provid.

Works Cited

Alber, Erdmute. 2003. Denying Biological Parenthood: Fosterage in Northern Benin. *Ethnos* 68 (4): 487–506.

American Community Survey (ACS) 2006-08. 2010. Accessed from Steven Ruggles, J. Trent Alexander, Katie Genadek, Ronald Goeken, Matthew B. Schroeder, and Matthew Sobek. *Integrated Public Use Microdata Series: Version 5.0* [Machine-readable database]. Minneapolis: University of Minnesota.

Ardayfio-Schandorf, Elizabeth and Margaret Amissah. 1996. Incidence of Child Fostering among School Children in Ghana. In *The Changing Family in Ghana*, ed. Elizabeth Ardayfio-Schandorf. Accra, Ghana: Ghana Universities Press.

Arthur, John A. 2008. *The African Diaspora in the United States and Europe: The Ghanaian Experience*. Burlington, VT: Ashgate.

Babou, Cheikh Anta. 2008. Migration and Cultural Change: Money, "Caste," Gender, and Social Status among Senegalese Female Hair Braiders in the United States. *Africa Today* 55 (2): 3–22.

Barnett, W. Steven, Dale J. Epstein, Megan E. Carolan, Jen Fitzgerald, Debra J. Ackerman, and Allison H. Friedman. 2010. *The State of Preschool 2010*. New Brunswick, NJ: National Institute for Early Childhood Research. http://nieer.org/publications/state-preschool-2010.

Blanc, Ann K. and Cynthia B. Lloyd. 1994. Women's Work, Child-Bearing, and Child-Rearing over the Lifecycle in Ghana. In *Gender, Work, and Population in Sub-Saharan Africa*, eds. Aderanti Adepoju and Christine Oppong. London: James Currey.

Bohr, Yvonne and Connie Tse. 2009. Satellite Babies in Transnational Families: A Study of Parents' Decisions to Separate from their Infants. *Infant Mental Health Journal* 30 (3): 265–86.

Brydon, Lynne. 1979. Women at Work: Some Changes in Family Structure in Amedzofe-Avatime, Ghana. *Africa* 49 (2): 97–111.

Bureau of Labor Statistics. 2011 (BLS). Nursing and Psychiatric Aides. In *Occupational Outlook Handbook, 2010-2011 Edition*. Washington, DC: BLS. www.bls.gov/oco/ocos327.htm.

_____. 2010. Occupational Employment Statistics: Occupational Employment and Wages, May 2010: Nursing Aides, Orderlies, and Attendants. www.bls.gov/oes/current/oes311012.htm#(2)).

Capps, Randy, Kristen McCabe, and Michael Fix. 2011. New Streams: Black African Migration to the United States. In *Young Children of Black Immigrants in America: Changing Flows, Changing Faces*, eds. Randy Capps and Michael Fix. Washington, DC: Migration Policy Institute.

Cervantes, Wendy. 2011. *Improving the Wellbeing of Children of Immigrants: Priorities for the 112th Congress*. Washington, DC: First Focus. www.firstfocus.net/library/fact-sheets/improving-the-wellbeing-of-children-of-immigrants-priorities-for-the-112th-congress.html.

Children's Defense Fund. 2010. *The State of America's Children: Early Childhood Development*. Washington, DC: Children's Defense Fund. www.childrens-defense.org/child-research-data-publications/data/the-state-of-ameri-cas-children-2010-report-early-childhood-development.pdf.

Clark, Gracia. 2001. "Nursing Mother Work" in Ghana: Power and Frustration in Akan Market Women's Lives. In *Women Traders in Cross-Cultural Perspective: Mediating Identities, Marketing Wares*, ed. Linda J. Seligmann. Stanford: Stanford University Press.

Coe, Cati. In press. How International Migration Has Affected the Distribution of Childcare in Ghana. In *Youth and Identity in Africa*, eds. Abubakar Momoh and Ndiouga Benga. Dakar, Senegal: Council for the Development of Social Science Research in Africa.

_____. 2011. What is Love? The Materiality of Care in Ghanaian Transnational Families. *International Migration* 49 (6): 7–24.

_____. 2008. The Structuring of Feeling in Ghanaian Transnational Families. *City & Society* 20 (2): 222-50.

Etienne, Mona. 1979. Maternité Sociale, Rapports d'Adoption et Pouvoir des Femmes chez les Baoulé (Côte d'Ivoire). *L'Homme* 19 (3–4): 63–107.

Forde, Maarit. 2011. Modes of Transnational Relatedness: Caribbean Migrants' Networks of Child Care and Ritual Kinship. In *Everyday Ruptures: Children, Youth, and Migration in Global Perspective*, eds. Cati Coe, Rachel R. Reynolds, Deborah A. Boehm, Julia Meredith Hess, and Heather Rae-Espinoza. Nashville, TN: Vanderbilt University Press.

Ghana Statistical Service. 1998. *Ghana Demographic and Health Survey, 1998*. Accra, Ghana: Ghana Statistical Service.

Gindling, Thomas H. and Sara Poggio. 2008. *Family Separation and Reunification as a Factor in the Educational Success of Immigrant Children*. Baltimore, MD: Maryland Institute for Policy Analysis and Research, University of Maryland, Baltimore County.

Goody, Esther. 1982. *Parenting and Social Reproduction: Fostering and Occupational Roles in West Africa*. Cambridge, UK: Cambridge University Press.

Gottlieb, Alma. 2004. *The Afterlife is Where We Come From: The Culture of Infancy in West Africa*. Chicago: University of Chicago Press.

Graham, Elspeth and Lucy P. Jordan. 2011. Migrant Parents and the Psychological Well-Being of Left-Behind Children in Southeast Asia. *Journal of Marriage and Family* 73: 763–87.

Greenhouse, Steven. 2007. Justices to Hear Case on Wages of Home Aides. *The New York Times*, March 25, 2007. www.nytimes.com/2007/03/25/nyre-gion/25aides.html?_r=2&oref=slogin&.

Hernandez, Donald J. 2012. Young Children in Black Immigrant Families from Africa and the Caribbean. In *Young Children of Black Immigrants in America: Changing Flows, Changing Faces*, eds. Randy Capps and Michael Fix. Washington, DC: Migration Policy Institute.

Hernandez, Donald J. and Wendy D. Cervantes. 2011. *Children in Immigrant Families: Ensuring Opportunity for Every Child in America*. Washington, DC: First Focus. www.firstfocus.net/library/reports/children-in-immigrant-families-ensuring-opportunity-for-every-child-in-america.

Hirsch, Jennifer S. 2003. *A Courtship after Marriage: Sexuality and Love in Mexican Transnational Families*. Berkeley, CA: University of California Press.

Hondagneu-Sotelo, Pierrette. 1994. *Gendered Transitions: Mexican Experiences of Immigration*. Berkeley, CA: University of California Press.

International Organization for Migration (IOM). Migration in Ghana: A Country Profile, 2009. www.iom.int/jahia/Jahia/about-migration/lang/en.

Isiugo-Abanihe, Uche C. 1985. Child Fostering in West Africa. *Population and Development Review* 11 (1): 53–73.

Katigback, Jose. 2011. Pinoy Teachers in US Fight Back. *The Philippine Star*, July 17, 2011.

Kent, Mary Mederios. 2007. Immigration and America's Black Population. In *Population Bulletin* 62 (4). Washington, DC: Population Reference Bureau. www.prb.org/pdf07/62.4immigration.pdf.

Kozol, Jonathan. 2005. *The Shame of the Nation: The Restoration of Apartheid Schooling in America*. New York: Crown Publishers.

Leinaweaver, Jessaca B. 2010. Outsourcing Care: How Peruvian Migrants Meet Transnational Family Obligations. *Latin American Perspectives* 37 (5): 67–87.

Manuh, Takyiwaa. 1998. Migrants and Citizens: Economic Crisis in Ghana and the Search for Opportunity in Toronto, Canada. PhD dissertation, Indiana University.

Mareschal, Patrice. 2006. Innovation and Adaptation: Contrasting Efforts to Organize Home Care Workers in Four States. *Labor Studies Journal* 31 (1): 25–49.

Martin, Douglas. 2009. Evelyn Coke, Home Care Aide Who Fought Pay Rule, is Dead at 74. *New York Times*, August 9, 2009. www.nytimes.com/2009/08/10/nyregion/10coke.html?scp=1&sq=evelyn%20coke&st=cse.

Mazzucato, Valentina and Djamila Schans. 2011. Transnational Families and the Well-Being of Children: Conceptual and Methodological Challenges. *Journal of Marriage and Family* 73: 704–12.

Moe, Karina and Dianna Shandy. 2010. *Glass Ceilings and 100-Hour Couples: What the Opt-Out Phenomenon Can Teach Us about Work and Family*. Athens, GA: University of Georgia Press.

Moscardino, Ughetta, Oge Nwobu, and Giovanna Axia. 2006. Cultural Beliefs and Practices Related to Infant Health and Development among Nigerian Immigrant Mothers in Italy. *Journal of Reproductive and Infant Psychology* 24 (3): 241–55.

Newman, Andy. 2006. Fire Puts a Sad Ending on an Optimistic Immigrant Tale. *New York Times*, February 25, 2006. www.nytimes.com/2006/02/25/nyregion/25victims.html?pagewanted=print&_r=0.

Office of Management and Budget. 2011. The Federal Budget, Fiscal Year 2011: Department of Health and Human Services. Fact Sheet. Washington, DC: The White House. www.whitehouse.gov/omb/factsheet_department_health/.

Olwig, Karen Fog. 1999. Narratives of the Children Left Behind: Home and Identity in Globalised Caribbean Families. *Journal of Ethnic and Migration Studies* 25 (2): 267–84.

Page, Hilary. 1989. Childrearing versus Childbearing: Coresidence of Mother and Child in Sub-Saharan Africa. In *Reproduction and Social Organization in Sub-Saharan Africa*, ed. Ron J. Lesthaeghe. Berkeley, CA: University of California Press.

Portes, Alejandro and Rubén G. Rumbaut. 2001. *Legacies: The Story of the Immigrant Second Generation.* Berkeley, CA: University of California Press.

Rae-Espinoza, Heather. 2011. The Children of Émigrés in Ecuador: Narratives of Cultural Reproduction and Emotion in Transnational Social Fields. In *Everyday Ruptures: Children, Youth, and Migration in Global Perspective*, eds. Cati Coe, Rachel R. Reynolds, Deborah A. Boehm, Julia Meredith Hess, and Heather Rae-Espinoza. Nashville, TN: Vanderbilt University Press.

Robertson, Claire C. 1984. *Sharing the Same Bowl: A Socioeconomic History of Women and Class in Accra, Ghana.* Bloomington, IN: Indiana University Press.

Schmalzbauer, Leah. 2004. Searching for Wages and Mothering from Afar: The Case of Honduran Transnational Families. *Journal of Marriage and Family* 66: 1317–31.

Smith, Andrea, Richard Lalonde, and Simone Johnson. 2004. Serial Migration and Its Implications for the Parent-Child Relationship: A Retrospective Analysis of the Experiences of the Children of Caribbean Immigrants. *Cultural Diversity and Ethnic Minority Psychology* 10 (2): 107–22.

Smith, Robert Courtney. 2006. *Mexican New York: Transnational Lives of New Immigrants.* Berkeley, CA: University of California Press.

Soto, Isa Maria. 1987. West Indian Child Fostering: Its Role in Migrant Exchange. In *Caribbean Life in New York City: Sociocultural Dimensions*, eds. Constance R. Sutton and Elsa M. Chaney. Staten Island, NY: Center for Migration Studies of New York.

Suárez-Orozco, Carola, Irina L. G. Todorova, and Josephine Louie. 2002. Making Up for Lost Time: The Experience of Separation and Reunification among Immigrant Families. *Family Process* 41 (4): 625–43.

Tetteh, Ernestina. 2008. Voices of Left Behind Children: A Study of International Families in Accra, Ghana. Master's thesis, Nordic Afrika Institute.

Thomas, Kevin J. A. 2011. What Explains the Increasing Trend in African Emigration to the US? *International Migration Review* 45 (1): 3–28.

Twum-Baah, Kwaku, A. 2005. Volume and Characteristics of International Ghanaian Migration. In *At Home in the World? International Migration and Development in Contemporary Ghana and West Africa*, ed. Takyiwaa Manuh. Accra, Ghana: Sub-Saharan Publishers.

Twum-Baah, Kwaku A., John S. Nabila, and Andrews F. Aryee, eds. 1995. *Migration Research Study in Ghana.* Accra, Ghana: Ghana Statistical Service.

United Nations Educational, Scientific and Cultural Organization (UNESCO) Institute for Statistics. Ghana profile. Accessed June 12, 2012. http://stats.uis.unesco.org.

UNESCO, International Bureau of Education. 2006. *Ghana: Early Childhood Care and Education (ECCE) Programmes.* Geneva: UNESCO International Bureau of Education. http://unesdoc.unesco.org/images/0014/001471/147192e.pdf.

US Department of Homeland Security (DHS), Office of Immigration Statistics. 2009. *2008 Yearbook of Immigration Statistics.* Washington, DC: DHS. www.dhs.gov/xlibrary/assets/statistics/yearbook/2008/ois_yb_2008.pdf.

US Department of Labor, Wage and Hour Division. 2011. Notice of Proposed Rulemaking to Amend the Companionship and Live-In Worker Regulations. Washington, DC: Department of Labor. http://webapps.dol.gov/FederalRegister/HtmlDisplay.aspx?DocId=25639&Month=12&Year=2011.

US Department of State. Diversity Visa Lottery 2010 (DV-2010) Results. http://travel.state.gov/visa/immigrants/types/types_4574.html.

_____. Instructions for the 2011 Diversity Immigrant Visa Program. Accessed October 16, 2012. www.travel.state.gov/pdf/DV-2011instructions.pdf.

Wall, Karin and José São José. 2004. Managing Work and Care: A Difficult Challenge for Immigrant Families. *Social Policy and Administration* 38 (6): 591–621.

Watanabe, Teresa. 2009. Filipino Teachers Exchange Homeland for Jobs in America. *Los Angeles Times*, March 18, 2009.

Wilson, Jill H. and Shelly Habecker. 2008. The Lure of the Capital City: An Anthro-Geographical Analysis of Recent African Immigration to Washington, DC. *Population, Space, and Place* 14: 433–48.

White House, Office of the Press Secretary. 2011. We Can't Wait: President Obama Will Announce Administrative Action to Provide Minimum Wage and Overtime Protections for Nearly 2 Million In-Home Care Workers. Press release, December 15, 2011. www.whitehouse.gov/the-press-office/2011/12/15/we-can-t-wait-president-obama-will-announce-administrative-action-provid.

Whitehouse, Bruce. 2009. Transnational Childrearing and the Preservation of Transnational Identity in Brazzaville, Congo. *Global Networks* 9 (1): 82–99.

World Bank. World Development Indicators. School enrollment, preprimary (% gross). Accessed October 16, 2012. http://data.worldbank.org/indicator/SE.PRE.ENRR.

Yoshikawa, Hirokazu. 2011. *Immigrants Raising Citizens: Undocumented Parents and Their Young Children.* New York: Russell Sage Foundation.

Zeng, Zhen and Yu Xie. 2004. Asian-Americans' Earnings Disadvantage Reexamined: The Role of Place in Education. *American Journal of Sociology* 109 (5): 1075–108.

Zontini, Elisabetta. 2010. *Transnational Families, Migration, and Gender: Moroccan and Filipino Women in Bologna and Barcelona.* New York: Berghahn Books.

PART THREE

EDUCATIONAL EXPERIENCES AND ACADEMIC ACHIEVEMENT

CHAPTER 9

BEYOND BLACK: DIVERSITY AMONG BLACK IMMIGRANT STUDENTS IN NEW YORK CITY PUBLIC SCHOOLS

Fabienne Doucet, Amy Ellen Schwartz, and Elizabeth Debraggio

New York University

Introduction: Background and Context

Fueled by the inflows of immigrants to public schools and increased availability of quantitative education data, a large and growing literature has examined the education of immigrant students. Much of this work focuses on Hispanics and Asians due, in part, to the size of these populations in US schools and in conventionally used national education data sets. In contrast, there has been comparatively little quantitative research examining the education of Black immigrants, hampered by the scarcity of data on this population.

At the same time, Black immigrants form a significant part of the population of Black students nationally and in New York City's public elementary and middle schools, which is the nation's largest school district.

Taking a mixed-methods approach, we use rich longitudinal quantitative data from the New York City Department of Education (NYCDOE) and in-depth qualitative interviews with educators serving Black immigrant students. This chapter explores the characteristics of Black immigrant students in elementary and middle schools and generates a set of key findings around social isolation and segregation within Black immigrant populations, factors influencing academic performance, and the impact of students' sending contexts and backgrounds.

Existing evidence suggests Black immigrants face considerable challenges and, perhaps as a consequence, fare poorly in New York City's public schools. In 2010, for example, New York City educated nearly 70,000 foreign-born students in grades 1 to 8, nearly 13,000 of whom were Black. These students performed almost as poorly on standardized tests as Hispanic immigrants, despite much higher rates of English proficiency. Although 71 percent of Black immigrant students did not report speaking a language other than English at home and only 14 percent were considered English Language Learners (ELLs), their performance on the New York State test in English Language Arts significantly trailed the average performance of students in their grade as well as Asian and white immigrants, who were more likely to be ELLs and speak another language at home (see Table 1).

Table 1. New York City Student Characteristics, Foreign-Born 1st-8th Graders, by Race/Ethnicity, 2010

	Number of Students	English Language Learner	Speaks Language Other than English at Home	Low-Income	Graded Special Ed	ELA z-score	Math z-score
Foreign Born	69,669	35.0%	76.8%	89.9%	6.1%	-0.132	-0.023
Asian	23,222	32.0%	80.9%	90.0%	4.0%	0.128	0.444
Hispanic	25,232	51.5%	94.6%	94.4%	7.8%	-0.439	-0.392
Black	12,921	14.4%	28.6%	88.6%	6.9%	-0.220	-0.347
White	8,294	25.0%	85.9%	78.1%	5.9%	0.243	0.340

Notes: English language learners are those considered Limited English Proficient (LEP). Students are considered low-income if they are eligible for free or reduced-price lunch (FRPL, family income below 185 percent of the federal poverty level) or attend a universal free meal school. Special education does not include students in citywide special education (District 75) schools or students in ungraded full-time special education settings. Students are tested in English language arts and math in grades 3-8 only. Z-scores are standardized within each grade across the city to have a mean of 0 and a standard deviation of 1. This means that a third grader with a z-score of 0 performs at grade-level average. A third grader with a z-score above 0 performs above average relative to other New York City third graders and third graders with z-scores below 0 perform below average relative to other New York City third graders.

Source: Data from the New York City Department of Education (NYCDOE).

At the same time, Black immigrants form a significant part of the population of Black students in New York's public elementary and middle schools — meaning their success (and failure) shapes the context and success not only for Black students, in particular, but also for the students sharing their schools as a whole.

The past decade has seen noticeable shifts in the size of the Black immigrant population in New York City public elementary and middle schools. While the number of foreign-born Black students decreased 30 percent, from almost 18,500 students in 2000 to slightly under 13,000 students a decade later, their share of the overall Black student population decreased only slightly because the native-born Black student population declined by about the same amount (see Table 2). To be specific, in 2010, foreign-born Black students comprised 9 percent of the Black students in grades 1 to 8 in New York City public schools, representing an important part of the Black student body and, undoubtedly, one of the largest and most diverse populations of Black immigrant students in US schools. Though there is tremendous linguistic, cultural, and historical diversity within Black immigrant communities, they often are conceived as a monolithic group.[1] Yet, shifts and changes within this broad group of students attest to an evolving, diverse, and complex set of dynamics that affect their education. In this chapter, we explore the diversity and variation in the Black immigrant population in New York City public schools and the differences in their achievement and experiences in school.

Large shares of New York City's Black immigrants come from the Caribbean and Africa, alongside significant numbers from Guyana. In 2010 the largest share of the city's Black immigrant students hailed from the Caribbean (7,900 students or 61 percent), while roughly one in five were born in Africa (2,500 students), and another one in five came from non-Caribbean/non-African countries (2,500 students). The shares of African immigrant students changed rapidly over the decade: in 2000 only 12 percent were African.

Table 2. Foreign-Born Black 1st-8th Grade Students in New York City Public Schools, by Country of Origin, 2000 and 2010

	Number		% Change	% of Blacks from that Region	
	2000	2010		2000	2010
All Blacks	202,049	147,496	-27.0%		
Native-Born	183,599	134,575	-26.7%		
Foreign-Born	18,450	12,921	-30.0%		
Foreign-Born Caribbean Blacks	12,645	7,874	-37.7%	100.0%	100.0%
Antigua & Barbuda	158	95	-39.9%	1.2%	1.2%
Barbados	387	103	-73.4%	3.1%	1.3%
British West Indies	123	22	-82.1%	1.0%	0.3%
Dominican Republic	140	62	-55.7%	1.1%	0.8%
Grenada	472	227	-51.9%	3.7%	2.9%
Haiti	2,150	2,258	5.0%	17.0%	28.7%
Jamaica	5,912	3,600	-39.1%	46.8%	45.7%
St. Lucia	257	265	3.1%	2.0%	3.4%
St. Vincent & the Grenadines	277	182	-34.3%	2.2%	2.3%
Trinidad and Tobago	2,328	857	-63.2%	18.4%	10.9%

---

1   Carla O'Connor, Amanda Lewis, and Jennifer Mueller, "Researching 'Black' Educational Experiences and Outcomes: Theoretical and Methodological Considerations," *Educational Researcher* 36, No. 9 (2007): 541–52.

	Number		% Change	% of Blacks from that Region	
	2000	2010		2000	2010
British Virgin Islands	145	58	-60.0%	1.1%	0.7%
Other Caribbean countries	296	145	-51.0%	2.3%	1.8%
Foreign-Born African Blacks	*2,211*	*2,519*	*13.9%*	*100.0%*	*100.0%*
Ghana	517	542	4.8%	23.4%	21.5%
Guinea	75	306	308.0%	3.4%	12.1%
Liberia	246	127	-48.4%	11.1%	5.0%
Nigeria	617	582	-5.7%	27.9%	23.1%
Senegal	96	106	10.4%	4.3%	4.2%
Sierra Leone	45	128	184.4%	2.0%	5.1%
Other African countries	615	728	18.4%	27.8%	28.9%
Foreign-Born Blacks, Other Regions	*3,594*	*2,528*	*-29.7%*	*100.0%*	*100.0%*
Belize	128	75	-41.4%	3.6%	3.0%
Canada	281	136	-51.6%	7.8%	5.4%
Germany	173	46	-73.4%	4.8%	1.8%
Guyana	1,859	1,472	-20.8%	51.7%	58.2%
Japan	245	132	-46.1%	6.8%	5.2%
United Kingdom	153	76	-50.3%	4.3%	3.0%
Other countries	755	591	-21.7%	21.0%	23.4%

Notes: Countries in the region with over 100 Black students enrolled in at least one year in New York City public schools are shown. All other countries in the region are represented in the "other countries" category.

Source: NYCDOE data.

Roughly 85 percent of the Black Caribbean immigrant students in New York City schools came from just three countries: Jamaica (3,600 students or 46 percent), Haiti (2,300 students or 29 percent), and Trinidad and Tobago (900 students or 11 percent). Among these, only Haitians increased in number over the decade; the number of students from other Caribbean countries generally declined. Perhaps most significant was the decline in Jamaican students, who numbered more than 5,900 in 2000.

African immigrant students' origins were somewhat less concentrated. Slightly more than one in five students came from Nigeria, slightly more than one in five came from Ghana, 12 percent came from Guinea, and no other country represented more than 5 percent. This diversity was seen in both 2000 and 2010.

Interestingly, there were slightly more Black immigrants from countries outside of Africa and the Caribbean than from Africa itself. Among these, Guyana was particularly noticeable. In 2010 over half of Black immigrant students from other regions came from Guyana; this group fell in number, but not in its share of all Black immigrant students since

2000. Relatively small numbers of Black immigrant students come from a wide range of countries around the world — some, undoubtedly, born to immigrants to those countries (perhaps en route to the United States) and a small number to Americans living (temporarily) overseas.

Our analyses of the diversity among Black immigrant elementary and middle school students and of the implications for policy and practice that such diversity suggests have been driven by the following research questions:

- What demographic differences exist within and among Black immigrant students in New York City public schools?

- What differences exist in racial isolation and intergroup relations among Black immigrant students in New York City public schools?

- What differences can be seen in academic performance within and among Black immigrant students in New York City public schools?

- How are Black immigrant students in New York City public schools perceived and/or treated by teachers, educators, and peers?

- How are these factors changing over time?

I. Determinants of Academic Performance

A well-established economics literature provides a useful foundation and understanding of factors associated with differences in academic performance. These relationships are usually described in an economic model called an "education production function" where differences in students' academic achievement are related to differences in their demographics, family and school inputs, and innate abilities.[2] Family and school inputs include race, poverty, English proficiency, parents' education, and school resources such as class size and teacher experience. Broadly, the research highlights the importance of family char-

---

2   Eric A. Hanushek, "The Economics of Schooling: Production and Efficiency in Public Schools," *Journal of Economic Literature* 24, No. 3 (1986): 1141–477; Petra E. Todd and Kenneth I. Wolpin, "On the Specification and Estimation of the Production Function for Cognitive Achievement," *Economic Journal* 113, No. 485 (2003): 3–33.

acteristics,[3] differences across racial and/or ethnic groups,[4] and the influence of teacher quality[5] in explaining differences in performance. Specifically, students who are white or Asian, English proficient, and who come from wealthy and well-educated families will outperform their peers from more disadvantaged backgrounds.

In their recent work, Amy Schwartz and Leanna Stiefel[6] note several reasons why nativity might matter in understanding determinants of performance.[7] First, the extent to which immigrant students come from families or homes with different levels of income, education, household composition, or marital status may influence their academic achievement.[8] Second, foreign-born students immigrate at different points in their childhood and bring with them different educational backgrounds that could hinder or enhance performance. Third, there are cultural differences in the emphasis, support, and encouragement that immigrant families and communities place on education, and these may cause students to succeed or struggle academically.[9] Finally, immigrants may experience schools differently due to differences in resources or services (such as special language classes).

New York City school district policies dictate that school resources be distributed according to formulas that allocate resources based on *student* and *school* characteristics. Differences in student characteristics drive some of the differences in school resources: a variety of federal and state programs direct additional resources to schools

3   See Meredith Phillips, James Crouse, and John Ralph, "Does the Black-White Test Score Gap Widen after Children Enter School?" in *The Black-White Test Score Gap*, eds. Christopher Jencks and Meredith Phillips (Washington, DC: Brookings Institution Press, 1998); Petra E. Todd and Kenneth I. Wolpin, "The Production of Cognitive Achievement in Children: Home, School, and Racial Test Score Gaps," *Journal of Human Capital* 1, No. 1 (2007): 91–136.

4   See Roland G. Fryer Jr. and Steven D. Levitt, "Understanding the Black-White Test Score Gap in the First Two Years of School," *The Review of Economics and Statistics* 86, No. 2 (2004): 447–64; Roland G. Fryer Jr. and Steven D. Levitt, "The Black-White Test Score Gap through Third Grade," *American Law and Economics Review* 8, No. 2 (2006): 249–81; Phillips, Crouse, and Ralph, "Does the Black-White Test Score Gap Widen after Children Enter School?"; Todd and Wolpin, "The Production of Cognitive Achievement in Children."

5   See Eric A. Hanushek, Steven G. Rivkin, and John F. Kain, "Teachers, Schools, and Academic Achievement," *Econometrica* 73, No. 2 (2005): 417–58.

6   Amy E. Schwartz and Leanna Stiefel, "Immigrants and Inequality in Public Schools," in *Whither Opportunity? Rising Inequality and the Uncertain Life Chances of Low-Income Children*, eds. Greg Duncan and Richard Murnane (New York: Russell Sage Foundation, 2011).

7   See also Amy E. Schwartz and Leanna Stiefel, "Is There a Nativity Gap? New Evidence on the Academic Performance of Immigrant Students," *Education Finance and Policy* 1, No. 1 (2006): 17–49.

8   Jennifer E. Glick and Michael J. White, "The Academic Trajectories of Immigrant Youths: Analysis within and across Cohorts," *Demography* 40, No. 4 (2003): 759–83; Grace Kao, "Psychological Well-Being and Educational Achievement among Immigrant Youth," in *Children of Immigrants: Health, Adjustment, and Public Assistance*, ed. Donald J. Hernandez (Washington, DC: National Academy Press, 1999).

9   Mary C. Waters, Black Identities: *West Indian Immigrant Dreams and American Realities* (New York and Cambridge, MA: Russell Sage Foundation and Harvard University Press, 1999).

serving students who are economically disadvantaged (e.g., the federal No Child Left Behind or Title I program), are English Language Learners (e.g., the federal Title III program that provides English as a Second Language services), require special education, and so on. A well-established literature documenting the relationship between resources and school populations finds that schools with higher percentages of poor and minority students receive more money and have higher numbers of teachers per student than otherwise similar schools.[10] These teachers, however, tend to be inexperienced and receive lower salaries.[11]

II. Black Immigrant Children and Schooling: Reviewing the Literature

While there is a large and growing literature examining disparities between Blacks and whites (or Latinos or Asians), there is, in contrast, very limited research on educational outcomes that differentiates Blacks by ethnic group or immigrant origin.[12] The work that does exist often focuses on comparing US-born Blacks to foreign-born Blacks and their children.[13] Such comparisons tend to paint foreign-born Blacks as a model minority. Indeed, demographic analyses have shown that foreign-born Blacks have higher median incomes, live in less racially segregated neighborhoods, have higher levels of educational attainment, and are disproportionately represented among Black university students.[14]

---

10 See Ross Rubenstein, Amy E. Schwartz, Leanna Stiefel, and Hella B. H. Amor, "From Districts to Schools: The Distribution of Resources across Schools in Big City School Districts," *Economics of Education Review* 26, No. 5 (2007): 532–45.

11 See, for example, Charles T. Clotfelter, Helen F. Ladd, and Jacob L. Vigdor, "Teacher-Student Matching and the Assessment of Teacher Effectiveness," *The Journal of Human Resources* 41, No. 4 (2006): 778–820; Patrice Iatarola and Leanna Stiefel, "Intra-district Equity of Public Education Resources and Performance," *Economics of Education Review* 22 No. 1 (2003): 69–78; Hamilton Lankford, Susanna Loeb, and James Wyckoff, "Teacher Sorting and the Plight of Urban Schools: A Descriptive Analysis," *Educational Evaluation and Policy Analysis* 24, No. 1 (2002): 37–62; Rubenstein et al., "From Districts to Schools."

12 O'Connor et al., "Researching 'Black' Educational Experiences and Outcomes."

13 Signithia Fordham, and John U. Ogbu, "Black Students' School Success: Coping with the 'Burden of "Acting White',"" *The Urban Review* 18, No. 3 (1986): 176–206; John U. Ogbu and Herber D. Simons, "Voluntary and Involuntary Minorities: A Cultural-Ecological Theory of School Performance with Some Implications for Education," *Anthropology and Education Quarterly* 29 (1998): 155–88.

14 Mary Mederios Kent, "Immigration and America's Black Population" (*Population Bulletin* 62, No. 4, Population Reference Bureau, December 2007), www.prb.org/pdf07/62.4immigration.pdf; Douglas S. Massey, Margarita Mooney, Kimberly C. Torres, and Camille Z. Charles, "Black Immigrants and Black Natives Attending Selective Colleges and Universities in the United States," *American Journal of Education* 113, No. 2 (2007): 243–71; Chapter 1 of this volume, Kevin J. A. Thomas, "Contemporary Black Caribbean Immigrants in the United States;" and Chapter 2 of this volume, Randy Capps, Kristen McCabe, and Michael Fix, "New Streams: African Migration to the United States."

It is important to note, however, that in the United States — where race is a master status, that is, an identifying characteristic that overshadows other potential identity markers[15] — foreign-born Blacks are subject to the same racism as their native counterparts because of the color of their skin. In the school context, racist assumptions have been shown to predispose teachers to have lower expectations of Black and brown children, to target them more often as behavioral problems, and to presuppose that their parents do not value education.[16]

Moreover, the standing of race as a master status means Black immigrants are "invisible," in the sense that their individual nationalities, ethnic affiliations, and cultural traditions often are unrecognized or unknown. Consequently, a number of studies have shown that foreign-born Black immigrants have gone to great lengths to identify themselves as immigrants in an effort to distinguish themselves from US-born Blacks.[17]

A. Linguistic Needs of Black Immigrant Students

One unique characteristic of foreign-born Black students is the vast diversity of languages they speak, including English, Spanish, French, Creole, African languages, and indigenous languages. Sometimes, and especially in the case of African immigrants, these children are multilingual, speaking both the "official" language of their country and at least one other local, tribal, or regional language or dialect. Though bilingual education has been a source of controversy across the United States, large metropolitan areas generally have been able to offer language support to their English Language Learner (ELL) students. Since groups of immigrants from the same country tend to settle near one another, school districts often are able to provide programs for the most commonly spoken languages in a district or town. But in school districts where immigrant students are scarce or where there is great diversity in students' countries of origin, English as a Second Language (ESL) programs are more manageable, since the instructor does not have to know the students' language. There is some evidence that newcomer schools — where immigrant children (typically in middle school or high school) from all over the world study together in small classroom settings — have proven successful in easing immigrant

---

15 Ivor L. Livingston, *Handbook of Black American Health: The Mosaic of Conditions, Issues, Policies, and Proposals* (Westport, CT: Greenwood Press, 1994).

16 Lisa Delpit, *Other People's Children: Cultural Conflict in the Classroom* (New York: New Press, 1995); Fabienne Doucet, "How African American Parents Understand Their and Teachers Roles in Children's Schooling and What This Means for Preparing Preservice Teachers," *Journal of Early Childhood Teacher Education [Special Issue on Multicultural Teacher Education in Honor of Leslie R. Williams]* 29, No. 2 (2008): 108–39; Fabienne Doucet, "(Re)Constructing Home and School: Immigrant Parents, Agency, and the (Un)desirability of Bridging Multiple Worlds," *Teachers College Record* 113, No. 12 (2011): 2705-38.

17 Waters, *Black Identities*; Flore Zéphir, *Trends in Ethnic Identification among Second-Generation Haitian Immigrants in New York City* (Westport, CT: Bergin and Garvey, 2001).

youth into learning English and acclimating to US culture.[18] Though newcomer schools tend to be more popular in urban school districts, smaller suburban and rural districts offer similar programs for immigrant students within their schools.[19]

Another area of controversy in the linguistic education of foreign-born Blacks concerns those coming from countries where English is spoken — as is the case for the majority of Black Caribbean students. Research has shown that these students typically understand themselves as native English speakers. Yet in school, they discover that their "other Englishes" are considered substandard to academic English, that their accents are not understood and sometimes ridiculed, and that they have difficulty with reading and/or writing assignments.[20] This body of work argues for approaches to teaching speakers of "other Englishes" that are nuanced, acknowledging the legitimacy of these variations on English, and sensitizing teachers to the patterns and distinctions of other Englishes so they can better assist their students in learning academic English.

B. *Previous Schooling Experiences*

Many African, Afro-Caribbean, and Afro–Latin American children come to the United States under circumstances of religious, ethnic, political, or economic persecution — from the child soldiers of Sudan, to children of victims of political persecution and earthquake survivors in Haiti, to children of human-rights activists in Cuba. Many of these children arrive with gaps in learning that result from their interrupted schooling. In Haiti between 1986 and 1996, for example, there was not a single school year that was not temporarily suspended due to political violence. This means that thousands of children had as little as five

---

18   Lesley Bartlett and Ofelia García, *Additive Schooling in Subtractive Times: Bilingual Education and Dominican Immigrant Youth in the Heights* (Nashville, TN: Vanderbilt University Press, 2011); Deborah J. Short and Beverly A. Boyson, *Creating Access: Language and Academic Programs for Secondary School Newcomers* (Washington, DC and McHenry, IL: Center for Applied Linguistics and Delta Publishing Company, 2004).

19   Tamara Lucas, Rosemary Henze, and Ruben Donato, "Promoting the Success of Latino Language-Minority Students: An Exploratory Study of Six High Schools," *Harvard Educational Review* 60, No. 3 (1990): 315–40.

20   Jennifer Jenkins, "Current Perspectives on Teaching World Englishes and English as a Lingua Franca," *TESOL Quarterly* 40, No. 1 (2006): 157–81; Constant Leung, Roxy Harris, and Ben Rampton, "The Idealised Native Speaker, Reified Ethnicities, and Classroom Realities," *TESOL Quarterly* 31, No. 3 (1997): 543–60; Shondel Nero, "Language, Identity, and Education of Caribbean English Speakers," *World Englishes* 25, No. 3/4 (2006): 501–11; Shondel Nero, "Language, Literacy, and Pedagogy of Caribbean Creole English Speakers," in *Ethnolinguistic Diversity and Education: Language, Literacy, and Culture,* eds. Marcia Farr, Lisya Seloni, and Juyoung Song (New York: Routledge/Taylor and Francis, 2010): 212–40; Ben Rampton, "A Critique of Some Educational Attitudes to the English of British Asian Schoolchildren, and their Implications," in *English as a Second Language in the United Kingdom: Linguistic and Educational Contexts,* eds. Christopher Brumfit, Rod Ellis, and Josie Levine (Oxford: Pergamon Press, 1985): 187–98.

academic years' worth of content spread out over ten years, a pattern that unfortunately has repeated itself from 2000 to the present day, as a result of civil unrest, political upheaval, and natural disasters.[21] The formal educational classification for children under these circumstances is "Students with Interrupted Formal Education" (SIFE), and the New York City public school system estimates that roughly one in ten ELL students is also a SIFE.[22] The strategies teachers employ to meet their needs tend to be highly individualized, given the wide range of possible configurations in their learning strengths and weaknesses. Beyond their academic needs, SIFEs also arrive with various psychological and socioemotional problems like post-traumatic stress disorder, depression and anxiety, and difficulties with social integration.[23] It is also the case that many children from countries plagued by war, extreme poverty, and civil unrest never start formal schooling until they leave their countries of origin, even at advanced ages. Since the US model of grade promotion tends to be based on age rather than mastery, modifications and special considerations need to be given in order to provide these children with the best education possible. In this sense, Haitian students may have more in common with students from countries with official "refugee" designations (including several African countries) than with Black students from nonrefugee countries in the Caribbean.

III. Methods

A. Research Design

In order to answer our research questions, we employed a mixed-methods design that allowed us to cross-validate quantitative administrative data on Black immigrant students with qualitative interviews with adults involved in educating these students. The qualitative interviews provided further insights for interpreting our analyses of the demographic and academic profiles of Black immigrant children.

B. Participants and Data Sources

I. Quantitative Component

We use rich, longitudinal administrative data from the New York

---

21 Paul Farmer's book, *Haiti After the Earthquake*, provides an up-to-date and compelling overview of Haiti's modern history, detailing various crises in the past decade that would have disrupted daily life and imposed interruptions on the academic calendar. See Paul Farmer, *Haiti after the Earthquake* (New York: Public Affairs, 2011).

22 Advocates for Children of New York, *Students with Interrupted Formal Education: A Challenge for New York City Public Schools* (New York: Advocates for Children of New York, 2010), www.advocatesforchildren.org/SIFE%20Paper%20final.pdf?pt=1.

23 Andrea DeCapua, William Smathers, and Lixing F. Tang, "Schooling, Interrupted," *Educational Leadership* 64, No. 6 (2007): 40–6.

City Department of Education (NYCDOE) on students enrolled in the city's public schools to provide comprehensive information on all foreign-born Black students in grades 1 through 8. These data include sociodemographic characteristics (age, gender, race/ethnicity, birthplace), educational needs (special education, English proficiency, eligibility for free/reduced price lunches), and standardized test scores (statewide English and math tests in grades 3 through 8). Importantly, the detailed birthplace variable allows us to not only identify students born outside of the United States, but also their region and country of birth. We define all students with birthplaces outside of the United States as being foreign born. Note, however, this means that the foreign-born population includes those students who have recently immigrated as well as those who arrived in the United States as infants and those born on US military bases in other countries. School districts do not collect data on parental nativity, and so second-generation students — those who are US born but have immigrant parents — cannot be identified. Nationally, the vast majority of children in immigrant families generally and Black immigrant families specifically are US born and therefore not included in this sample; however these children generally reside in the same families as students who are immigrants themselves and are therefore likely have many common characteristics. On the other hand, immigration status, interrupted education, and other factors related to instability and trauma in the home country are specific to first-generation students and do not apply to the larger group of US-born children, except indirectly through their parents. As we are interested in the Black immigrant population specifically (i.e., the first generation), we focus our analysis on these students, disaggregating by region (Caribbean, African, non-Caribbean/non-African) and by country.

2. Qualitative Component

To complement the quantitative data, we designed semi-structured qualitative interviews conducted with adults who provide educational support to young immigrant children, either as classroom teachers, ESL teachers, or leaders in academic community organizations (e.g., tutoring centers). These participants were recruited through schools, churches, and community organizations in enclaves with high populations of Haitian and other Black immigrants throughout New York City. Participants were also asked to identify colleagues who might be eligible and interested to be interviewed, and we followed up on their recommendations.

A total of ten educators participated in the qualitative component of the study. All were highly educated women who had master's degrees or above (one had two master's degrees, another was writing her dissertation, and a third had begun a program of doctoral study), and they ranged in age from 28 to 55 (the median age was 48). Four of the participants were born outside of the United States and migrated as young adults (over age 20) and one was born in the United States to African immigrant parents. All but one identified English as her native language, though all spoke at least one other language. Racially and ethnically, the group was quite mixed: two identified as Black/African American, two as Black/Afro-Caribbean, one as Black/African, four as non-Latino white, and one as being of mixed race or ethnicity.

Of the ten participants, eight reported being classroom teachers, though one explained that she split her time evenly between teaching and working as a project coordinator at a community organization serving African immigrant families. She was new to teaching, having done so for about two years, but the other seven were evenly split with respect to their years of teaching experience — four had been teaching for ten years or more and three had taught for at least four but no more than nine years. With respect to the grade levels in which they taught, four teachers worked in elementary schools, two in middle schools, and two in high schools.[24] All but one teacher taught in a program for ELLs, though all teachers had at least four years of experience working with linguistically and culturally diverse students. The two nonteachers in the group were a counselor and a program director at the same community organization serving African immigrant families where the teacher/administrator worked. The counselor worked with children of elementary school age, and the administrator with high school students; both had at least seven years of experience working with culturally and linguistically diverse students.

C. Instruments, Variables, and Measures

Descriptive comparisons and analyses. In our analysis, we explore the demographic characteristics of Black immigrants in grades 1 to 8, comparing students from different countries and regions and examining changes in the composition of this population of students over the past decade. We pay particular attention to the Black immigrant population from the Caribbean region as they comprised 60 percent of New York City's Black students in grades 1 through 8 in 2010. We focus our demographic comparisons on variables capturing English proficiency, home language, poverty, participation in special education services, and scores on standardized English language arts (ELA) and math exams.[25] These provide some insight into the educational services Black immigrant students may require. Further, because we can link students to the schools they attend, we also examine the degree of racial isolation and type of intergroup relations experienced by different groups of Black immigrants, calculating exposure indices to shed

---

24 We attempted to restrict the participants to educators working with students in grades 1 to 8 to parallel the quantitative data set, but recruitment was difficult, and ultimately we opened up eligibility to educators working with high school students.

25 New York State tests students in grades 3 through 8 annually in English language arts (ELA) and math. We use data on the scores on each exam.

light on the extent to which Black immigrants attend schools with other Black students and co-ethnic peers.

Students' academic performance. We introduce an education production function linking student performance on standardized ELA and math exams to demographic characteristics.[26] In our baseline models, we estimate the differences in performance among Caribbean immigrants, African immigrants, and Black immigrants born in countries outside of the Caribbean and Africa, and, importantly, the differences between Haitian and Jamaican students and other Caribbeans. We examine Jamaicans and Haitians separately because they are the two largest origin countries for Black immigrant students and have contrasting language profiles: virtually no Black immigrants from Jamaica are classified as ELLs while almost half of Haitian Black students are considered ELLs. We then extend the model to examine whether — and to what extent — these differences in ELA and math scores change between spring 2009 and spring 2010. In this way, we explore the changes in performance over time.

Semi-structured interviews and analyses. Interview questions were divided into five major sections: (1) background and demographic characteristics, (2) institutional support for Black immigrant children, (3) educator responses to Black immigrant children, (4) demographic differences among groups of Black immigrant children, and (5) academic and social differences among groups of Black immigrant children. Interviews lasted approximately one hour. Nine of the interviews were conducted in person and one was conducted via Skype because the participant was traveling during the time of data collection. Interviews were conducted by the first author and two trained student research assistants (RAs) and were audio recorded.

IV. Findings

A. *Black Immigrants by the Numbers: Quantitative Findings*

I. Demographic Differences

There are important differences in the demographic and educational characteristics of foreign-born Black students relative to their native-born Black peers (see Table 3).

---

26 An education production function is a statistical model that describes relationships between differences in students' academic achievement and differences in their demographics, family and school inputs, and innate abilities. For more see Hanushek, "The Economics of Schooling."

Table 3. New York City Public School Student Characteristics, Black 1st-8th graders, by Nativity and Origin, 2010

	Number of Students	English Language Learner	Speaks Language Other than English at Home	Low-Income	Graded Special Ed	ELA z-score	Math z-score
All Blacks	*147,496*	*2.4%*	*6.5%*	*88.7%*	*11.6%*	*-0.191*	*-0.314*
Native-Born	134,575	1.3%	4.3%	88.7%	12.0%	-0.188	-0.310
Foreign-Born	12,921	14.4%	28.6%	88.5%	6.9%	-0.220	-0.347
Non-Caribbean	5,047	15.8%	32.6%	88.5%	6.7%	-0.161	-0.282
African	2,519	26.0%	51.8%	89.7%	4.4%	-0.189	-0.312
Other region	2,528	5.6%	13.4%	87.3%	8.9%	-0.134	-0.252
Caribbean	7,874	13.5%	26.0%	88.6%	7.0%	-0.256	-0.387
Antigua & Barbuda	95	0.0%	1.1%	86.3%	8.4%	-0.277	-0.456
Barbados	103	0.0%	0.0%	82.5%	12.6%	-0.209	-0.255
British West Indies	22	0.0%	4.5%	77.3%	0.0%	0.112	0.044
Dominican Republic	62	45.2%	71.0%	96.8%	4.8%	-0.523	-0.911
Grenada	227	0.0%	0.0%	89.4%	8.4%	-0.277	-0.323
Haiti	2,258	45.5%	87.7%	91.5%	6.8%	-0.401	-0.551
Jamaica	3,600	0.1%	0.1%	86.9%	6.9%	-0.239	-0.361
St. Lucia	265	0.4%	3.0%	90.2%	5.7%	-0.105	-0.236
St. Vincent & the Grenadines	182	0.0%	0.0%	87.9%	6.0%	-0.219	-0.239
Trinidad and Tobago	857	0.0%	0.1%	88.7%	8.1%	-0.084	-0.206
British Virgin Islands	58	0.0%	0.0%	93.1%	5.2%	-0.084	-0.324
Other Caribbean countries	145	3.4%	7.6%	83.4%	6.9%	-0.197	-0.260

Notes: "Other region" includes all Black students not from Africa or the Caribbean. English language learners are those considered Limited English Proficient (LEP). Students are considered low-income if they are eligible for free or reduced-price lunch (FRPL, family income below 185 percent of the federal poverty level) or attend a universal free meal school. Special education does not include students in citywide special education (District 75) schools or students in ungraded full-time special education settings. Students are tested in English language arts and math in grades 3-8 only. Z-scores are standardized within each grade across the city to have a mean of 0 and a standard deviation of 1. This means that a third grader with a z-score of 0 performs at grade-level average. A third grader with a z-score above 0 performs above average relative to other New York City third graders and third graders with z-scores below 0 perform below average relative to other New York City third graders.

Source: NYCDOE data.

Notably, while 99 percent of native-born Black students in grades 1 through 8 are considered English proficient and 96 percent speak English at home, the same is not true for foreign-born Black students: 86 percent are English proficient and 71 percent speak English at home. There is considerable diversity in English proficiency within the Black foreign-born population — with many countries reporting near 100 percent proficiency (Jamaica, Barbados, British West Indies, Trinidad and Tobago, Virgin Islands, etc.) and others, such as Haiti or some of the African countries, reporting significant ELL populations.

Among those speaking a language other than English at home, two languages are most common: French (5 percent) and Haitian-Creole (12 percent). Roughly 3 percent of all Black immigrants also report speaking "French-Haitian."[27] Again, there is diversity across and within the regions: while Jamaicans almost universally speak English at home, more than two-thirds of Haitians report speaking Haitian-Creole, with another one in five speaking French or French-Haitian (see Table 4). Roughly one in six Black immigrants from Africa reports speaking French at home.

Table 4. Home Language of Black Immigrant 1st-8th Grade Students in New York City Public Schools, 2010

	Number	Speaks English at Home	Speaks Haitian-Creole	Speaks French	Speaks French-Haitian
All Foreign-Born Blacks	*12,921*	*71.4%*	*11.9%*	*5.1%*	*2.5%*
Caribbean	7,874	74.0%	19.5%	2.0%	3.9%
Haitian	2,258	12.3%	67.5%	6.6%	13.4%
Jamaican	3,600	99.9%	0.1%	0.0%	0.0%
Non-Caribbean	5,047	67.4%	0.2%	9.9%	0.4%
African	2,519	48.6%	0.1%	17.1%	0.6%
Other non-Caribbean	2,528	86.2%	0.3%	2.7%	0.2%

Notes: Black immigrants from non-Caribbean countries speak 79 different languages. After English and French, the most reported home languages are Fulani (4.2 percent) and Twi (2.9 percent). The same is true for Black immigrants from African countries (8.1 percent report speaking Fulani at home and 5.5 percent report speaking Twi). Black immigrants from other non-Caribbean regions also report speaking Spanish (1.8 percent), Bengali (1.6 percent), Arabic (1.3 percent), and Dutch (1.1 percent).

Source: NYCDOE data.

---

27 Though a full discussion of the sociolinguistic implications of this distinction is beyond the scope of this chapter, it is useful to note that the French spoken in Haiti is different from the French spoken in, say, France or Canada, much as the English spoken in the United States is different from the English spoken in the United Kingdom or Australia. Furthermore, the statuses of French and Haitian-Creole are contentious issues in Haitian society, where it is widely estimated that about 10 percent of the people speak French, while almost all speak Haitian-Creole. (For deeper discussions of these issues, see Michel DeGraff, "Creole Exceptionalism and the (Mis)education of the Creole Speaker," in *The Languages of Africa and the Diaspora: Educating for Language Awareness,* eds. Jo A. Kleifgen and George C. Bond (Bristol, UK: Multilingual Matters, 2009); and Bambi B. Schiefflin and Rachelle C. Doucet, "The 'Real' Haitian Creole: Ideology, Metalinguistics, and Orthography," *American Ethnologist* 21, No. 1 (1994): 176–200.

Almost 90 percent of both foreign- and native-born Black students live in low-income families — those that are eligible for free or reduced-price lunches (FRPL) (see Table 3).[28] Although some origin groups have low-income rates below 85 percent, these are very few in number. The vast majority are quite poor — with students from Haiti, St. Lucia, the British Virgin Islands, and the Dominican Republic all having low-income rates of over 90 percent.

Participation in special education is low among foreign-born Blacks: native-born Blacks are almost twice as likely to participate in special education. While there is variation across countries and regions, foreign-born Blacks from Africa have particularly low participation rates (less than 5 percent).

Turning to differences in performance, we compare ELA and math z-scores within the Black student population. Z-scores are standardized across students in the same grade within a given year so that the average performance for test takers in that grade is 0. Students performing above average for their grade have positive z-scores and those performing below average have negative z-scores. As seen in Table 3, both native-born and foreign-born Black students perform below the grade-level average for all students on both the ELA and math exams. Foreign-born Blacks, as a whole, lag their native-born peers, scoring 0.220 standard deviations below the mean (i.e., below average) on the ELA exam and 0.347 standard deviations below the mean on the math exam. Again, there is significant variation between regions and, within regions, between countries. Students from African and other non-Caribbean/non-African countries perform below average, but better than their Caribbean peers on both exams, with students from African countries performing roughly on par with native-born Black students. Caribbean students overall and those from Haiti and the Dominican Republic in particular have lower scores. Haitians perform 0.401 standard deviations below the mean on the ELA exam and 0.551 standard deviations below the mean on the math exam, and students from the Dominican Republic perform 0.523 and 0.911 standard deviations below the mean on the ELA and math exams respectively. Note that these two countries also have the highest shares of ELL students: Haiti has 46 percent and the Dominican Republic 45 percent.

2. Racial Isolation and Intergroup Relations

Black students on the whole attend schools where a majority of students are Black (see Table 5). While the average Black student attends school where 58 percent of his/her peers are Black, this share rises to 65 percent for the average foreign-born Black student and 71 percent for the average Black Caribbean student. This share is lower for Black African students (46 percent).

---

28 The federal government subsidizes lunches for students with family incomes below 185 percent of the federal poverty level.

Foreign-born Black students overall also have greater exposure to *foreign-born* Black peers in school: 9 percent compared to only 3 percent in the citywide student population. This is especially true for Caribbean Blacks, which suggests that sorting into ethnic neighborhoods and communities may result in sorting across schools. As an example, Haitian students, on average, have higher exposures to other Haitian students in school than their Black peers of any other origin. Although Haitians are less than 1 percent of the total student population in grades 1 through 8, the average Haitian student attends school where the student population is 5 percent Haitian. This is much higher than the exposure for all Blacks (1 percent), foreign-born Blacks overall (2 percent), or Caribbean Blacks specifically (3 percent). While sorting has a particular connotation, these differences in exposure may not necessarily be negative. It is possible that Haitian students benefit to the extent that this segregation translates into community support or a critical mass of same-language peers.

Table 5. Exposure Indices: Black Students by Nativity and Origin, 1st-8th Graders, New York City Public Schools, 2010

	Black	NB Black	FB Black	Caribbean Black	Haitian Black	Non-Caribbean Black
% in total population	28.2	25.7	2.5	1.5	0.4	1.0
All Blacks	*57.9*	*52.3*	*5.6*	*3.8*	*1.1*	*1.9*
Native-Born	57.3	52.0	5.3	3.5	1.0	1.8
Foreign-Born	64.5	55.2	9.2	6.5	2.1	2.7
Caribbean	70.9	60.3	10.7	8.0	2.7	2.7
Haitian	72.7	60.6	12.1	9.3	4.7	2.8
Non-Caribbean	54.4	47.4	7.0	4.2	1.3	2.8
African	45.9	40.4	5.5	2.8	0.8	2.8
Other non-Caribbean	62.9	54.4	8.5	5.6	1.8	2.8

Notes: NB = native born; FB = foreign born. Exposure indices tell us for the average student of group A, the share of his/her school's population belonging to group B. If students were evenly distributed across schools, the exposure to a particular group would always equal that group's share of the population. For example, in the absence of sorting we would expect exposure to Haitian Blacks to be roughly 0.4 percent for the average student of any race, nativity, or origin. As shown, however, the average Black student attends schools where 1.1 percent of the students are Haitian and the average Haitian Black student attends schools where almost 5 percent of the students are Black Haitians.
Source: NYCDOE data.

Black students, on average, have lower exposure to ELLs in their schools (see Table 6). Although ELLs comprise 12 percent of the total student population in grades 1 through 8, the average Black student — native or foreign born — attends school where the ELL population is only 8 percent. Black immigrants from Africa have the highest exposure to ELLs (12 percent) among all Black students, both foreign and native born. However, their exposure to Black ELLs (2 percent) is similar to that for the average foreign-born Black student (2 percent). Among Caribbean Blacks, Haitians have higher exposure to ELLs in school — likely in part attributable to their higher exposure to Haitians generally.[29]

Table 6. Exposure Indices: ELL 1st-8th Graders, by Nativity and Origin, New York City Public Schools, 2010

	ELL	Black ELL	NB Black ELL	FB Black ELL	Caribbean Black ELL	Haitian ELL
% in total population	12.1	0.7	0.3	0.4	0.2	0.2
All Blacks	*8.0*	*1.3*	*0.6*	*0.8*	*0.5*	*0.5*
Native-Born	8.0	1.3	0.6	0.7	0.5	0.5
Foreign-Born	8.1	2.1	0.7	1.4	1.0	1.0
Caribbean	7.0	2.3	0.7	1.6	1.3	1.3
Haitian	8.8	3.6	0.9	2.7	2.3	2.3
Non-Caribbean	9.7	1.8	0.7	1.1	0.6	0.6
African	12.0	1.8	0.7	1.1	0.4	0.4
Other non-Caribbean	7.4	1.8	0.6	1.2	0.8	0.8

Notes: NB = native born; FB = foreign born. See Table 5 notes for explanation of exposure indices.

Source: NYCDOE data.

3. Differences in Academic Performance

The unadjusted z-scores shown in Table 3 fail to account for demographic and educational differences within the foreign-born Black population. Haitian Blacks, as shown earlier, depart from most of their Caribbean-born Black peers in their higher rates of ELL status, lack of English at home, and exposure to other Black students. To address these factors, we estimate a set of regression models linking student performance on the ELA and math exams with a set of demographic and educational controls. Here, we limit our sample to only the foreign-born Black population in grades 3 to 8 (because these are the grades in which testing occurs) in the 2009 and 2010 academic years in order to estimate differences in the performance of specific groups of foreign-born Blacks. The reference group in these models are Black immigrants from countries outside of the Caribbean, Africa, and Guyana. We also include indicators for students born in Haiti and Jamaica. These coefficients should be interpreted as the difference between students from Haiti and Jamaica relative to the average performance of students from the Caribbean.

We begin by controlling for demographic characteristics (i.e., characteristics outside of the educational context, such as gender, home language, poverty, and borough of residence within New York City). Due

---

29   As seen earlier in Table 3, among Caribbean Blacks, Haitians and Dominicans have the highest rates of Limited English Proficiency.

to the significant variation across regions and countries in the share of students speaking English at home, we begin by only controlling for gender, low income, and residence borough. As seen in column 1 of Tables 7a and 7b, Caribbean students perform below Black immigrants from outside of the Caribbean, Africa, and Guyana, but they outperform their peers from African countries and Guyana on both the ELA and math exams. Haitians and Jamaicans have lower performance than the Caribbean average — with Haitians in particular performing 0.276 standard deviations worse on the ELA exam and 0.320 standard deviations worse on the math exam.

In order to focus on differences in populations separate and apart from their language skills, we add a control variable for whether the student speaks a language other than English at home. This factor may be particularly important for Haitian students, a large share of whom speak a language other than English at home. After adding a control for home language, we find Caribbean students perform slightly better than the Guyanese and have lower performance compared to foreign-born Blacks from countries outside of the Caribbean, Africa, and Guyana on both the ELA and math exams (see Table 7a, column 2, and Table 7b, column 2). While Caribbean students outperformed their African peers (as shown in the model shown in column 1) this is no longer the case. Moreover, while Haitian students had significantly lower ELA and math z-scores than their Caribbean peers, after controlling for home language, Haitian students perform no differently from their otherwise similar Caribbean peers on either the ELA or math exam. When we control for characteristics related to the student's educational needs and ability (English proficiency, special education participation, and prior performance on standardized tests) and include school fixed effects (that broadly control for the differing characteristics of schools), we see that within schools, Caribbeans still perform worse than their foreign-born Black peers (except for the Guyanese) on both exams, but Haitian students perform slightly better than their otherwise equivalent Caribbean peers on the ELA exam (Table 7a, column 3) and no differently on the math exam (Table 7b, column 3).[30]

---

30 To include school fixed effects, we essentially add a dummy variable identifying the school a student attends. Thus, we have a dummy variable for school A, a second for school B, and so on.

Table 7a. Performance on ELA Exam, Foreign-Born Black 3rd-8th Graders, New York City Public Schools, Spring 2009 and Spring 2010

	ELA		
	Demographic Controls - Excluding Home Language	Demographic Controls - Including Home Language	Demographic Controls and Controls for Educational Services and Prior Achievement
	(1)	(2)	(3)
Caribbean	-0.080**	-0.181***	-0.078***
	(0.032)	(0.032)	(0.021)
Haitian	-0.276***	0.058	0.064**
	(0.033)	(0.043)	(0.026)
Jamaican	-0.102***	-0.114***	-0.045***
	(0.021)	(0.021)	(0.015)
African	-0.156***	-0.074*	0.026
	(0.040)	(0.039)	(0.027)
Guyanese	-0.154***	-0.259***	-0.106***
	(0.035)	(0.035)	(0.025)
Female	0.216***	0.213***	0.113***
	(0.013)	(0.013)	(0.010)
Low-income	-0.087***	-0.079***	-0.019
	(0.025)	(0.025)	(0.016)
Non-English at home		-0.391***	-0.002
		(0.033)	(0.022)
ELL			-0.588***
			(0.028)
Graded special ed			-0.327***
			(0.021)
Lagged test score			0.471***
			(0.012)
Constant	-0.192***	-0.041	-0.265***
	(0.069)	(0.068)	(0.069)
Observations	22,059	22,059	22,059
R-squared	0.030	0.045	0.421
School fixed effects	N	N	Y
Borough controls	Y	Y	Y

Notes: Robust standard errors, adjusted for within school clusters, in parentheses (*** $p<0.01$, ** $p<0.05$, * $p<0.1$). Z-scores are standardized within each grade across the city to have a mean of 0 and a standard deviation of 1. This means that a third grader with a z-score of 0 performs at grade-level average. A third grader with a z-score above 0 performs above average relative to other New York City third graders and third graders with z-scores below 0 perform below average relative to other New York City third graders. Students are considered low-income if they are eligible for free or reduced-price lunch eligibility (family income below 185 percent of federal poverty level) or attend a universal free meal school. English Language Learners are those considered Limited English Proficient. Ungraded special education students are excluded. All models include controls for grade, year, and an indicator for students missing prior performance. The reference group is all other foreign-born Black students.

Source: Authors' calculations using NYCDOE data.

Table 7b. Performance on Math Exam, Foreign-Born Black 3rd-8th Graders, New York City Public Schools, Spring 2009 and Spring 2010

	Math		
	Demographic Controls - Excluding Home Language	Demographic Controls - Including Home Language	Demographic Controls and Controls for Educational Services and Prior Achievement
	(1)	(2)	(3)
Caribbean	-0.070**	-0.165***	-0.065***
	(0.035)	(0.035)	(0.023)
Haitian	-0.320***	-0.018	0.005
	(0.045)	(0.050)	(0.026)
Jamaican	-0.086***	-0.098***	-0.032**
	(0.024)	(0.024)	(0.015)
African	-0.093**	-0.019	0.048*
	(0.042)	(0.041)	(0.026)
Guyanese	-0.088**	-0.189***	-0.077***
	(0.036)	(0.036)	(0.025)
Female	0.134***	0.131***	0.068***
	(0.015)	(0.015)	(0.011)
Low-income	-0.050*	-0.043*	0.002
	(0.026)	(0.026)	(0.015)
Non-English at home		-0.350***	0.053***
		(0.035)	(0.020)
ELL			-0.510***
			(0.029)
Graded special ed			-0.310***
			(0.021)
Lagged test score			0.540***
			(0.011)
Constant	**-0.211***	**-0.065**	**-0.204***
	(0.077)	(0.077)	(0.074)
Observations	22,799	22,799	22,799
R-squared	**0.024**	**0.035**	**0.455**
School fixed effects	N	N	Y
Borough controls	Y	Y	Y

Notes: See notes under Table 7a.

Source: Authors' calculations using NYCDOE data.

These results provide some evidence that within schools, relative to otherwise similar Caribbean Blacks, Haitian students perform slightly better on the ELA exam and fare no differently on the math exam.

Notice that the magnitude of the estimated coefficients capturing English proficiency (ELL status) are large, significant, and negative, which speaks to the importance of facility with English on student performance. While the estimated coefficients for Haitian students indicate they perform no differently from or even better than their Caribbean peers, it is important to remember that this compares *otherwise similar* students (i.e., students with similar language proficiencies). Controlling for language proficiency and exposure, therefore, appears to explain a significant amount of the difference in raw, unadjusted test scores (shown earlier in Table 3) between Haitians and their Caribbean peers.

We then extend our model to examine changes in the performance of Black immigrant students on standardized tests in ELA and math between spring 2009 and spring 2010 (see Tables 8a and 8b).[31] The results are intriguing: in 2009 Caribbean students as a whole earned lower scores than other Black foreign-born students on the ELA exam, and among the Caribbean students Jamaicans performed particularly poorly — matched in their poor performance only by the Guyanese (see Table 8a, column 1). Math results are similar and there is little evidence of any change between spring 2009 and spring 2010 on either exam, as all the interaction effects between specific student origin groups and the testing year are insignificant.

That said, it is possible that unobserved differences between students are affecting the results. Thus, we re-estimate the models using student fixed effects, which essentially control for the characteristics of students that do not vary over time. In other words, these models describe the change in test scores *for the same students* between the two school years.

In the fixed-effects models, we see the performance of Haitians *gaining significantly* between spring 2009 and spring 2010 in both ELA and math, and Africans gaining significantly in math but not ELA performance (see column 2 in Tables 8a and 8b). Whether these improvements are due to changes in the social context following the tragic earthquake in Haiti in January 2010 or evidence that Haitians (and Africans) improve their performance over time, alongside growing

---

31   To be clear, we include only the students registered prior to October 31, 2009, and tested in the spring of 2010.

familiarity with English and increasing assimilation, is unclear.[32] This is clearly a topic worthy of future study.

Table 8a. Performance on ELA Exam, Foreign-Born Black 3rd-8th Graders, New York City Public Schools, Spring 2009 and Spring 2010, Extended Model

	ELA	
	Demographic and Educational Controls	Demographic, Educational and Student Fixed Effects Controls
	(1)	(2)
Caribbean	-0.063*	---
	(0.036)	---
Caribbean * Spring 2010	-0.033	-0.060
	(0.048)	(0.071)
Haitian	0.056	---
	(0.037)	---
Haitian * Spring 2010	0.048	0.108**
	(0.031)	(0.044)
Jamaican	-0.099***	---
	(0.025)	---
Jamaican * Spring 2010	0.008	0.065
	(0.028)	(0.042)
African	-0.005	---
	(0.040)	---
African * Spring 2010	0.073	0.112
	(0.049)	(0.070)
Guyanese	-0.139***	---
	(0.041)	---
Guyanese * Spring 2010	-0.001	0.009
	(0.049)	(0.069)
Observations	22,059	22,059
R-squared	0.265	0.875
School fixed effects	Y	N
Student fixed effects	N	Y

Notes: Robust standard errors, adjusted for within school clusters, in parentheses (*** $p<0.01$, ** $p<0.05$, * $p<0.1$). Z-scores are standardized within each grade across the city to have a mean of 0 and a standard deviation of 1. This means that a third grader with a z-score of

---

32   Following the earthquake, there was a great outpouring of support and empathy for Haitians. Schools provided counseling services, raised funds for affected families, and so on. These services were not restricted to students who had recently arrived from Haiti but to all students of Haitian descent (and in some schools with the resources, trauma and grief counseling were made available to the entire student body). It is plausible that within this context of positivity and support, all Haitian students would have received more attention, assistance, and/or even forbearance from teachers and other school people.

0 performs at grade-level average. A third grader with a z-score above 0 performs above average relative to other New York City third graders and third graders with z-scores below 0 perform below average relative to other New York City third graders. Models include controls for gender, ELL, home language, low-income, participation in special education, grade, year, residence borough, and in column (2), fixed effects for individual students over time. Estimates in column (2) capture differences in performance for the same student over time. The reference group is all other foreign-born Black students.

Source: Authors' calculations using NYCDOE data.

Table 8b. Performance on Math Exam, Foreign-Born Black 3rd-8th Graders, New York City Public Schools, Spring 2009 and Spring 2010, Extended Model

	Math	
	Demographic and Educational Controls	Demographic, Educational and Student Fixed Effects Controls
	(1)	(2)
Caribbean	-0.095**	---
	(0.038)	---
Caribbean * Spring 2010	0.037	-0.017
	(0.045)	(0.054)
Haitian	-0.013	---
	(0.041)	---
Haitian * Spring 2010	0.034	0.134**
	(0.039)	(0.062)
Jamaican	-0.057**	---
	(0.025)	---
Jamaican * Spring 2010	-0.023	0.020
	(0.029)	(0.036)
African	0.036	---
	(0.043)	---
African * Spring 2010	0.063	0.139***
	(0.048)	(0.053)
Guyanese	-0.098**	---
	(0.041)	---
Guyanese * Spring 2010	0.022	0.039
	(0.046)	(0.055)
Observations	22,799	22,799
R-squared	**0.258**	**0.902**
School fixed effects	Y	N
Student fixed effects	N	Y

Notes: See Table 8a notes.

Source: Authors' calculations using NYCDOE data.

B. Probing Deeper: Qualitative Findings on the School Experiences of Black Immigrant Students

Participants in the qualitative research reported contrasting stories with respect to how Black immigrant students are perceived and treated in school. Half of the participants reported that regular content area teachers seemed largely "clueless" about working with Black immigrant students and with immigrant students more generally. The five ESL teachers in particular pointed out that regular content area teachers had little preparation for and understanding of the complicated processes involved in learning another language.

Rather than attributing students' educational and social issues to ethnicity or race, the educators participating in the study were more likely to talk about family background, parents' educational levels, and perceptions of social class. Middle-school social studies teacher Lisa[33] stated, "The parents that have a bit more wealth, or seem to have a bit more wealth, their students . . . have the resources to achieve academically a bit more than students with less. And that could be because of actual materials, like a place to sit and read, paper, and pens, and glasses." As echoed by other participants, this pattern was consistent among middle-class and/or educated parents, irrespective of whether parents were newcomers or not. Lisa further clarified that newcomer parents tended to take a more active role in terms of working with their children on homework and by enforcing discipline.

Two of the participants in our qualitative research linked social class differences to parental literacy and educational background. Elsie, an ESL teacher, stated:

> One of the real challenges of teaching the ESL population that I work with: most of them come from families whose parents are illiterate. Which is a completely different thing. Like if you move to Greece right now, learning Greek for you would be a completely different experience than if you didn't understand what a sentence is, what a paragraph is, what a verb is, what the concepts of language are . . . And the kids that I teach, they aren't spoken to, they don't read magazines, there's no magazines in their homes, there's nothing, so they're trying to acquire literacy at the same time . . . [as acquiring] literacy in a foreign language. Which was not the case with those European immigrants, most of them. Even if they didn't have a lot of money, most of them were literate, because that was the thing to be in Europe. In Europe . . . people [had] . . . scholarship and books, you know, it was considered a valuable thing.

Similarly, Assiatou, whose parents had migrated from Sierra Leone in the late 1960s, noted that the newer wave of African immigrants seemed less educated than her parents' generation. She attributed this,

---

33   All participant names are pseudonyms.

in part, to historical changes, explaining that in the 1960s and 1970s, the school systems of many African countries had "not collapsed yet, at least in Sierra Leone, and so they came in very well educated, above and beyond their peers a lot of the time." By contrast, she found that with newer African immigrants:

> The countries are in worse shape . . . the education system has completely collapsed in a lot of the countries that the kids are coming from, and if they haven't collapsed there is such huge disparity in what people have access to, so you don't even know . . . the basic education that people should have access to. There's no baseline. They're either coming far beyond their peers or they come and . . . can't read or write anything, in any language.

Reinforcing her point about the importance of sending context, she further explained:

> And then we have some of our students, particularly those from like either extremely affluent backgrounds — countries like Ghana and Nigeria . . . or even Ivory Coast, where the school system was relatively solid, those students tend to come a little bit better prepared. Students that are coming from Guinea, it really depends on their background, their socioeconomic background, and then students coming from Mali — almost across the board, they struggle.[34]

These comments reinforce the need for more research that links the conditions of schooling in countries of origin to immigrant children's academic performance in host countries.[35]

Many participants raised the topic of interrupted schooling when asked to reflect on the academic performance of immigrant students. They indicated that SIFE status put students at a severe disadvantage, certainly with respect to academic performance, but also in terms of understanding the routines and social expectations of school. About one-tenth of ELL students in New York City schools also have SIFE status. About two-thirds of SIFE students speak Spanish and about 5 percent speak Haitian Creole, the third most common language for SIFE students.[36] According to Iveline, a Caribbean American high school teacher:

> We have both ends of the spectrum. We have some kids who we think are SIFE — kids with interrupted education who came and

---

34 This statement comes from Assiatou's personal experience with immigrant students from these African countries and should not be interpreted as definitive conclusions on the educational contexts of these sending nations.

35 Conger, Schwartz, and Stiefel examine the effect of economic conditions in students' home countries and the human capital characteristics of co-ethnic immigrant communities on foreign-born students' performance on standardized exams. See Dylan Conger, Leanna Stiefel, and Amy E. Schwartz, "The Effects of Immigrant Communities on Foreign-Born Student Achievement," *International Migration Review* 45, No. 3 (2011): 675-701.

36 Advocates for Children of New York, *Students with Interrupted Formal Education.*

have may have gone to school in their country for two years or
something and they really and truly need from the basics up. So
those kids struggle, but then you have the other kids who went
to private schools or did go to schools in the countries that they
came from and they have a ... history of excelling.

There has been a recent surge in advocacy for, and attention given to, SIFE students in New York City.[37] The Department of Education has hosted professional development sessions for administrators, teachers, and other school staff to learn about the unique challenges facing these students, and promising initiatives have emerged in schools and community organizations that address them. As these are only initial efforts, teachers still feel unprepared to meet the needs of students with such divergent schooling experiences. Participant Kai's comment (below) suggests that as US school systems develop policies and practices for working with SIFE students, they might be well served to look to other countries where interrupted schooling is more of a norm and where teachers may be better equipped for working with these students:

I taught most of the time in Tanzania where everybody is SIFE,
everybody has interrupted formal education. I don't mean to
demean it at all, but I didn't realize it was a big deal. I actually
thought it was the norm. So teachers in Tanzania have to be so
versatile around that because you know that any given year, there
are going to be people in the room who haven't been here for a
year, or two, or three.

Some participants spoke with great enthusiasm about working with immigrant students. High school ESL teacher Pauline explained her favorable views of immigrant students in this way:

I am generally thankful that I teach ESL because the kids tend
to be nicer. I think that it is because the teacher is valued a little
bit differently in different parts of the world than in the United
States. A lot of students also understand that in their country the
teacher has a lot of authority ... The students change after two,
three years. It could be because their real personality comes out
after they have learned English. Or because they have become
Americanized. And it's probably not just becoming Americanized.
I should probably be careful with that. They're probably taking
on the cultures of the schools of America.

Within schools, the institutional supports for immigrant students, such as ESL classes, were available to all students irrespective of background. In schools with large populations of students from a given region or speaking a given language, participants mentioned resources such as dedicated sections of the library, translators, and translated versions of tests. Iveline explained how helpful it was for Haitian students to be able to take their state regents exams in Haitian-Creole:

---

37 Advocates for Children of New York, *Students with Interrupted Formal Education.*

"Taking tests in Creole is advantageous — many students pass. I mean, this year for our ... what was it? Global History, I think 97 percent of them, because they would take it in Creole, passed." By and large, participants spoke about the pressures of testing in negative terms, highlighting both the inherent difficulties in forcing newly arrived students to take high-stakes exams and the personal toll such pressure took on their students. Elementary ESL teacher Jocelyn asserted that she spoke for all ESL teachers in claiming:

> Our hearts as teachers, our hearts bleed for these children. Because they are so nervous when it comes to the test day. They show up, they shake, we have to say OK, it's just a test, take some water, it's going to be OK. And we are, the ESL teachers more than anybody else, we are like their advocates in every school in this public school system. When they leave their parents, the ESL teachers become their parents. They hug (we're not supposed to hug), boys wanna hug, girls wanna hug, it's like you come to get them out of their classroom for their ESL session, it's like they see some ... something, you know, and they just get up and they come. And they run. In fact [ESL class is] the only time they get to talk, express themselves, what are their feelings, cause the groups are small. When they're in the general population of 33 children in the classroom, sometimes they can't say, "I wanna go to the bathroom." They're afraid to raise their hand because "bathroom" may sound funny and all of these children may laugh at them. So they're under stress.

V. Synthesis and Discussion of Findings

We conducted a mixed-methods study of Black immigrants in New York City public schools in order to capture the diversity represented within this population of students, often discussed in the literature as a monolithic category. Though Black immigrants are predominantly English proficient and speak English at home, countries such as the Dominican Republic, Haiti, Guinea, and Senegal — where English does not predominate — also send large numbers of ELL students to New York City schools. Using rich longitudinal quantitative data from the city's Department of Education and in-depth qualitative interviews with educators serving Black immigrant students, we explore the characteristics of Black foreign-born students in elementary and middle schools and generate a set of key findings around social isolation and segregation within Black immigrant populations, factors influencing academic performance, and the impact of students' sending contexts and backgrounds.

With respect to social isolation among Black immigrants, we find that foreign-born Blacks are more likely than native-born Blacks to be in schools attended by same-race peers, while Haitian students are overconcentrated in schools with their same–country, same-race peers. Prior research has suggested such isolation can be a risk factor for academic failure.[38] The comparatively poor performance of Haitian immigrant students would seem to support these theories. However, other data presented in this volume do not.[39]

Turning to academic performance, our quantitative data show that foreign-born Blacks perform below grade-level average and below the performance of their native-born counterparts, with Caribbean Blacks performing even worse. We also find that Caribbean immigrants perform worse than their counterparts from other regions of the world. Haitian students, however, perform better or no differently from other Caribbean immigrants, after controlling for English proficiency and exposure to English at home. More importantly, our findings show that English proficiency is one of the most important factors, if not the most important factor, associated with academic performance. Thus, students from countries in which the primary language is not English face a different set of challenges than students from English-speaking countries. The importance of English language skills suggests that rather than distinguishing groups of immigrants by the geographic region of their home country — Africa versus the Caribbean, for example — it might be more useful and appropriate to distinguish by home language. While not surprising, this finding points to the importance of disaggregating data on the diverse group of Black immigrant students. On a broader level, the findings presented here suggest that English language exposure and proficiency are strongly associated with differences in immigrant students' ELA and math test scores.

The qualitative data highlight three other important, related dimensions in the diversity of Black immigrant students: social class in the home country, parental literacy and educational attainment, and the quality and consistency of home-country schooling. Quantitatively we do not find much variability in income levels across Black immigrant groups or between native-born Blacks and foreign-born Blacks.

Educators also spoke to the importance of parental literacy in supporting their children's education — for instance, through reading books to children at home and supporting children with their homework. It is important to note that this notion of literacy can be abstracted and extended to encompass the kind of familiarity with the US schooling system that puts mainstream families at an advantage when compared to immigrant, ethnic minority, and/or low-income families — what Lisa Delpit has termed access to the culture of power.[40] More quantitative data are needed to help confirm or challenge these educators' perceptions.

---

38 Carola Suárez-Orozco, Marcelo M. Suárez-Orozco, and Irina Todorova, *Learning a New Land: Immigrant Students in American Society* (Cambridge, MA: Harvard University Press, 2008).
39 See also Chapter 10 of this volume, Dylan Conger and Megan Hatch, "The Academic Development of Black Foreign-Born Students in Miami-Dade County Schools."
40 Delpit, *Other People's Children*.

Our qualitative findings point to the significance of interrupted schooling in shaping the academic performance of Black immigrant students. A comprehensive understanding of SIFE students will require much more data than now exist. Most of the literature available on SIFE students and how to work with them emerges from the realms of policy and practice and would be strengthened by empirical evidence to support recommendations and guidelines for addressing the needs of these students.

In spite of decreases in the size of the population of Black immigrant students overall, the growing numbers of immigrant students in New York City public schools from a number of African nations and from Haiti attests to the fact that these students' experiences, strengths, and challenges must be explored and understood. Deliberate attention to the rich diversity present among Black immigrant students will help create programs and policies designed to meet their unique needs and help them to succeed. ⤴

Works Cited

Advocates for Children of New York. 2010. *Students with Interrupted Formal Education: A Challenge for New York City Public Schools.* New York: Advocates for Children of New York. http://www.advocatesforchildren.org/SIFE%20 Paper%20final.pdf?pt=1

Bartlett, Lesley and Ofelia García. 2011. *Additive Schooling in Subtractive Times: Bilingual Education and Dominican Immigrant Youth in the Heights.* Nashville, TN: Vanderbilt University Press.

Capps, Randy, Kristen McCabe, and Michael Fix. 2012. New Streams: African Migration to the United States. In *Young Children of Black Immigrants in America: Changing Flows, Changing Faces,* eds. Randy Capps and Michael Fix. Washington, DC: Migration Policy Institute.

Clotfelter, Charles T., Helen F. Ladd, and Jacob L. Vigdor. 2006. Teacher-Student Matching and the Assessment of Teacher Effectiveness. *The Journal of Human Resources* 41 (4): 778–820.

Conger, Dylan and Megan Hatch. 2012. The Academic Development of Black Foreign-Born Students in Miami-Dade County Schools. In *Young Children of Black Immigrants in America: Changing Flows, Changing Faces,* eds. Randy Capps and Michael Fix. Washington, DC: Migration Policy Institute.

Conger, Dylan, Leanna Stiefel, and Amy E. Schwartz. 2011. The Effects of Immigrant Communities on Foreign-Born Student Achievement. *International Migration Review* 45 (3): 675-701.

DeCapua, Andrea, William Smathers, and Lixing F. Tang. 2007. Schooling, Interrupted. *Educational Leadership* 64 (6): 40–6.

DeGraff, Michel. 2009. Creole Exceptionalism and the (Mis)education of the Creole Speaker. In *The Languages of Africa and the Diaspora: Educating for Language Awareness,* eds. Jo A. Kleifgen and George C. Bond. Bristol, UK: Multilingual Matters.

Delpit, Lisa. 1995. *Other People's Children: Cultural Conflict in the Classroom.* New York: New Press.

Doucet, Fabienne. 2008. How African American Parents Understand Their and Teachers Roles in Children's Schooling and What This Means for Preparing Preservice Teachers. *Journal of Early Childhood Teacher Education [Special Issue on Multicultural Teacher Education in Honor of Leslie R. Williams]* 29 (2): 108–39.

_____. 2011. (Re)Constructing Home and School: Immigrant Parents, Agency, and the (Un)desirability of Bridging Multiple Worlds. *Teachers College Record* 113 (12): 2705-38.

Farmer, Paul. 2011. *Haiti after the Earthquake.* New York: Public Affairs.

Fordham, Signithia, and John U. Ogbu. 1986. Black Students' School Success: Coping with the "Burden of 'Acting White'." *The Urban Review* 18 (3): 176–206.

Fryer Jr., Roland G. and Steven D. Levitt. 2004. Understanding the Black-White Test Score Gap in the First Two Years of School. *The Review of Economics and Statistics* 86 (2): 447–64.

_____. 2006. The Black-White Test Score Gap through Third Grade. *American Law and Economics Review* 8 (2): 249–81.

Glick, Jennifer E. and Michael J. White. 2003. The Academic Trajectories of Immigrant Youths: Analysis within and across Cohorts. *Demography* 40 (4): 759–83.

Hanushek, Eric A. 1986. The Economics of Schooling: Production and Efficiency in Public Schools. *Journal of Economic Literature* 24 (3): 1141–477.

Hanushek, Eric A., Steven G. Rivkin, and John F. Kain. 2005. Teachers, Schools, and Academic Achievement. *Econometrica* 73 (2): 417–58.

Iatarola, Patrice and Leanna Stiefel. 2003. Intra-District Equity of Public Education Resources and Performance. *Economics of Education Review* 22 (1): 69–78.

Jenkins, Jennifer. 2006. Current Perspectives on Teaching World Englishes and English as a Lingua Franca. *TESOL Quarterly* 40 (1): 157–81.

Kao, Grace. 1999. Psychological Well-Being and Educational Achievement among Immigrant Youth. In *Children of Immigrants: Health, Adjustment, and Public Assistance,* ed. Donald J. Hernandez. Washington, DC: National Academy Press.

Kent, Mary Mederios. 2007. Immigration and America's Black Population. *Population Bulletin* 62, Population Reference Bureau, Washington, DC. www.prb.org/pdf07/62.4immigration.pdf.

Lankford, Hamilton, Susanna Loeb, and James Wyckoff. 2002. Teacher Sorting and the Plight of Urban Schools: A Descriptive Analysis. *Educational Evaluation and Policy Analysis* 24 (1): 37–62.

Leung, Constant, Roxy Harris, and Ben Rampton. 1997. The Idealised Native Speaker, Reified Ethnicities, and Classroom Realities. *TESOL Quarterly* 31 (3): 543–60.

Livingston, Ivor L. 1994. *Handbook of Black American Health: The Mosaic of Conditions, Issues, Policies, and Proposals.* Westport, CT: Greenwood Press.

Lucas, Tamara, Rosemary Henze, and Ruben Donato. 1990. Promoting the Success of Latino Language-Minority Students: An Exploratory Study of Six High Schools. *Harvard Educational Review* 60 (3): 315–40.

Massey, Douglas S., Margarita Mooney, Kimberly C. Torres, and Camille Z. Charles. 2007. Black Immigrants and Black Natives Attending Selective Colleges and Universities in the United States. *American Journal of Education* 113 (2): 243–71.

Nero, Shondel. 2006. Language, Identity, and Education of Caribbean English Speakers. *World Englishes* 25 (3/4): 501–11.

_____. 2010. Language, Literacy, and Pedagogy of Caribbean Creole English Speakers. In *Ethnolinguistic Diversity and Education: Language, Literacy, and Culture,* eds. Marcia Farr, Lisya Seloni, and Juyoung Song, 212–40. New York: Routledge/Taylor and Francis.

O'Connor, Carla, Amanda Lewis, and Jennifer Mueller. 2007. Researching "Black" Educational Experiences And Outcomes: Theoretical and Methodological Considerations. *Educational Researcher* 36 (9): 541–52.

Ogbu, John U. and Herber D. Simons. 1998. Voluntary and Involuntary Minorities: A Cultural-Ecological Theory of School Performance with Some Implications for Education. *Anthropology and Education Quarterly* 29: 155–88.

Phillips, Meredith, James Crouse, and John Ralph. 1998. Does the Black-White Test Score Gap Widen after Children Enter School? In *The Black-White Test Score Gap,* eds. Christopher Jencks and Meredith Phillips. Washington, DC: Brookings Institution Press.

Rampton, Ben. 1985. A Critique of Some Educational Attitudes to the English of British Asian Schoolchildren, and their Implications. In *English as a Second Language in the United Kingdom: Linguistic and Educational Contexts,* eds. Christopher Brumfit, Rod Ellis, and Josie Levine, 187–98. Oxford: Pergamon Press.

Rubenstein, Ross, Amy E. Schwartz, Leanna Stiefel, and Hella B. H. Amor. 2007. From Districts to Schools: The Distribution of Resources across Schools in Big City School Districts. *Economics of Education Review* 26 (5): 532–45.

Schiefflin, Bambi B. and Rachelle C. Doucet. 1994. The "Real" Haitian Creole: Ideology, Metalinguistics, and Orthography. *American Ethnologist* 21 (1): 176–200.

Schwartz, Amy E., and Leanna Stiefel. 2006. Is There a Nativity Gap? New Evidence on the Academic Performance of Immigrant Students. *Education Finance and Policy* 1 (1): 17–49.

_____. 2011. Immigrants and Inequality in Public Schools. In *Whither Opportunity? Rising Inequality and the Uncertain Life Chances of Low-Income Children,* eds. Greg Duncan and Richard Murnane. New York: Russell Sage Foundation.

Short, Deborah J. and Beverly A. Boyson. 2004. *Creating Access: Language and Academic Programs for Secondary School Newcomers.* Washington, DC and McHenry, IL: Center for Applied Linguistics and Delta Publishing Company.

Suárez-Orozco, Carola, Marcelo M. Suárez-Orozco, and Irina Todorova. 2008. *Learning a New Land: Immigrant Students in American Society.* Cambridge, MA: Harvard University Press.

Thomas, Kevin J. A. 2012. Contemporary Black Caribbean Immigrants in the United States. In *Young Children of Black Immigrants in America: Changing Flows, Changing Faces,* eds. Randy Capps and Michael Fix. Washington, DC: Migration Policy Institute.

Todd, Petra E., and Kenneth I. Wolpin. 2003. On the Specification and Estimation of the Production Function for Cognitive Achievement. *Economic Journal* 113 (485): 3–33.

_____. 2007. The Production of Cognitive Achievement in Children: Home, School, and Racial Test Score Gaps. *Journal of Human Capital* 1 (1): 91–136.

Waters, Mary C. 1999. *Black Identities: West Indian Immigrant Dreams and American Realities.* New York and Cambridge, MA: Russell Sage Foundation and Harvard University Press.

Zéphir, Flore. 2001. *Trends in Ethnic Identification among Second-Generation Haitian Immigrants in New York City.* Westport, CT: Bergin and Garvey.

CHAPTER 10

THE ACADEMIC DEVELOPMENT OF BLACK FOREIGN-BORN STUDENTS IN MIAMI-DADE COUNTY SCHOOLS

Dylan Conger and Megan Hatch

The George Washington University

Introduction: Setting the Stage and Related Literature

Research on the academic adjustment of immigrant children from the second great wave of migration to the United States has grown substantially in recent years. Much of the research documents a decrease in academic performance across generations, with immigrant children (the first generation) or US-born children of immigrants (the second generation) outperforming their later-generation peers in school.[1] Explanations for this phenomenon, which has been termed an "immigrant paradox" and "downward assimilation," often point to the potential risks of growing up in specific communities in the United States. One common concern is that immigrant youth arrive with positive values that help them excel in school (such as high regard for educational attainment, a strong work ethic, and respect for teachers and other authority figures), but that these academically beneficial values erode as students are exposed to low-income, native-born

---

1   Andrew Fuligni, "The Academic Achievement of Adolescents from Immigrant Families: The Roles of Family Background, Attitudes, and Behavior," *Child Development* 68, No. 2 (1997): 351–63; Grace Kao and Marta Tienda, "Optimism and Achievement: The Educational Performance of Immigrant Youth," *Social Science Quarterly* 76 (1995): 1–19; Amy Ellen Schwartz and Leanna Stiefel, "Is There a Nativity Gap? Achievement of New York City Elementary and Middle School Immigrant Students," *Education Finance and Policy* 1 (2006): 17–49.

youth in under-resourced communities.[2] Such findings pose significant challenges for educators because they contradict the assumption that exposing young newcomers to native-born youth, the English language, and US schools will universally promote their academic and social development.

Yet, the existing literature on the educational adjustment of immigrant children is deficient in at least two major ways, in part due to data constraints.

First, because of a shortage of large-scale longitudinal data sets, most prior quantitative research relied on cross-sectional data that compare children across generations (first, second, and third or later) or according to their length of residency in the United States. Both of these approaches fail to isolate acculturative changes in immigrant children. The first approach (comparing generations) does not account for cohort quality — whether, for instance, the second generation in a given year is born to a cohort of immigrants that have higher human capital than the first generation in that year. The second approach (comparing length of residency) fails to isolate the effect of time in the country from the effect of age of entry because the two variables are inversely related.

Second, most prior research has examined children from Hispanic and Asian families, with very little attention paid to children from Black families. This gap in the literature can be primarily attributed to the relatively small numbers of Black immigrant children who, when studied using national survey data, do not yield sufficient samples for statistically reliable analysis. As a consequence, many of the prior theories regarding the acculturation of immigrant children have been untested on Black immigrants, a group that may experience integration differently than other immigrant groups.

In this chapter, we aim to fill these gaps in the literature by examining the academic development of young Black foreign-born children as they age in the United States. Our analysis is made possible with administrative data on large numbers of Black foreign-born students enrolled in the Miami-Dade County Public Schools (M-DCPS). We use regression analysis to identify initial gaps in achievement between Black foreign-born and native-born students in the third grade, controlling for students' gender, poverty status, identified disability, and English proficiency. We then examine how gaps in achievement change as the students progress to the eighth grade. By comparing changes in Black foreign-born students' test scores to those of Black native-born students of the same ages and in the same years, we are able to control for normal developmental changes that occur as children age and to determine whether Black immigrant youth experience a trajectory that departs from that of native-born youth.

---

2   Alejandro Portes and Rubén G. Rumbaut, *Legacies: The Story of the Immigrant Second Generation* (Los Angeles: University of California Press and Russell Sage Foundation, 2001).

Our analysis first focuses on comparisons between all Black first-generation immigrants and all Black native-born youth. We then examine variation in the academic trajectories of Black foreign-born and native-born students by whether English is spoken in the students' homes. For comparison, we also analyze a sample of Hispanic students. The purposes of our study are to test for evidence of downward assimilation (an important theory in the sociological and child-development literature) among Black foreign-born children and to shed new light, for the benefit of educators and policymakers, on how this population in particular adjusts to the host culture.

Related Literature

The majority of research on immigrant youth focuses on their paths to acculturation. There are several competing theories about these paths. One hypothesis is that today's newcomers will follow a trajectory of upward assimilation similar to that taken by European immigrants coming to the United States at the turn of the 20th century. This implies that, though of humble origins, young immigrant children will rapidly learn the English language and American customs and later outpace their parents on measures of educational attainment, labor-market performance, and other indicators of assimilation.[3] In short, the theory is that becoming more "American" will lead to developmental, academic, and other gains. An alternative view is that many of today's newcomers will show signs of downward assimilation because they are poor, are racial and ethnic minorities, and are growing up in inner-city public schools where resources are scarce and peers have negative attitudes about school.[4]

These competing expectations can be applied to inter- and intra-generational changes. When first-generation children, for example, outperform later-generation children, this is consistent with a pattern of downward assimilation across generations. When immigrant children who are newly arrived outperform immigrant children who have resided in the United States longer, this is consistent with a pattern of downward assimilation within the first generation. In the child-development literature, these patterns have been referred to as an "immigrant paradox": some recently arrived immigrants who face significant barriers to educational progress (such as limited proficiency in English and high rates of poverty) tend to experience better educational, health, psychosocial, behavioral, and academic outcomes than

---

3   Richard Alba and Victor Nee, *Remaking the American Mainstream: Assimilation and Contemporary Immigration* (Cambridge, MA and London: Harvard University Press, 2003).

4   Alejandro Portes and Rubén G. Rumbaut, *Immigrant America: A Portrait* (Los Angeles: University of California Press, 1996); Portes and Rumbaut, *Legacies*; Alejandro Portes and Min Zhou, "The New Second Generation: Segmented Assimilation and its Variants," *Annals of the American Academy of Political and Social Science* 530 (1993): 74–96.

other immigrant youth with longer residence in the United States or than native-born youth.[5]

Sociologists Alejandro Portes and Rubén Rumbaut[6] and Min Zhou[7] hypothesize this phenomenon as a process whereby young children of immigrants face certain structural conditions in school and in their communities that change the course on which their parents intended to set them. Children of immigrants benefit initially from the high expectations of their immigrant parents, yet for some, the positive start is reversed or altered by their exposure to American students and norms. That is, those immigrant youth who lose attachments to their immigrant communities may trend downward. There are several rich ethnographies about immigrant groups in specific localities that document many of the positive social and cultural attributes that buffer immigrant children from decline (e.g., about a Vietnamese community in New Orleans that fosters strong family systems and highly connected co-ethnic social networks).[8]

Despite the ample theoretical and qualitative description of trajectories among first-generation immigrants, there have been very few quantitative attempts to track large groups of foreign-born children over time and almost none that compare foreign-born changes to native-born changes. The native-born trend provides an important benchmark because it tracks the developmental changes that students in the United States experience as they age. If the foreign-born trajectory differs from the native-born trajectory, this suggests that foreign-born status (e.g., different language abilities, cultural practices, lack of citizenship or legal status, acculturative stress) and/or immigrant parentage (e.g., stricter control over social lives, emphasis on traditions and cultural norms, academic expectations) influence development and socialization in school.

In one of the only large studies to use this approach, Wen-Jui Han,[9] a scholar on social work, uses the Early Childhood Longitudinal Survey–Kindergarten Cohort (ECLS-K), a national probability sample of kindergarteners in 1998, to track changes in children's reading and math achievement from kindergarten to the third grade. Han finds that children of immigrants (i.e., foreign-born children and the US-born children of immigrants) from most Latin American countries score lower than their white American counterparts in kindergarten, yet on

<hr />

5   Cynthia García Coll and Amy Marks, eds., *Is Becoming an American a Developmental Risk?* (Washington, DC: American Psychological Association Books, 2011).

6   Portes and Rumbaut, *Immigrant America*; Portes and Rumbaut, *Legacies*.

7   Min Zhou, "Segmented Assimilation: Issues, Controversies, and Recent Research on the New Second Generation," *International Migration Review* 31, No. 4 (1997): 975–1008.

8   Min Zhou and Carl L. Bankston III, *Growing Up American: How Vietnamese Children Adapt to Life in the United States* (New York: Russell Sage Foundation, 1998); Nathan Caplan, John K. Whitmore, and Marcella H. Choy, *The Boat People and Achievement in America* (Ann Arbor, MI: The University of Michigan Press, 1989).

9   Wen-Jui Han, "The Academic Trajectories of Children of Immigrants and Their School Environments," *Developmental Psychology* 44, No. 6 (2008): 1572–90.

average, their achievement increases over time and, for some groups, reaches parity with white, native-born children. Asian immigrant children experience an opposite pattern: relatively high early achievement, followed by slight decreases, with few Asian immigrants dropping to the native-born average by the third grade. In part because of insufficient numbers of students, Han's analysis was restricted to students who were born in Asia or Latin America or had at least one parent born in these regions; thus, the results may not generalize to most Black immigrant children.

This study builds upon the Han analysis by focusing on the experiences of Black immigrants, a group that may experience acculturation differently from Hispanic and Asian immigrant peers. We also distinguish among Black immigrants whose primary home language is English and those whose home language is not English, since this is one of the unique features of the Black immigrant population.[10] In Miami-Dade County, as across the nation, a large percentage of Black immigrants hail from English-speaking nations and thus arrive to the United States with what may appear to be an advantage over immigrants who come with relatively limited English exposure. At the same time, Black immigrants with high levels of English familiarity might be more socially integrated with their native-born classmates and, if the "immigrant paradox" holds true, pulled downward by the low achievement of the same-race native born. We thus examine whether, and how, English in the home matters for Black immigrant children as they progress through the school system.

I. Data and Methods

A. Data

Miami-Dade County has the fourth-largest school system in the United States, with approximately 347,000 students in 435 schools. According to census records, between 2005 and 2009 approximately 49 percent of Miami-Dade residents were foreign born, reflecting Miami-Dade's long history as a traditional gateway for immigrants to the United States.

M-DCPS officials provided us with data on all students enrolled in the public school system in school years (SY) 2003 through 2008. To examine changes in reading test scores, we restrict the sample to the 14,531 students whose first reading exam was taken in the third grade in 2003 and who were tested annually through the eighth grade without repeating a grade. The data are organized hierarchically in student years, resulting in 87,186 student-year observations.

---

10 For more on the diversity of Black immigration flows, see Chapter 3 in this volume, Donald J. Hernandez, *Young Children in Black Immigrant Families from Africa and the Caribbean.*

The dependent variable for the analysis is students' reading scores on the Florida Comprehensive Achievement Test (FCAT). The FCAT is a criterion-referenced statewide exam that has been administered since the mid-1990s to evaluate students and schools against the state's curriculum and performance standards, known as the Sunshine State Standards. Using data on all test-takers in each year, we standardize the test scores to an average of 0 and a standard deviation of 1 at the level of each grade within each school year.[11] Standardizing FCAT scores makes it possible to evaluate children relative to their peers across all the Miami-Dade County public schools.

For each student, the data also contain key demographic (race, gender) and educational (receipt of services for disabilities and English Language Learner [ELL] status) indicators.[12] Information is also available on the poverty status of the family through the students' participation in the free and reduced-price lunch (FRPL) program. Students with family incomes below 130 percent of the federal poverty level are eligible for free lunch, and those with incomes between 130 percent and 185 percent of the poverty level are eligible for reduced-price lunch.[13]

Of key relevance to this study, the data also identify each student's country of birth, which allows us to identify foreign-born students. In addition, though the data do not record the birthplace of the parents, data are available on the languages most frequently spoken at home and by the student. Using these data, we distinguish among native-born Black students according to whether a language other than English is the primary language spoken in the home or by the student.

B. Methodology

Our primary aim is to determine whether the academic trajectories of Black foreign-born youth differ from those of their native-born Black peers. To model these dynamics, we use regression analyses, allowing us to identify the initial (third grade) test score gaps between foreign-born and native-born children as well as changes over time in

---

11 This conversion to standardized test scores is done by subtracting the average for all test-takers in a grade and year from an individual student's score, and dividing by the standard deviation in test scores for all test-takers in the grade and year.

12 The racial categories recorded by the school system are as follows: Asian, Black, Hispanic, white, multiracial, and other. Like most school systems, Miami-Dade County Public Schools (M-DCPS) does not identify Hispanic ethnicity separately from race.

13 In 2008 the federal poverty level was $21,200 for a family of four, and slightly higher for larger families and lower for smaller families. See US Department of Health and Human Services (DHSS), "The 2008 HHS Poverty Guidelines," last revised January 29, 2010, http://aspe.hhs.gov/poverty/08poverty.shtml.

these gaps, controlling for several student attributes.[14]

Our control variables include students' gender, their eligibility for free or reduced-price lunch, disability status, and whether they were designated as ELLs in the third grade (the first year of the test).

Using this regression framework, we make three comparisons using three different samples. For our first comparison, we use the full sample of students to examine the initial test scores and changes in test scores of all students by their race and nativity status. More specifically, we compare the following eight groups:

- Foreign-born Black
- Native-born Black
- Foreign-born Hispanic
- Native-born Hispanic
- Foreign-born Asian
- Native-born Asian
- Foreign-born white
- Native-born white

For our second comparison, we restrict the sample to only Black students then examine the initial test scores and changes in test scores for the following four groups:

- Native-born and home language is English
- Native-born and home language is not English
- Foreign-born and home language is English
- Foreign-born and home language is not English

---

14 The following equation captures the basic regression framework:

$$(1) \quad test_{ig} = \beta_{00} + \beta_{10} grade_{ig} + \beta_{01} fb_i + \beta_{11}(fb_i \, x \, grade_{ig}) + \varepsilon_{0i} + \varepsilon_{1i}(grade_{ig}) + \varepsilon_{ig}$$

where *test* is the FCAT reading score for student *i* in grade *g*; *grade* is a counter for each grade that the student is tested, set to 0 in the third grade; and *fb* is a dummy variable set to 1 if the student is foreign born and 0 if the student is native born. In this equation, the intercept captures the mean native-born reading performance in the third grade, while the estimated coefficient on *fb* captures the difference between foreign-born and native-born students in the third grade. The grade variables then permit comparisons of foreign born to native born as they age. Specifically, the coefficient on the grade variable provides the slope for native-born students (their average annual rate of change) and the coefficient on the interaction *fb* and *grade* captures the difference between the slopes of foreign-born and native-born students. The model also provides estimation of three random error components; the between-student residual in the initial (grade 3) scores; the between-student residual in the annual rate of change; and the within-student residual variance from grade to grade.

For our final comparison, we restrict the sample to Hispanic students and examine the academic trajectories for Hispanic students who are native or foreign born. We separate out those from Cuba and Venezuela, the largest groups among Hispanic foreign-born students in M-DCPS. Specifically, we examine the academic development of the following four groups:

- Native born

- Cuban born

- Venezuelan born

- Other foreign born

C. Description of Sample

Table 1 provides a descriptive snapshot of the students in the sample by their race and nativity status. Approximately 19 percent of the sample is foreign born, with the highest share of immigrants found among Hispanic and Asian students. Among Black students, foreign- and native-born students are about equally likely to be eligible for FRPL: 87 percent and 86 percent, respectively. For the other three racial groups, foreign-born students have higher rates of both FRPL and ELL status. Though they possess higher rates of socioeconomic disadvantage, immigrant students of all racial groups are less likely than their native-born peers to have identified disabilities, such as learning or physical disabilities. The lower rates of special needs among the foreign born, which is consistent with research on students nationwide and in other large urban areas (such as New York City), may result from selective migration (i.e., families with disabled children may be less likely to leave their birth countries) and/or to lower rates of disability identification among foreign-born students.[15]

---

15 Dylan Conger, Amy Ellen Schwartz, and Leanna Stiefel, "Immigrant and Native-born Differences in School Stability and Special Education: Evidence from New York City," *International Migration Review* 41, No. 2 (2007): 402–31; Dylan Conger and Elena Grigorenko, "Special Educational Needs of Children in Immigrant Families," in *Immigration, Diversity, and Education*, eds. Elena L. Grigorenko and Ruby Takanishi (New York, NY and Abingdon, UK: Routledge/Taylor and Francis Group, 2009).

Table 1. Mean Characteristics of Sample, Miami-Dade Public Schools, 2003

	All	Black		Hispanic		Asian		White	
Percent of column group who are foreign born:	19	7		25		22		8	
Percent of column group who are:		FB	NB	FB	NB	FB	NB	FB	NB
Male	48	43	45	48	48	68	46	49	48
Free or reduced-price lunch (FRPL) eligible	66	87	86	76	64	59	33	35	26
Disabled	7	1	7	4	8	2	8	5	9
English Language Learner (ELL)	12	26	5	40	9	32	5	17	2
Number of students	14,531	225	3,007	2,287	6,974	44	153	125	1,454

Notes: Sample includes all students who first took the reading exam in the third grade in 2003 and who were continuously tested without repeating a grade through the eighth grade. FB refers to foreign born; NB refers to native born. FRPL, disability, and ELL status are determined in the first test year (the third grade).
Source: Miami-Dade County Public Schools.

Table 2 provides greater detail on the background characteristics of the 3,232 Black students in the sample according to their nativity status and whether English is the primary language spoken in the home. Among the native-born students whose home language is not English, 89 percent are in homes where Haitian Creole is the primary language. Thus, this group can almost be considered second-generation Haitian (US-born children with a Haitian-born parent).[16] Approximately 52 percent of the immigrant students in English homes are Jamaican born, with the remainder of these students born in the British Virgin Islands and other Caribbean countries. Finally, approximately 86 percent of the foreign-born students in homes where English is not the primary language are from Haiti, with another 6 percent from the Bahamas. The native-born students in English-speaking homes include a mixture of third- or later-generation African American and second-generation children from Jamaica and other Caribbean nations.

Among native-born students, those who speak or whose families speak Haitian Creole are more likely than other Black native-born students to be male, FRPL, and ELL. There is only a small difference in the disability rate of native-born students from English- and non-English-speaking homes: approximately 7 percent and 6 percent, respectively. Similar patterns are found among foreign-born children, with those who are less exposed to English more likely to be male, FRPL, and ELL and equally likely to have a disability as their peers in homes where English is not the primary language.

---

16 Importantly, we note that language at home only approximates Haitian immigrant household status. It is possible that some native-born children in Haitian-Creole-speaking homes are third or later generation (i.e., have US-born parents), and that some native-born children in non-Haitian-Creole-speaking homes are second-generation Haitian.

Table 2. Characteristics of Black Students by Nativity and Language At Home, 2003

	Native Born, English at Home	Native Born, Another Language at Home	Foreign Born, English at Home	Foreign Born, Another Language at Home
Percent of Black students who belong to column group:	74	19	2	5
Percent of column group who are:				
Male	44	50	34	48
Free or reduced-price lunch (FRPL) eligible	83	96	75	94
Disabled	7	6	1	1
English Language Learner (ELL)	<1	23	0	40
Number of students	2,405	602	79	146

Notes: Sample includes all 3,232 Black students who first took the reading exam in the third grade in 2003 and who were continuously tested without repeating a grade through the eighth grade. FRPL, disability, and ELL status are determined in the first test year (the third grade).
Source: Miami-Dade County Public Schools.

II. Results: Academic Trajectories of Immigrant and Native-Born Students in Miami-Dade Public Schools

Here, we provide and interpret the results of the test score analyses. The first section discusses the test score differences between all students in the sample by their race and nativity status. The second section discusses the test score differences between Black students in the sample by their home language and nativity status. The final section discusses the test score differences between Hispanic students in the sample by their nativity status. These three sections correspond to the three separate analyses outlined earlier in the methodology section.

A. *Trajectories of All Students, by Race and Nativity*

Figure 1 provides a graphic portrayal of the trajectories that emerge from the first version of the regression equation: the full sample of students, focusing on differences between all eight nativity and race groups (regression results can be found in Appendix Table A-1). The figure provides predicted reading scores at each grade and for each race/nativity group for students who are female, not FRPL-eligible, not disabled, and not ELL (that is, students who are likely to have the highest reading test scores). By selecting one prototype for the predictions, the figure provides comparisons between the race and nativity groups that control for the composition of those groups (at least on gender, FRPL eligibility, disability, and ELL status).[17]

Figure 1. Predicted Reading Scores of Sample, Third to Eighth Grade, by Race and Nativity, 2003-08

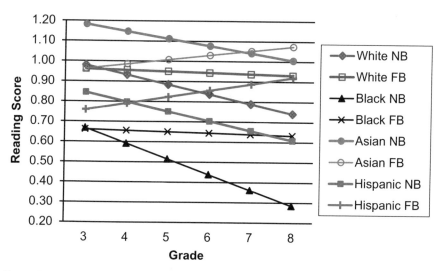

Notes: Sample includes all M-DCPS students who took the third grade reading test in 2003 and were continuously tested through the eighth grade without repeating a grade. The figure shows predicted values from models of reading test scores where the predictions are calculated using students who are female, not eligible for free or reduced-price lunch, not disabled, and not ELLs. FB refers to foreign born and NB refers to native born.

Source: Miami-Dade County Public Schools.

Figure 1 shows that Black native-born and Black foreign-born students start out with the lowest scores of all groups in the third grade, and their scores are equal to one another when controlling for gender, family income, disability, and English language ability. Over time, the academic trajectories of Black foreign-born and native-born students are, however, quite different. Black native-born students experience a sharp decline in their reading performance, while Black immigrant students experience no change in their reading scores. By the eighth grade, Black native-born students score far lower than any other group, while Black immigrant students have reached near parity with Hispanic native born. The decrease in scores for Black native born, from approximately 0.67 standard deviations to 0.28 standard deviations above 0, is roughly equivalent to a decrease of 15 percentile points on the test.

---

17 Gaps among the race and nativity groups and changes over time in these gaps are the same irrespective of the prototype chosen. For instance, students who are male, FRPL, disabled, and ELL would show lower scores across the board for all groups, but the gaps among the groups would not be different than those displayed in Figure 1.

Comparisons of native born to foreign born within each racial group reveal a consistent pattern. Irrespective of the level of their performance in the third grade, all of the foreign-born groups hold steady or trend upwards, while all of the native-born groups trend slightly downward. Thus, foreign-born students of all racial groups experience improvements in their annual scores relative to their native-born same-race peers. The difference is largest between Black foreign-born and native-born students, primarily because Black native born experience such a large decrease in their reading achievement. Despite their success relative to Black and Hispanic native-born students, Black immigrant students fail to reach parity with Hispanic foreign-born, white, and Asian students.

It is important to note the role of "regression to the mean" as a partial explanation for the trends shown in Figure 1. Regression to the mean is a statistical artifact that is attributed to the fact that students test scores at any given point are a combination of their true achievement or skill and the error that is involved in measuring achievement. If a student, for example, achieves the highest score possible in the third grade, the score is very likely a combination of the student's true (high) achievement and some luck. The next time the student takes the exam, she is unlikely to be so lucky and, even if her actual skill level does not change, she will likely score a bit lower on the exam. All of this means that when groups are compared over time, those who score at the very top initially are likely to show small amounts of decline, while those who score at the very bottom are likely to show small amounts of improvement, even if they experience no real changes in their achievement.

In the context of Figure 1, this means that some of the downward movement of the very highest-performing groups is a consequence of regression downward toward the mean, while some of the upward movement of the very lowest-performing groups is a consequence of regression upward toward the mean. What is notable, however, and inconsistent with what one would expect from statistical regression, is that Black native-born and foreign-born pupils start with the same low test scores in the third grade and the Black native-born trend downward. In addition, all groups of foreign-born students hold steady or trend upward, even those that are initially performing above the mean, which for this prototypical student is about 0.8 standard deviations in the third grade and 0.6 standard deviations in the eighth grade. In short, the patterns found in Figure 1 cannot entirely be attributed to statistical regression toward the mean.

B. Trajectories of Black Students, by Nativity and Language at Home

Figure 2 shows trajectories of test scores for Black students disaggregated by nativity and language spoken at home (regression results can be found in Appendix Table A-2). In the third grade, the two high-est-performing groups are foreign-born students with English at home and native-born students with non-English languages in the home. The two other groups — the native born with English at home and foreign born with a language other than English at home — score lower than the two other groups and similar to one another.

The changes over time are somewhat remarkable. The foreign-born students whose home language is not English (primarily Haitian students) are the only group to experience an increase in their test scores between third and eighth grade. All other groups show declining scores, with the declines steepest among the English, native-born group. By the eighth grade, the reading scores of non-English foreign-born students have surpassed all other groups.

Again, some of the trends in Figure 2 reflect regression upward and downward due to the challenges of accurately measuring test scores. Nevertheless, the improvements of the Black foreign-born students whose home language is not English — relative to their peers — is quite steep, and the crossing of the lines exceeds what one would expect from statistical regression. Instead, the students appear to be making real gains in their learning that continue after they reach parity with native-born students. In contrast, the foreign-born students in English-speaking homes show declines, much like their native-born peers.

Figure 2. Predicted Reading Scores of Black Students, Third to Eighth Grade, by Nativity and Language at Home, 2003-08

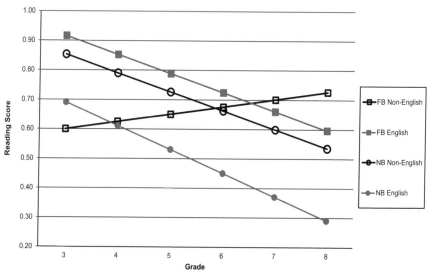

Notes: Sample includes all M-DCPS Black students who took the third grade reading test in 2003 and were continuously tested through the eighth grade without repeating a grade. The figure shows predicted values from models of reading test scores where the predictions are calculated using students who are female, not eligible for free or reduced-price lunch, not disabled, and not ELLs. FB refers to foreign born and NB refers to native born.

Source: Miami-Dade County Public Schools.

C. Trajectories of Hispanic Students, by Nativity

The results so far suggest a pattern of improving test scores for Black foreign-born students relative to Black native-born students. Figure 1 also revealed that this pattern seems to be true for all immigrant students, including Asian, Hispanic, and white students. Given that Hispanic students represent the largest share of the M-DCPS population, they provide a useful contrast to Black students.

Table 3 provides summary statistics on the demographic and educational background characteristics of Hispanic students by their country of origin, with Cuban- and Venezuelan-born students representing the top two origin groups.[18] Cuban students are the most economically disadvantaged of the four groups, with the highest rates of FRPL eligibility. Native-born students have the lowest rates of limited English proficiency but the highest rates of disability.

Table 3. Characteristics of Hispanic Students, by Nativity, 2003

	Native Born	Cuban Born	Venezuelan Born	Other Foreign Born
Percent of Hispanic students who belong to column group:	75	10	3	12
Percent of column group who are:				
Male	48	47	42	49
Free or reduced-price lunch (FRPL) eligible	64	85	52	74
Disabled	8	6	4	3
English Language Learner (ELL)	9	35	43	41
Number of students	6,974	942	271	1,094

Note: Sample includes all 9,281 Hispanic students who first took the reading exam in the third grade in 2003 and who were continuously tested without repeating a grade through the eighth grade. FRPL, disability, and ELL status are determined in the first test year (the third grade).
Source: Miami-Dade County Public Schools.

Figure 3 provides the test-score trajectories of Hispanic students according to their country of origin (regression results can be found in Appendix Table A-3). In grade 3, Cuban-born students earn very low scores, while all other groups score similar to one another. Over time, all groups of foreign-born students experience a large improvement in test scores, while the native born experience a sharp decrease. By

---

18 We were unable to reliably disaggregate among Hispanic foreign-born students by whether English is spoken in the home due to the very small numbers of Hispanic immigrants from English-speaking homes.

the eighth grade, all groups of foreign-born Hispanic students are far outperforming their native-born peers, and Cuban-born students have closed some of the gap with other foreign-born Hispanics. Thus, even within the Hispanic foreign-born population, we observe relatively large increases in reading achievement among foreign-born students from the major sending countries.

Figure 3. Predicted Reading Scores of Hispanic Students, Third to Eighth Grade, by Country of Origin, 2003-08

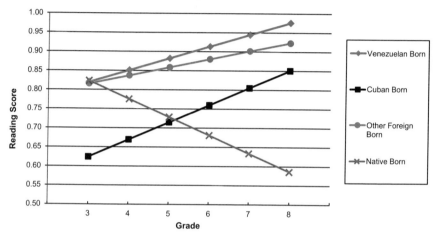

Notes: Sample includes all M-DCPS Hispanic students who took the third grade reading test in 2003 and were continuously tested through the eighth grade without repeating a grade. The figure shows predicted values from models of reading test scores where the predictions are calculated using students who are female, not eligible for free or reduced-price lunch, not disabled, and not ELLs. FB refers to foreign born and NB refers to native born.

Source: Authors' Calculations, using Miami-Dade County Public Schools data.

D. Sensitivity Analyses

In order to interpret the results shown thus far, it is important to consider the composition of students who are in the sample, which consists of students who were continuously enrolled and repeatedly tested from the third to the eighth grade. If the most motivated native-born students exit the public school system by eighth grade, comparisons of the students who remain in the public schools may overstate the academic growth of foreign-born students relative to their native-born peers. Similarly, if immigrant students are disproportionately held back a grade or not tested, then the remaining sample leaves out some of the poorest-performing foreign-born students.

To investigate this issue, we compared the mean reading test scores of Black students who were continuously tested to the eighth grade (i.e., those included in the sample with the results described above) to those who were tested in the third grade, but who dropped out of the sample because they were not continuously tested. The "not continuously tested" group could have exited the public school system, been retained in a grade, or not taken an exam for some reason.

These comparisons reveal that the continuously tested students (those in our sample) scored higher than those not continuously tested in the third grade. However, the differences between the continuously tested and not continuously tested students are similar for native-born and foreign-born students. Thus, while students in the analytic sample are a higher achieving group than the full population of M-DCPS students who take tests, this is true for both the foreign-born and native-born students. This result indicates that the relative gains we find among Black foreign-born students in our sample are unlikely to be driven by the composition of the students who are retained or who exit the sample over time.

To improve our set of control variables, we also estimated regression models that removed the student characteristics (gender, FRPL eligibility, disability, and ELL status) and replaced them with a set of student fixed effects, or indicator variables for each student. These fixed effects control for attributes of students that do not change over time but that matter to their test scores, such as early childhood education and other earlier parental investments. The fixed effects prevent us from comparing their third grade scores, but should yield less biased estimates of the changes from the third to the eighth grade. The results from these models are remarkably similar to the results presented in the chapter.

III. Discussion and Conclusion

Using longitudinal data from M-DCPS, we examine changes in reading test scores across the third through eighth grades for Black immigrants in comparison to those of native-born students, both Black and non-Black. The results point to improvement in test scores for Black foreign-born students relative to their Black native-born peers. The higher academic gains for immigrants relative to their native-born peers is also found among students who are Asian, Hispanic, and white.

We also observe variation in the trajectories of Black immigrant students according to the language at home. Foreign-born students whose home language is not English (most in Haitian-Creole-speaking homes), begin with the lowest third-grade scores of any Black group, but show a steep improvement in their scores by eighth grade. While some of this upward trend is likely driven by a regression toward the mean, these students outperform their native-born peers by the eighth grade. At the same time, Black foreign-born students in English-speaking homes appear to follow a pattern of downward assimilation, scoring quite high in the third grade then decreasing at nearly the same rate as their native-born same-race peers. In addition, though native-born children in non-English-speaking households show decreases in achievement, their declines are not as steep as those of native-born children in English-speaking homes.

Taken together, these results suggest that among Black students, immigrant status may serve as a protective factor in school. The pattern of relative academic improvement among Black foreign-born students in non-English-speaking homes is found among other foreign-born students in the Miami-Dade public schools, including Hispanic students from different countries of origin. At the same time, Black immigrants from English-speaking households show slight decreases in their achievement over time. These results suggest that being an immigrant, and in particular an immigrant with a language other than English in the home, may serve as a protective factor in school, limiting the decreases in test scores seen in other nativity and home language groups.

The differences in the trajectories we observe could also be driven by family expectations, neighborhood quality, support from the surrounding co-ethnic community, and so on. Further study of the differing rates of academic development for these groups of Black immigrants as well as Black immigrants from other parts of the world — such as Latin America, Europe, and Africa —would greatly enhance our understanding of the academic experiences of young immigrants in the United States. ⁊

Appendices

Tables A-1 through A-3 provide regression coefficients and standard errors (in parentheses) from the three analyses described in the methodology section above. For each table, there are two columns of results: Column I provides the results of a regression of standardized reading achievement with just the nativity and grade variables as independent variables. Column II provides the results of a regression of standardized reading achievement with the nativity and grade variable along with controls for students' free and reduced-price lunch (FRPL) eligibility, gender, disability, and English Language Learner (ELL) status. As an example of an interpretation, the coefficient on the Black foreign-born variable in Column I of Table A-1 indicates that Black foreign-born students score 0.569 standard deviations lower than white native-born students in the third grade.

Table A-1. Results from Growth Models: All Students, by Race and Nativity

Initial (third grade)	I	II
Black FB	-0.569***	-0.319***
	(0.052)	(0.049)
Black NB	-0.496***	-0.312***
	(0.022)	(0.022)
Hispanic FB	-0.517***	-0.222***
	(0.023)	(0.023)
Hispanic NB	-0.277***	-0.135***
	(0.020)	(0.019)
Asian FB	-0.223**	-0.017
	(0.112)	(0.104)
Asian NB	0.177***	0.202***
	(0.062)	(0.058)
White FB	-0.091	-0.019
	(0.068)	(0.063)

Slope (change over time)	I	II
Grade	-0.048***	-0.048***
	(0.003)	(0.003)
Black FB x grade	0.042***	0.042***
	(0.008)	(0.008)
Black NB x grade	-0.029***	-0.029***
	(0.004)	(0.004)
Hispanic FB x grade	0.080***	0.080***
	(0.004)	(0.004)
Hispanic NB x grade	0.000	0.000
	(0.003)	(0.003)
Asian FB x grade	0.070***	0.070***
	(0.018)	(0.018)
Asian NB x grade	0.012	0.012
	(0.010)	(0.010)
White FB x grade	0.042***	0.042***
	(0.011)	(0.011)
Student-level controls	No	Yes
Number of student years	87,186	87,186

Notes: (i) Standard errors in parentheses; (ii) FB refers to foreign born, NB refers to native born; (iii) all specifications include an intercept; (iv) student-level controls include indicator variables for eligibility for free or reduced-price lunch (FRPL), male, disabled, and English Language Learner (ELL); (v) * p<0.10, ** p<0.05, *** p<0.01.

Source: Authors' calculations, using Miami-Dade County Public Schools data.

Table A-2. Results from Growth Models: Black Students, by Language at Home

	I	II
FB, English spoken at home	0.294***	0.225***
	(0.077)	(0.072)
FB, English not spoken at home	-0.264***	-0.091
	(0.057)	(0.057)
NB, English not spoken at home	0.022	0.162***
	(0.031)	(0.031)
Grade	-0.080***	-0.080***
	(0.002)	(0.002)
FB, English spoken at home X grade	0.016	0.016
	(0.013)	(0.013)
FB, English not spoken at home X grade	0.105***	0.105***
	(0.009)	(0.009)
NB, English not spoken at home X grade	0.016***	0.016***
	(0.005)	(0.005)
Student-level controls	No	Yes
Number of student -years	19,392	19,392

Notes: (i) Standard errors in parentheses; (ii) all specifications include an intercept; (iii) student-level controls include indicator variables for eligibility for free or reduced-price lunch, male, disabled, and English Language Learner; and (iv) * p<0.10, ** p<0.05, *** p<0.01.

Source: Authors' calculations, using Miami-Dade County Public Schools data.

Table A-3. Results from Growth Models: Hispanic Students, by Country of Origin

	I	II
Cuban Born	-0.371***	-0.199***
	(0.026)	(0.025)
Venezuelan Born	-0.108**	-0.004
	(0.048)	(0.045)
Other Foreign Born	-0.160***	-0.008
	(0.025)	(0.024)
Grade	-0.047***	-0.047***
	(0.001)	(0.001)
Cuban Born x grade	0.093***	0.093***
	(0.004)	(0.004)
Venezuelan Born x grade	0.079***	0.079***
	(0.008)	(0.008)
Other Foreign Born x grade	0.069***	0.069***
	(0.004)	(0.004)
Student-level controls	No	Yes
Number of student -years	55,566	55,566

Note: (i) Standard errors in parentheses; (ii) all specifications include an intercept; (iii) student-level controls include indicator variables for eligibility for free or reduced-price lunch, male, disabled, and English Language Learner; and (iv) * p<0.10, ** p<0.05 *** p<0.01

Source: Authors' calculations, using Miami-Dade County Public Schools data.

.

Works Cited

Alba, Richard and Victor Nee. 2003. *Remaking the American Mainstream: Assimilation and Contemporary Immigration.* Cambridge, MA, and London: Harvard University Press.

Caplan, Nathan, John K. Whitmore, and Marcella H. Choy. 1989. *The Boat People and Achievement in America.* Ann Arbor, MI: The University of Michigan Press.

Conger, Dylan and Elena Grigorenko. 2009. Special Educational Needs of Children in Immigrant Families. In *Immigration, Diversity, and Education,* eds., Elena L. Grigorenko and Ruby Takanishi, New York and Abingdon, UK: Routledge/ Taylor and Francis Group.

Conger, Dylan, Amy Ellen Schwartz, and Leanna Stiefel. 2007. Immigrant and Native-born Differences in School Stability and Special Education: Evidence from New York City. *International Migration Review* 41 (2): 402–31.

Fuligni, Andrew. 1997. The Academic Achievement of Adolescents from Immigrant Families: The Roles of Family Background, Attitudes, and Behavior. *Child Development* 68 (2): 351–63.

García Coll, Cynthia and Amy Marks, eds. 2011. *Is Becoming an American a Developmental Risk?* Washington, DC: American Psychological Association Books.

Han, Wen-Jui. 2008. The Academic Trajectories of Children of Immigrants and Their School Environments. *Developmental Psychology* 44 (6): 1572–90.

Hernandez, Donald J. 2012. Young Children in Black Immigrant Families from Africa and the Caribbean. In *Young Children of Black Immigrants in America: Changing Flows, Changing Faces,* eds. Randy Capps and Michael Fix. Washington, DC: Migration Policy Institute.

Kao, Grace and Marta Tienda. 1995. Optimism and Achievement: The Educational Performance of Immigrant Youth. *Social Science Quarterly* 76: 1–19.

Portes, Alejandro and Min Zhou. 1993. The New Second Generation: Segmented Assimilation and its Variants. *Annals of the American Academy of Political and Social Science* 530: 74–96.

Portes, Alejandro and Rubén G. Rumbaut. 1996. *Immigrant America: A Portrait.* Los Angeles: University of California Press.

———. 2001. *Legacies: The Story of the Immigrant Second Generation.* Los Angeles: University of California Press and Russell Sage Foundation.

Schwartz, Amy Ellen and Leanna Stiefel. 2006. Is There a Nativity Gap? Achievement of New York City Elementary and Middle School Immigrant Students. *Education Finance and Policy* 1: 17–49.

US Department of Health and Human Services (DHSS). 2010. The 2008 HHS Poverty Guidelines. Last revised January 29, 2010. http://aspe.hhs.gov/poverty/08poverty.shtml.

Zhou, Min. 1997. Segmented Assimilation: Issues, Controversies, and Recent Research on the New Second Generation. *International Migration Review* 31 (4): 975–1008.

Zhou, Min and Carl L. Bankston III. 1998. *Growing Up American: How Vietnamese Children Adapt to Life in the United States.* New York: Russell Sage Foundation.

CHAPTER 11

WILL THE PARADOX HOLD? UNCOVERING THE PATH TO ACADEMIC SUCCESS FOR YOUNG CHILDREN OF BLACK IMMIGRANTS

By Carola Suárez-Orozco

University of California, Los Angeles

Introduction

Research from a variety of disciplines has shown that immigrant groups demonstrate a remarkable and sometimes counterintuitive pattern of strengths. The body of work examining the well-being of immigrant-origin populations across generations reveals a pattern that contradicts conventional expectations: first-generation immigrant populations tend to demonstrate the best performance on a variety of physical health, behavioral health, and educational outcomes, followed by a decline across subsequent generations.[1] These declines in performance can also occur within generations as immigrants adjust and adapt to US society and norms.[2] Although many recently arrived immigrants face a wide range of stressors and risks (e.g., poverty, discrimination, taxing occupations, relatively low formal education, limited English skills, and social isolation), they do better — on a wide

---

1   Cynthia García-Coll and Amy Kerivan Marks, eds., *The Immigrant Paradox in Children and Adolescents: Is Becoming American a Developmental Risk?* (Washington, DC: American Psychological Association Press, 2011); American Psychological Association (APA), *Crossroads: The Psychology of Immigration in the 21st Century,* Report of the 2011 APA Presidential Task Force on Immigration (Washington, DC: APA, 2012), www.apa.org/topics/immigration/report.aspx.

2   See Chapter 10 in this volume, Dylan Conger and Megan Hatch, "The Academic Development of Black Foreign-Born Students in Miami-Dade County Schools."

range of outcomes — than both their counterparts who remain in the country of origin and second-generation immigrants in the United States.[3]

I. Accounting for the Immigrant Paradox

A number of arguments have been made to explain this "immigrant paradox" of better performance despite risks and stressors,[4] but no one explanation fully accounts for it.[5] Possibilities include the notion that individuals who undertake the migration journey are selectively healthier than those who remain in the country of origin;[6] that the continual hardships of migration select for persistence and resilience;[7] and that immigrant populations bring with them cultural values and behaviors that enhance health, before such values and behaviors fade alongside acculturation to the host country.[8] For instance, health declines in the second and subsequent generations have been ascribed to the adoption of high-risk behaviors that predominate in the United States, such as drug abuse and changes in dietary practices (e.g., an increase in "super-sized" fast-food meals). The stress of racial/ethnic minority status and the concomitant experiences of discrimination — in terms of both structural obstacles to mobility and a negative self-

3   Margarita Alegría, Norah Mulvaney-Day, Maria Torres, Antonio Polo, Zhun Cao, and Glorisa Canino, "Prevalence of Psychiatric Disorders across Latino Subgroups in the United States," *American Journal of Public Health* 97, No. 1 (2007): 68–75; APA, *Crossroads*; García-Coll and Marks, *The Immigrant Paradox in Children and Adolescents.*

4   García-Coll and Marks, *The Immigrant Paradox in Children and Adolescents;* Donald J. Hernandez and Evan Charney, eds., *From Generation to Generation: The Health and Well-Being of Children of Immigrant Families* (Washington, DC: National Academy Press, 1998); Carola Suárez-Orozco, Jean Rhodes, and Michael Milburn, "Unraveling the Immigrant Paradox: Academic Engagement and Disengagement among Recently Arrived Immigrant Youth," *Youth and Society* 41, No. 2 (2009): 151–85.

5   See, for a discussion, Carola Suárez-Orozco, Irina Todorova, and Desirée Baolian Qin, "The Well-Being of Immigrant Adolescents: A Longitudinal Perspective on Risk and Protective Factors," in *The Crisis in Youth Mental Health: Critical Issues and Effective Program, Volume 2: Disorders and in Adolescence. Child Psychology and Mental Health,* eds., Francisco A. Villarruel and Tom Luster (Thousand Oaks, CA: Sage Press, 2006): 53–83.

6   Alberto Palloni and Jeffrey D. Morenoff, "Interpreting the Paradoxical in the Hispanic Paradox: Demographic and Epidemiological Approaches," *Annals of the New York Academy of Sciences* 954 (2001): 140–74.

7   Ana F. Abraido-Lanza, Bruce P. Dohrenwend, Daisy S. Ng-Mak, and J. Blake Turner, "The Latino Mortality Paradox: A Test of the 'Salmon Bias' and Healthy Migrant Hypothesis," *American Journal of Public Health* 89, No. 10 (1999): 1543–48, http://ajph.aphapublications.org/doi/pdf/10.2105/AJPH.89.10.1543.

8   Andres J. Pumariega, Eugenio Rothe, and JoAnne B. Pumariega, "Mental Health of Immigrants and Refugees," *Community Mental Health Journal* 41, No. 5 (2005): 581–97.

image derived from others' perceptions — are also likely contributors to poor health outcomes and academic performance.[9]

In some instances, first- and second-generation students share experiences that work to their advantage; for instance, many immigrant parents expect their children to respect teachers and other adults in positions of authority[10] — an expectation that is often lost by the third generation. Other common experiences reflect shared risks: many first- and second-generation children have parents who do not know how to navigate an unfamiliar US educational system.[11] Similarly, many first- and second-generation students grow up in homes where English is not spoken, and enter school needing to acquire basic conversational English just as they learn to read. This limited exposure to English places them at a temporary disadvantage in absorbing academic content if they are not provided adequate educational supports.[12]

At the same time, the second generation has some unique advantages compared to the first generation. All are by definition US citizens by birth, and some will not face a language acquisition hurdle, particularly if they live in neighborhoods where they are regularly exposed to English language models.[13] On the other hand the second generation may be less buffered by the optimism of their foreign-born peers, whose view of life in the United States is framed by presumably more negative home-country experiences.[14] The second generation may also be more susceptible to the corrosive effects of discrimination and racism.[15]

9   APA, *Crossroads*; Cynthia García-Coll and Katherine Magnuson, "The Psychological Experience of Immigration: A Developmental Perspective," in *Immigration and the Family*, eds., Alan Booth, Ann C. Crouter, and Nancy Landale (Mahwah, NJ: Lawrence Erlbaum, 1997): 91–132; Carola Suárez-Orozco, "Identities under Siege: Immigration Stress and Social Mirroring among the Children of Immigrants" in *Cultures under Siege: Social Violence and Trauma*, eds. Antonius C.G.M. Robben and Marcelo Suárez-Orozco (Cambridge, UK: Cambridge University Press, 2000): 194-226.

10   García-Coll and Marks, *The Immigrant Paradox in Children and Adolescents*; Carola Suárez-Orozco and Marcelo Suárez-Orozco, *Children of Immigration* (Cambridge, MA: Harvard University Press, 2001).

11   Carola Suárez-Orozco, Marcelo Suárez-Orozco, and Irina Todorova, *Learning a New Land: Immigrant Students in American Society* (Cambridge, MA: Harvard University Press, 2008).

12   Ellen Bialystok, Shilpi Majumder, and Michelle M. Martin, "Developing Phonological Awareness: Is There a Bilingual Advantage?" *Applied Psycholinguistics* 24, No. 1 (2003): 27–44; Ofelia García, *Bilingual Education in the 21st Century: A Global Perspective* (Malden, MA: Wiley-Blackwell Publishing, 2009).

13   Suárez-Orozco and Suárez-Orozco, *Children of Immigration*.

14   Grace Kao and Marta Tienda, "Optimism and Achievement: The Educational Performance of Immigrant Youth," *Social Science Quarterly* 76, No.1 (1995): 1–19.

15   APA, *Crossroads*.

II. The Paradox Revisited: Nuances Across Origin Groups

While this pattern of an immigrant paradox holds true across a number of immigrant groups studied to date, there is increasing evidence that there are subtle nuances across groups. Whether the paradox holds depends in part on which outcomes and origin groups are considered, especially when it comes to academic outcomes.[16] When compared to their US-born peers, the literature shows that first-generation students have stronger-than-expected attendance rates,[17] attitudes toward their teachers,[18] attitudes about school,[19] attachment to school,[20] and grades.[21] Furthermore, a number of studies have found declines in academic aspirations, academic engagement, and academic performance among immigrant students over time[22] and across generations.[23]

On the other hand, many groups of first-generation students do not perform as well as their US-born peers on standardized achievement tests. The test performance of first-generation students often suffers as

---

16 Andrew Fuligini, "The Intersection of Aspirations and Resources in the Development of Children from Immigrant Families," in *The Immigrant Paradox in Children and Adolescents: Is Becoming American a Developmental Risk?* eds. Cynthia García-Coll and Amy Kerivan Marks (Washington, DC: APA Press, 2011).

17 García-Coll and Marks, *The Immigrant Paradox in Children and Adolescents.*

18 Carola Suárez-Orozco and Marcelo Suárez-Orozco, *Transformations: Immigration, Family Life, and Achievement Motivation among Latino Adolescents* (Stanford, CA: Stanford University, 1995).

19 Andrew Fuligni, "The Academic Achievement of Adolescents from Immigrant Families: The Roles of Family Background, Attitudes, and Behavior," *Child Development* 69, No. 2 (2007): 351-63.

20 García-Coll and Marks, *The Immigrant Paradox in Children and Adolescents;* Suárez-Orozco and Suárez-Orozco, *Transformations: Immigration, Family Life, and Achievement Motivation.*

21 García-Coll and Marks, *The Immigrant Paradox in Children and Adolescents;* Donald J. Hernandez, Nancy A. Denton, Suzanne Macartney, and Victoria L. Blanchard, "Children in Immigrant Families: Demography, Policy, and Evidence for the Immigrant Paradox" in *The Immigrant Paradox in Children and Adolescents: Is Becoming American a Developmental Risk?* Cynthia García Coll & Amy Kerivan Marks (Washington, DC: APA, 2011); Alejandro Portes and Rubén G. Rumbaut, *Immigrant America: A Portrait* (Berkeley, CA: University of California Press, 2006).

22 Carola Suárez-Orozco, Francisco X. Gaytán, Hee Jin Bang, Juliana Pakes, Erin O'Connor, and Jean Rhodes, "Academic Trajectories of Newcomer Immigrant Youth," *Developmental Psychology* 46, No. 3 (2010): 602-18, https://steinhardt.nyu.edu/scmsAdmin/uploads/005/785/Trajectories%20Dev%20Psych%202010%20.pdf.

23 Fuligni, "The Academic Achievement of Adolescents from Immigrant Families;" Alejandro Portes and Rubén G. Rumbaut, *Legacies: The Story of the Second Generation* (Berkeley, CA: University of California Press, 2001); Suárez-Orozco and Suárez-Orozco, *Transformations: Immigration, Family Life, and Achievement Motivation.*

these results depend upon academic English proficiency, reading skills, and exposure to cultural knowledge and content.[24]

Studies have found that certain characteristics place children from varying immigrant origins at particular risk for poor academic outcomes. I delineate these characteristics and briefly consider how they may apply to academic outcomes for the diverse populations of Black children of immigrants described in this volume.

First, some Black immigrants — notably Haitians and some recent African groups — have fled political persecution, social instability, and/or natural disaster. Refugees and asylum seekers face particular stressors that can affect both mental health as well as educational outcomes.[25] "Cultural bereavement" can result from the experience of losing loved ones in conflict or disaster, and from the inability to return to the country of origin. A legacy of loss and exposure to trauma accompanies already complex acculturation and adjustment processes and is associated with psychological symptoms such as anxiety, depression, and posttraumatic stress disorder.[26] Ongoing separation from loved ones who continue to be in danger also predicts psychological problems.[27] Survivors of torture and those who have been in detention facilities have especially severe mental health needs, including treatment for posttraumatic stress syndrome, depression, anxiety, psychosis, and dissociation.[28]

24 APA, Crossroads; Kao and Tienda, "Optimism and Achievement;" Kate Menken, *English Language Learners Left Behind: Standardized Testing As Language Policy* (Clevedon, UK: Multilingual Matters, 2008); Jorge Ruiz-de-Velasco, Michael Fix, and Beatriz Chu Clewell, *Overlooked & Underserved: Immigrant Students in U.S. Secondary Schools* (Washington, DC: The Urban Institute, 2000); Suárez-Orozco, Suárez-Orozco, and Todorova, *Learning a New Land*; Nellie Tran and Dina Birman, "Questioning the Model Minority: Studies of Asian American Academic Performance," *Asian American Journal of Psychology* 1, No. 2 (2010): 106-18.

25 APA, *Resilience and Recovery after War: Refugee Children and Families in the United States,* Report of the APA Task Force on the Psychosocial Effects of War on Children and Families Who Are Refugees From Armed Conflict Residing in the United States (Washington, DC: APA, 2010), www.apa.org/pubs/info/reports/refugees.aspx.

26 Hikmet Jamil, Mohamed Farrag, Julie Hakim-Larson, Talib Kafaji, Husam Abdulkhaleq, and Adnan Hammad, "Mental Health Symptoms in Iraqi Refugees: Posttraumatic Stress Disorder, Anxiety, and Depression," *Journal of Cultural Diversity* 14, No. 1 (2007): 19–25; Minoru Masuda, Keh-Ming Lin, and Laurie Tazuma, "Adaptation Problems of Vietnamese Refugees: Life Changes and Perception of Life Events," *Archives of General Psychiatry* 37, No. 4 (1980): 447–50.

27 Angela Nickerson, Richard A. Bryant, Robert Brooks, Zachary Steel, and Derrick Silove, "The Impact of Fear for Family on Mental Health in a Resettled Iraqi Refugee Community," *Journal of Psychiatric Research* 44, No. 4 (2010): 229–35.

28 Emily F. Keyes, "Mental Health Status in Refugees: An Integrative Review of Current Research," *Issues in Mental Health Nursing* 21, No. 4 (2000): 397–410.

While pre-migration trauma and loss influence the mental health of refugees, particularly in the early stages of resettlement,[29] post-migration factors also have an impact.[30] For example, permanent housing and economic opportunity have been found to be associated with improved mental health outcomes. Better mental health is also associated with English-language use[31] and fluency[32] as well as social support, particularly from within the same refugee community.[33]

Experiencing discrimination, on the other hand, has negative mental and physical health consequences.[34] Further, higher levels of education and socioeconomic status prior to displacement are associated with worse mental and physical health outcomes, which may reflect highly skilled immigrants' frustration with their social standing in the United States compared with that enjoyed in the home country.[35] In turn, these cumulative mental health issues are associated with negative educational outcomes.[36]

Immigrant students whose education has been interrupted (commonly referred to as students with interrupted formal education, or SIFE) and those with no prior formal education face particular challenges in transitioning to US schools. Students from the Caribbean in general — including some of the major groups such as Haitians, Jamaicans, Guyanese, and Dominicans — often have interrupted formal education. Many refugee children, including those from African origins such as Liberia, Somalia, and the Sudan, arrive after prolonged stays in refugee camps, with some never having been in school and/or coming from cultures with no tradition of literacy in any language.[37] It has been estimated that

29 Morton Beiser, "Longitudinal Research to Promote Effective Refugee Resettlement," *Transcultural Psychiatry* 43, No. 1 (2006): 56–71.

30 Dina Birman and Nellie Tran, "The Impact of Pre- and Post-Migration Factors on Psychological Distress and Adjustment of Vietnamese Refugees in the U.S.," *American Journal of Orthopsychiatry* 78 (2008): 109-20.

31 Dung Ngo, Thank V. Tran, Judith L. Gibbons, and Joan M. Oliver, "Acculturation, Pre-Migration Traumatic Experiences and Depression among Vietnamese Americans," *Journal of Human Behavior in the Social Environment* 3, No. 3–4 (2000): 225–42.

32 Beiser, "Longitudinal Research to Promote Effective Refugee Resettlement."

33 Laura Simich, Morton Beiser, and Farah N. Mawani, "Social Support and the Significance of Shared Experience in Refugee Migration and Resettlement," *Western Journal of Nursing Research* 25, No. 7 (2003): 872–91.

34 Ibrahim A. Kira, Linda Lewandowski, Thomas Templin, Vidya Ramaswamy, Bulent Ozkan, and Jamal Mohanesh, "The Effects of Perceived Discrimination and Backlash on Iraqi Refugees' Mental and Physical Health," *Journal of Muslim Mental Health* 5, No. 1 (2010): 59–81; APA, *Resilience and Recovery after War.*

35 Mathew Porter and Nick Haslam, "Predisplacement and Postdisplacement Factors Associated with Mental Health of Refugees and Internally Displaced Persons: A Meta-analysis," *Journal of the American Medical Association* 294, No. 5 (2005): 602–12, http://jama.jamanetwork.com/article.aspx?articleid=201335.

36 APA, *Crossroads.*

37 Dan Van Lehman and Omar Eno, "The Somali Bantu: Their History and Culture" (*Culture Profile* No. 16, Center for Applied Linguistics, Washington, DC, 2003), http://hartfordinfo.org/issues/wsd/immigrants/somali_bantu.pdf.

SIFEs comprise 10 percent of English language learner students in the New York City public school system.[38] In addition to needing to master a new language, SIFEs arrive with limited literacy skills in their native languages and gaps in knowledge across academic subjects.[39] They face distinct challenges in adjusting to school: many lack the expected skills to complete homework assignments or participate in most classroom activities[40] and, in extreme cases, even knowledge of how to act in the classroom and perform pencil-and-paper tasks.[41]

Students who are unauthorized immigrants are another group at risk of failing to thrive in schools, though many do well despite their lack of legal status. Unauthorized status is generally less common among Black immigrants than other groups — particularly Latino immigrants — although it is found among some origin groups such as Haitians.

Many unauthorized immigrant children have faced lengthy family separations followed by complicated family reunifications. Post-migration, these children — as well as an estimated 4.5 million US citizen children living in households with an unauthorized parent — often experience fear and anxiety over being separated from family members and friends who might be apprehended or deported. Psychological and emotional duress can take a heavy toll on the well-being and academic experiences of children growing up in these homes.[42] Further, while unauthorized youth have a legal right to public K–12 education, they do not have equal access to public health insurance coverage or social services.[43] These and other barriers to academic access, economic advancement, and full integration into US society can lower both the mental health outcomes as well as the academic expectations of unau-

38 Advocates for Children of New York, *Students with Interrupted Formal Education: A Challenge for New York City Public Schools* (New York, NY: Advocates for Children of New York, 2010).

39 Dina Birman and Nellie Tran, "When Worlds Collide: Newly Arriving Somali Bantu Students in a U.S. Elementary School," *American Educational Research Journal* (2012, forthcoming).

40 Karen Dooley, "Re-Thinking Pedagogy for Middle School Students with Little, No or Severely Interrupted Schooling," *English Teaching: Practice and Critique* 8, No. 1 (2009.): 5–22, http://education.waikato.ac.nz/research/files/etpc/files/2009v8n1art1.pdf; Elizabeth Cassity and Greg Gow, "Making up for Lost Time: The Experiences of Southern Sudanese Young Refugees in High Schools," *Youth Studies Australia* 24, No. 3 (2005): 51-5.

41 Beverly Alsleben, "Preliterate English Learners: Refugee Camp to the U.S. Classroom," *California English* 11, No. 4 (2006), www.nwp.org/cs/public/print/resource/2335; Birman and Tran, "When Worlds Collide;" Cynthia H. Brock, "Exploring an English Language Learner's Literacy Learning Opportunities: A Collaborative Case Study Analysis," *Urban Education* 42, No. 5 (2007): 470-501.

42 Randolph Capps, Rosa Maria Castaneda, Ajay Chaudry, and Robert Santos, "Paying the Price: The Impact of Immigration Raids on America's Children" (Discussion Paper, Urban Institute, Washington, DC, October 31, 2007), www.urban.org/publications/411566.html; Carola Suárez-Orozco, Hirokazu Yoshikawa, Robert T. Teranishi, and Marcelo Suárez-Orozco, "Growing Up in the Shadows: The Developmental Implications of Unauthorized Status," *Harvard Educational Review* 81, No. 3 (2011): 438–72, www.hepg.org/document/163/.

43 Patricia Gándara and Frances Contreras, *Understanding the Latino Education Gap—Why Latinos Don't Go to College* (Cambridge, MA: Harvard University Press, 2009).

thorized children and youth.[44] Further, there is growing evidence of the adverse developmental implications of the unauthorized status of parents on their US citizen children.[45]

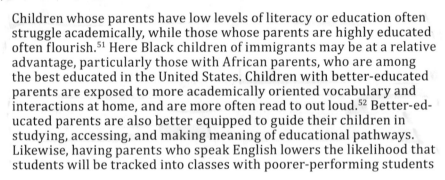

The role of family capital in structuring opportunity for children has been well documented.[46] For children of immigrant origin, parental poverty, education, and linguistic resources play a particularly crucial role.[47]

Black immigrant families have low incomes relative to most immigrant and native families, with the important exceptions of Latino immigrant and Black native families.[48] Children raised in socioeconomic deprivation are vulnerable to an array of stressors including anxiety, depression, and difficulties concentrating and sleeping. These can significantly impede academic performance.[49] Further, poverty frequently coexists with other factors that augment risks, such as residence in neighborhoods plagued with violence, gang activity, and drug trade, and school environments that are segregated, overcrowded, and poorly funded.[50]

Children whose parents have low levels of literacy or education often struggle academically, while those whose parents are highly educated often flourish.[51] Here Black children of immigrants may be at a relative advantage, particularly those with African parents, who are among the best educated in the United States. Children with better-educated parents are exposed to more academically oriented vocabulary and interactions at home, and are more often read to out loud.[52] Better-educated parents are also better equipped to guide their children in studying, accessing, and making meaning of educational pathways. Likewise, having parents who speak English lowers the likelihood that students will be tracked into classes with poorer-performing students

44   Suárez-Orozco et al., "Growing Up in the Shadows."
45   Ibid.
46   Suniya S. Luthar, *Poverty and Children's Adjustment* (Thousand Oaks, CA: Sage Publications, 1999); Richard Weissbourd, *The Vulnerable Child: What Really Hurts America's Children and What We Can Do about It* (Reading, MA: Perseus Books, 1996); Carola Suárez-Orozco, Francisco X. Gaytán, and Ha Yeon Kim, "Facing the Challenges of Educating Latino Immigrant Origin Students," in *Growing up Hispanic: Health and Development of Children*, eds., Susan McHale and Alan Booth (Washington, DC: The Urban Institute, 2010): 189–239.
47   Krista M. Perreira, Kathleen M. Harris, and Dohoon Lee, "Making it in America: High School Completion by Immigrant and Native Youth," *Demography* 43, No. 3 (2006): 1–26.
48   For more, see earlier chapters in this volume.
49   Luthar, *Poverty and Children's Adjustment*; Weissbourd, The Vulnerable Child.
50   Gary Orfield and Chungmei Lee, *Racial Transformation and the Changing Nature of Segregation* (Cambridge, MA: The Civil Rights Project at Harvard University, 2006), www.swannfellowship.org/research/files07/racialtransformation.pdf.
51   Portes and Rumbaut, Legacies; Philip Kasinitz, John Mollenkopf, Mary Waters, and Jennifer Holdaway, *Inheriting the City: The Children of Immigrants Come of Age* (Cambridge, MA and New York, NY: Harvard University Press and Russell Sage Foundation, 2008).
52   Claude Goldenberg, Robert S. Rueda, and Dianne August, "Synthesis: Sociocultural Contexts and Literacy Development," in *Developing Reading and Writing in Second-Language Learners: Report of the National Literacy Panel on Language-Minority Children and Youth*, eds., Dianne August and Timothy Shanahan (New York: Routledge, 2008): 95–130.

— and facilitates communication among parents, teachers and school administrators. English proficiency also makes it easier for parents to participate in culturally valued parent involvement activities.[53] Here, too, most groups of Black immigrants' children — with the important exceptions of those from Haiti, the Spanish-speaking Caribbean, and a small group from African origins — have an advantage over children whose parents did not come from Anglophone countries.

Xenophobia and discrimination significantly affect the lives of immigrants in the United States,[54] and in this context Black immigrants may be doubly disadvantaged by their skin color and foreign birth. Immigrant adults and their children are identified by their accented English, "unusual" names, and manners of dress. Fears of job competition[55] and of new, undesirable cultural practices,[56] have led to discrimination against immigrants in neighborhoods, workplaces, service agencies, and schools.[57] Immigrants may also be subject to negative media coverage,[58] hate crimes,[59] and exclusionary political legislation.[60] Immigrants who are racially distinct from the majority are at particular risk for experiencing discrimination.[61] There is clear and well-documented evidence

---

53   Suárez-Orozco, Gaytán, and Kim, "Facing the Challenges of Educating Latino Immigrant Origin Students."

54   APA, *Crossroads*; Kay Deaux, *To Be an Immigrant* (New York, NY: Russell Sage Foundation, 2006).

55   German Marshall Fund of the United States (GMFUS), *Transatlantic Trends: Immigration 2010* (Washington, DC: GMFUS, 2010), www.gmfus.org/archives/transatlantic-trends-immigration-2010/.

56   Michael A. Zárate, Berenice Garcia, Azenett A. Garza, and Robert T. Hitlan, "Cultural Threat and Perceived Realistic Group Conflict as Predictors of Attitudes towards Mexican Immigrants," *Journal of Experimental Social Psychology* 40, No. 1 (2004): 99–105.

57   Rubén G. Rumbaut, "Sites of Belonging: Acculturation, Discrimination, and Ethnic Identity among Children of Immigrants," in *Discovering Successful Pathways in Children's Development: Mixed Methods in the Study of Childhood and Family Life,* ed., Thomas S. Weiner (Chicago, IL: University of Chicago Press, 2005): 111–64; Susan Stone and Meekyung Han, "Perceived School Environments, Perceived Discrimination, and School Performance among Children of Mexican Immigrants," *Children and Youth Services Review* 27, No. 1 (2005): 51–66.

58   Douglas S. Massey, *New Faces in New Places: The Changing Geography of American Immigration* (New York, NY: Russell Sage Foundation, 2010); Roberto Suro, "Preface," in *Writing Immigration: Academics and Journalists in Dialogue,* eds. Marcelo Suárez-Orozco, Vivian Louie, and Roberto Suro (Berkeley, CA: University of California Press, 2011).

59   Leadership Conference on Civil Rights (LCCR) Education Fund, *Confronting the New Faces of Hate: Hate Crimes in America 2009* (Washington, DC: LCCR, 2009), www.protectcivilrights.org/pdf/reports/hatecrimes/lccref_hate_crimes_report.pdf.

60   National Conference of State Legislatures (NCSL), *2011 Immigration-related Laws, Bills, and Resolutions in the States: Jan. 1-March 31, 2011* (Washington, DC: NCSL, 2011), www.ncsl.org/default.aspx?tabid=13114.

61   John W. Berry and Colette Sabatier, "Acculturation, Discrimination and Adaptation among Second Generation Immigrant Youth in Montreal and Paris," *International Journal of Intercultural Relations* 34, No. 3 (2010): 91–207; Karmela A. Liebkind and Inga Jasinskaja-Lahti, "The Influence of Experiences of Discrimination on Psychological Stress: A Comparison of Seven Immigrant Groups," *Journal of Community and Applied Social Psychology* 10, No. 1 (2000): 1–16.

of the negative physical and mental health consequences of living with prejudice as well as its detrimental educational implications.[62]

III. Children of Black Immigrants, the Paradox, and Research Moving Forward

How does the immigrant paradox apply to Black children of immigrants from differing origins? The answer is: it is too soon to tell. Black Caribbean migration streams are well established but small and understudied, while Black African migration streams are very recent, and smaller still but growing rapidly. Moreover, as described in this volume, it is challenging to place Black immigrants within a single category given the variety of their family origins and resources — from English-speaking immigrants with the most educated backgrounds to those arriving without literacy from war-torn conditions. But we can begin to venture some hypotheses and to search for patterns of evidence based on the research about other immigrant groups and the research included in this volume.

As we consider the constellation of factors that place immigrant children more generally at risk, there is reason to believe that some children of Black immigrants are at lower risk than other immigrant groups while others bear a greater weight of accumulated risk. The fact that fewer face the dilemmas of living in the shadows of unauthorized status than their Latino peers is a considerable advantage, but does not apply to all groups — particularly those whose parents are from Haiti and some other Caribbean origins. Because the barriers to migration from Africa to the United States remain high, many Black African immigrant children have parents from the more educated elite and middle class in their home countries, and this relatively high parental social status confers advantages on these children. At the same time, many Caribbean and African students with refugee backgrounds have had interrupted formal education, which puts them at a great disadvantage. English speakers, who predominate among both African and Caribbean immigrants, can enter the classroom without having to first clear the hurdle of acquiring a new language, especially at the conversational level. Still, English-language dialects — particularly those from Caribbean countries such as Jamaica — present similar issues to learning a second language when it comes to classroom English assignments and assessments (including high-stakes testing). Further, in a society with long-standing, unresolved issues around race, the Black phenotype is likely to affect daily experiences — including exposure to discrimination and prejudice — that can slow economic advancement for many of

---

62 APA, *Resolution on Prejudice, Stereotypes, and Discrimination* (Washington, DC: APA, 2006), www.apa.org/about/policy/prejudice.pdf.

these children.[63] The effects of these barriers to opportunity have been documented in the Black Caribbean immigrant community, which has had more exposure to US discrimination than the more recent group of African immigrants.[64]

Moving forward, issues of racial self-identification need to be explored more deeply. Two examples in the Caribbean immigrant population, which is particularly racially diverse, come to mind. Residents of the Dominican Republic typically do not think of themselves as Black but may be placed within that racial category after immigrating to the United States. Compared to some other Caribbean-origin immigrants, a relatively small percentage of Dominicans self-identify as Black in national survey data collected by the US Census Bureau.[65] Racial identification is something that may change across generations and is not easily captured by a survey label.[66] In another example, about half of Guyanese immigrants identify themselves as Black while the other half identify their origin as South Asian (primarily Indian); in reality, many Guyanese are mixtures of the two. In characterizations of the Black immigrant experience in the United States, how and in what way can racial and ethnic data from these diverse groups be captured accurately?

In the research going forward, it is important not to make sweeping generalizations about children in Black immigrant families. As documented in this volume, there is wide variability depending upon the sending origin, the receiving context, and the circumstances surrounding migration as well as settlement. Analyses of large data sets are unlikely to address subtleties in the adaptation, health, well-being, and educational outcomes of these diverse populations. Large-scale surveys include data on national origins, racial self-identification, spoken English proficiency, parental education, and some other relevant measures, but research going forward will also need to consider factors that are harder to capture, such as interrupted education in the sending country, migration experiences, trauma histories, exposure to discrimination, and proficiency in academic written English. Mixed-methods approaches that combine large-scale survey data with in-depth fieldwork will be fundamental to determining the nature of these more nuanced experiences and to accurately representing the full range of Black immigrants' academic outcomes. ⤴

---

63 Ibid.

64 Portes and Rumbaut, *Immigrant America*; Mary Waters, *Ethnic Options: Choosing Identities in America* (Berkeley, CA: University of California Press, 1990).

65 See Chapter 1 in this volume, Kevin J. A. Thomas, *Contemporary Black Caribbean Immigrants in the United States* (Washington, DC: Migration Policy Institute, 2012); and Chapter 3, Donald J. Hernandez, *Young Children in Black Immigrant Families from Africa and the Caribbean* (Washington, DC: Migration Policy Institute, 2012).

66 Benjamin H. Bailey, "Dominican-American Ethnic/Racial Identities and United States Social Categories," *International Migration Review* 35, No. 3 (2001): 677–708.

Works Cited

Abraido-Lanza, Ana F., Bruce P. Dohrenwend, Daisy S. Ng-Mak, and J. Blake Turner. 1999. The Latino Mortality Paradox: A Test of the "Salmon Bias" and Healthy Migrant Hypothesis. *American Journal of Public Health* 89 (10): 1543–48. http://ajph.aphapublications.org/doi/pdf/10.2105/AJPH.89.10.1543.

Advocates for Children of New York. 2010. *Students with Interrupted Formal Education: A Challenge for New York City Public Schools.* New York, NY: Advocates for Children of New York.

Alegría, Margarita, Norah Mulvaney-Day, Maria Torres, Antonio Polo, Zhun Cao, and Glorisa Canino. 2007. Prevalence of Psychiatric Disorders across Latino Subgroups in the United States. *American Journal of Public Health* 97 (1): 68–75.

Alsleben, Beverly. 2006. Preliterate English Learners: Refugee Camp to the U.S. Classroom. *California English* 11 (4). www.nwp.org/cs/public/print/resource/2335.

American Psychological Association (APA). 2006. *Resolution on Prejudice, Stereotypes, and Discrimination.* Washington, DC: APA. www.apa.org/about/policy/prejudice.pdf.

_____. 2010. *Resilience and Recovery after War: Refugee Children and Families in the United States.* Report of the APA Task Force on the Psychosocial Effects of War on Children and Families Who Are Refugees from Armed Conflict Residing in the United States. Washington, DC: APA. www.apa.org/pubs/info/reports/refugees.aspx.

_____. 2012. *Crossroads: The Psychology of Immigration in the 21st Century.* Report of the 2011 APA Presidential Task Force on Immigration. Washington, DC: APA. www.apa.org/topics/immigration/report.aspx.

Bailey, Benjamin H. 2001. Dominican-American Ethnic/Racial Identities and United States Social Categories. *International Migration Review* 35 (3): 677–708.

Beiser, Morton. 2006. Longitudinal Research to Promote Effective Refugee Resettlement. *Transcultural Psychiatry* 43 (1): 56–71.

Berry, John W. and Colette Sabatier. 2010. Acculturation, Discrimination and Adaptation among Second Generation Immigrant Youth in Montreal and Paris. *International Journal of Intercultural Relations* 34 (3): 91–207.

Bialystok, Ellen, Shilpi Majumder, and Michelle M. Martin. 2003. Developing Phonological Awareness: Is There a Bilingual Advantage? *Applied Psycholinguistics* 24 (1): 27–44.

Birman, Dina and Nellie Tran. 2008. The Impact of Pre- and Post-Migration Factors on Psychological Distress and Adjustment of Vietnamese Refugees in the U.S. *American Journal of Orthopsychiatry* 78: 109-20.

_____. 2012 forthcoming. When Worlds Collide: Newly Arriving Somali Bantu Students in a U.S. Elementary School. *American Educational Research Journal.*

Brock, Cynthia H. 2007. Exploring an English Language Learner's Literacy Learning Opportunities: A Collaborative Case Study Analysis," *Urban Education* 42 (5): 470-501.

Capps, Randolph, Rosa Maria Castaneda, Ajay Chaudry, and Robert Santos. 2007. Paying the Price: The Impact of Immigration Raids on America's Children. Discussion Paper, Urban Institute. Washington, DC. www.urban.org/publications/411566.html.

Cassity, Elizabeth and Greg Gow. 2005. Making up for Lost Time: The Experiences of Southern Sudanese Young Refugees in High Schools. *Youth Studies Australia* 24 (3): 51-5.

Deaux, Kay. 2006. *To Be an Immigrant.* New York, NY: Russell Sage Foundation.

Dooley, Karen. 2009. Re-Thinking Pedagogy for Middle School Students with Little, No or Severely Interrupted Schooling. *English Teaching: Practice and Critique* 8 (1): 5–22. http://education.waikato.ac.nz/research/files/etpc/files/2009v8n1art1.pdf.

Eisenbruch, Maurice. 1988. The Mental Health of Refugee Children and Their Cultural Development. *International Migration Review* 22 (2): 282–300.

Fuligni, Andrew. 1997. The Academic Achievement of Adolescents from Immigrant Families: The Roles of Family Background, Attitudes, and Behavior. *Child Development* 69(2): 351-63.

_____. 2011. The Intersection of Aspirations and Resources in the Development of Children from Immigrant Families. In *The Immigrant Paradox in Children and Adolescents: Is Becoming American a Developmental Risk?* eds. Cynthia García-Coll and Amy Kerivan Marks. Washington, DC: American Psychological Association Press.

Gándara, Patricia and Frances Contreras. 2009. *Understanding the Latino Education Gap—Why Latinos Don't Go to College.* Cambridge, MA: Harvard University Press, 2009.

García, Ofelia. 2009. *Bilingual Education in the 21st Century: A Global Perspective.* Malden, MA: Wiley-Blackwell Publishing.

García-Coll, Cynthia and Katherine Magnuson. 1997. The Psychological Experience of Immigration: A Developmental Perspective. In *Immigration and the Family,* eds. Alan Booth, Ann C. Crouter, and Nancy Landale. Mahwah, NJ: Lawrence Erlbaum.

García-Coll, Cynthia and Amy Kerivan Marks, eds. 2011. *The Immigrant Paradox in Children and Adolescents: Is Becoming American a Developmental Risk?* Washington, DC: American Psychological Association Press.

German Marshall Fund of the United States (GMFUS). *Transatlantic Trends: Immigration 2010.* Washington, DC: GMF. www.gmfus.org/archives/transatlantic-trends-immigration-2010/.

Goldenberg, Claude, Robert S. Rueda, and Dianne August. 2008. Synthesis: Sociocultural Contexts and Literacy Development. In *Developing Reading and Writing in Second-Language Learners: Report of the National Literacy Panel on Language-Minority Children and Youth,* eds. Dianne August and Timothy Shanahan. New York, NY: Routledge.

Hernandez, Donald J. 2012. Young Children in Black Immigrant Families from Africa and the Caribbean. In *Young Children of Black Immigrants in America: Changing Flows, Changing Faces,* eds. Michael Fix and Randy Capps. Washington, DC: Migration Policy Institute.

Hernandez, Donald J. and Evan Charney, eds. 1998. *From Generation to Generation: The Health and Well-Being of Children of Immigrant Families.* Washington, DC: National Academy Press.

Hernandez, Donald J. Nancy A. Denton, Suzanne Macartney, and Victoria L. Blanchard. 2011. Children in Immigrant Families: Demography, Policy, and Evidence for the Immigrant Paradox. In *The Immigrant Paradox in Children and Adolescents: Is Becoming American a Developmental Risk?* eds., Cynthia García Coll & Amy Kerivan Marks. Washington, DC: American Psychological Association.

Jamil, Hikmet, Mohamed Farrag, Julie Hakim-Larson, Talib Kafaji, Husam Abdulkhaleq, and Adnan Hammad. 2007. Mental Health Symptoms in Iraqi Refugees: Posttraumatic Stress Disorder, Anxiety, and Depression. *Journal of Cultural Diversity* 14 (1): 19–25.

Kao, Grace and Marta Tienda. 1995. Optimism and Achievement: The Educational Performance of Immigrant Youth. *Social Science Quarterly* 76 (1): 1–19.

Kasinitz, Philip, John Mollenkopf, Mary Waters, and Jennifer Holdaway. 2008. *Inheriting the City: The Children of Immigrants Come of Age.* Cambridge, MA, and New York, NY: Harvard University Press and Russell Sage Foundation.

Keyes, Emily F. 2000. Mental Health Status in Refugees: An Integrative Review of Current Research. *Issues in Mental Health Nursing* 21 (4): 397–410.

Kira, Ibrahim A., Linda Lewandowski, Thomas Templin, Vidya Ramaswamy, Bulent Ozkan, and Jamal Mohanesh. 2010. The Effects of Perceived Discrimination and Backlash on Iraqi Refugees' Mental and Physical Health. *Journal of Muslim Mental Health* 5 (1): 59–81.

Leadership Conference on Civil Rights (LCCR) Education Fund. 2009. *Confronting the New Faces of Hate: Hate Crimes in America 2009.* Washington, DC: LCCR. www.protectcivilrights.org/pdf/reports/hatecrimes/lccref_hate_crimes_report.pdf.

Liebkind, Karmela A. and Inga Jasinskaja-Lahti. 2000. The Influence of Experiences of Discrimination on Psychological Stress: A Comparison of Seven Immigrant Groups. *Journal of Community and Applied Social Psychology* 10 (1): 1–16.

Luthar, Suniya S. 1999. *Poverty and Children's Adjustment.* Thousand Oaks, CA: Sage Publications.

Orfield, Gary and Chungmei Lee. 2006. *Racial Transformation and the Changing Nature of Segregation.* Cambridge, MA: The Civil Rights Project at Harvard University. www.swannfellowship.org/research/files07/racialtransformation.pdf.

Massey, Douglas S. 2010. *New Faces in New Places: The Changing Geography of American Immigration.* New York, NY: Russell Sage Foundation.

Masuda, Minoru, Keh-Ming Lin, and Laurie Tazuma. 1980. Adaptation Problems of Vietnamese Refugees: Life Changes and Perception of Life Events. *Archives of General Psychiatry* 37 (4): 447–50.

Menken, Kate. 2008. *English Language Learners Left Behind: Standardized Testing As Language Policy.* Clevedon, UK: Multilingual Matters.

National Conference of State Legislatures (NCSL). 2011. *2011 Immigration-related Laws, Bills, and Resolutions in the States: Jan. 1-March 31, 2011.* Washington, DC: NCSL. www.ncsl.org/default.aspx?tabid=13114.

Nickerson, Angela, Richard A. Bryant, Robert Brooks, Zachary Steel, and Derrick Silove. 2010. The Impact of Fear for Family on Mental Health in a Resettled Iraqi Refugee Community. *Journal of Psychiatric Research* 44 (4): 229–35.

Ngo, Dung, Thank V. Tran, Judith L. Gibbons, and Joan M. Oliver. 2000. Acculturation, Pre-Migration Traumatic Experiences and Depression among Vietnamese Americans. *Journal of Human Behavior in the Social Environment* 3 (3–4): 225–42.

Palloni, Alberto and Jeffrey D. Morenoff. 2001. Interpreting the Paradoxical in the Hispanic Paradox: Demographic and Epidemiological Approaches. *Annals of the New York Academy of Sciences* 954: 140–74.

Perreira, Krista M., Kathleen M. Harris, and Dohoon Lee. 2006. Making it in America: High School Completion by Immigrant and Native Youth. *Demography* 43 (3): 1–26.

Porter, Mathew and Nick Haslam. 2005. Predisplacement and Postdisplacement Factors Associated with Mental Health of Refugees and Internally Displaced Persons: A Meta-analysis. *Journal of the American Medical Association* 294 (5): 602–12. http://jama.jamanetwork.com/article.aspx?articleid=201335.

Portes, Alejandro and Rubén G. Rumbaut. 2001. *Legacies: The Story of the Second Generation.* Berkeley, CA: University of California Press.

_____. 2006. *Immigrant America: A Portrait.* Berkeley, CA: University of California Press.

Pumariega, Andres J., Eugenio Rothe, and JoAnne B. Pumariega. 2005. Mental Health of Immigrants and Refugees. *Community Mental Health Journal* 41 (5): 581–97.

Ruiz-de-Velasco, Jorge, Michael Fix, and Beatriz Chu Clewell. 2000. *Overlooked & Underserved: Immigrant Students in U.S. Secondary Schools.* Washington, DC: The Urban Institute.

Rumbaut, Rubén G. 2005. Sites of Belonging: Acculturation, Discrimination, and Ethnic Identity among Children of Immigrants. In *Discovering Successful Pathways in Children's Development: Mixed Methods in the Study of Childhood and Family Life,* ed. Thomas S. Weiner. Chicago, IL: University of Chicago Press.

Simich, Laura, Morton Beiser, and Farah N. Mawani. 2003. Social Support and the Significance of Shared Experience in Refugee Migration and Resettlement. *Western Journal of Nursing Research* 25 (7): 872–91.

Stone, Susan and Meekyung Han. 2005. Perceived School Environments, Perceived Discrimination, and School Performance among Children of Mexican Immigrants. *Children and Youth Services Review* 27 (1): 51–66.

Suárez-Orozco, Carola. 2000. Identities under Siege: Immigration Stress and Social Mirroring among the Children of Immigrants. In *Cultures under Siege: Social Violence and Trauma,* eds. Antonius C.G.M.. Robben and Marcelo Suárez-Orozco. Cambridge, UK: Cambridge University Press.

Suárez-Orozco, Carola, Francisco X. Gaytán, Hee Jin Bang, Juliana Pakes, Erin O'Connor, and Jean Rhodes. 2010. Academic Trajectories of Newcomer Immigrant Youth. *Developmental Psychology* 46(3): 602-18. https://steinhardt.nyu.edu/scmsAdmin/uploads/005/785/Trajectories%20Dev%20Psych%20 2010%20.pdf.

Suárez-Orozco, Carola, Francisco X. Gaytán, and Ha Yeon Kim. 2010. Facing the Challenges of Educating Latino Immigrant Origin Students. In *Growing up Hispanic: Health and Development of Children,* eds. Susan McHale and Alan Booth. Washington, DC: The Urban Institute.

Suárez-Orozco, Carola, Jean Rhodes, and Michael Milburn. 2009. Unraveling the Immigrant Paradox: Academic Engagement and Disengagement among Recently Arrived Immigrant Youth. *Youth and Society* 41 (2): 151–85.

Suárez-Orozco, Carola and Marcelo Suárez-Orozco. 1995. *Transformations: Immigration, Family Life, and Achievement Motivation among Latino Adolescents.* Stanford, CA: Stanford University Press.

Suárez-Orozco, Carola and Marcelo Suárez-Orozco. 2001. *Children of Immigration.* Cambridge, MA: Harvard University Press.

Suárez-Orozco, Carola, Marcelo Suárez-Orozco, and Irina Todorova. 2008. *Learning a New Land: Immigrant Students in American Society.* Cambridge, MA: Harvard University Press.

Suárez-Orozco, Carola, Irina Todorova, and Desirée Baolian Qin. 2006. The Well-Being of Immigrant Adolescents: A Longitudinal Perspective on Risk and Protective Factors. In *The Crisis in Youth Mental Health: Critical Issues and Effective Program, Volume 2: Disorders and in Adolescence. Child Psychology and Mental Health,* eds. Francisco A. Villarruel and Tom Luster. Thousand Oaks, CA: Sage Press.

Suárez-Orozco, Carola, Hirokazu Yoshikawa, Robert T. Teranishi, and Marcelo Suárez-Orozco. 2011. Growing Up in the Shadows: The Developmental Implications of Unauthorized Status. *Harvard Educational Review* 81 (3): 438–72.
www.hepg.org/document/163/.

Suro, Roberto. 2011. Preface. In *Writing Immigration: Academics and Journalists in Dialogue,* eds. Marcelo Suárez-Orozco, Vivian Louie, and Roberto Suro. Berkeley, CA: University of California Press.

Thomas, Kevin J. A. 2012. Contemporary Black Caribbean Immigrants in the United States. *In Young Children of Black Immigrants in America: Changing Flows, Changing Faces,* eds. Michael Fix and Randy Capps. Washington, DC: Migration Policy Institute.

Tran, Nellie and Dina Birman. 2010. Questioning the Model Minority: Studies of Asian American Academic Performance. *Asian American Journal of Psychology* 1: 106-18.

Van Lehman, Dan and Omar Eno. 2003. The Somali Bantu: Their History and Culture. *Culture Profile* No. 16, Center for Applied Linguistics, Washington, DC. http://hartfordinfo.org/issues/wsd/immigrants/somali_bantu.pdf.

Waters, Mary. 1990. *Ethnic Options: Choosing Identities in America.* Berkeley, CA: University of California Press.

Weissbourd, Richard. 1996. *The Vulnerable Child: What Really Hurts America's Children and What We Can Do about It.* Reading, MA: Perseus Books.

Zárate, Michael A., Berenice Garcia, Azenett A. Garza, and Robert T. Hitlan. 2004. Cultural Threat and Perceived Realistic Group Conflict as Predictors of Attitudes towards Mexican Immigrants. *Journal of Experimental Social Psychology* 40 (1): 99–105.

ACKNOWLEDGMENTS

The editors would like to thank Ruby Takanishi, former president of the Foundation for Child Development, for her vision and support in making this Young Children in Black Immigrant Families research initiative and book a reality. We would also like to deeply thank the Foundation for its financial support.

We would like to acknowledge the thoughtful guidance given us by an ad hoc committee convened by the Migration Policy Institute early in the project. Participants included Vivian Gadsden (University of Pennsylvania), Eugene García (Arizona State University), Donald Hernandez (Hunter College and the Graduate Center, City University of New York), Micere Keels (University of Chicago), Anne Masten (University of Minnesota), Margie McHugh (MPI), Demetrios G. Papademetriou (MPI), Alex Stepick (Florida International University), and Kevin Thomas (Pennsylvania State University).

We are also indebted to a number of participants at a September 2011 authors' seminar at MPI whose comments sharpened the papers and this volume.

Michelle Mittelstadt, MPI's Director of Communications, has worked tirelessly on the volume and our colleague Kristen McCabe has made many contributions, not the least of which has been helping us manage this rewarding, complex project.

Randy Capps   Michael Fix

About the Editors

Randy Capps is a demographer and Senior Policy Analyst with the Migration Policy Institute's National Center on Immigrant Integration Policy. His areas of expertise include immigration trends, the unauthorized population, immigrants in the US labor force, and children of immigrants.

Prior to joining MPI, Dr. Capps was a researcher in the Immigration Studies Program at the Urban Institute (1993-96, and 2000-08).

His published works include *New Streams: Black African Migration to the United States* (co-author), *Delegation and Divergence: A Study of 287(g) State and Local Immigration Enforcement* (co-author), *Still an Hourglass? Immigrant Workers in Middle-Skilled Jobs* (co-author), *Immigrants and Health Care Reform: What's Really at Stake?* (co-author), *Paying the Price: The Impact of Immigration Raids on America's Children, A Comparative Analysis of Immigrant Integration in Low-Income Urban Neighborhoods, Trends in the Low-Wage Immigrant Labor Force 2000-2005*, and *Immigration and Child and Family Policy*. He has also published widely on immigrant integration at the state and local level.

Dr. Capps received his PhD in sociology from the University of Texas in 1999 and his master of public affairs degree, also from the University of Texas, in 1992.

Michael Fix is Senior Vice President and Director of Studies at the Migration Policy Institute (MPI), as well as Co-Director of MPI's National Center on Immigrant Integration Policy. His work focuses on immigrant integration, citizenship policy, immigrant children and families, the education of immigrant students, the effect of welfare reform on immigrants, and the impact of immigrants on the US labor force.

Mr. Fix, who is an attorney, previously was at the Urban Institute, where he directed the Immigration Studies Program (1998-2004). His research there focused on immigrants and integration, regulatory reform, federalism, race, and the measurement of discrimination.

Mr. Fix is a Research Fellow with IZA in Bonn, Germany. He served on the National Academy of Sciences' Committee on the Redesign of US Naturalization Tests. In 2005, Mr. Fix was a New Millennium Distinguished Visiting Scholar at Columbia University's School of Social Work.

His recent publications include *Still an Hourglass? Immigrant Workers in Middle-Skilled Jobs* (co-author), *Immigrants and Welfare* (editor), *Los Angeles on the Leading Edge: Immigrant Integration Indicators and Their Policy Implications, Adult English Language Instruction in the United States: Determining Need and Investing Wisely, Measures of Change: The Demography and Literacy of Adolescent English Learners,* and *Securing the Future: US Immigrant Integration Policy, A Reader* (editor). His past research explored the implementation of employer sanctions and other reforms introduced by the 1986 *Immigration Reform and Control Act.*

Mr. Fix received a JD from the University of Virginia and a bachelor of the arts degree from Princeton University. He did additional graduate work at the London School of Economics.

About the Authors

Cati Coe is an Associate Professor of Anthropology in the Department of Sociology, Anthropology, and Criminal Justice at Rutgers University. Her areas of expertise include education, nationalism, and transnational migration in Ghana.

Her work on nationalism and schools has been published in a book, *The Dilemmas of Culture in African Schools: Nationalism, Youth, and the Transformation of Knowledge* (University of Chicago Press, 2005) and numerous journal articles.

Dr. Coe is one of the founders of the Working Group on Childhood and Migration, a network of scholars from around the world and a variety of disciplines who collaborate in their research on various aspects of the effects of migration on children, both those who migrate and those who are left behind by migrant relatives. The working group produced two conferences in 2008, resulting in edited volumes of selected and revised papers. *Everyday Ruptures: Children, Youth, and Migration in Global Perspective*, edited by Cati Coe, Rachel R. Reynolds, Deborah Boehm, Julia Meredith Hess, and Heather Rae-Espinoza, was published by Vanderbilt University Press in April 2011. The other collection is forthcoming online through Drexel University's iDea Repository.

Dr. Coe received her MA and PhD in folklore and folklife from the University of Pennsylvania and a BA from Wesleyan University.

Dylan Conger is an Associate Professor and Director of the Master of Public Policy (MPP) Program at The George Washington University, Trachtenberg School of Public Policy and Public Administration. She is also a research affiliate at The George Washington Institute of Public Policy and the Institute for Education and Social Policy.

Before joining the Trachtenberg School faculty, Dr. Conger held research positions at the Vera Institute of Justice, Abt Associates Inc, and the Institute for Education and Social Policy at New York University.

Dr. Conger's research concerns disadvantaged and minority youth, with a focus on educational policies and urban areas. Current projects concern the role that advanced high school courses play in racial, socioeconomic, and gender disparities in educational outcomes; gender disparities in higher education; the public policies that influence English Language Learners' ability to learn English; and the educational outcomes of immigrant students.

She serves on the Board of Directors of the Association for Education Finance and Policy and is a Technical Panel Member for the National Center for Education Statistics' National Assessment of Educational Progress High School Transcript Study.

Dr. Conger received her BA in ethnic studies from the University of California at Berkeley, her MPP from the University of Michigan, and her PhD in public policy/public administration from New York University.

Danielle A. Crosby is an Associate Professor of Human Development and Family Studies at the University of North Carolina at Greensboro, School of Health and Human Sciences. Her research focuses on understanding and promoting child development in the context of poverty, and includes studies of the effects of welfare and employment policies on families, and the early care and education experiences of children in low-income, ethnic minority, and immigrant families.

As a recipient of the *Changing Faces of America's Children* Young Scholars Award from the Foundation for Child Development, Dr. Crosby is conducting a project that uses national, longitudinal data to examine the role of social safety-net programs in supporting the development of young children in immigrant families. She is also collaborating on two National Institutes of Health-funded grants examining the impacts of parents' nonstandard employment on child health and well-being and the mediators and moderators of Head Start program participation.

Prior to her current position, she was a postdoctoral scholar at the University of Chicago's Center for Human Potential and Public Policy from 2004-06.

Dr. Crosby received her BA in psychology from the University of North Carolina at Chapel Hill, and both her MS and PhD in human development and family sciences from the University of Texas at Austin.

Elizabeth Debraggio is a Research Associate at the NYU Institute for Education and Social Policy (IESP). Currently she is studying the academic performance of immigrant children, the effects of mobility on the achievement of students in New York City, the relationship between school food policies and obesity, and the ways neighborhood and community factors affect local schools and students. Prior to joining IESP, she worked as a Research Assistant in the Industrial Relations and Education Research Sections at Princeton University, and previously worked at Goldman Sachs.

As an undergraduate, she conducted research on the labor market outcomes of immigrants for the Arthur Levitt Public Affairs Center at

Hamilton College and spent a year studying at Oxford University.

She is pursuing her master of public administration at the Wagner School and graduated magna cum laude from Hamilton College in 2007.

Fabienne Doucet is Chair of the Haiti Working Group at the New York University (NYU) Steinhardt Institute for Human Development and Social Change, an affiliated faculty member of the NYU Center for Latin American and Caribbean Studies. She is also a Research Associate at the Interuniversity Institute for Research and Development (INURED), Haiti.

Her research program addresses the educational experiences of immigrant and US-born children of color and their families, with a particular focus on Haitian immigrants. Using ethnography, Dr. Doucet seeks to understand how structural factors such as race, nationality, immigrant status, and socioeconomic status affect children's educational experiences and contribute to parents' interactions with and understandings of the educational project.

She was a postdoctoral fellow at the Harvard University Graduate School of Education, with fellowships from the National Science Foundation and the Spencer Foundation, and recently received a grant from the Society for Research in Child Development to launch a research initiative on child development in Haiti, as well as a Fulbright-Hays fellowship to conduct research on educational reform in Haiti.

Dr. Doucet has a PhD in human development and family studies from the University of North Carolina at Greensboro.

Angel S. Dunbar is a PhD student in the Department of Human Development and Family Studies at the University of North Carolina at Greensboro. Her research interests include child development in ethnic minority and immigrant families, child poverty, resiliency, and social policy. She has also conducted research in the areas of attachment and maternal sensitivity, and toddler emotional knowledge and regulation.

Ms. Dunbar received her BA degree with honors in psychology from the University of Delaware and a MS in human development and family studies from the University of North Carolina at Greensboro.

Tiffany Green, a health economist, is Assistant Professor in the Department of Healthcare Policy and Research at Virginia Commonwealth University.

During her time as a Robert Wood Johnson Health and Society Scholar (2007-09) and a Health Disparities Research Scholar (2009-11) at the University of Wisconsin-Madison, Dr. Green continued her research on child health, with a focus on infant health outcomes as well as the intersections between pediatric asthma and obesity.

Dr. Green is a member of the data team for the Dane County Infant Mortality Collaborative, an interdisciplinary initiative created to understand the reasons behind the dramatic improvements in the Black infant mortality rate in Dane County, WI. In this project, she is exploring the role of Medicaid policy on infant mortality and maternal well-being.

She received her PhD in economics from the University of North Carolina at Chapel Hill in 2007. Her dissertation research focused the impact of maternal behaviors on asthma diagnosis and morbidity.

Megan Hatch is a PhD student in public policy at The George Washington University, concentrating on urban and social policy. Her research interests include poverty, housing policy, and access to education.

She received her BA in government and psychology from Georgetown University and her MPA from Cornell University.

Donald J. Hernandez is a Professor in the Department of Sociology at Hunter College and The Graduate Center, City University of New York, as well as Senior Advisor at the Foundation for Child Development.

He is the author of *America's Children: Resources from Family, Government, and the Economy* (Russell Sage Foundation, 1993), the first national research using children as the unit of analysis to document the timing, magnitude, and reasons for revolutionary changes experienced by children since the Great Depression in family composition, parent's education, father's and mother's work, and family income and poverty. He currently is using the Foundation for Child Development's Child Well-Being Index (CWI) to study disparities in child well-being by race-ethnic, immigrant, and socioeconomic status.

His publications include *Children in Immigrant Families in Eight Affluent Countries: Their Family, National, and International Context* (UNICEF Innocenti Research Centre, 2009), *Double Jeopardy: How Third-Grade Reading Skills and Poverty Influence High School Graduation* (Annie E. Casey Foundation, 2011), *Children in Immigrant Families: Ensuring Opportunity for Every Child in America* (First Focus & Foundation for Child Development, 2011), and *Declining Fortunes of Children in Middle-Class Families: Economic Inequality and Child Well-Being in the 21st Century* (Foundation for Child Development, 2011).

Dr. Hernandez earned his PhD in sociology, with specializations in demography, social stratification, and the family, from the University of California, Berkeley. He holds an MA from the University of California, Berkeley, and a BA from the University of Illinois, Urbana-Champaign.

Margot Jackson is an Assistant Professor of Sociology at Brown University, where she studies life-course and intergenerational aspects of the relationship between social circumstances and health, with a focus on the early life-cycle reproduction of social inequality and the role of child health in the production of social inequality.

Dr. Jackson's research reflects this multidimensional and longitudinal emphasis, examining how multiple contexts shape children's well-being and how the effects of these contexts, and of health itself, may vary over the life cycle.

She is currently working on two projects. First, using longitudinal data from the United States and the United Kingdom, she is studying the dynamics of child health and socioeconomic attainment — specifically, whether child health is a source of compounding disadvantage in academic achievement during the school years, as well as whether the shape and size of poor health's changing influence depends on its timing and persistence. In a second project she is examining health among children with migration backgrounds, among whom potentially divergent patterns of economic status and health with time in the United States complicate understanding of the socioeconomic gradient in health.

Kristen McCabe is an Associate Policy Analyst at the Migration Policy Institute (MPI), where she works for the National Center on Immigrant Integration Policy.

She has co-authored a number of publications, including most recently *Profile of Immigrants in Napa County, Diverse Streams: African Migration to the United States,* and *Labor Standards Enforcement and Low-Wage Immigrants.*

Prior to joining MPI, Ms. McCabe worked as a Legal Assistant at an immigration and nationality law firm in Boston. She holds a bachelor of the arts degree with honors from Tufts University, where she double majored in English and international relations.

Lauren Rich is a Senior Researcher at Chapin Hall at the University of Chicago. She is primarily interested in the family and school contexts of children living in poverty, particularly as these contexts relate to school readiness and elementary/middle school achievement among children. In addition to developing analyses of the Palm Beach County longitudinal data, Dr. Rich is currently conducting an evaluation of an initiative designed to bring schools and community-based agencies together to offer extracurricular activities and health and social supports to students and families in Chicago.

Previously she directed a project examining outcomes among disadvantaged children and youth attending residential schools. Prior to joining Chapin Hall, Dr. Rich was an Assistant Professor in the School of Social Work at the University of Pennsylvania, where she conducted and published research on youth employment, teen childbearing, welfare reform, child support enforcement, the educational attainment of teen mothers, and the economic status of low-income, noncustodial fathers.

Dr. Rich holds a PhD in economics from the University of Michigan.

Amy Ellen Schwartz is Professor of Public Policy, Education, and Economics and Director of the NYU Institute for Education and Social Policy (IESP). She teaches courses in public finance and policy at NYU's Wagner School of Public Administration and Steinhardt School of Culture, Education, and Human Development. Her research is primarily in applied econometrics, focusing on issues in urban policy, education policy, and public finance.

Her current research in K-12 education examines the relationship between student performance and housing and neighborhood change, the role of schools and neighborhoods in shaping childhood obesity, immigration and mobility in urban schools, and the efficacy of school reforms. Her research on urban economic development has included work on business improvement districts, housing investment, school choice, and investment in infrastructure, among other issues in public finance.

Dr. Schwartz received her PhD in economics from Columbia University.

Julie Spielberger is a Research Fellow at Chapin Hall with a background in child development and early childhood education, and particular interest in emergent literacy, school readiness, the role of play in children's learning and development, and improving program quality and professional development. In addition to the Palm Beach County family study, she currently leads several research projects and evaluations of system-building initiatives designed to improve the coordination and quality of a range of early childhood services, including home visitation, early care and education, and health and mental health.

Prior to joining Chapin Hall, Dr. Spielberger worked extensively in the training of Head Start teachers as a Child Development Associate (CDA) advisor and as a researcher and consultant with Head Start family literacy programs.

Dr. Spielberger received her PhD in child development from the Erikson Institute, Loyola University Chicago, and an MST in early childhood education from the University of Chicago.

Carola Suárez-Orozco is a Professor of Psychological Studies in Education at the University of California, Los Angeles and Co-Director of the Institute for Immigrant Children & Youth at UCLA's Graduate School of Education and Information Studies. Her areas of research include educational achievement among immigrant-origin youth, immigrant family separations, the role of mentors in facilitating youth development, the effects of unauthorized status on developing youth, gendered experiences of immigrant youth, the experiences of immigrant-origin youth in community college settings, and civic engagement among emerging adults of immigrant origin.

Prior to joining UCLA, she was a Professor of Applied Psychology at New York University's Steinhardt School of Culture, Education, & Human Development; Co-Director of Immigration Studies @ NYU; and Director of the School Psychology Program.

Her books include: *Learning a New Land: Immigrant Children in American Society; Children of Immigration; Transformations: Migration, Family Life, and Achievement Motivation Among Latino Adolescents;* and *The New Immigration: An Interdisciplinary Reader.*

She has been awarded an American Psychological Association (APA) Presidential Citation for her contributions to the understanding of cultural psychology of immigration and has served as the Chair of the APA Presidential Task Force on Immigration.

Kevin J. A. Thomas is an Assistant Professor of Sociology, Demography, and African Studies at The Pennsylvania State University. His research focuses on international migration, race, families, and the African diaspora.

Dr. Thomas completed his PhD in demography at the University of Pennsylvania in December 2004 and was a postdoctoral research fellow at both the Harvard Center for Population and Development Studies and the Harvard Initiative for Global Health. He was also a faculty associate at The Pennsylvania State University's Center for Family Research in Diverse Contexts and currently works as a research associate of the university's Population Research Institute.

Angela Valdovinos D'Angelo is a Harold A. Richman Postdoctoral Fellow at Chapin Hall at the University of Chicago. Dr. Valdovinos D'Angelo has expertise in immigrant and Latino fathering and families, the context of development for immigrant and minority children, as well as experience in policy-relevant research. She is currently pursuing training in applied policy research at Chapin Hall. She is part of the team conducting an implementation evaluation of the Elev8 program, a full-service schools initiative serving five low-income middle schools in Chicago.

Prior to joining Chapin Hall, she earned her PhD in human development and social policy at Northwestern University in 2009. While at Northwestern she received interdisciplinary research training and experience working with disadvantaged populations through her work on the *Welfare, Children, & Families: A Three-City Study.*

About the Young Children in Black Immigrant Families Research Initiative

The Young Children in Black Immigrant Families research initiative, undertaken by the Migration Policy Institute's National Center on Immigrant Integration Policy, aims to address gaps in knowledge about the well-being and development of young children (birth to age 10) in Black immigrant families.

There are 1.3 million children in Black immigrant families in the United States, most with parents from Africa and the Caribbean. Children in these families account for 11 percent of all Black children in America and represent a rapidly growing segment of the US population; yet they remain neglected by research studies.

To address this important gap in knowledge, MPI's National Center on Immigrant Integration Policy has conducted a project to examine the well-being and development of children in Black immigrant families in the first decade of life. Core support for the research initiative comes from the Foundation for Child Development. For more on the Foundation for Child Development and its work, visit http://fcd-us.org/.

Studies commissioned as part of the project, which are published in this volume, focus on risk and resilience factors for this population and how they may be uniquely mediated by race, immigration, and discrimination.

A key goal of the project is to ensure that research on this understudied, growing, and potentially vulnerable population is contextualized in an understanding of both theoretical models of child development and public policy. An equally important goal is to bring together and expand the field of researchers focused on immigrant families with African and Caribbean origins in the United States and other major receiving countries.

For more on the Young Children of Black Immigrants research initiative, please visit:

www.migrationpolicy.org/cbi

About MPI's National Center on Immigrant Integration Policy

Launched in 2007, the Migration Policy Institute's National Center on Immigrant Integration Policy is a crossroads for policymakers, state and local agency managers, local service providers, journalists, and others seeking to respond to the challenges and opportunities today's high rates of immigration create in local communities.

The National Center on Immigrant Integration Policy exists to:

- *Focus needed attention.* The Center works to bring often-over-looked issues of immigrant integration to the fore of national and local debates, promoting constructive solutions that will build stronger, more cohesive, and more successful communities.

- *Set the record straight.* The Center provides an unbiased look at the needs, costs, and contributions of immigrants and offers a balanced analysis of the integration policy options facing local communities and our nation.

- *Organize and strengthen a nascent field.* Groups and individuals tackling integration issues often work in isolation, unable to leverage their expertise and energy into more systemic outcomes. The Center connects them to one another, informs and nurtures their efforts, and promotes the entry of new actors into integration policy and its various subfields.

- *Identify and promote effective policies and practices.* The need for expertise has only grown with migration to "new destination" states, the continuing debate over illegal immigration, and more urgent concerns about the competitiveness of US workers and products in a globalized economy. The Center provides the research, data, and ideas that add value to stakeholders' own efforts and guides them toward effective policies and practices.

The Center's current areas of focus include: adult education and English instruction; preK-12 education; workforce preparation; citizenship and civic engagement; health; public benefits use; state and local immigration law enforcement; and translation and interpretation policy.

The Center is one of five programs at the Migration Policy Institute (MPI), an independent, nonpartisan, nonprofit think tank in Washington, DC dedicated to analysis of the movement of people worldwide. Founded in 2001, MPI provides analysis, development, and evaluation of migration and refugee policies at the local, national, and international levels. It aims to meet the rising demand for pragmatic and thoughtful responses to the challenges and opportunities that large-scale migration, whether voluntary or forced, presents to communities and institutions in an increasingly integrated world.

For more on the National Center on Immigrant
Integration Policy, please visit:
www.migrationpolicy.org/integration